Yuto Tsukuda

I had great fun traveling to the U.S. for Anime Expo last year. I want to go again sometime. Oh, and I'd like to take the Soma crew to Spain for a research trip. Thailand too. And Vietnam. And definitely one more trip to Europe. All right, I'd better get back to work!

Shun Saeki

We played in the park together! Is he all tuckered out now?

About the authors

Yuto Tsukuda won the 34th Jump Juniketsu Newcomers' Manga Award for his one-shot story *Kiba ni Naru*. He made his *Weekly Shonen Jump* debut in 2010 with the series *Shonen Shikku*. His follow-up series, *Food Wars!: Shokugeki no Soma*, is his first English-language release.

Shun Saeki made his *Jump NEXT!* debut in 2011 with the one-shot story *Kimi to Watashi no Renai Soudan*. *Food Wars!: Shokugeki no Soma* is his first *Shonen Jump* series.

Food Wars!
SHOKUGEKI NO SOMA

Volume 28
Shonen Jump Advanced Manga Edition
Story by Yuto Tsukuda, Art by Shun Saeki
Contributor Yuki Morisaki

Translation: Adrienne Beck
Touch-Up Art & Lettering: James Gaubatz, Mara Coman
Design: Alice Lewis
Editor: Jennifer LeBlanc

SHOKUGEKI NO SOMA © 2012 by Yuto Tsukuda, Shun Saeki
All rights reserved.
First published in Japan in 2012 by SHUEISHA Inc., Tokyo.
English translation rights arranged by SHUEISHA Inc.

The stories, characters and incidents mentioned in this publication
are entirely fictional.

Printed in the U.S.A.

Published by VIZ Media, LLC
P.O. Box 77010
San Francisco, CA 94107

10 9 8 7 6 5 4 3 2 1
First printing, February 2019

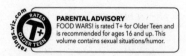

viz.com   shonenjump.com

Original Creator:
Yuto Tsukuda

Artist:
Shun Saeki

Contributor:
Yuki Morisaki

Food Wars! Shokugeki no Soma

FIRST-YEAR KID

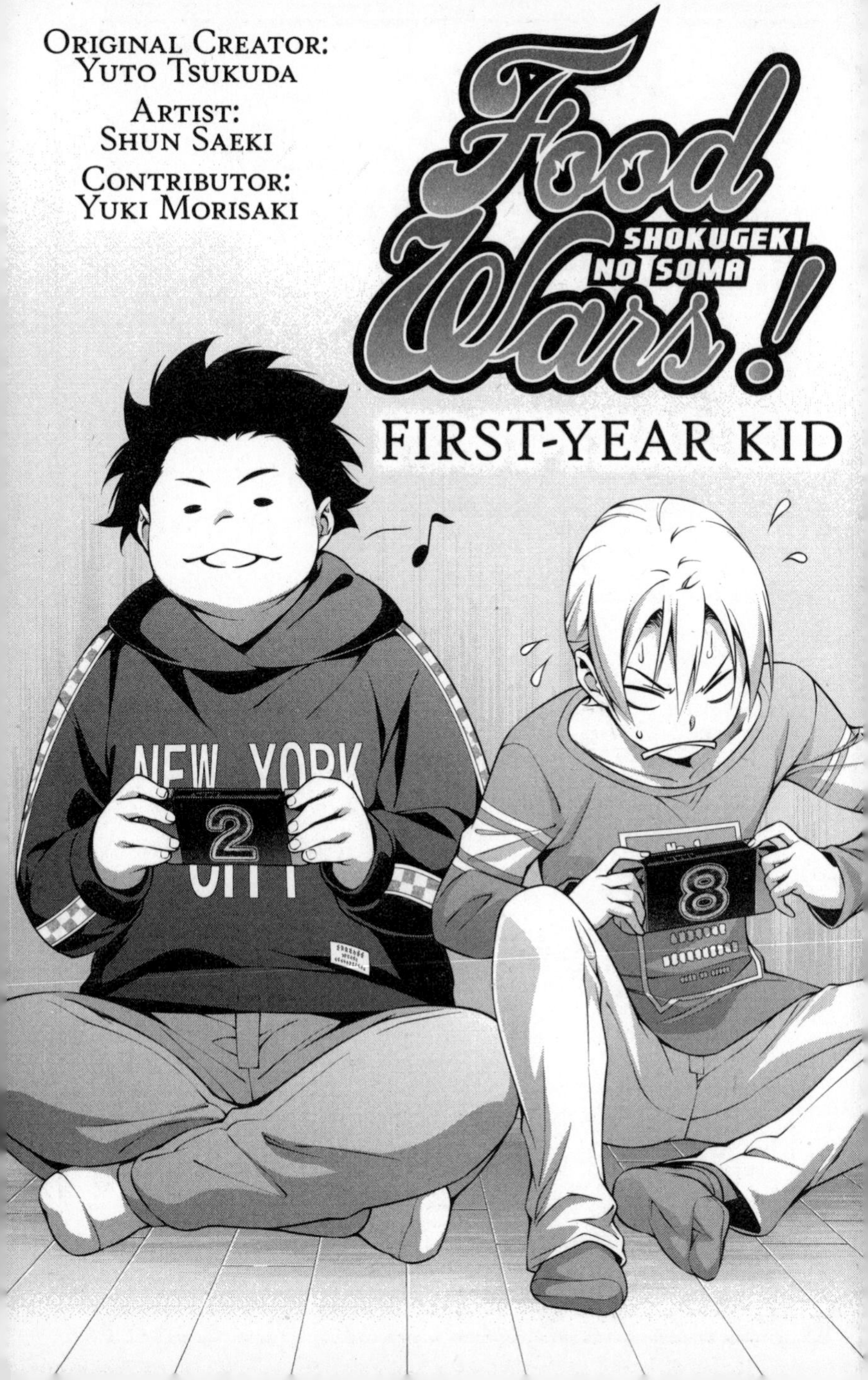
NEW YORK
2
8

CHARACTERS

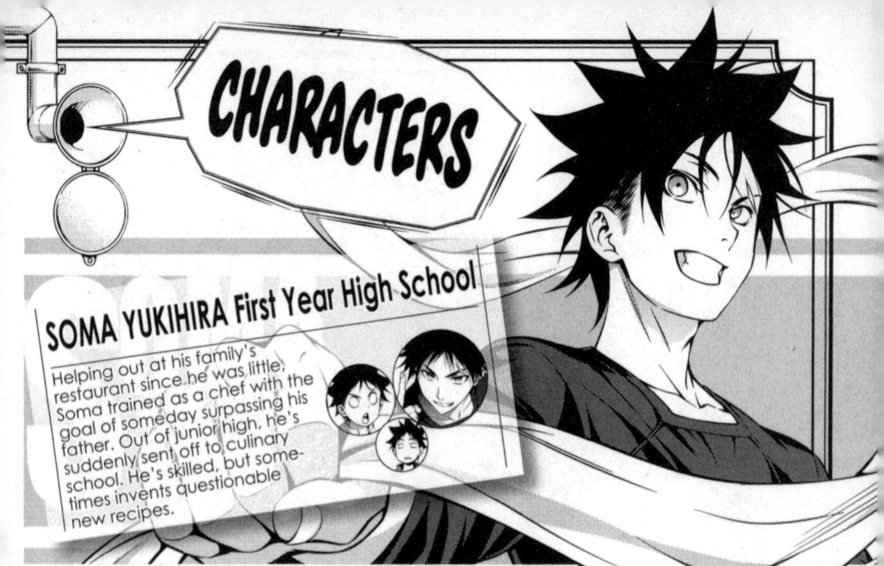

SOMA YUKIHIRA First Year High School

Helping out at his family's restaurant since he was little, Soma trained as a chef with the goal of someday surpassing his father. Out of junior high, he's suddenly sent off to culinary school. He's skilled, but sometimes invents questionable new recipes.

Shokugeki no SOMA

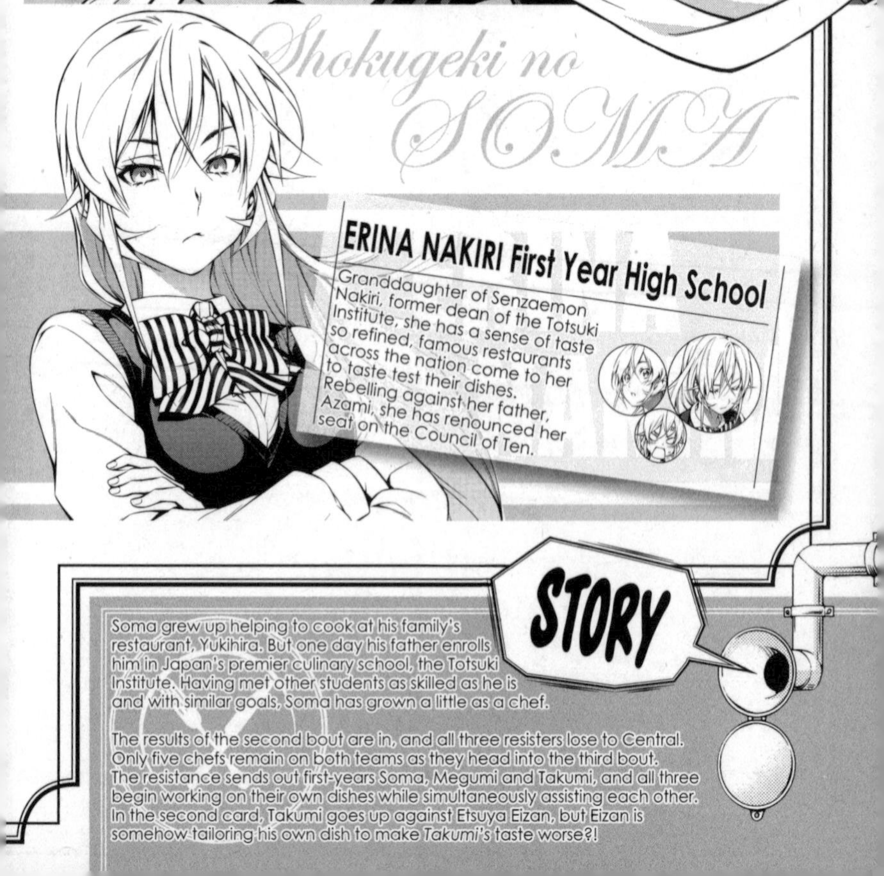

ERINA NAKIRI First Year High School

Granddaughter of Senzaemon Nakiri, former dean of the Totsuki Institute, she has a sense of taste so refined, famous restaurants across the nation come to her to taste test their dishes. Rebelling against her father, Azami, she has renounced her seat on the Council of Ten.

STORY

Soma grew up helping to cook at his family's restaurant, Yukihira. But one day his father enrolls him in Japan's premier culinary school, the Totsuki Institute. Having met other students as skilled as he is and with similar goals, Soma has grown a little as a chef.

The results of the second bout are in, and all three resisters lose to Central. Only five chefs remain on both teams as they head into the third bout. The resistance sends out first-years Soma, Megumi and Takumi, and all three begin working on their own dishes while simultaneously assisting each other. In the second card, Takumi goes up against Etsuya Eizan, but Eizan is somehow tailoring his own dish to make *Takumi's* taste worse?!

Shokugeki no SOMA

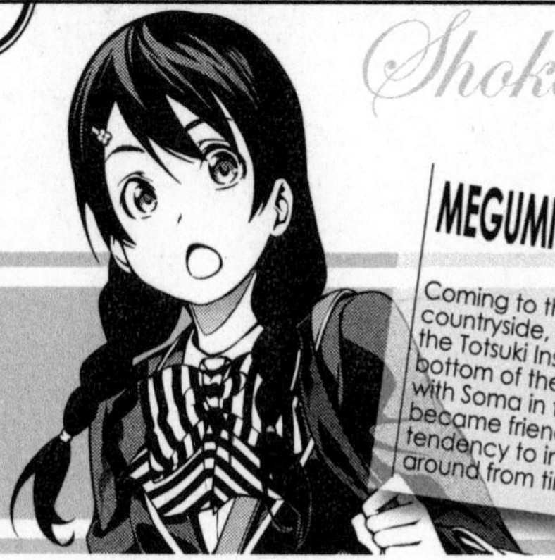

MEGUMI TADOKORO First Year High School

Coming to the big city from the countryside, Megumi made it into the Totsuki Institute at the very bottom of the rankings. Partnered with Soma in their first class, the two became friends. However, he has a tendency to inadvertently yank her around from time to time.

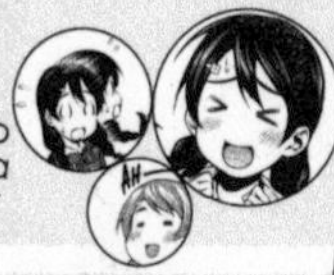
AH

TAKUMI ALDINI First Year High School

Working at his family's trattoria in Italy from a young age, he transferred into the Totsuki Institute in junior high. Isami is his younger twin brother.

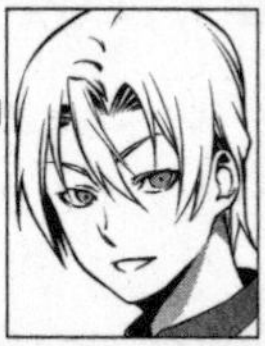

SUBARU MIMASAKA First Year High School

He cooks by tracing the actions of other chefs. After losing to Soma in a shokugeki, he reforms his cheating ways and begins to take his cooking seriously.

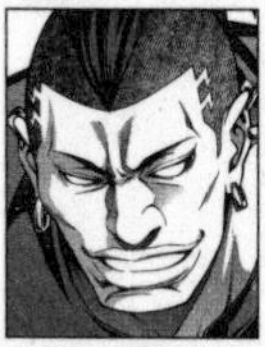

ETSUYA EIZAN Second Year High School

The seventh seat on the new Council of Ten. Not only does he have natural talent as a chef, his work as a consultant has given him connections throughout the industry.

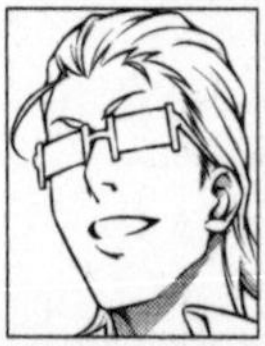

MOMO AKANEGAKUBO Third Year High School

The current third seat on the new Council of Ten, Momo specializes in baking and desserts. She is never without her stuffed animal named "Butchy."

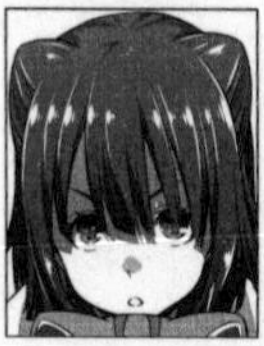

SOMEI SAITO Third Year High School

The current fourth seat on Totsuki's Council of Ten. A gifted sushi chef, he greatly values Bushido. He calls his favorite sword (i.e., butcher knife) *Isanakiri*.

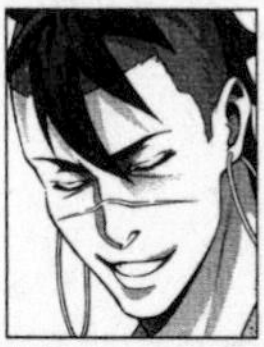

AZAMI NAKIRI

Erina's father, he convinced over half the Council of Ten to back him in staging a coup for taking control of the institute, forcing former dean Senzaemon Nakiri into retirement.

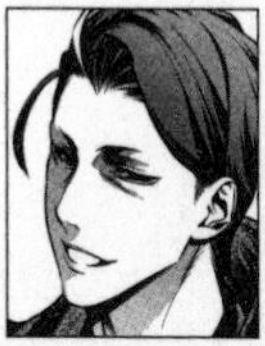

Food Wars!
SHOKUGEKI NO SOMA

28

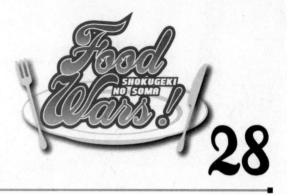

Table of Contents

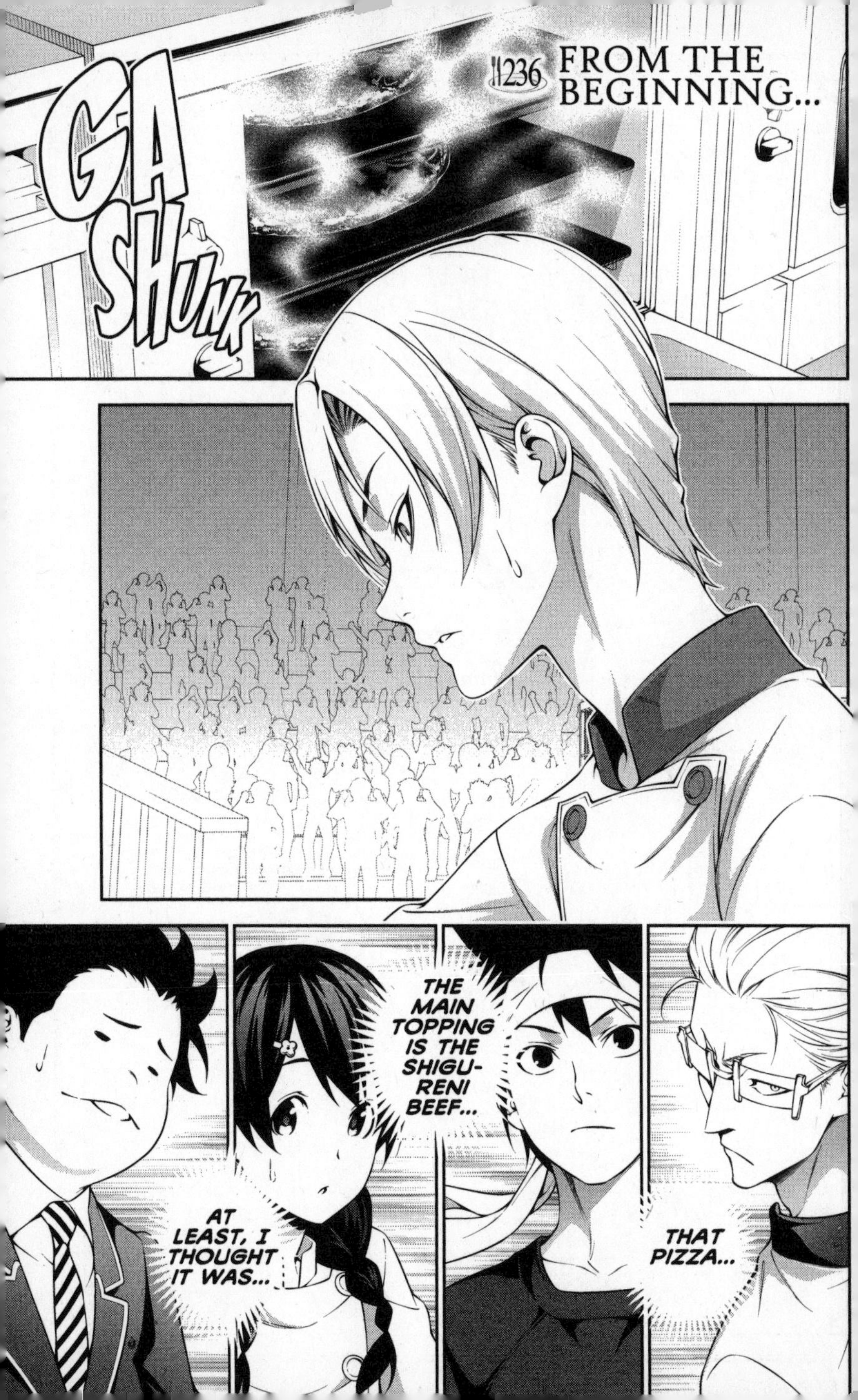

236 FROM THE BEGINNING...
GA SHUNK
THAT PIZZA...
THE MAIN TOPPING IS THE SHIGU-RENI BEEF...
AT LEAST, I THOUGHT IT WAS...

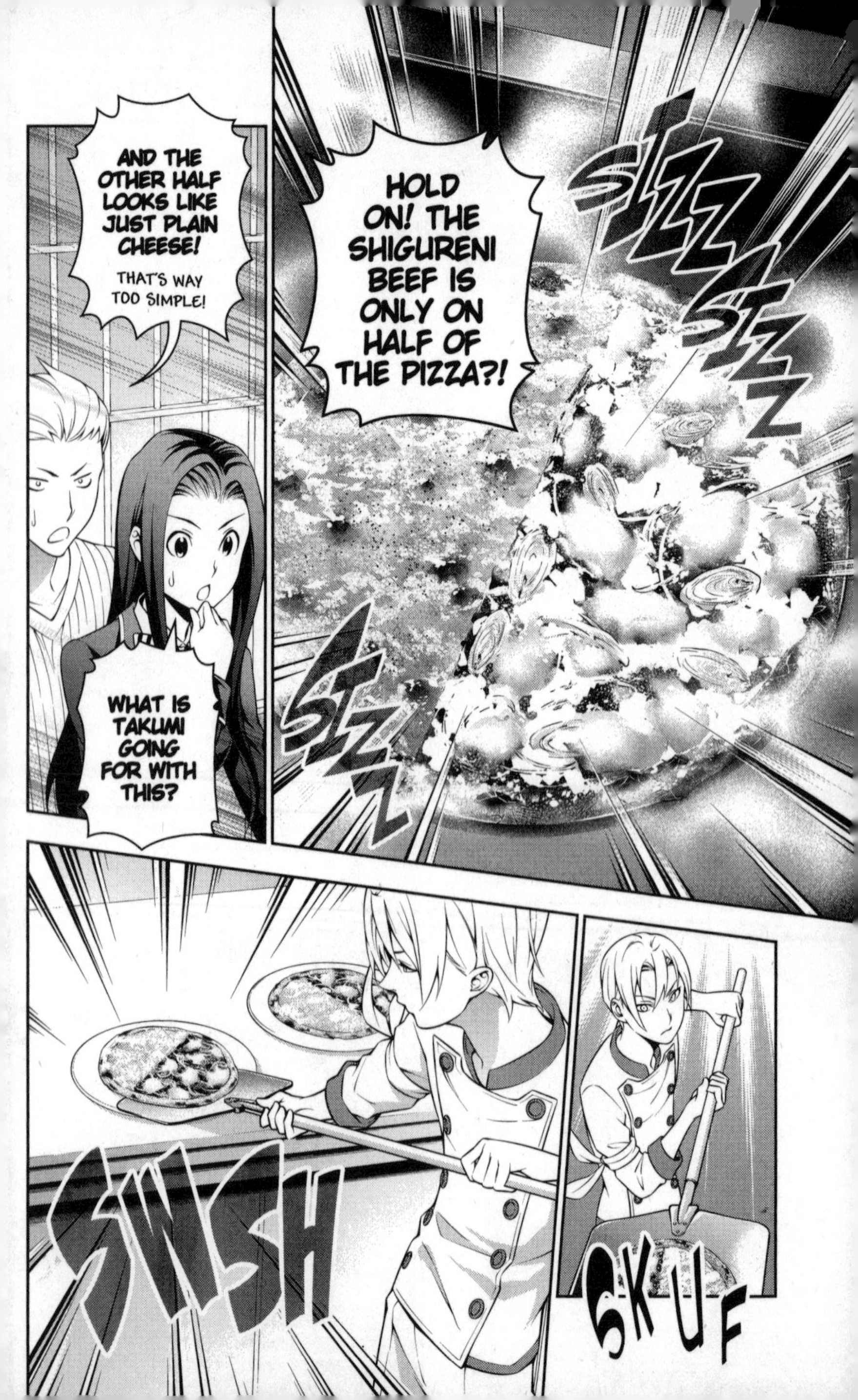
SIZZ
SIZZ
HOLD ON! THE SHIGURENI BEEF IS ONLY ON HALF OF THE PIZZA?!
SIZZ
AND THE OTHER HALF LOOKS LIKE JUST PLAIN CHEESE!
THAT'S WAY TOO SIMPLE!
WHAT IS TAKUMI GOING FOR WITH THIS?
SKUF
SWISH

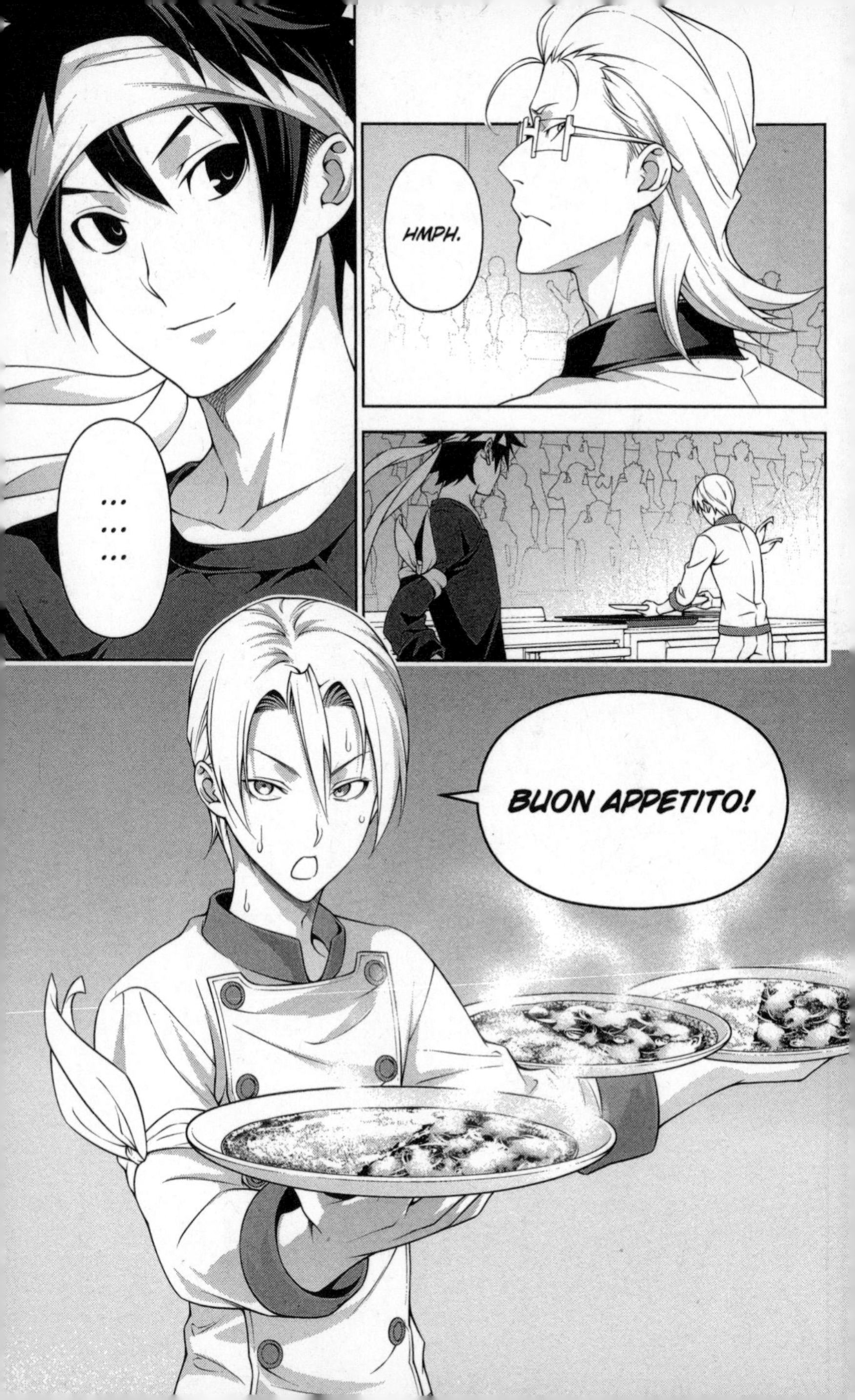
HMPH.
...
...
...
BUON APPETITO!

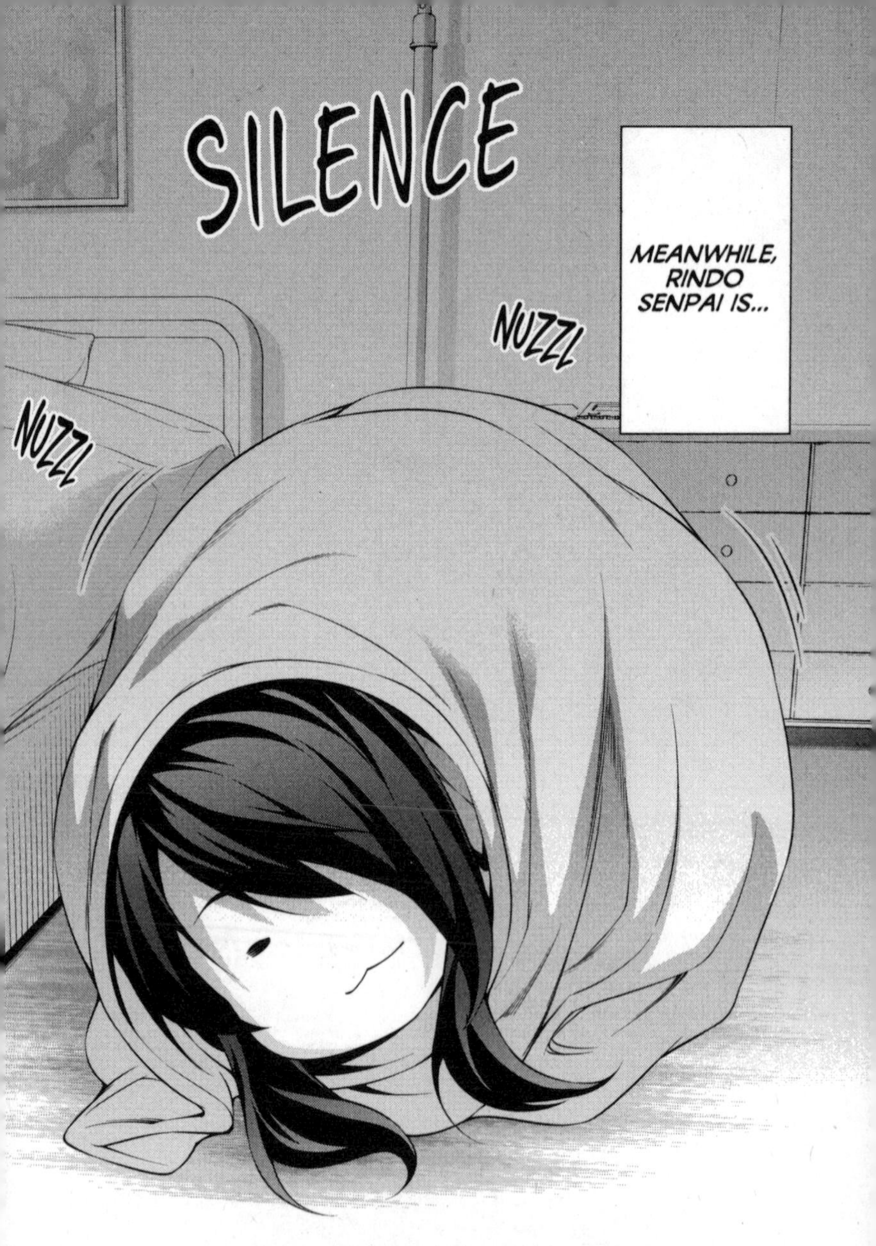
MEANWHILE, RINDO SENPAI IS...
SILENCE
NUZZL
NUZZL

236 FROM THE BEGINNING...

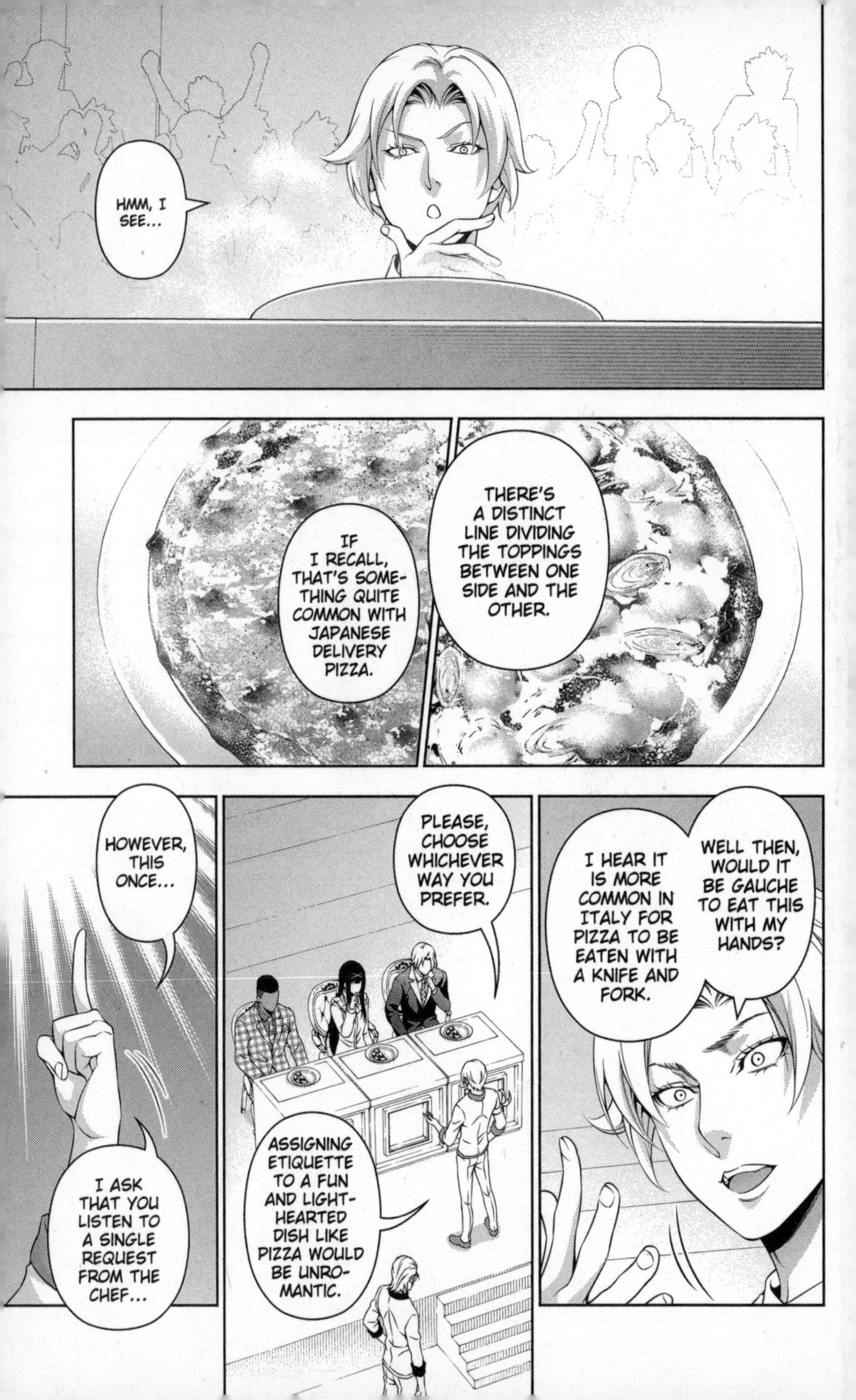
HMM, I SEE...
THERE'S A DISTINCT LINE DIVIDING THE TOPPINGS BETWEEN ONE SIDE AND THE OTHER.
IF I RECALL, THAT'S SOMETHING QUITE COMMON WITH JAPANESE DELIVERY PIZZA.
WELL THEN, WOULD IT BE GAUCHE TO EAT THIS WITH MY HANDS?
I HEAR IT IS MORE COMMON IN ITALY FOR PIZZA TO BE EATEN WITH A KNIFE AND FORK.
PLEASE, CHOOSE WHICHEVER WAY YOU PREFER.
ASSIGNING ETIQUETTE TO A FUN AND LIGHTHEARTED DISH LIKE PIZZA WOULD BE UNROMANTIC.
HOWEVER, THIS ONCE...
I ASK THAT YOU LISTEN TO A SINGLE REQUEST FROM THE CHEF...

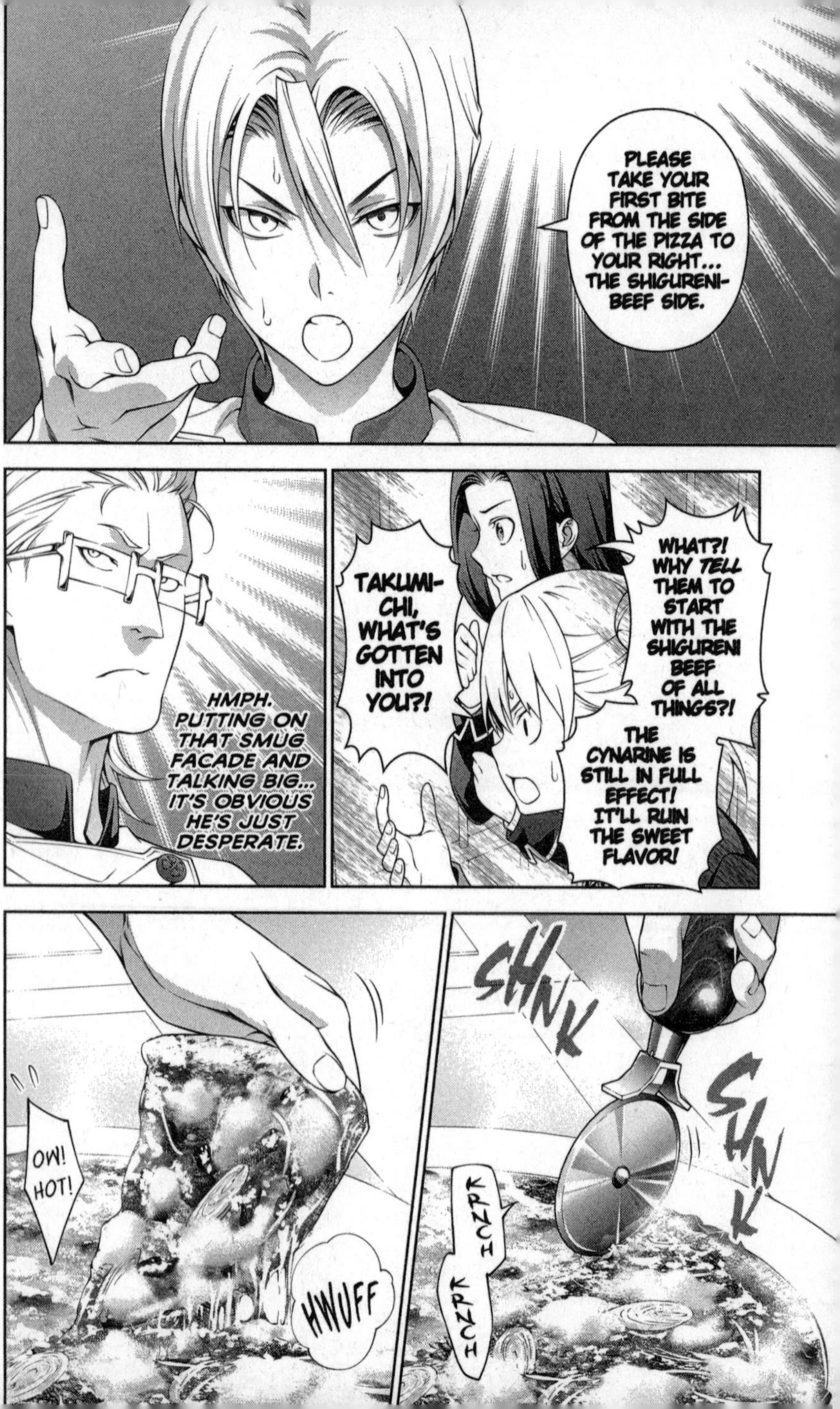
PLEASE TAKE YOUR FIRST BITE FROM THE SIDE OF THE PIZZA TO YOUR RIGHT... THE SHIGURENI-BEEF SIDE.
WHAT?! WHY TELL THEM TO START WITH THE SHIGURENI BEEF OF ALL THINGS?!
TAKUMI-CHI, WHAT'S GOTTEN INTO YOU?!
THE CYNARINE IS STILL IN FULL EFFECT! IT'LL RUIN THE SWEET FLAVOR!
HMPH. PUTTING ON THAT SMUG FACADE AND TALKING BIG... IT'S OBVIOUS HE'S JUST DESPERATE.
SHNK
SHNK
KRNCH
KRNCH
OW! HOT!
HWUFF

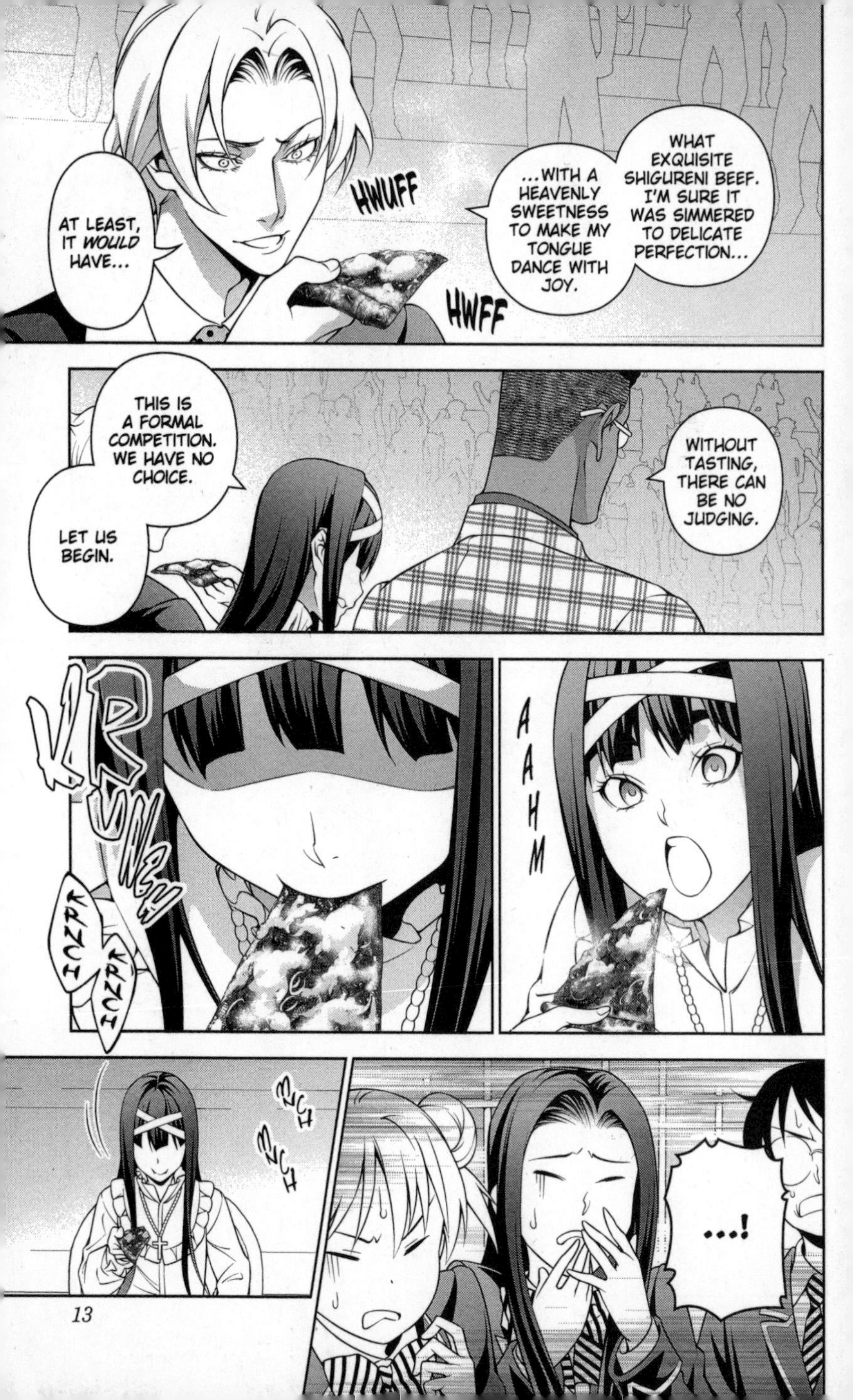

WHAT EXQUISITE SHIGURENI BEEF. I'M SURE IT WAS SIMMERED TO DELICATE PERFECTION...
...WITH A HEAVENLY SWEETNESS TO MAKE MY TONGUE DANCE WITH JOY.
HWUFF
HWFF
AT LEAST, IT *WOULD* HAVE...
WITHOUT TASTING, THERE CAN BE NO JUDGING.
THIS IS A FORMAL COMPETITION. WE HAVE NO CHOICE.
LET US BEGIN.
AAHM
KRNCH
KRNCH
...!
MNCH
MNCH

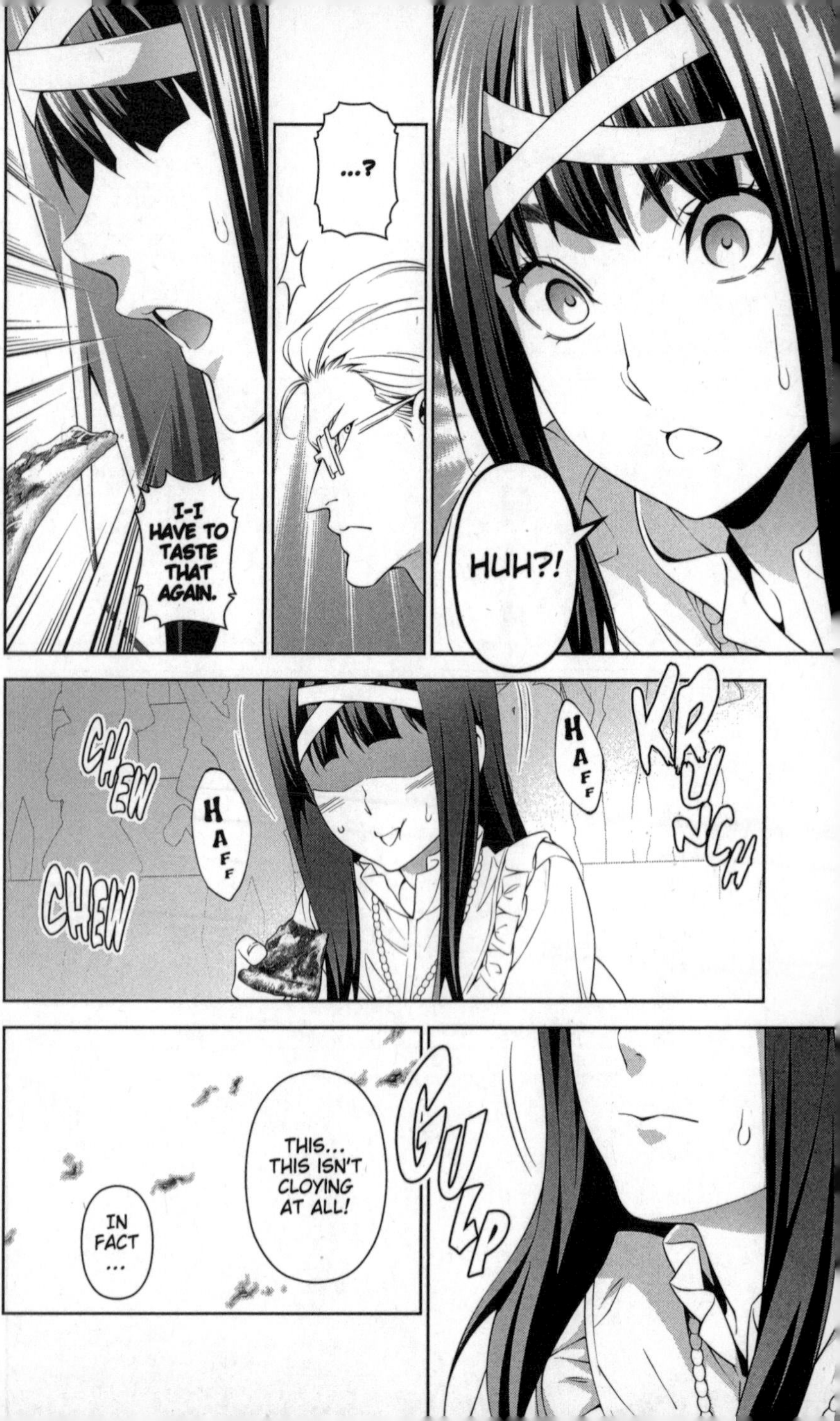
HUH?!
...?
I-I HAVE TO TASTE THAT AGAIN.
KRUNCH
HAFF
HAFF
CHEW
CHEW
GULP
THIS... THIS ISN'T CLOYING AT ALL!
IN FACT ...

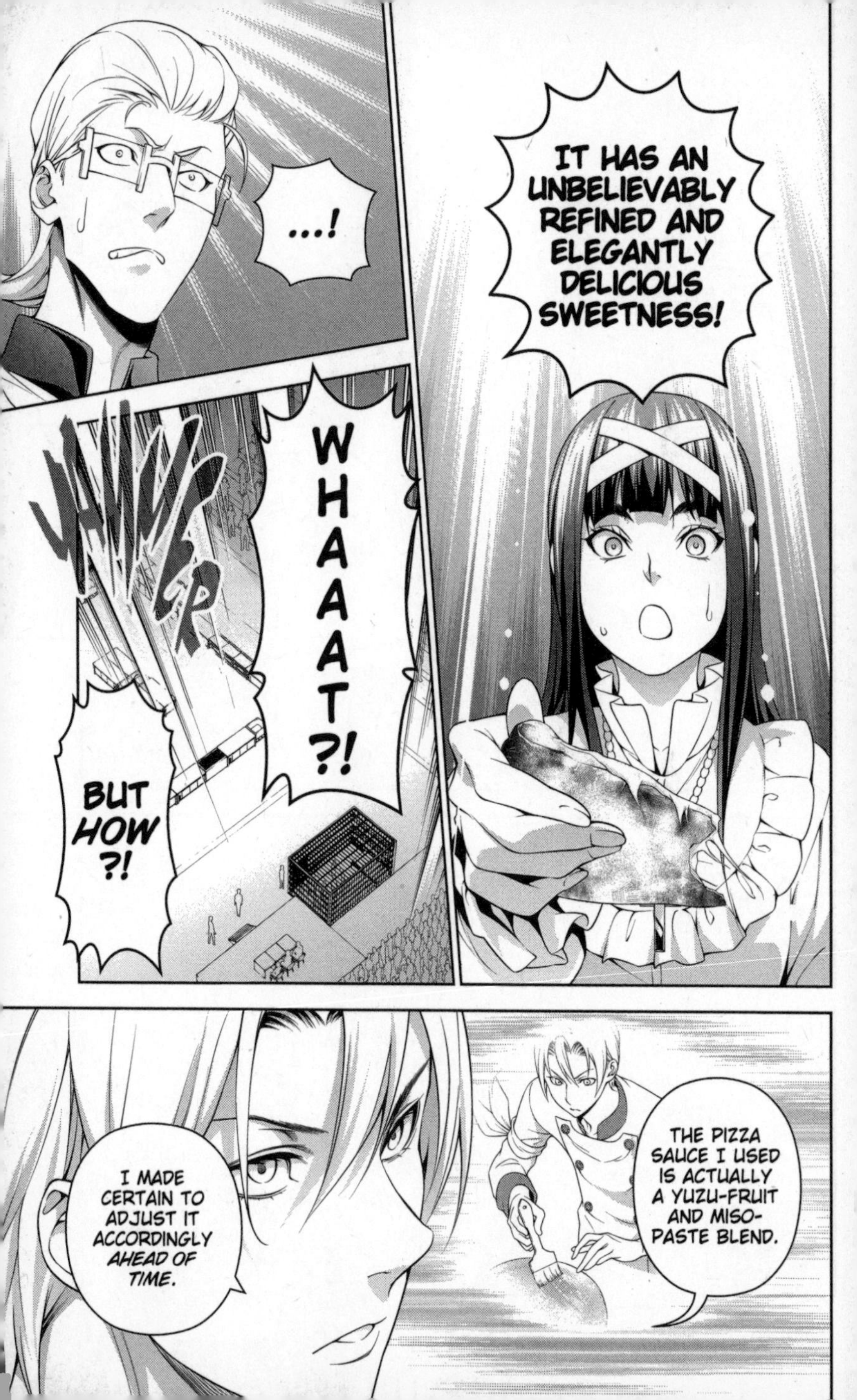
IT HAS AN UNBELIEVABLY REFINED AND ELEGANTLY DELICIOUS SWEETNESS!
...!
WHAAAAT?!
BUT HOW?!
THE PIZZA SAUCE I USED IS ACTUALLY A YUZU-FRUIT AND MISO-PASTE BLEND.
I MADE CERTAIN TO ADJUST IT ACCORDINGLY AHEAD OF TIME.

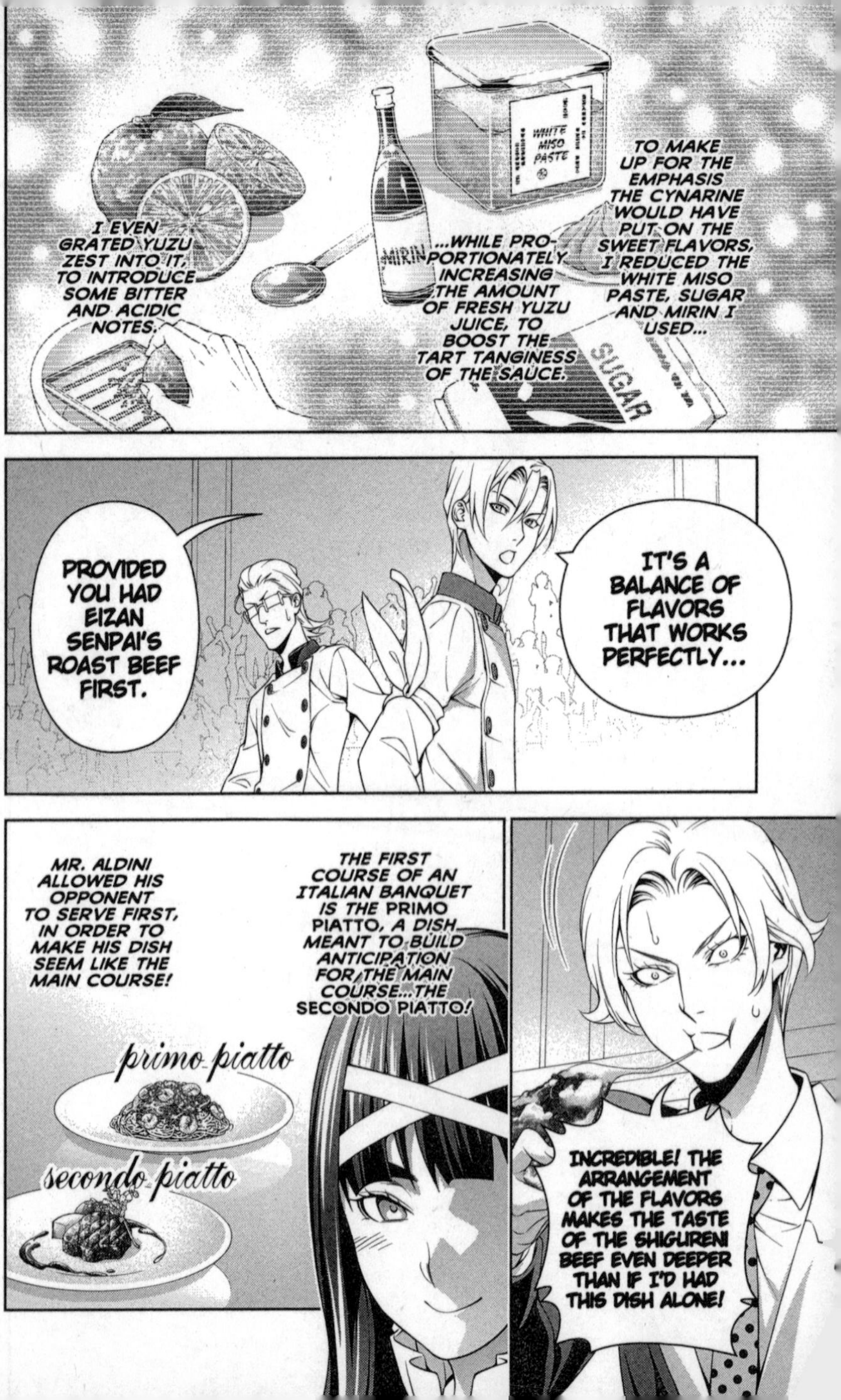
WHITE MISO PASTE
TO MAKE UP FOR THE EMPHASIS THE CYNARINE WOULD HAVE PUT ON THE SWEET FLAVORS, I REDUCED THE WHITE MISO PASTE, SUGAR AND MIRIN I USED...
MIRIN
...WHILE PROPORTIONATELY INCREASING THE AMOUNT OF FRESH YUZU JUICE, TO BOOST THE TART TANGINESS OF THE SAUCE.
SUGAR
I EVEN GRATED YUZU ZEST INTO IT, TO INTRODUCE SOME BITTER AND ACIDIC NOTES.
IT'S A BALANCE OF FLAVORS THAT WORKS PERFECTLY...
PROVIDED YOU HAD EIZAN SENPAI'S ROAST BEEF FIRST.
INCREDIBLE! THE ARRANGEMENT OF THE FLAVORS MAKES THE TASTE OF THE SHIGURENI BEEF EVEN DEEPER THAN IF I'D HAD THIS DISH ALONE!
THE FIRST COURSE OF AN ITALIAN BANQUET IS THE PRIMO PIATTO, A DISH MEANT TO BUILD ANTICIPATION FOR THE MAIN COURSE...THE SECONDO PIATTO!
MR. ALDINI ALLOWED HIS OPPONENT TO SERVE FIRST, IN ORDER TO MAKE HIS DISH SEEM LIKE THE MAIN COURSE!
primo piatto
secondo piatto

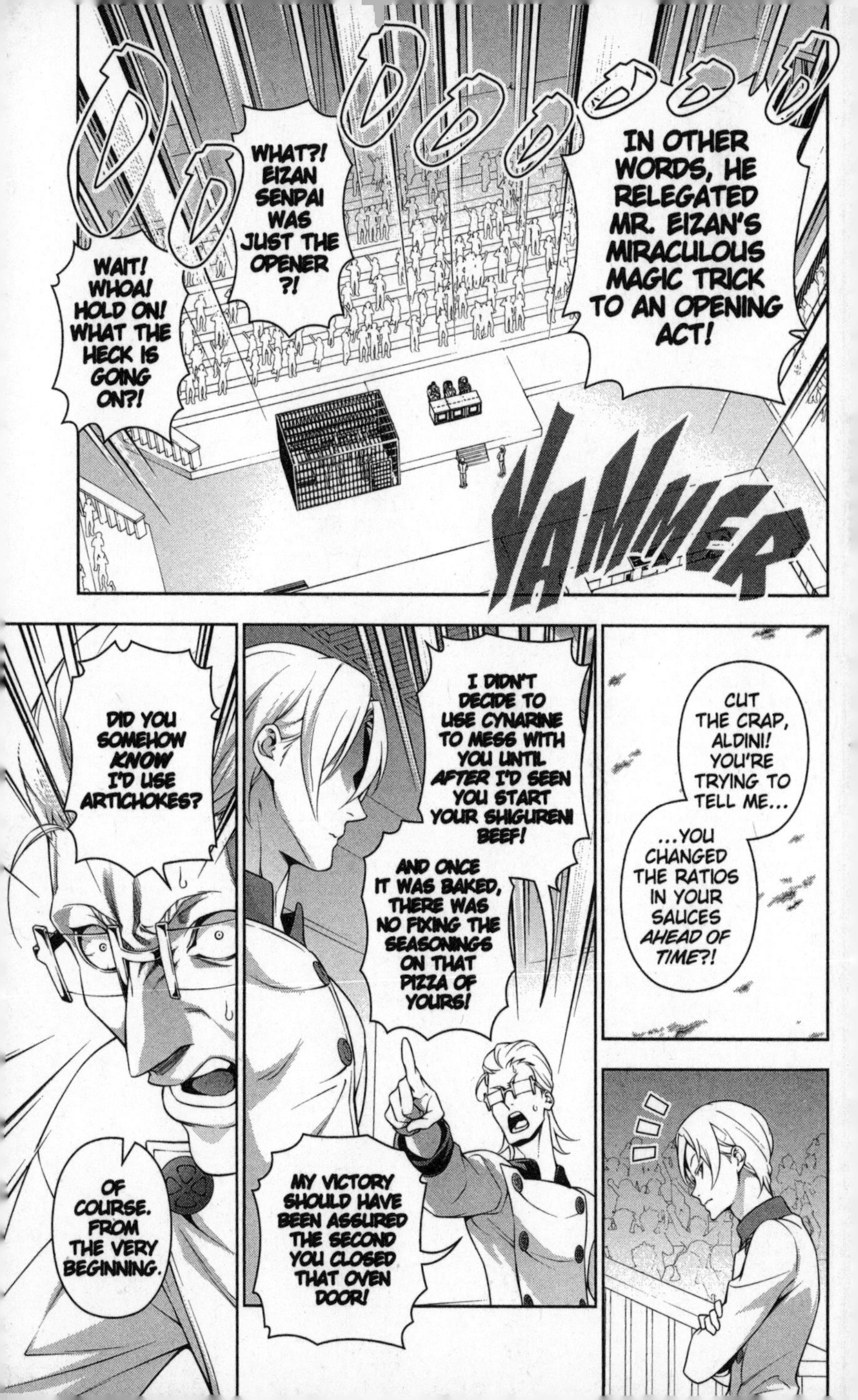
IN OTHER WORDS, HE RELEGATED MR. EIZAN'S MIRACULOUS MAGIC TRICK TO AN OPENING ACT!
WHAT?! EIZAN SENPAI WAS JUST THE OPENER?!
WAIT! WHOA! HOLD ON! WHAT THE HECK IS GOING ON?!
YAMMER
CUT THE CRAP, ALDINI! YOU'RE TRYING TO TELL ME...
...YOU CHANGED THE RATIOS IN YOUR SAUCES AHEAD OF TIME?!
I DIDN'T DECIDE TO USE CYNARINE TO MESS WITH YOU UNTIL AFTER I'D SEEN YOU START YOUR SHIGURENI BEEF!
AND ONCE IT WAS BAKED, THERE WAS NO FIXING THE SEASONINGS ON THAT PIZZA OF YOURS!
MY VICTORY SHOULD HAVE BEEN ASSURED THE SECOND YOU CLOSED THAT OVEN DOOR!
DID YOU SOMEHOW KNOW I'D USE ARTICHOKES?
OF COURSE. FROM THE VERY BEGINNING.

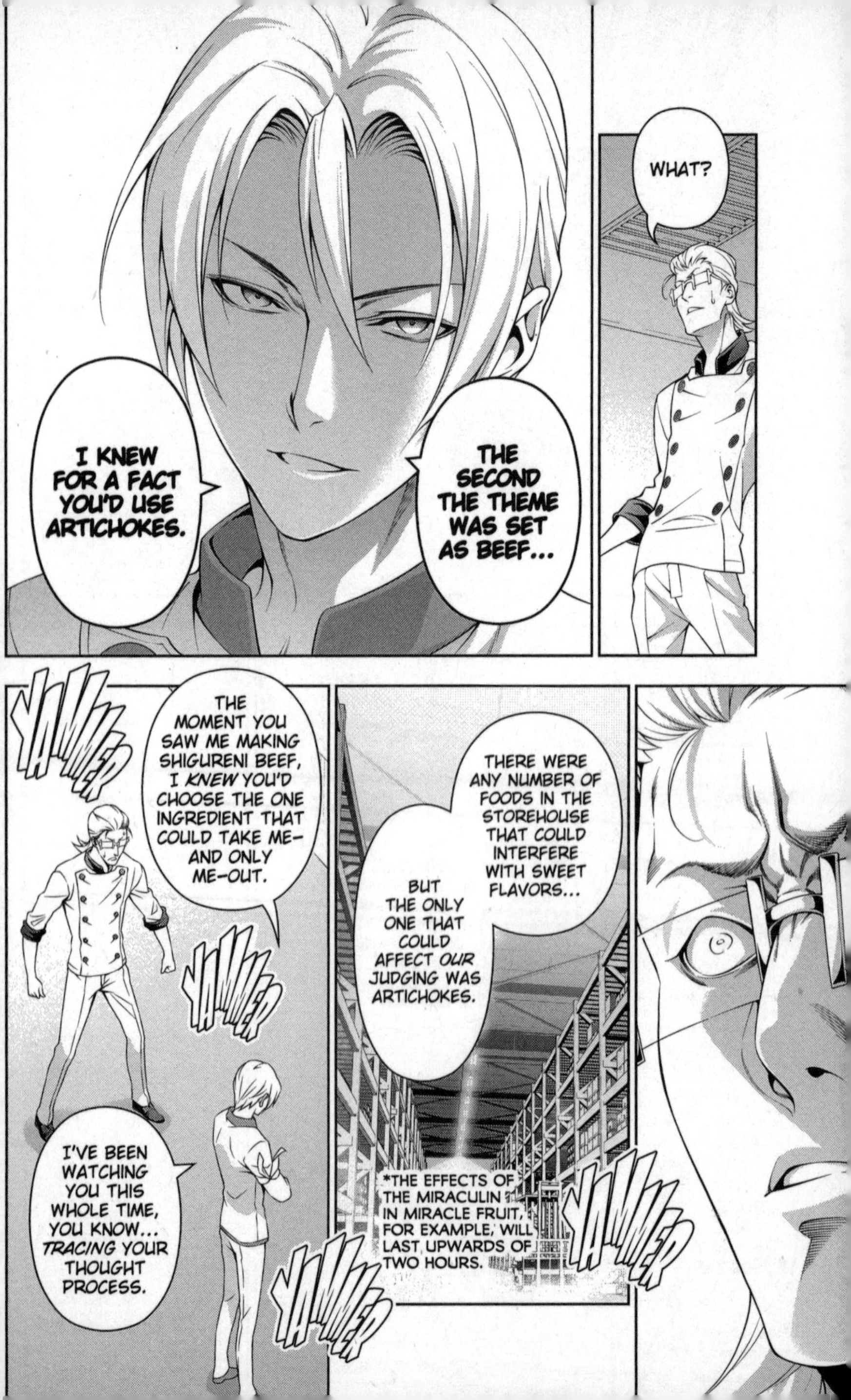
WHAT?
THE SECOND THE THEME WAS SET AS BEEF...
I KNEW FOR A FACT YOU'D USE ARTICHOKES.
YAMMER
THERE WERE ANY NUMBER OF FOODS IN THE STOREHOUSE THAT COULD INTERFERE WITH SWEET FLAVORS...
BUT THE ONLY ONE THAT COULD AFFECT *OUR* JUDGING WAS ARTICHOKES.
*THE EFFECTS OF THE MIRACULIN IN MIRACLE FRUIT, FOR EXAMPLE, WILL LAST UPWARDS OF TWO HOURS.
YAMMER
THE MOMENT YOU SAW ME MAKING SHIGURENI BEEF, I *KNEW* YOU'D CHOOSE THE ONE INGREDIENT THAT COULD TAKE ME—AND ONLY ME—OUT.
YAMMER
I'VE BEEN WATCHING YOU THIS WHOLE TIME, YOU KNOW... *TRACING* YOUR THOUGHT PROCESS.
YAMMER

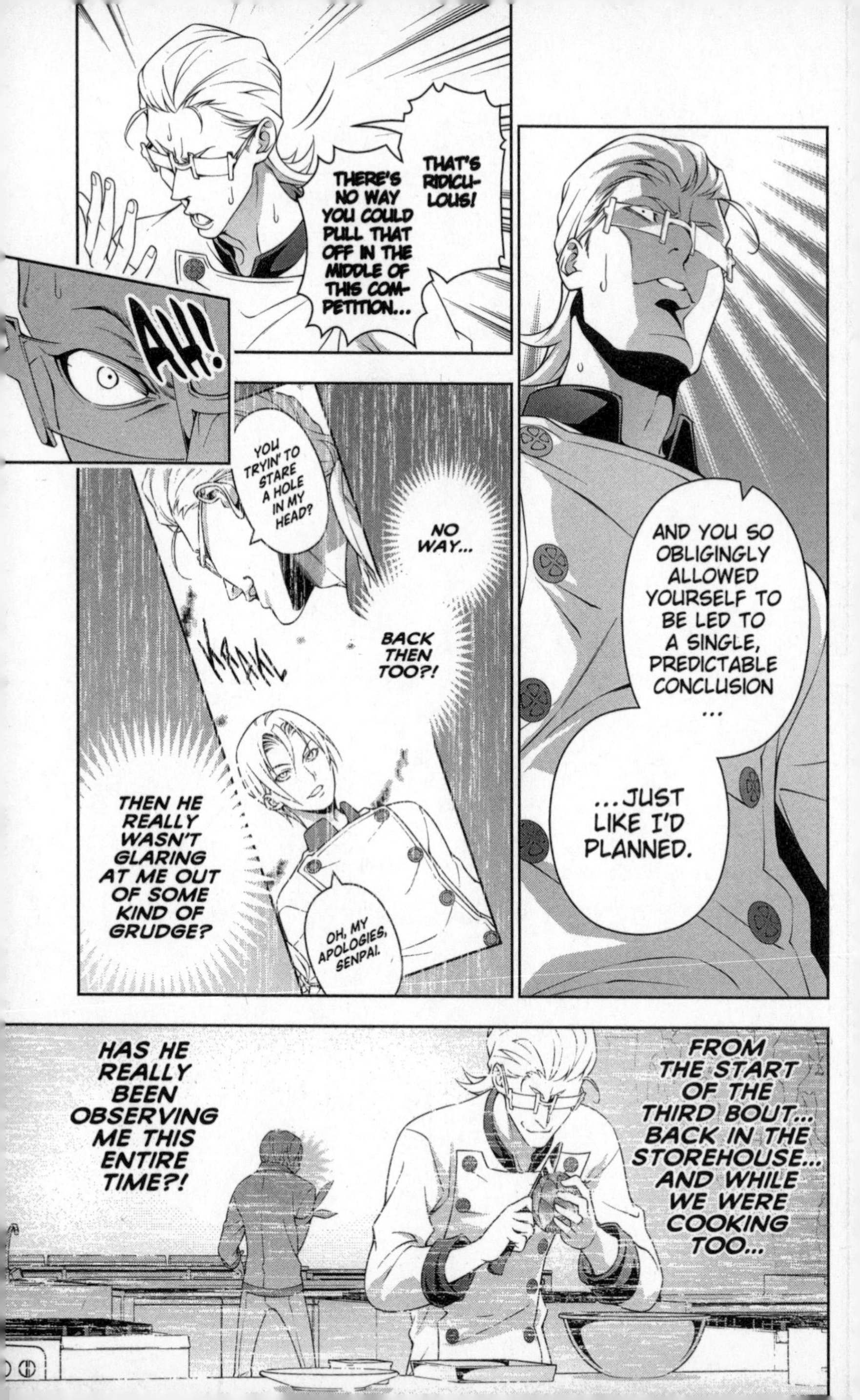
THAT'S RIDICU-LOUS!
THERE'S NO WAY YOU COULD PULL THAT OFF IN THE MIDDLE OF THIS COM-PETITION...
AND YOU SO OBLIGINGLY ALLOWED YOURSELF TO BE LED TO A SINGLE, PREDICTABLE CONCLUSION ...
...JUST LIKE I'D PLANNED.
AH!
YOU TRYIN' TO STARE A HOLE IN MY HEAD?
NO WAY...
BACK THEN TOO?!
OH, MY APOLOGIES, SENPAI.
THEN HE REALLY WASN'T GLARING AT ME OUT OF SOME KIND OF GRUDGE?
FROM THE START OF THE THIRD BOUT... BACK IN THE STOREHOUSE... AND WHILE WE WERE COOKING TOO...
HAS HE REALLY BEEN OBSERVING ME THIS ENTIRE TIME?!

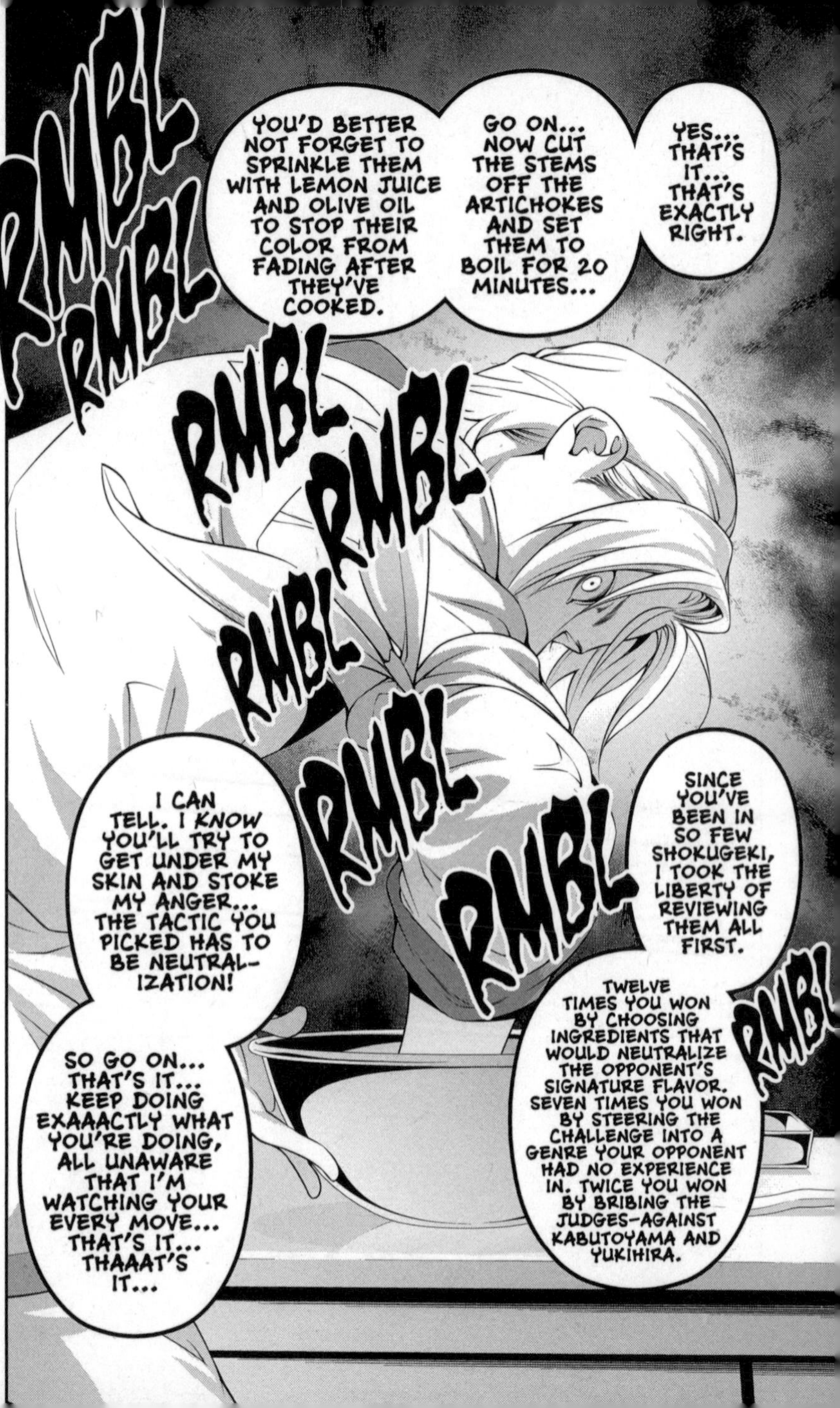
YES... THAT'S IT... THAT'S EXACTLY RIGHT.
GO ON... NOW CUT THE STEMS OFF THE ARTICHOKES AND SET THEM TO BOIL FOR 20 MINUTES...
YOU'D BETTER NOT FORGET TO SPRINKLE THEM WITH LEMON JUICE AND OLIVE OIL TO STOP THEIR COLOR FROM FADING AFTER THEY'VE COOKED.
RMBL RMBL
RMBL RMBL RMBL
RMBL RMBL RMBL
SINCE YOU'VE BEEN IN SO FEW SHOKUGEKI, I TOOK THE LIBERTY OF REVIEWING THEM ALL FIRST.
TWELVE TIMES YOU WON BY CHOOSING INGREDIENTS THAT WOULD NEUTRALIZE THE OPPONENT'S SIGNATURE FLAVOR. SEVEN TIMES YOU WON BY STEERING THE CHALLENGE INTO A GENRE YOUR OPPONENT HAD NO EXPERIENCE IN. TWICE YOU WON BY BRIBING THE JUDGES—AGAINST KABUTOYAMA AND YUKIHIRA.
RMBL
I CAN TELL. I KNOW YOU'LL TRY TO GET UNDER MY SKIN AND STOKE MY ANGER... THE TACTIC YOU PICKED HAS TO BE NEUTRALIZATION!
SO GO ON... THAT'S IT... KEEP DOING EXAAACTLY WHAT YOU'RE DOING, ALL UNAWARE THAT I'M WATCHING YOUR EVERY MOVE... THAT'S IT... THAAAT'S IT...

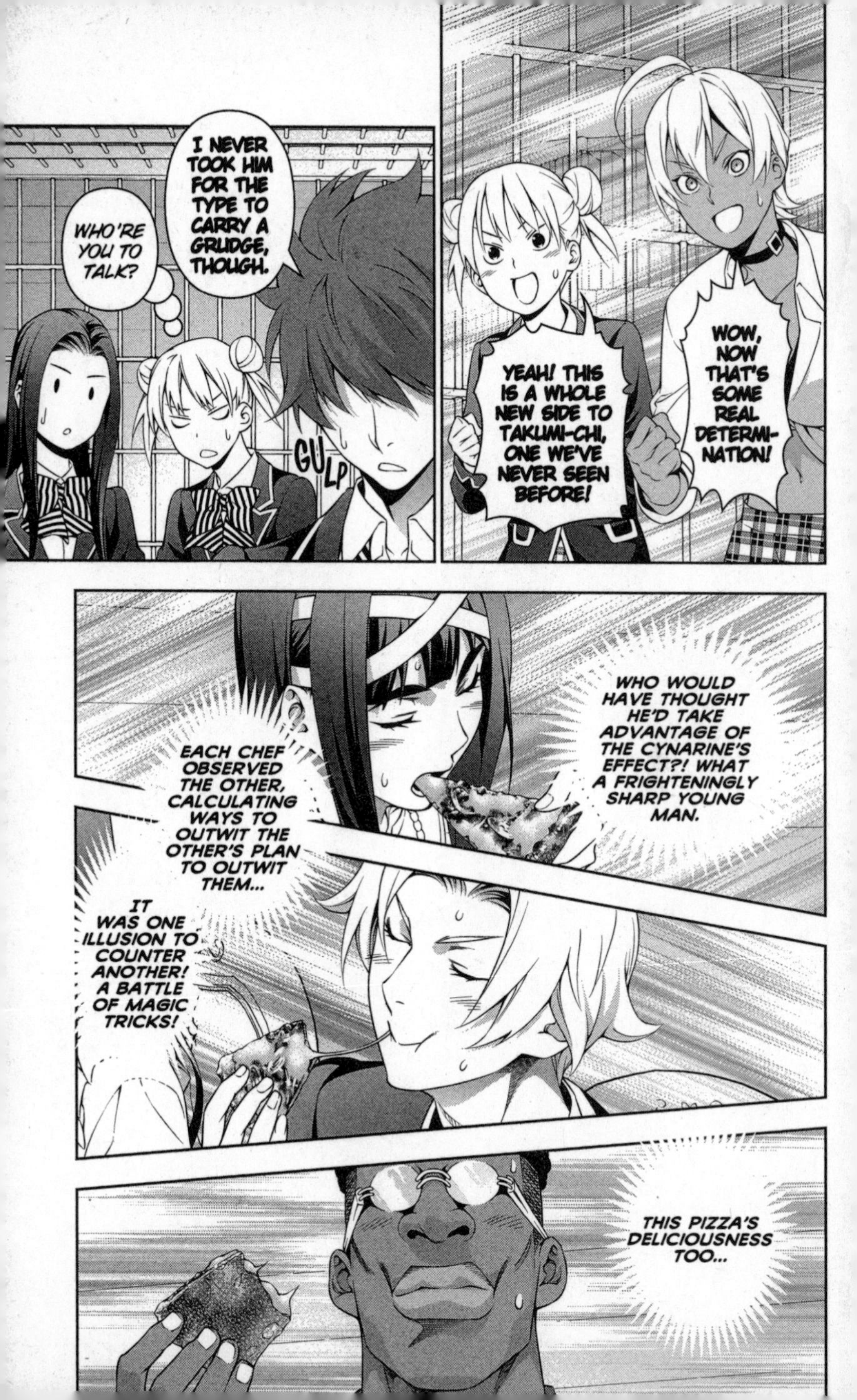
WOW, NOW THAT'S SOME REAL DETERMINATION!
YEAH! THIS IS A WHOLE NEW SIDE TO TAKUMI-CHI, ONE WE'VE NEVER SEEN BEFORE!
I NEVER TOOK HIM FOR THE TYPE TO CARRY A GRUDGE, THOUGH.
WHO'RE YOU TO TALK?
GULP
WHO WOULD HAVE THOUGHT HE'D TAKE ADVANTAGE OF THE CYNARINE'S EFFECT?! WHAT A FRIGHTENINGLY SHARP YOUNG MAN.
EACH CHEF OBSERVED THE OTHER, CALCULATING WAYS TO OUTWIT THE OTHER'S PLAN TO OUTWIT THEM...
IT WAS ONE ILLUSION TO COUNTER ANOTHER! A BATTLE OF MAGIC TRICKS!
THIS PIZZA'S DELICIOUSNESS TOO...

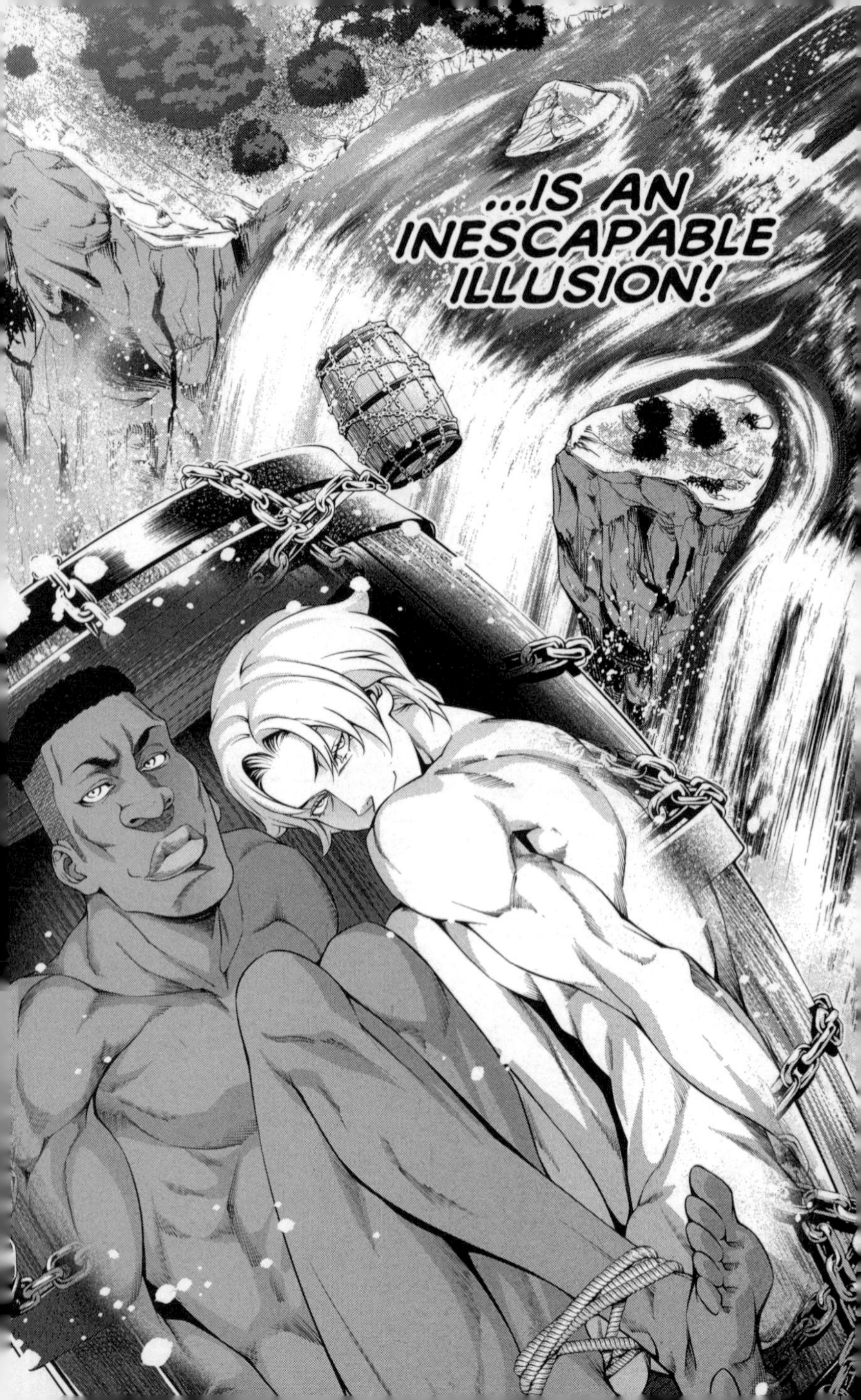
...IS AN INESCAPABLE ILLUSION!

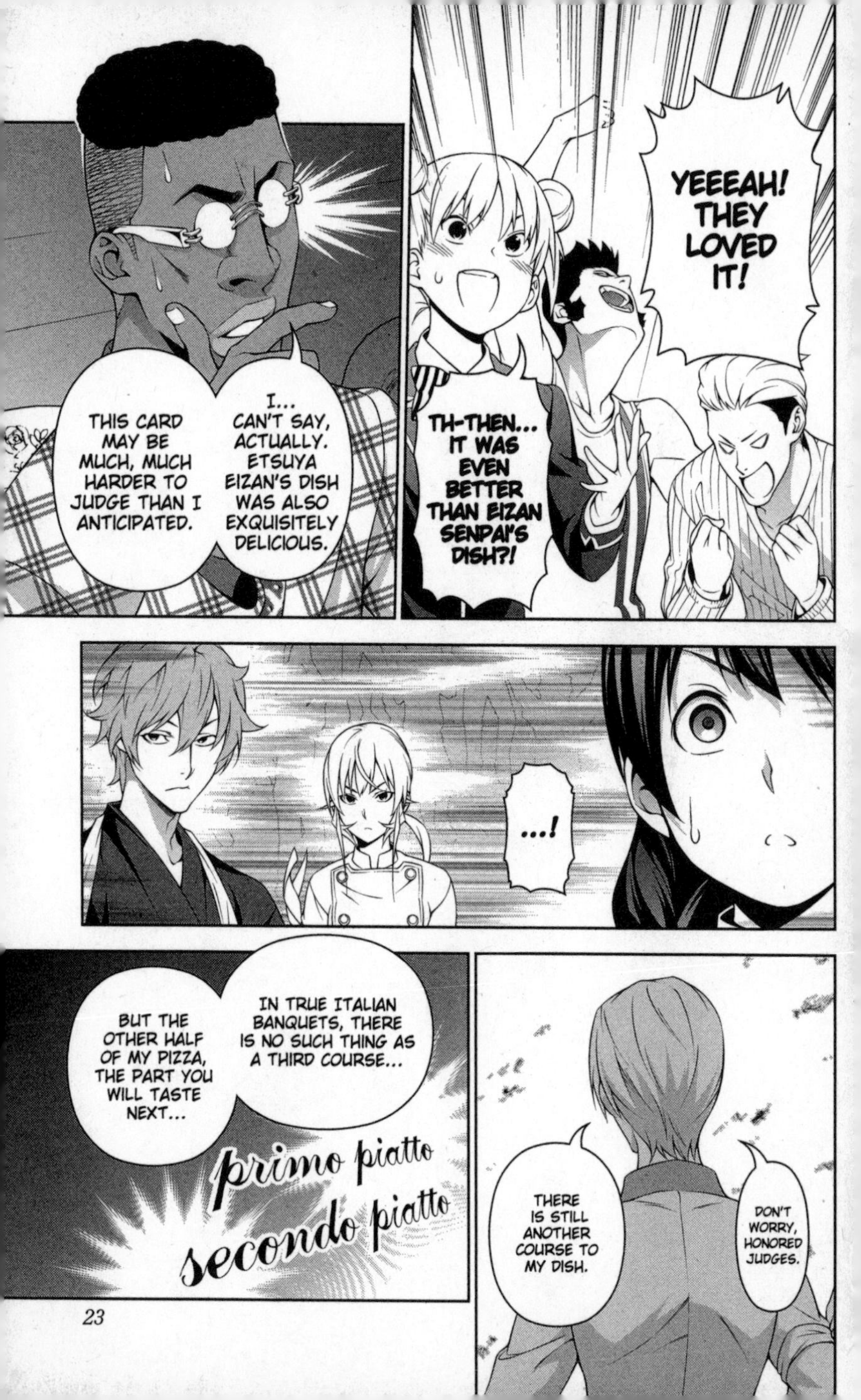

YEEEAH! THEY LOVED IT!
TH-THEN... IT WAS EVEN BETTER THAN EIZAN SENPAI'S DISH?!
I... CAN'T SAY, ACTUALLY. ETSUYA EIZAN'S DISH WAS ALSO EXQUISITELY DELICIOUS.
THIS CARD MAY BE MUCH, MUCH HARDER TO JUDGE THAN I ANTICIPATED.
...!
DON'T WORRY, HONORED JUDGES.
THERE IS STILL ANOTHER COURSE TO MY DISH.
IN TRUE ITALIAN BANQUETS, THERE IS NO SUCH THING AS A THIRD COURSE...
BUT THE OTHER HALF OF MY PIZZA, THE PART YOU WILL TASTE NEXT...
primo piatto
secondo piatto

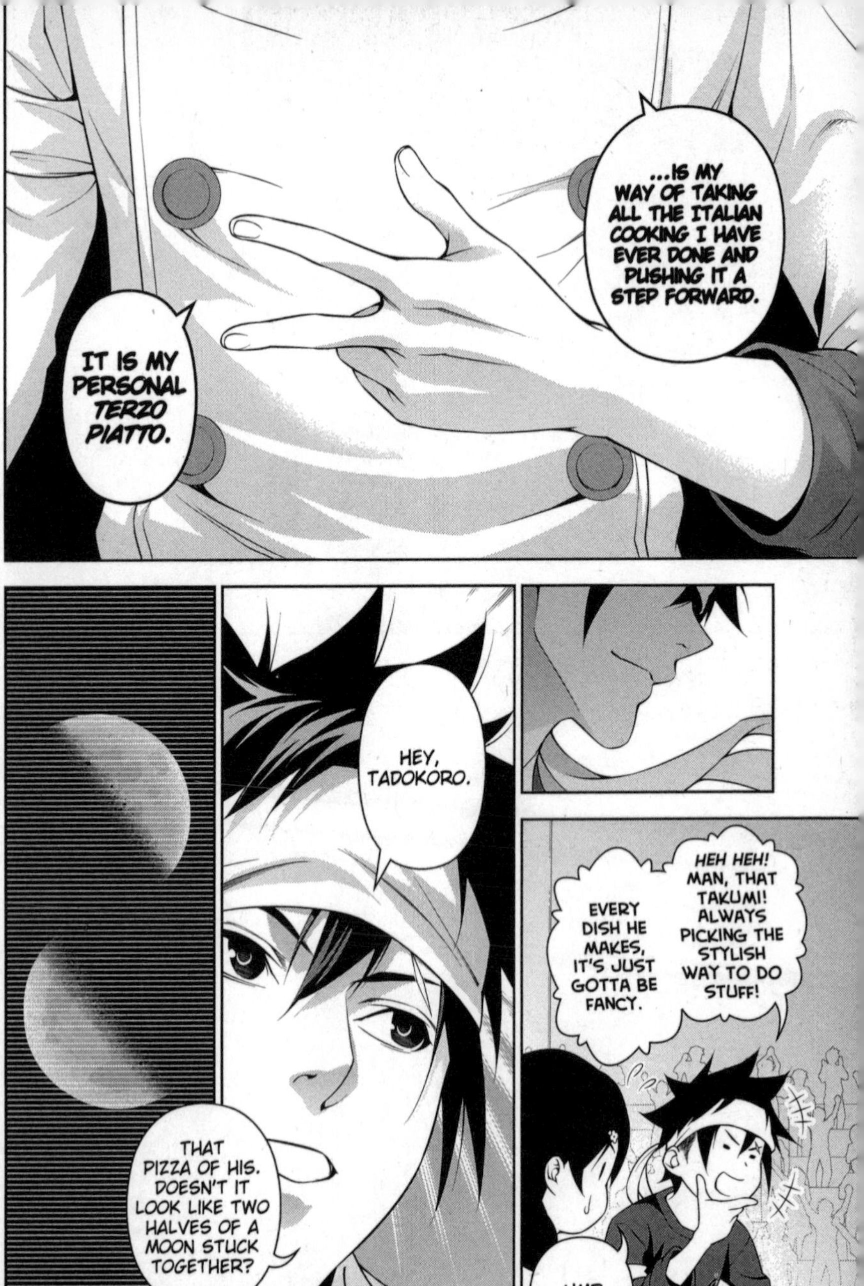
...IS MY WAY OF TAKING ALL THE ITALIAN COOKING I HAVE EVER DONE AND PUSHING IT A STEP FORWARD.
IT IS MY PERSONAL *TERZO PIATTO.*
HEH HEH! MAN, THAT TAKUMI! ALWAYS PICKING THE STYLISH WAY TO DO STUFF!
EVERY DISH HE MAKES, IT'S JUST GOTTA BE FANCY.
HM? SOMA?
HEY, TADOKORO.
THAT PIZZA OF HIS. DOESN'T IT LOOK LIKE TWO HALVES OF A MOON STUCK TOGETHER?

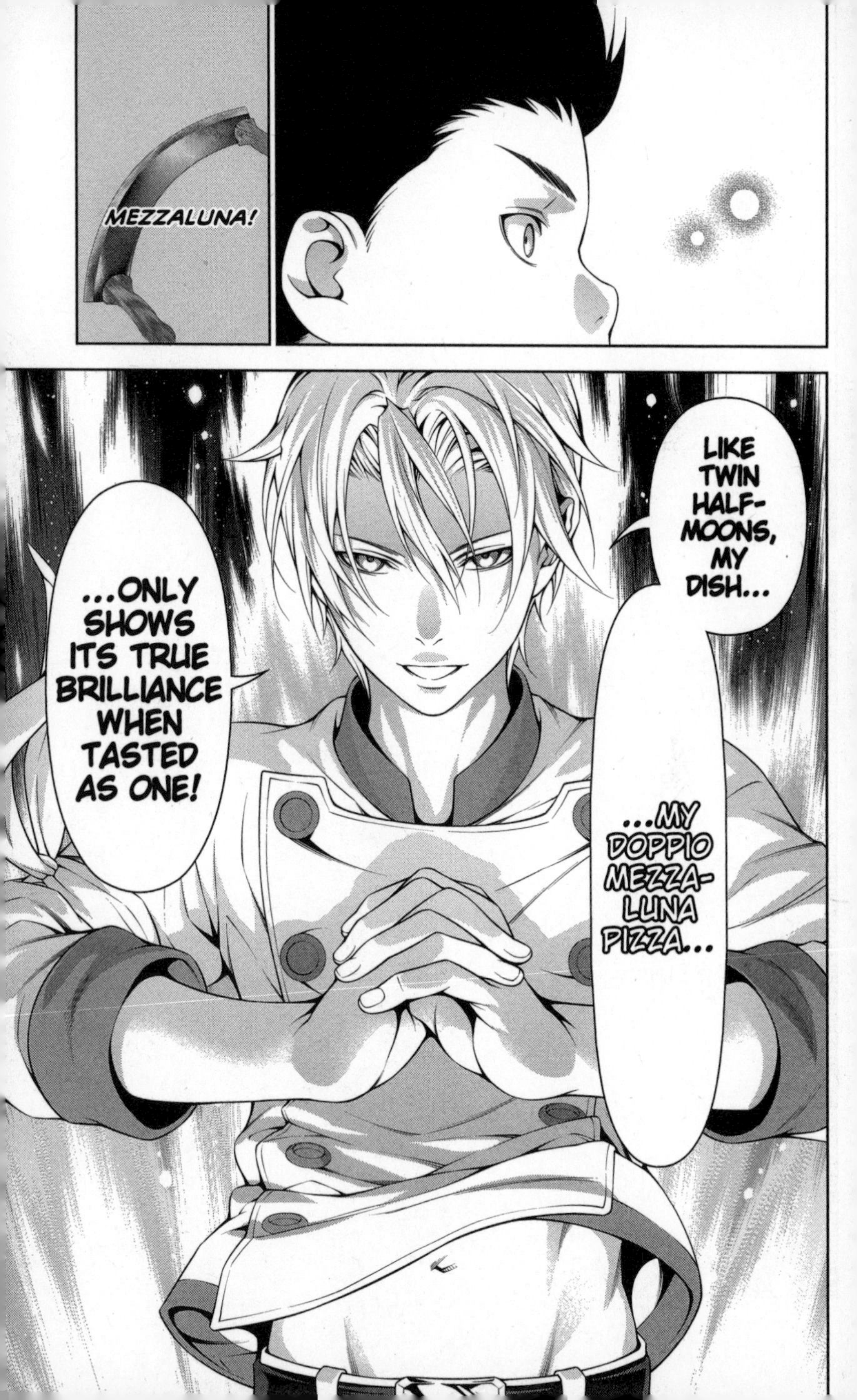
MEZZALUNA!
LIKE TWIN HALF-MOONS, MY DISH...
...MY DOPPIO MEZZALUNA PIZZA...
...ONLY SHOWS ITS TRUE BRILLIANCE WHEN TASTED AS ONE!

**Food Wars! The Third Plate!
Third Anime Season
Celebration**

*TERZO
PIATTO!*

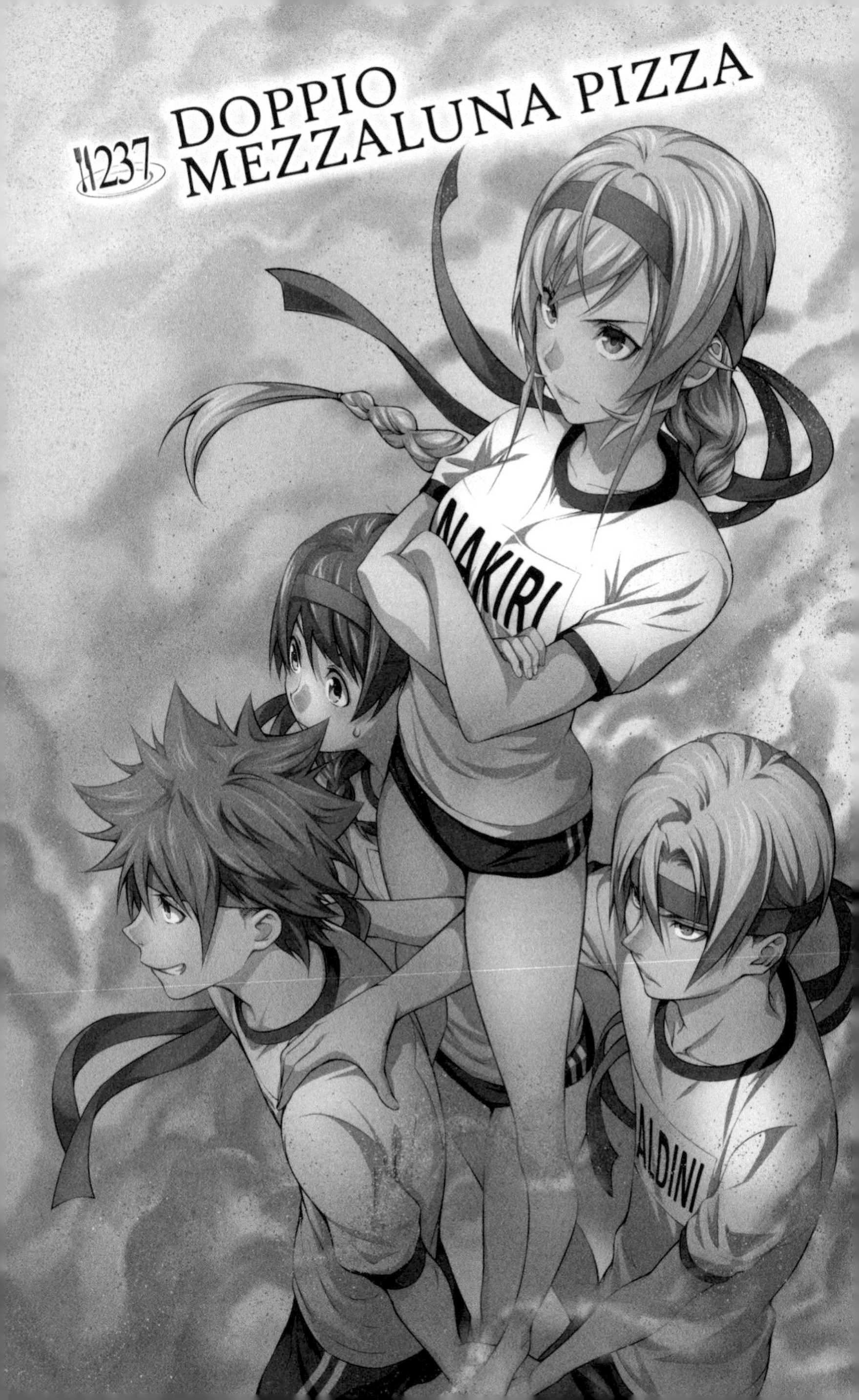
237
DOPPIO
MEZZALUNA PIZZA
NAKIRI
ALDINI

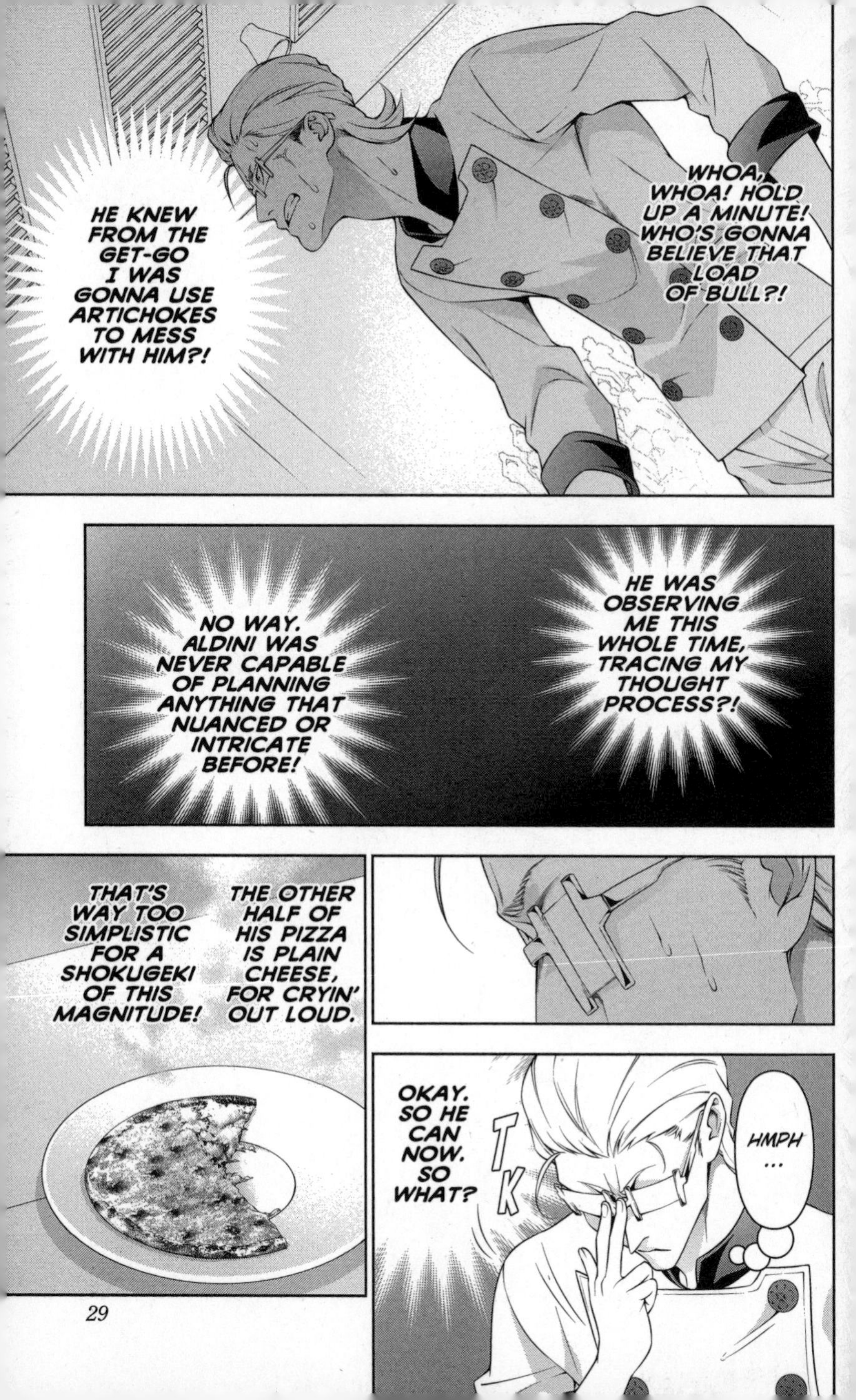
WHOA, WHOA! HOLD UP A MINUTE! WHO'S GONNA BELIEVE THAT LOAD OF BULL?!
HE KNEW FROM THE GET-GO I WAS GONNA USE ARTICHOKES TO MESS WITH HIM?!
HE WAS OBSERVING ME THIS WHOLE TIME, TRACING MY THOUGHT PROCESS?!
NO WAY. ALDINI WAS NEVER CAPABLE OF PLANNING ANYTHING THAT NUANCED OR INTRICATE BEFORE!
HMPH...
TK
OKAY. SO HE CAN NOW. SO WHAT?
THE OTHER HALF OF HIS PIZZA IS PLAIN CHEESE, FOR CRYIN' OUT LOUD.
THAT'S WAY TOO SIMPLISTIC FOR A SHOKUGEKI OF THIS MAGNITUDE!

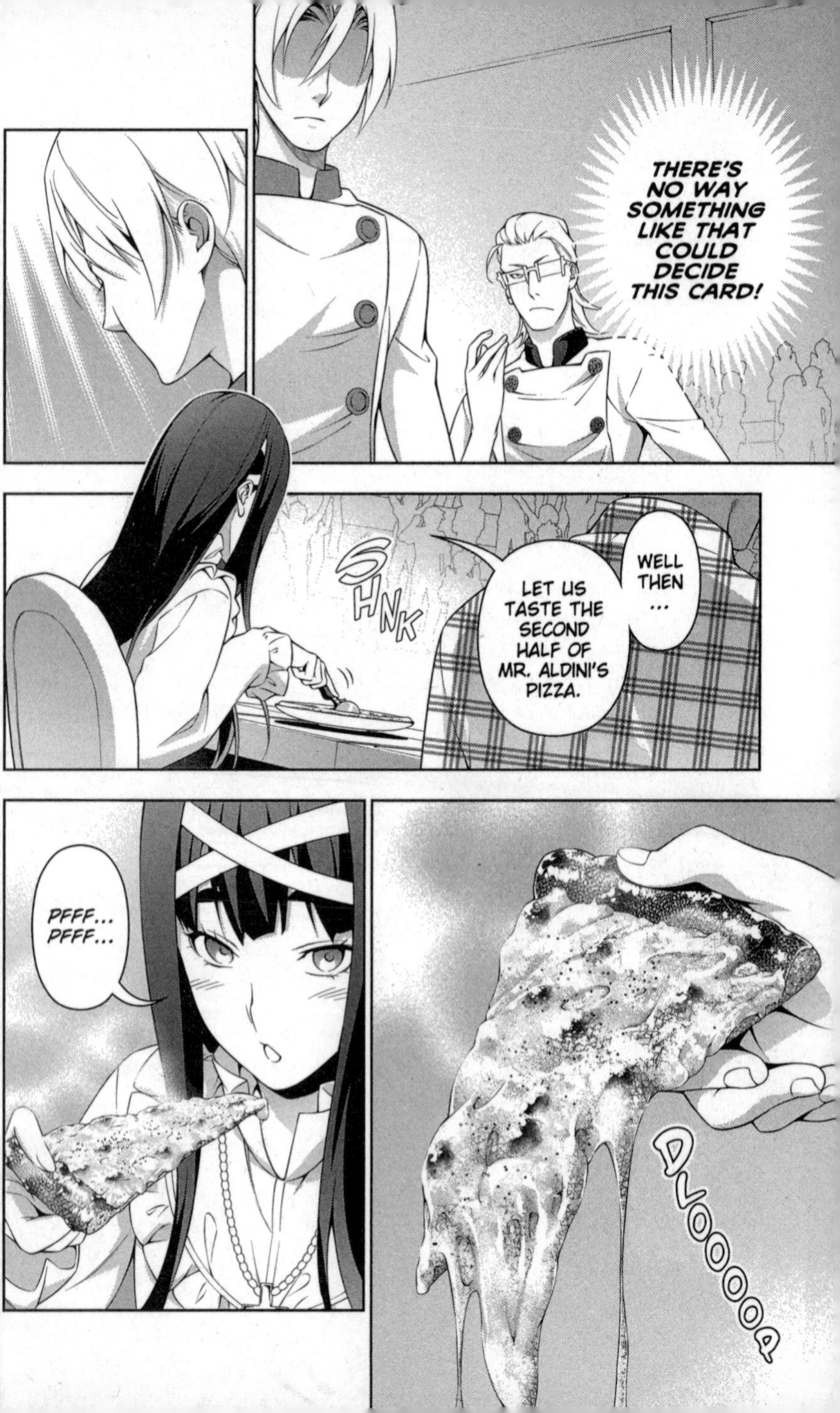
THERE'S NO WAY SOMETHING LIKE THAT COULD DECIDE THIS CARD!
WELL THEN...
LET US TASTE THE SECOND HALF OF MR. ALDINI'S PIZZA.
SHNK
DVOOOOA
PFFF... PFFF...

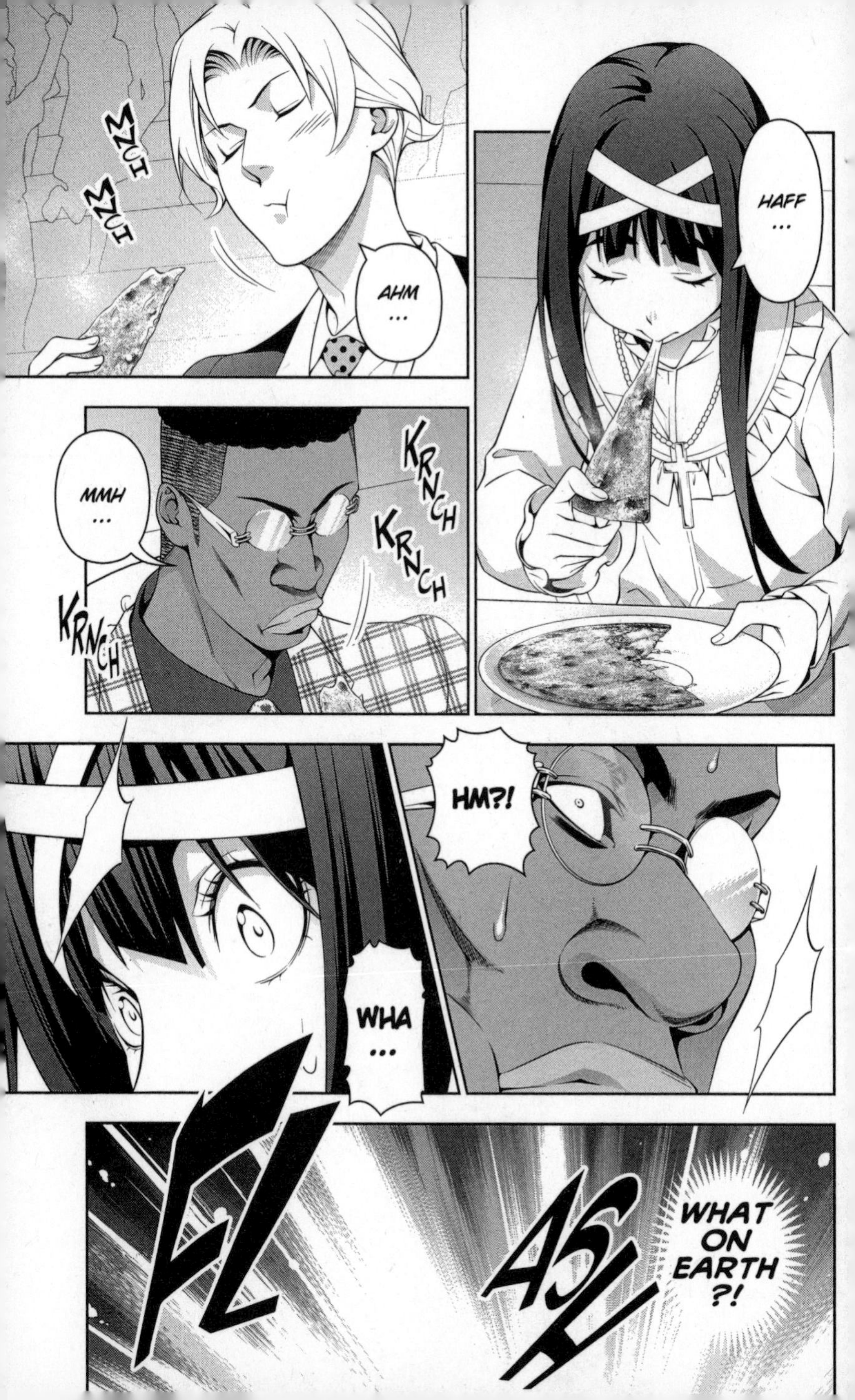
HAFF ...
AHM ...
MUNCH
MUNCH
MMH ...
KRNCH
KRNCH
KRNCH
HM?!
WHA ...
FLASH
WHAT ON EARTH ?!

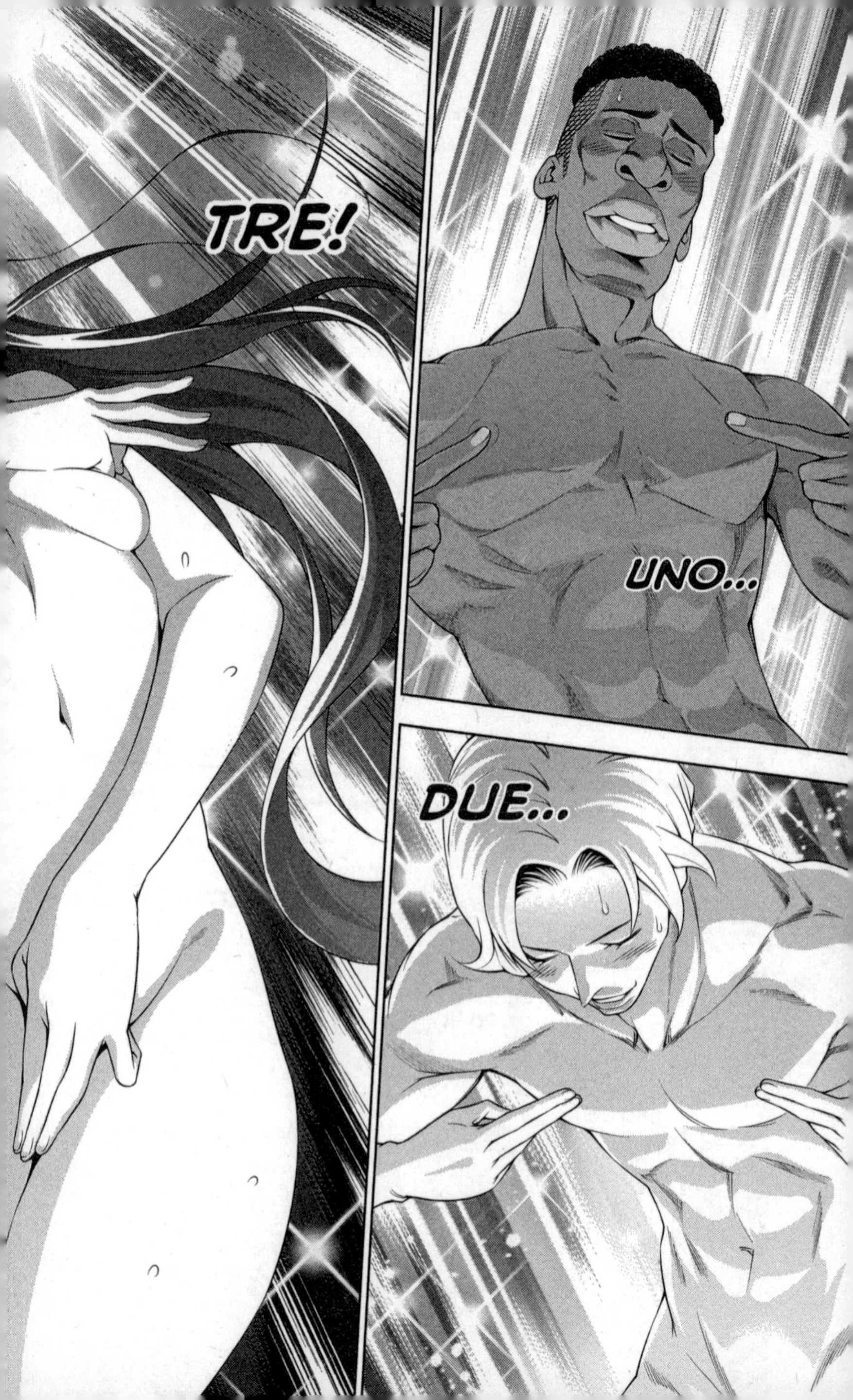
UNO...
DUE...
TRE!

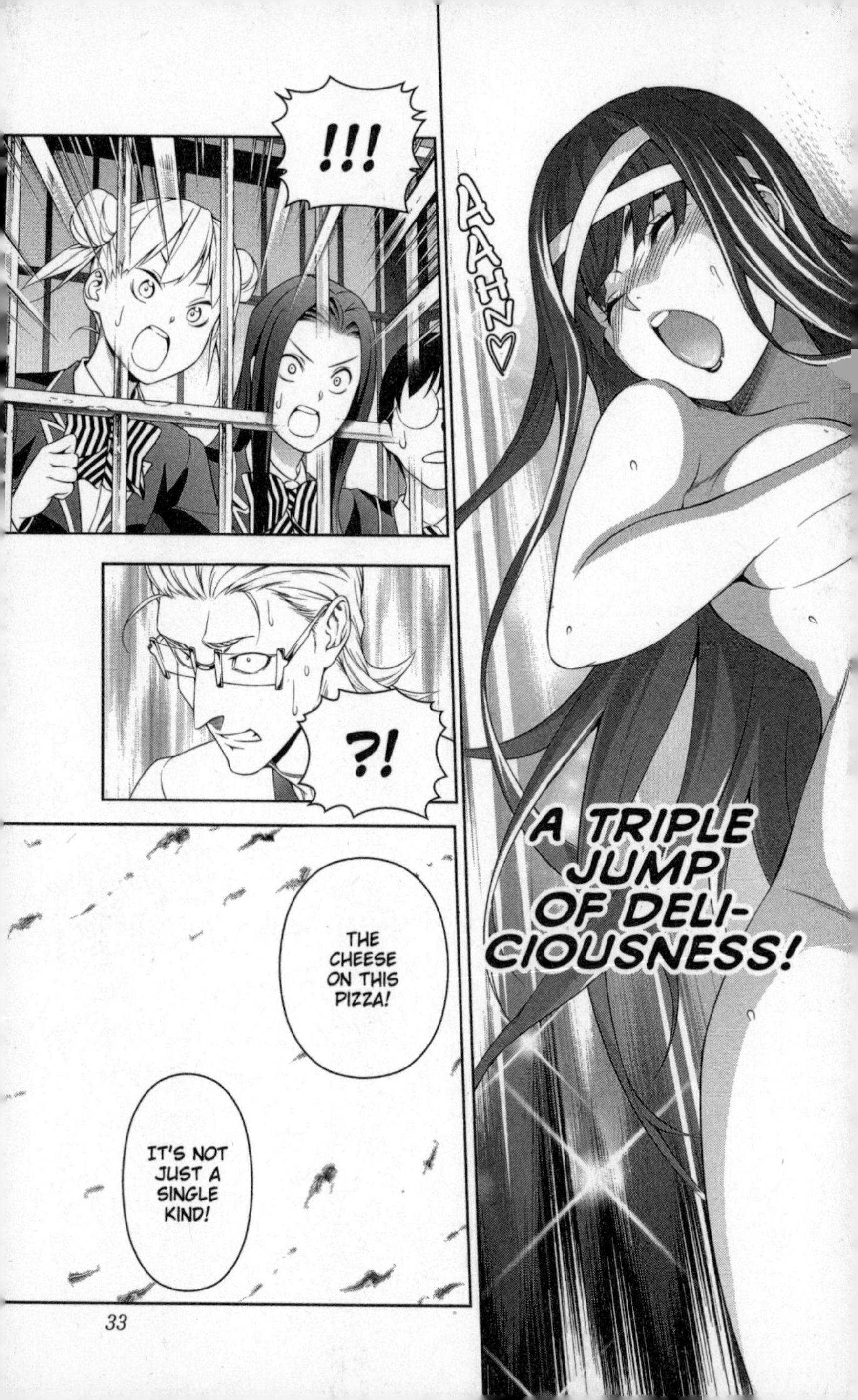
AAHN♡
A TRIPLE JUMP OF DELICIOUSNESS!
!!!
?!
THE CHEESE ON THIS PIZZA!
IT'S NOT JUST A SINGLE KIND!

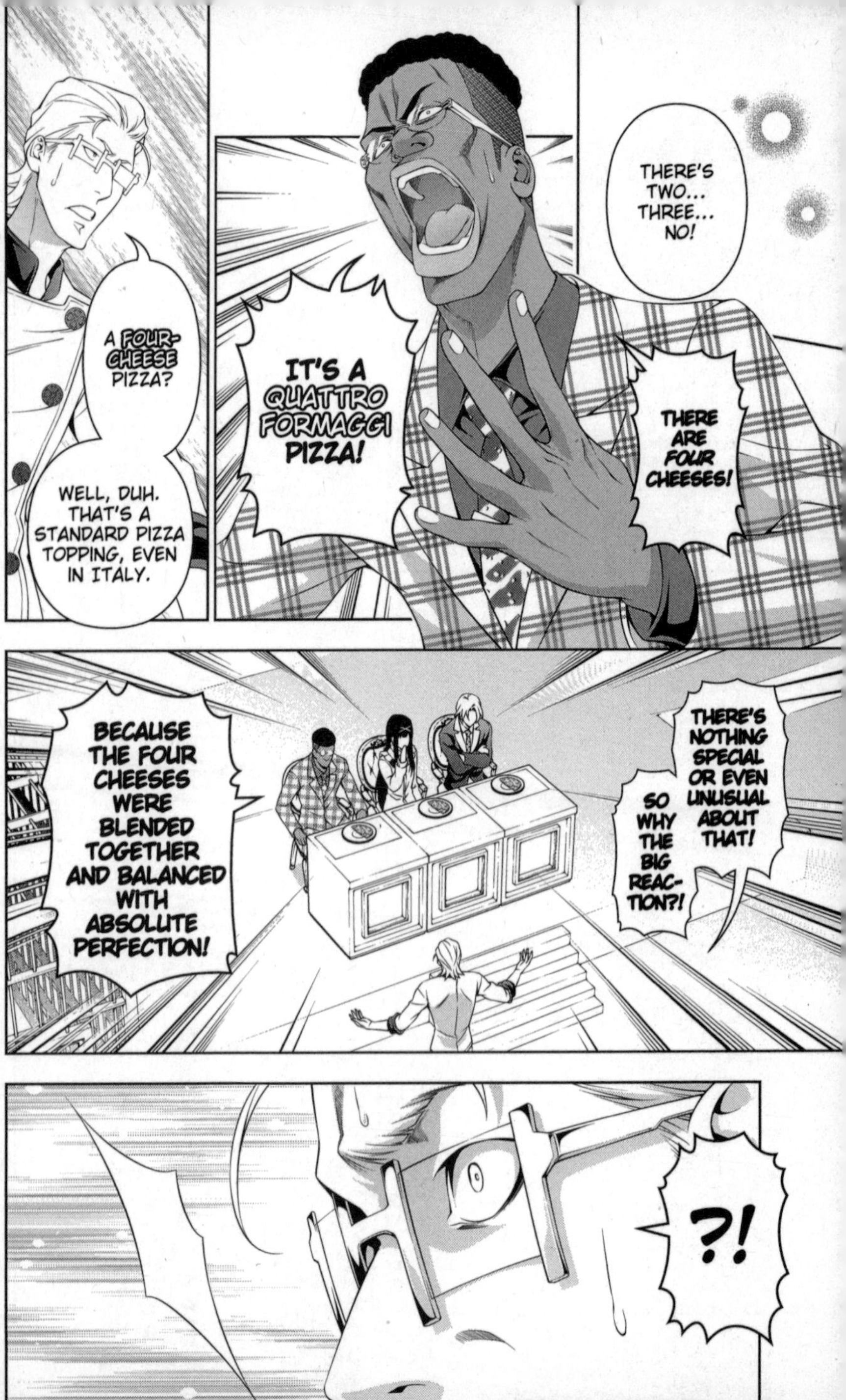
THERE'S TWO... THREE... NO!
THERE ARE FOUR CHEESES!
IT'S A QUATTRO FORMAGGI PIZZA!
A FOUR-CHEESE PIZZA?
WELL, DUH. THAT'S A STANDARD PIZZA TOPPING, EVEN IN ITALY.
THERE'S NOTHING SPECIAL OR EVEN UNUSUAL ABOUT THAT!
SO WHY THE BIG REACTION?!
BECAUSE THE FOUR CHEESES WERE BLENDED TOGETHER AND BALANCED WITH ABSOLUTE PERFECTION!
?!

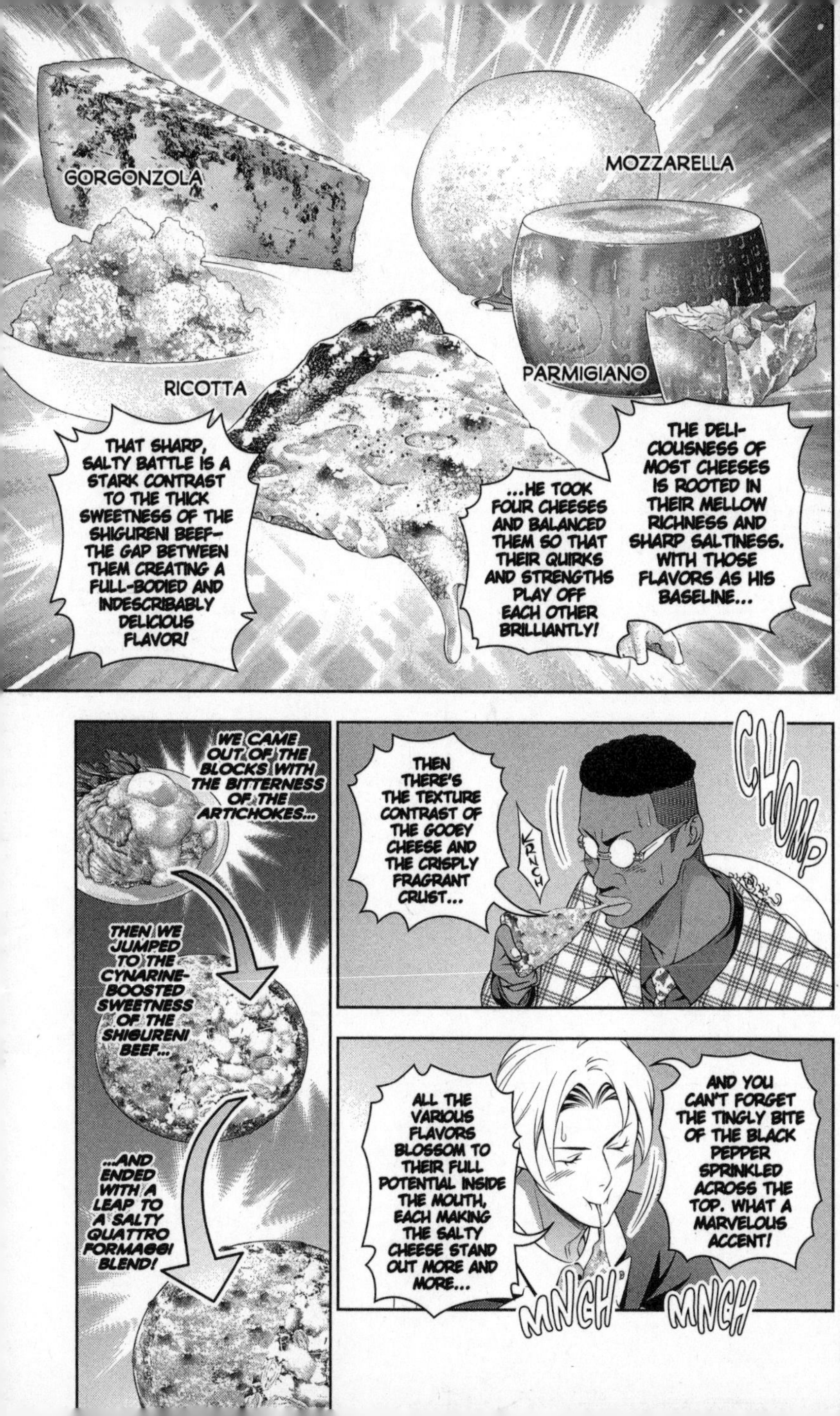
MOZZARELLA
GORGONZOLA
PARMIGIANO
RICOTTA
THE DELICIOUSNESS OF MOST CHEESES IS ROOTED IN THEIR MELLOW RICHNESS AND SHARP SALTINESS. WITH THOSE FLAVORS AS HIS BASELINE...
...HE TOOK FOUR CHEESES AND BALANCED THEM SO THAT THEIR QUIRKS AND STRENGTHS PLAY OFF EACH OTHER BRILLIANTLY!
THAT SHARP, SALTY BATTLE IS A STARK CONTRAST TO THE THICK SWEETNESS OF THE SHIGURENI BEEF–THE GAP BETWEEN THEM CREATING A FULL-BODIED AND INDESCRIBABLY DELICIOUS FLAVOR!
CHOMP
KRNCH
THEN THERE'S THE TEXTURE CONTRAST OF THE GOOEY CHEESE AND THE CRISPLY FRAGRANT CRUST...
AND YOU CAN'T FORGET THE TINGLY BITE OF THE BLACK PEPPER SPRINKLED ACROSS THE TOP. WHAT A MARVELOUS ACCENT!
ALL THE VARIOUS FLAVORS BLOSSOM TO THEIR FULL POTENTIAL INSIDE THE MOUTH, EACH MAKING THE SALTY CHEESE STAND OUT MORE AND MORE...
MNCH
MNCH
WE CAME OUT OF THE BLOCKS WITH THE BITTERNESS OF THE ARTICHOKES...
THEN WE JUMPED TO THE CYNARINE-BOOSTED SWEETNESS OF THE SHIGURENI BEEF...
...AND ENDED WITH A LEAP TO A SALTY QUATTRO FORMAGGI BLEND!

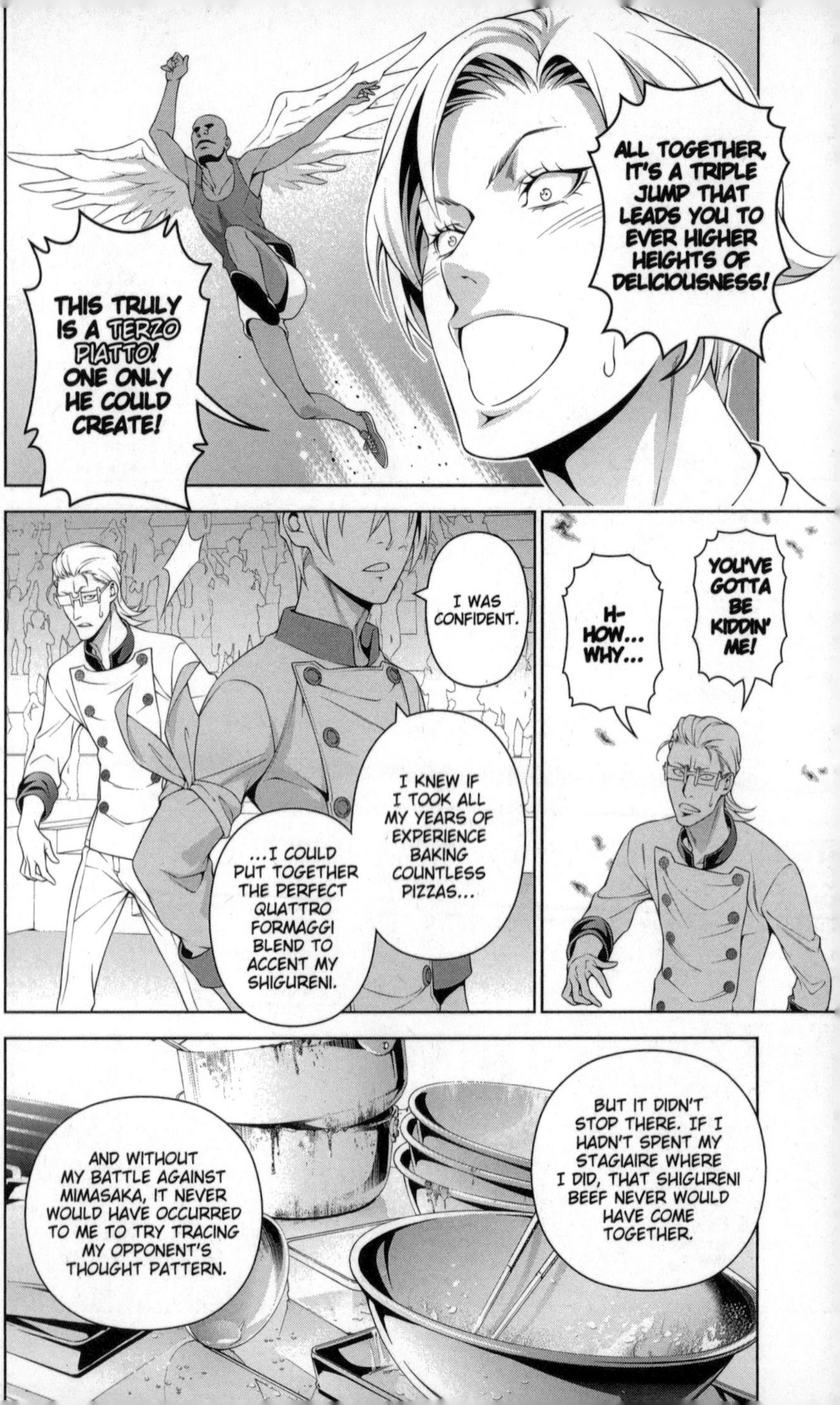

ALL TOGETHER, IT'S A TRIPLE JUMP THAT LEADS YOU TO EVER HIGHER HEIGHTS OF DELICIOUSNESS!
THIS TRULY IS A TERZO PIATTO! ONE ONLY HE COULD CREATE!
YOU'VE GOTTA BE KIDDIN' ME!
H-HOW... WHY...
I WAS CONFIDENT.
I KNEW IF I TOOK ALL MY YEARS OF EXPERIENCE BAKING COUNTLESS PIZZAS...
...I COULD PUT TOGETHER THE PERFECT QUATTRO FORMAGGI BLEND TO ACCENT MY SHIGURENI.
BUT IT DIDN'T STOP THERE. IF I HADN'T SPENT MY STAGIAIRE WHERE I DID, THAT SHIGURENI BEEF NEVER WOULD HAVE COME TOGETHER.
AND WITHOUT MY BATTLE AGAINST MIMASAKA, IT NEVER WOULD HAVE OCCURRED TO ME TO TRY TRACING MY OPPONENT'S THOUGHT PATTERN.

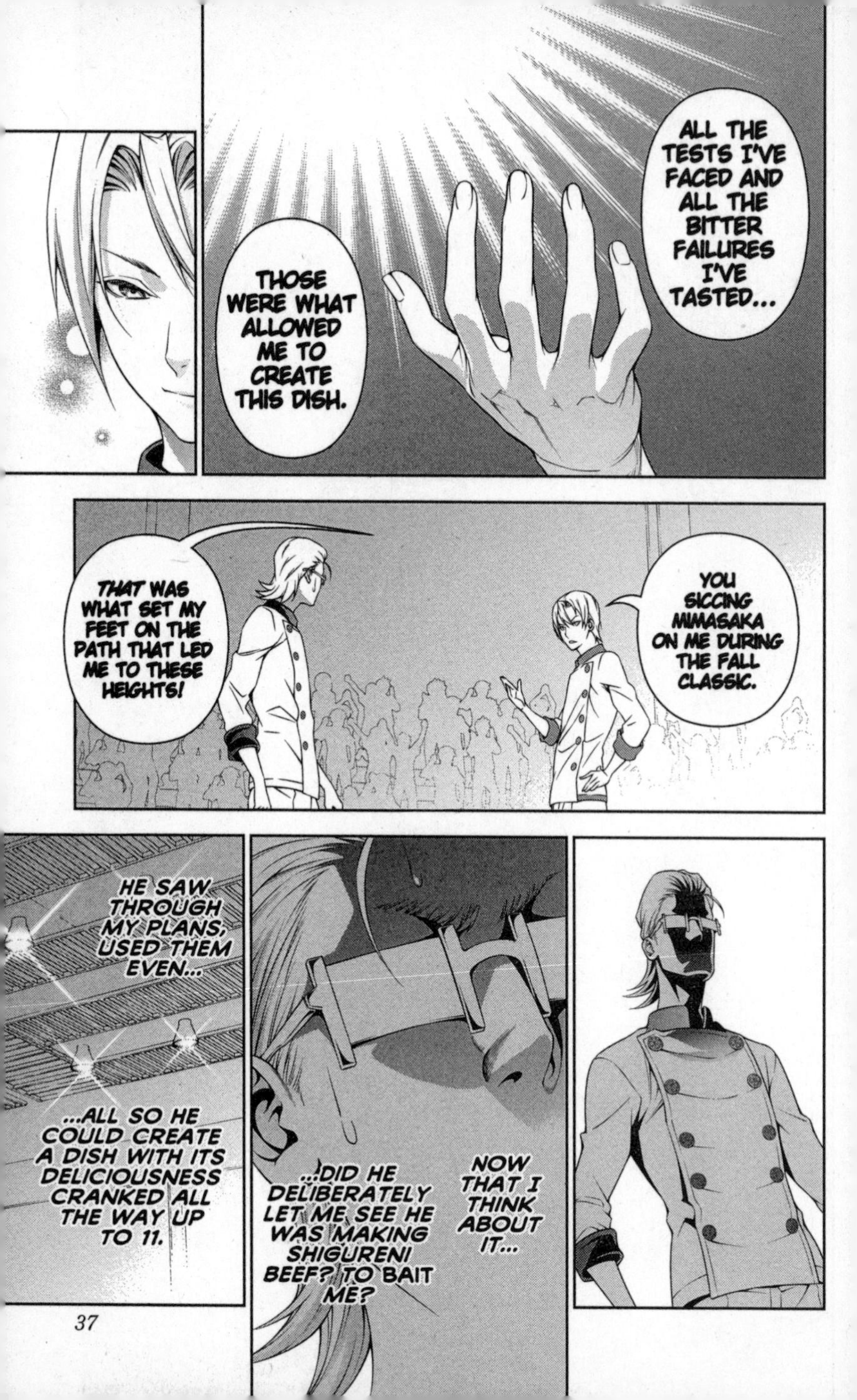
ALL THE TESTS I'VE FACED AND ALL THE BITTER FAILURES I'VE TASTED...
THOSE WERE WHAT ALLOWED ME TO CREATE THIS DISH.
YOU SICCING MIMASAKA ON ME DURING THE FALL CLASSIC.
THAT WAS WHAT SET MY FEET ON THE PATH THAT LED ME TO THESE HEIGHTS!
NOW THAT I THINK ABOUT IT...
...DID HE DELIBERATELY LET ME SEE HE WAS MAKING SHIGURENI BEEF? TO BAIT ME?
HE SAW THROUGH MY PLANS, USED THEM EVEN...
...ALL SO HE COULD CREATE A DISH WITH ITS DELICIOUSNESS CRANKED ALL THE WAY UP TO 11.

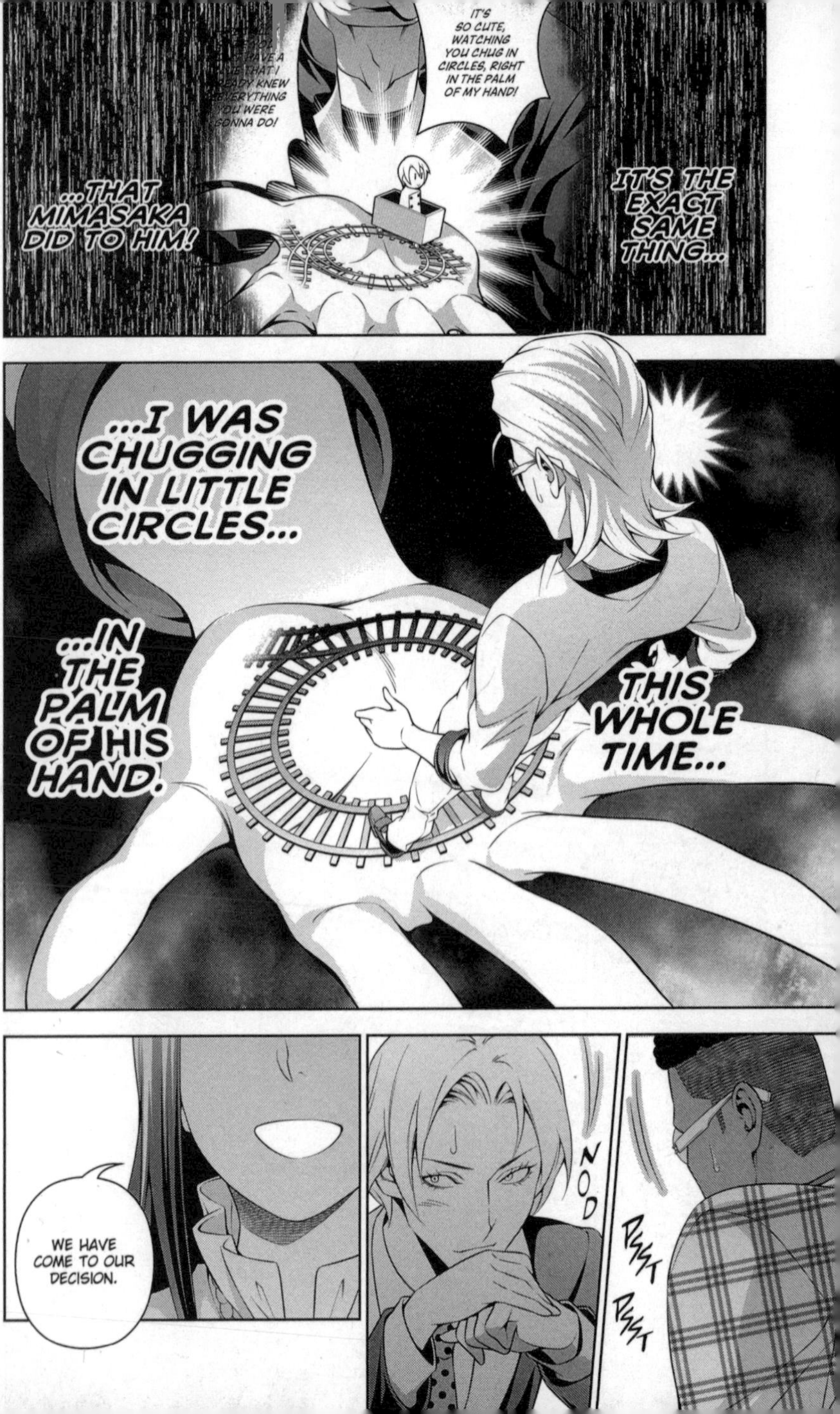
IT'S SO CUTE, WATCHING YOU CHUG IN CIRCLES, RIGHT IN THE PALM OF MY HAND!
KNEW EVERYTHING YOU WERE GONNA DO!
IT'S THE EXACT SAME THING...
...THAT MIMASAKA DID TO HIM!
THIS WHOLE TIME...
...I WAS CHUGGING IN LITTLE CIRCLES...
...IN THE PALM OF HIS HAND.
PSST PSST
NOD
WE HAVE COME TO OUR DECISION.

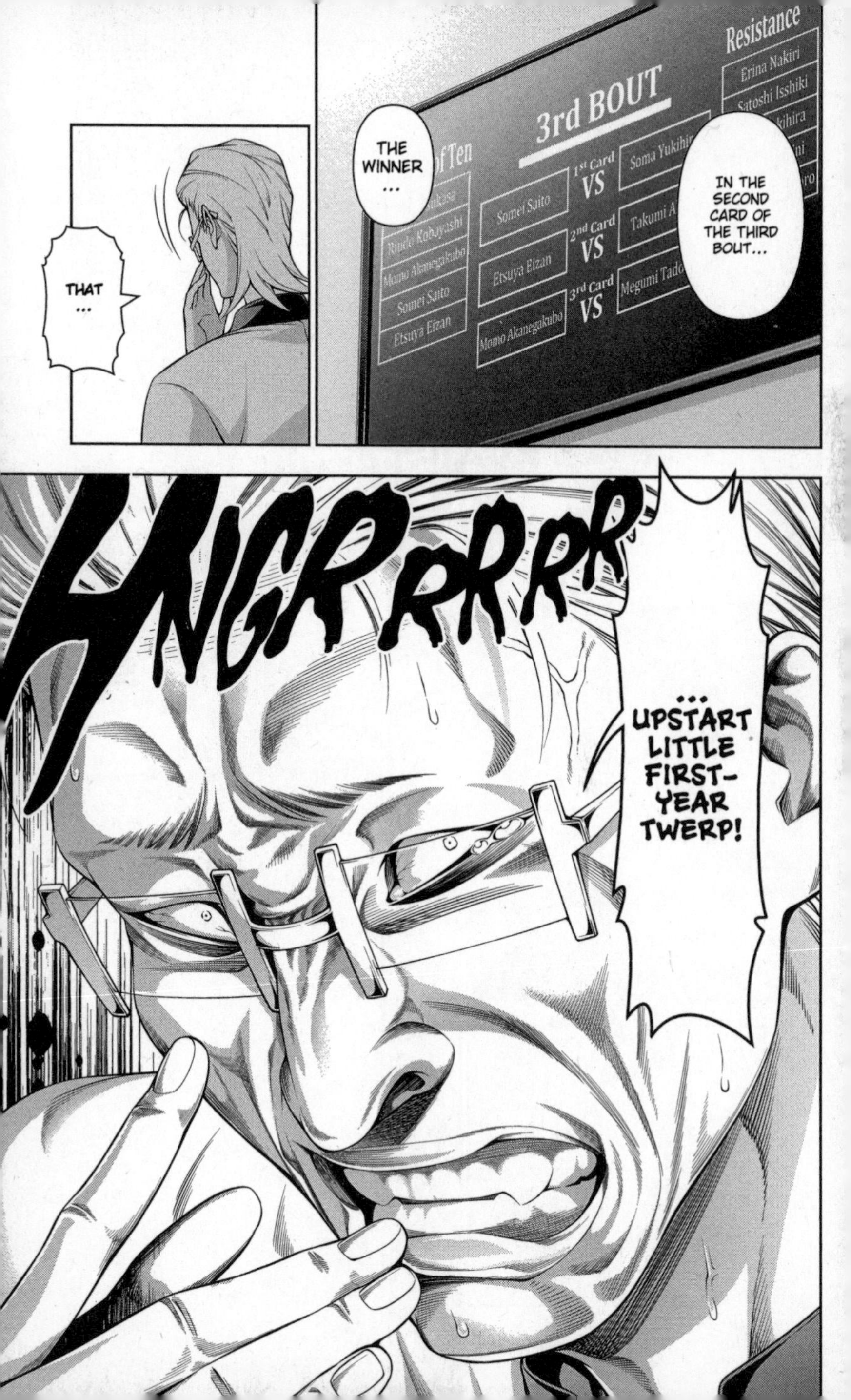
IN THE SECOND CARD OF THE THIRD BOUT...
Resistance
Erina Nakiri
Satoshi Isshiki
3rd BOUT
1st Card VS
2nd Card VS
3rd Card VS
Somei Saito
Etsuya Eizan
Momo Akanegakubo
Rindo Kobayashi
Momo Akanegakubo
Somei Saito
Etsuya Eizan
THE WINNER ...
THAT ...
HNGRRRRR
... UPSTART LITTLE FIRST-YEAR TWERP!

...IS TAKUMI ALDINI, OF THE RESISTANCE!

3rd BOUT

Somei Saito 1st Card VS Soma Yukihira

Etsuya Eizan 2nd Card VS Takumi Aldini
0   3

Momo Akanegakubo 3rd Card VS Megumi Tadokoro

Resista

Erina N
Satoshi
Soma Yu
Takumi
Megumi Ta

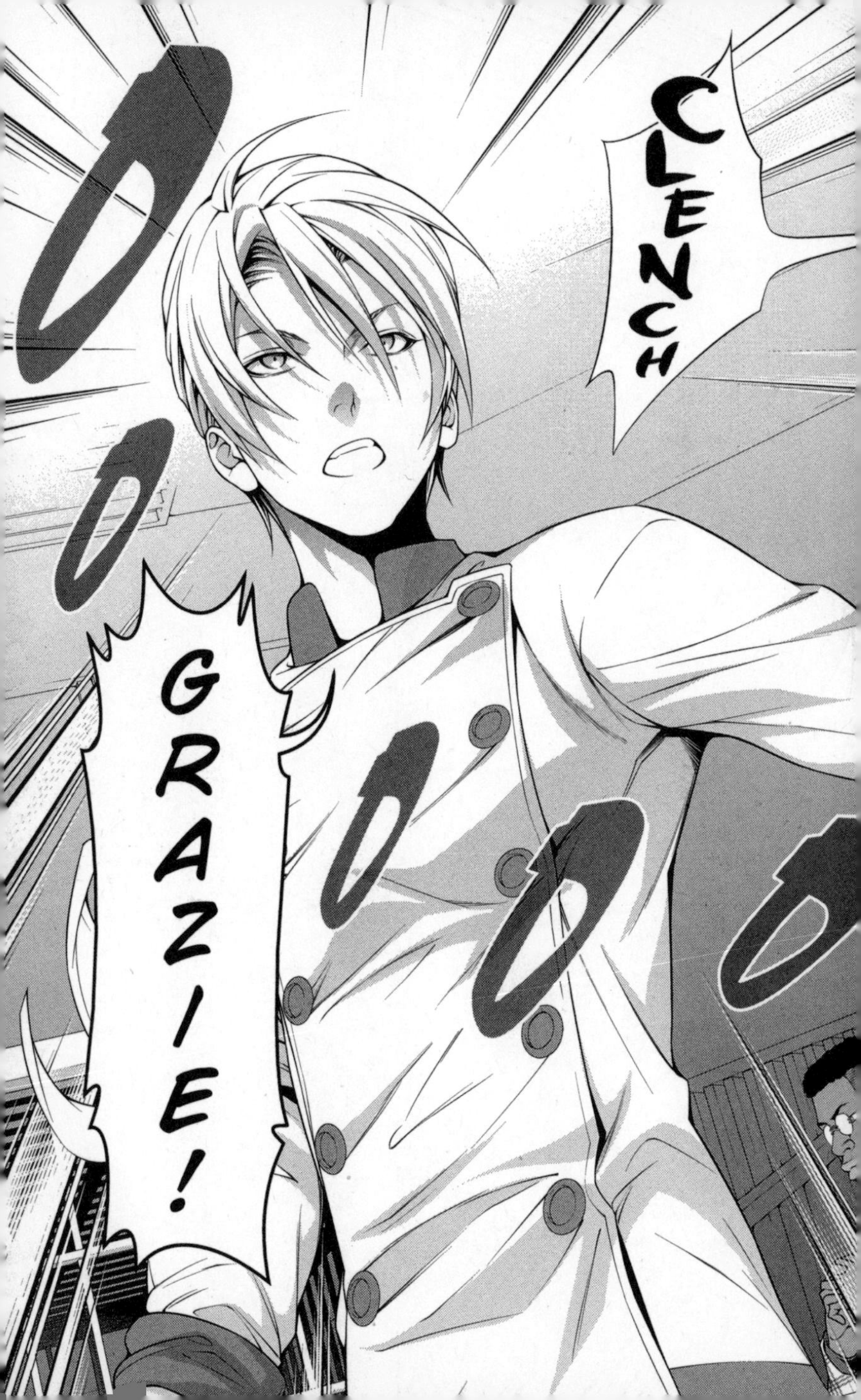

CLENCH
GRAZIE!

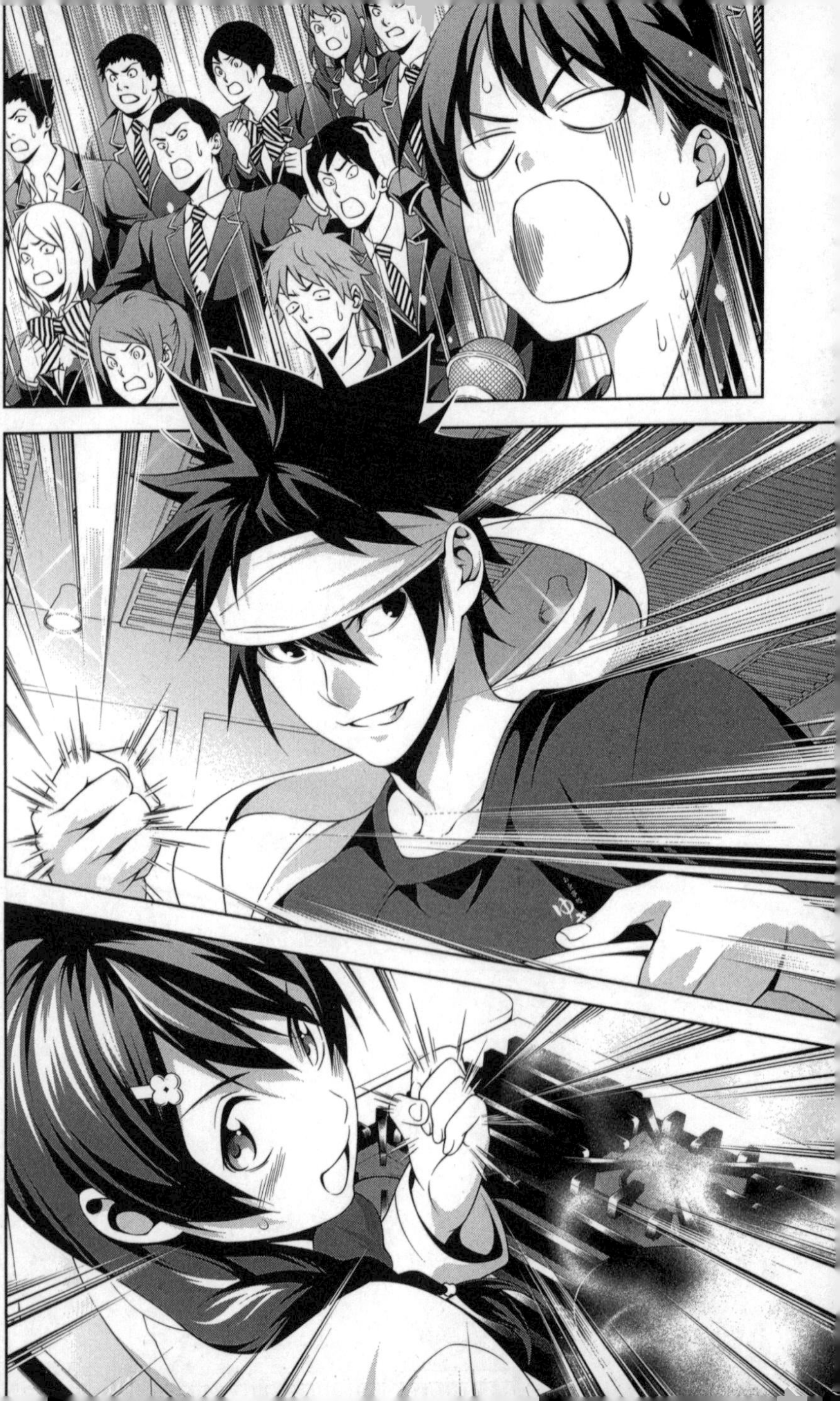

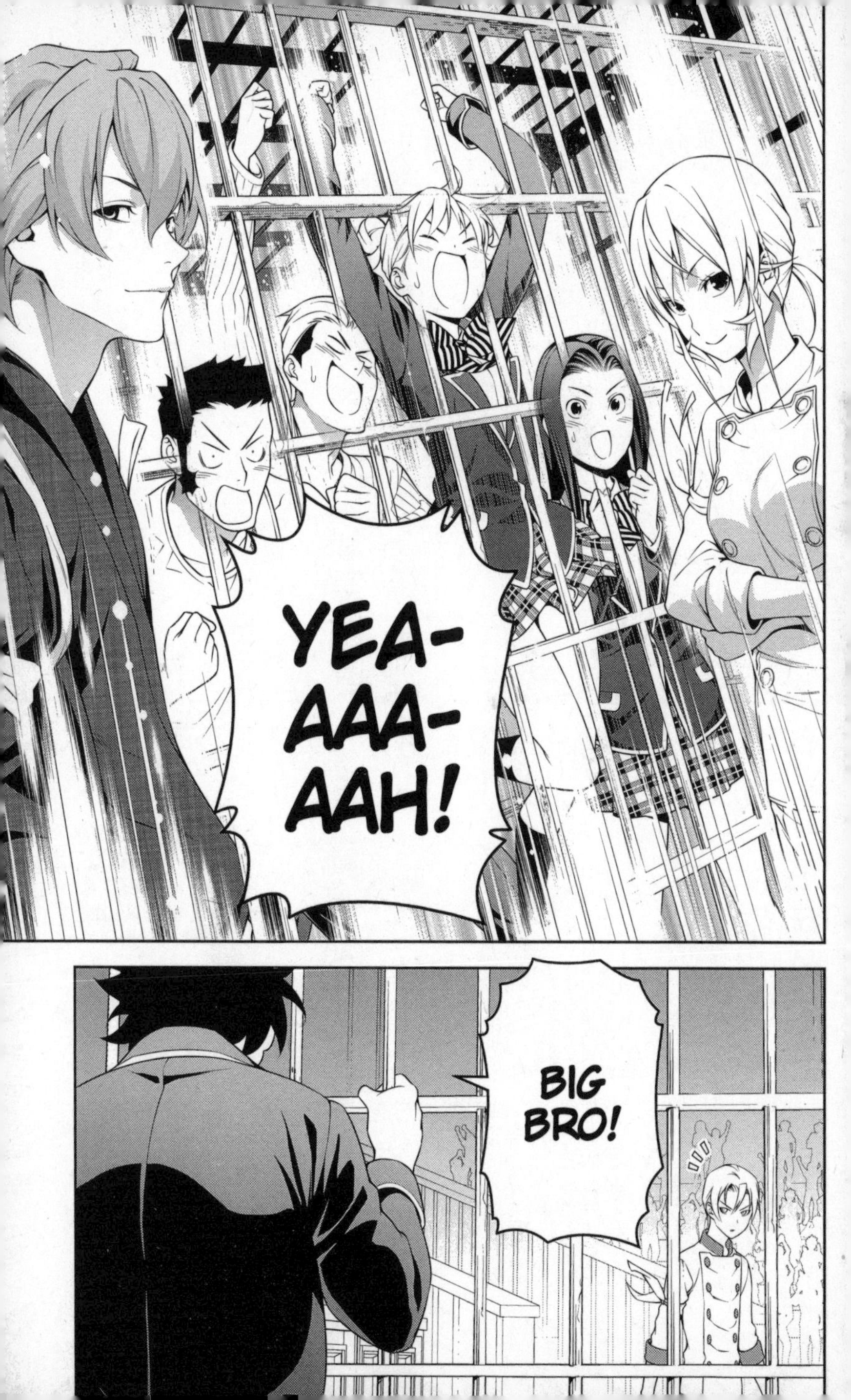
YEA-AAA-AAH!
BIG BRO!

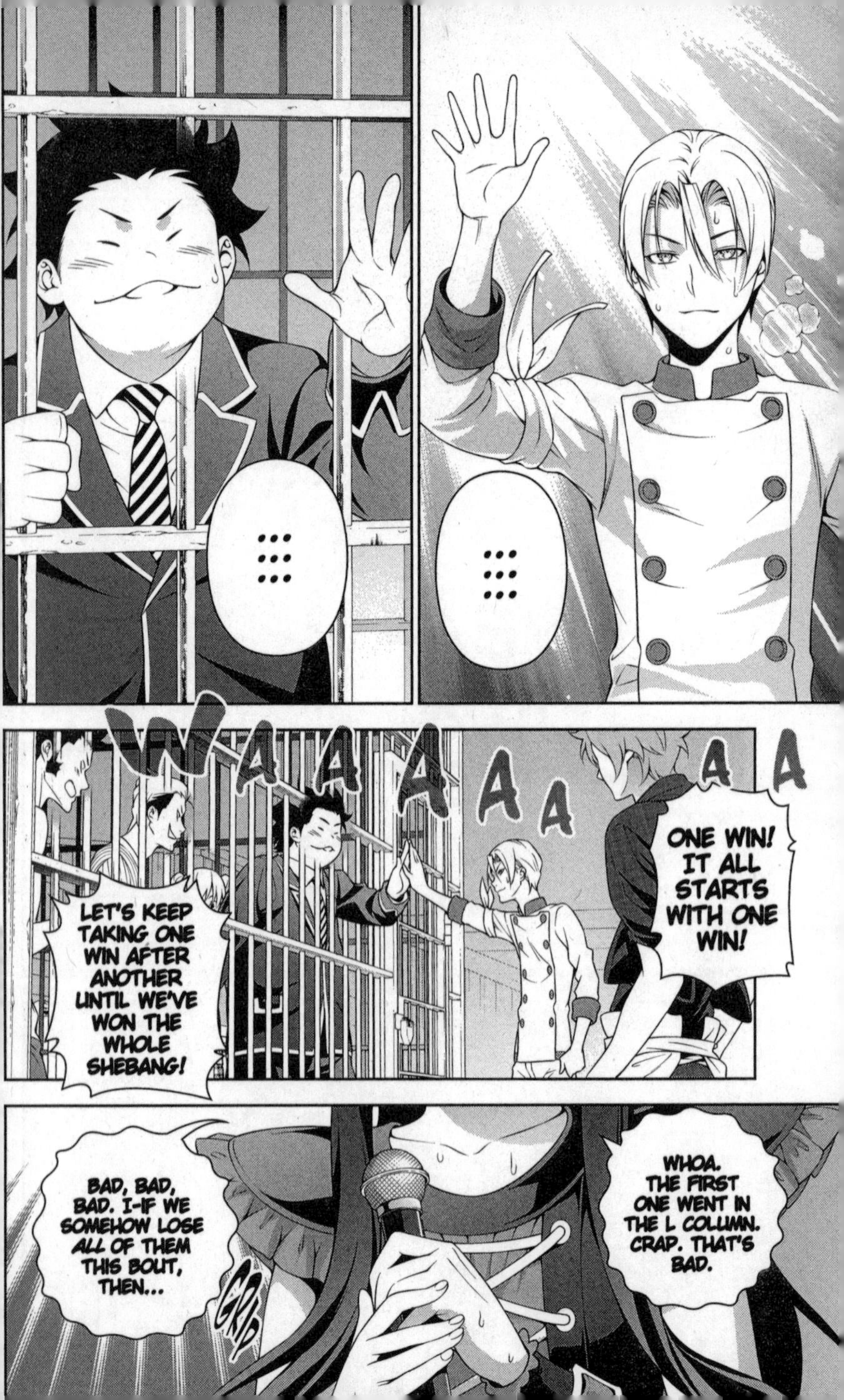
......
......
WAAAAAAAA
ONE WIN! IT ALL STARTS WITH ONE WIN!
LET'S KEEP TAKING ONE WIN AFTER ANOTHER UNTIL WE'VE WON THE WHOLE SHEBANG!
WHOA. THE FIRST ONE WENT IN THE L COLUMN. CRAP. THAT'S BAD.
BAD, BAD, BAD. I-IF WE SOMEHOW LOSE ALL OF THEM THIS BOUT, THEN...
GRIP

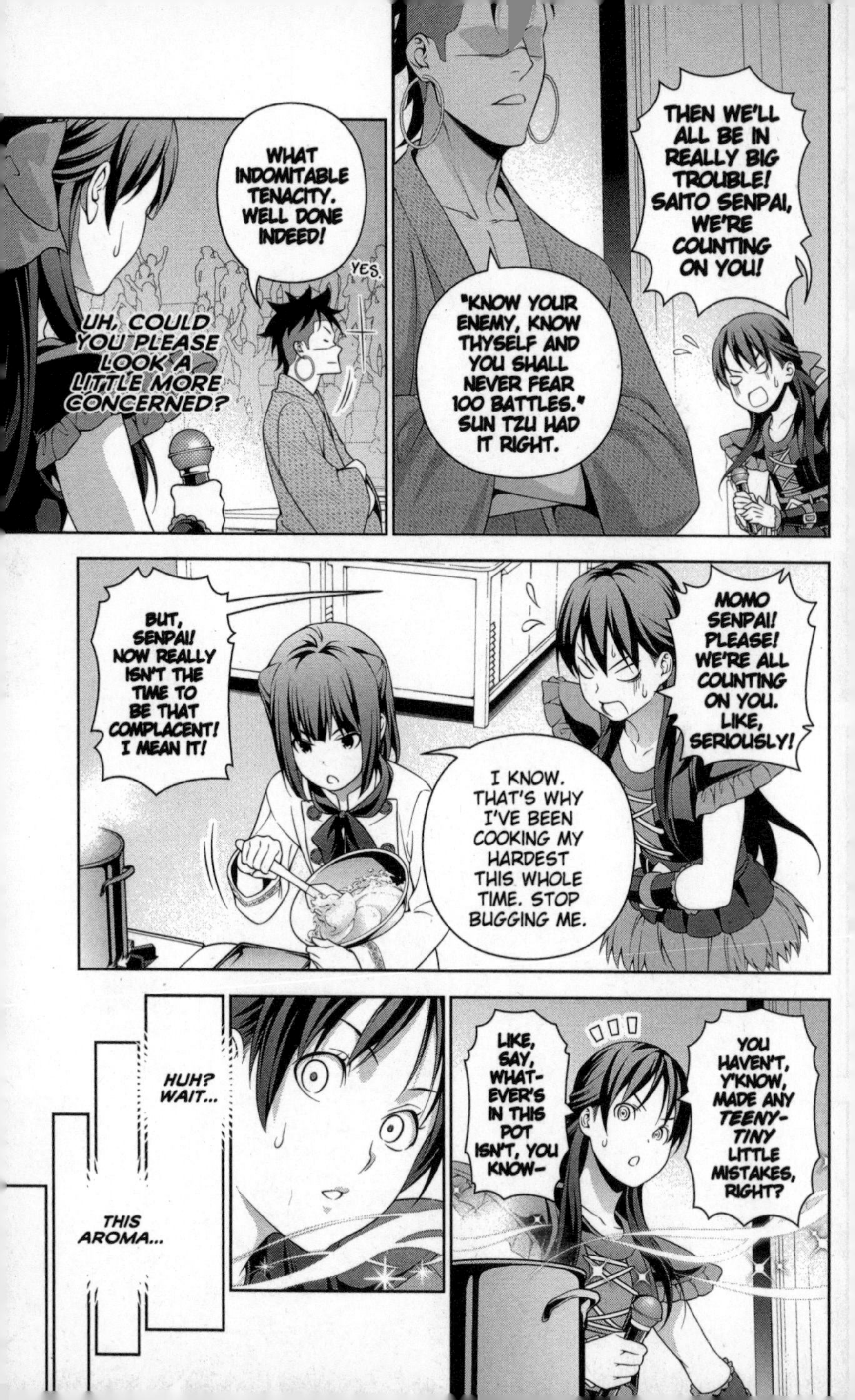
THEN WE'LL ALL BE IN REALLY BIG TROUBLE! SAITO SENPAI, WE'RE COUNTING ON YOU!
"KNOW YOUR ENEMY, KNOW THYSELF AND YOU SHALL NEVER FEAR 100 BATTLES." SUN TZU HAD IT RIGHT.
WHAT INDOMITABLE TENACITY. WELL DONE INDEED!
YES.
UH, COULD YOU PLEASE LOOK A LITTLE MORE CONCERNED?
MOMO SENPAI! PLEASE! WE'RE ALL COUNTING ON YOU. LIKE, SERIOUSLY!
BUT, SENPAI! NOW REALLY ISN'T THE TIME TO BE THAT COMPLACENT! I MEAN IT!
I KNOW. THAT'S WHY I'VE BEEN COOKING MY HARDEST THIS WHOLE TIME. STOP BUGGING ME.
YOU HAVEN'T, Y'KNOW, MADE ANY TEENY-TINY LITTLE MISTAKES, RIGHT?
LIKE, SAY, WHAT-EVER'S IN THIS POT ISN'T, YOU KNOW-
HUH? WAIT...
THIS AROMA...

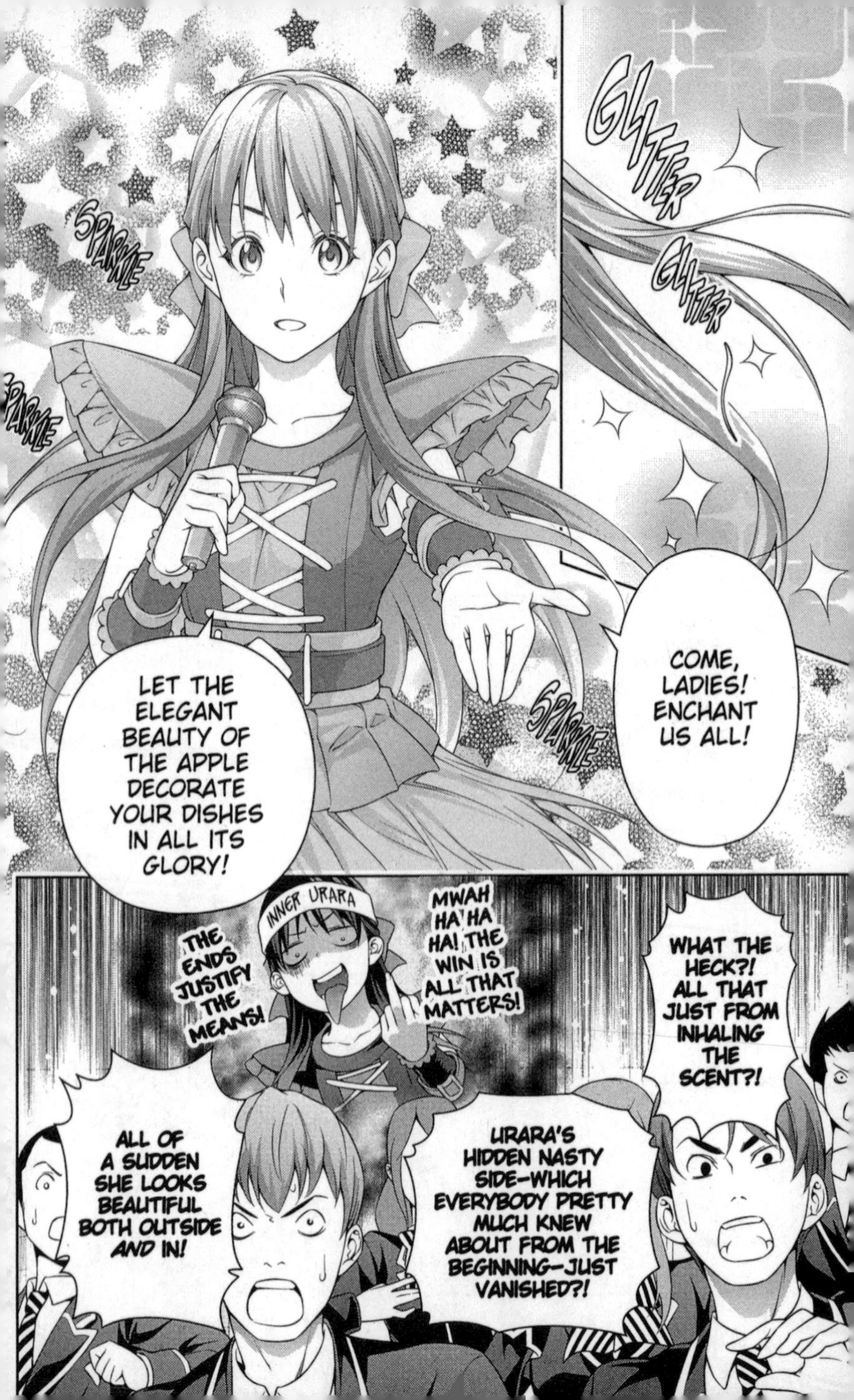
GLITTER
GLITTER
SPARKLE
SPARKLE
COME, LADIES! ENCHANT US ALL!
SPARKLE
LET THE ELEGANT BEAUTY OF THE APPLE DECORATE YOUR DISHES IN ALL ITS GLORY!
WHAT THE HECK?! ALL THAT JUST FROM INHALING THE SCENT?!
INNER URARA
MWAH HA HA HA! THE WIN IS ALL THAT MATTERS!
THE ENDS JUSTIFY THE MEANS!
URARA'S HIDDEN NASTY SIDE—WHICH EVERYBODY PRETTY MUCH KNEW ABOUT FROM THE BEGINNING—JUST VANISHED?!
ALL OF A SUDDEN SHE LOOKS BEAUTIFUL BOTH OUTSIDE AND IN!

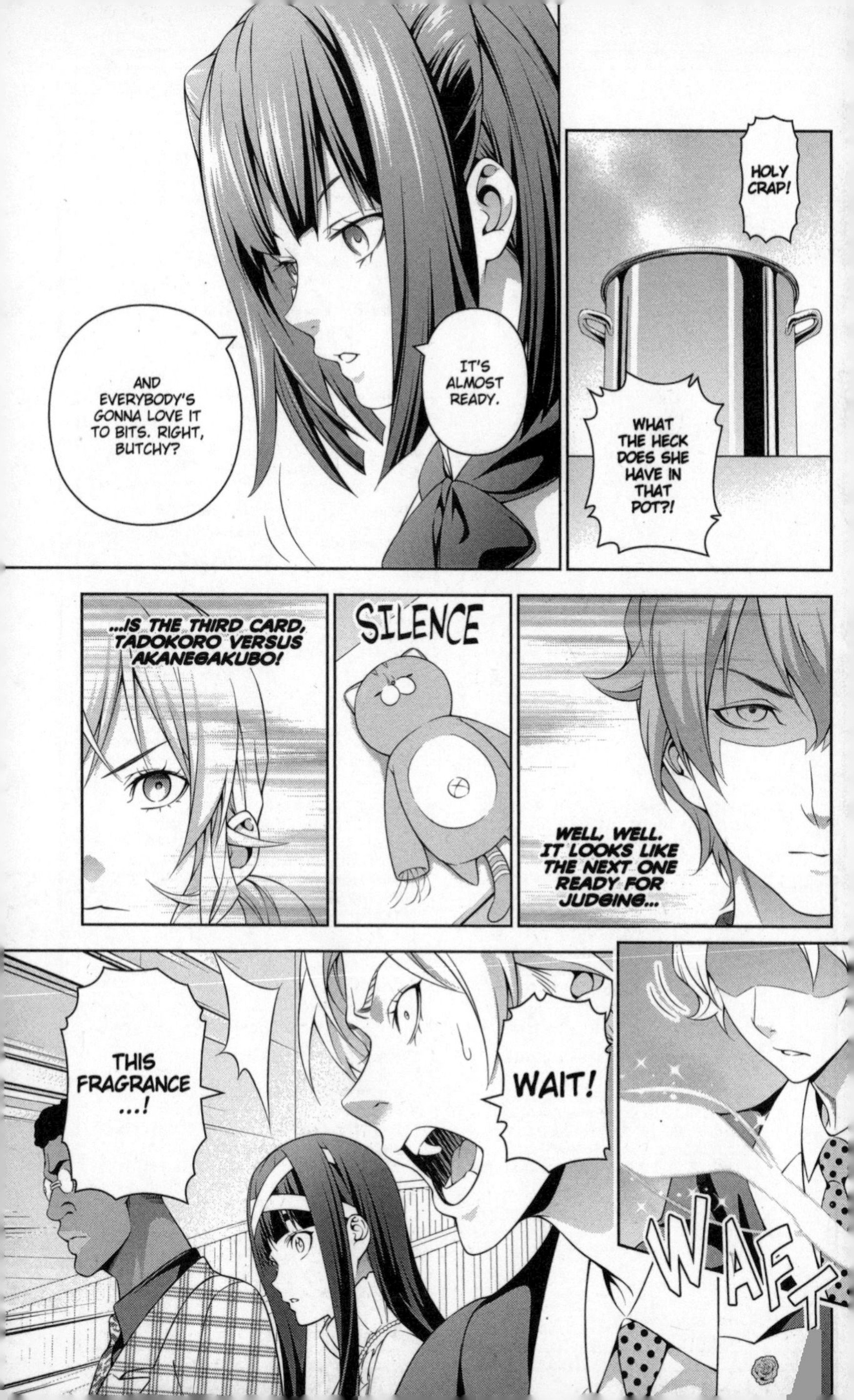
HOLY CRAP!
WHAT THE HECK DOES SHE HAVE IN THAT POT?!
IT'S ALMOST READY.
AND EVERYBODY'S GONNA LOVE IT TO BITS. RIGHT, BUTCHY?
WELL, WELL. IT LOOKS LIKE THE NEXT ONE READY FOR JUDGING...
SILENCE
...IS THE THIRD CARD, TADOKORO VERSUS AKANEGAKUBO!
WAFT
WAIT!
THIS FRAGRANCE...!

ARTIST: YUTO TSUKUDA RECIPE BY: YUKI MORISAKI

VOLUME 28
SPECIAL SUPPLEMENT!

PRACTICAL RECIPE #1

IT JUST MAKES YOU WANT TO TRY SAYING IT OUT LOUD.

DOPPIO MEZZALUNA PIZZA

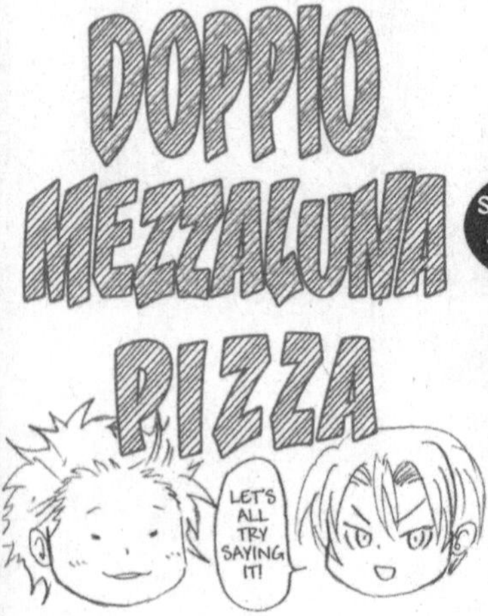
DOPPIO MEZZALUNA PIZZA
LET'S ALL TRY SAYING IT!

SIMPLIFIED HOME VERSION

● INGREDIENTS ●
(MAKES 2 PIZZAS)

★ **PIZZA DOUGH**

[A]
- 200 GRAMS BREAD FLOUR
- 100 GRAMS CAKE FLOUR
- 1/2 TABLESPOON DRY YEAST
- 1 TABLESPOON SUGAR
- 2/3 TEASPOON SALT
- 2 TABLESPOONS OLIVE OIL

180 CC WARM WATER

★ **BEEF SHIGURENI**

- 200 GRAMS THINLY SLICED BEEF
- 30 GRAMS GINGER

[B]
- 4 TABLESPOONS EACH WATER, COOKING SAKE
- 2 TABLESPOONS EACH SOY SAUCE, MIRIN, SUGAR

★ **PIZZA TOPPINGS**

- 4 SHREDDED CHEESES OF YOUR CHOICE (CREAM CHEESE, PIZZA CHEESE, GORGONZOLA CHEESE, PARMESAN CHEESE, ETC.)
- BLACK PEPPER, HONEY

1. POUR THE WARM WATER IN A BOWL AND ADD THE YEAST TO ACTIVATE IT. ADD THE REST OF (A) AND MIX WITH A SPATULA UNTIL A SHAGGY DOUGH FORMS. PUT THE DOUGH ON A LIGHTLY FLOURED SURFACE AND KNEAD UNTIL SMOOTH AND ELASTIC. SHAPE THE DOUGH INTO A BALL AND PUT IT INTO AN OILED BOWL. COVER AND LET SIT IN A WARM PLACE FOR ABOUT 20 MINUTES TO RISE.

2. WHILE THE DOUGH IS RISING, MAKE THE BEEF SHIGURENI. CUT THE BEEF STRIPS INTO BITE-SIZE LENGTHS. PEEL THE GINGER AND THEN FINELY JULIENNE IT. SOAK THE GINGER IN COLD WATER AND THEN LET DRY.

3. POUR (B) INTO A POT AND BRING TO A SIMMER. ADD THE BEEF STRIPS AND SIMMER UNTIL THE LIQUID REDUCES BY HALF. MIX THE JULIENNED GINGER IN AND LET IT ALL SIMMER FOR A FEW MINUTES. REMOVE FROM THE HEAT AND ALLOW IT TO COOL.

4. POKE THE DOUGH FROM (1) TO REMOVE THE AIR BUBBLES. CUT INTO TWO EQUAL PORTIONS AND FORM EACH INTO A BALL. PLACE ONE PORTION ON A LIGHTLY FLOURED SURFACE AND USE A ROLLING PIN TO ROLL IT OUT INTO A CIRCLE. TOP HALF OF THE CIRCLE WITH THE BEEF SHIGURENI FROM (3), AND TOP THE OTHER HALF WITH YOUR CHOICE OF A FOUR-CHEESE BLEND. SPRINKLE THE CHEESE HALF WITH BLACK PEPPER. REPEAT WITH THE SECOND DOUGH PORTION. PREHEAT THE OVEN TO 425°F, BAKE THE PIZZAS FOR ABOUT 15 MINUTES, AND DONE! (FOR SOMETHING DIFFERENT, TRY DRIZZLING HONEY OVER THE CHEESE HALF RIGHT AFTER IT COMES OUT OF THE OVEN. IT'S GOOD!)

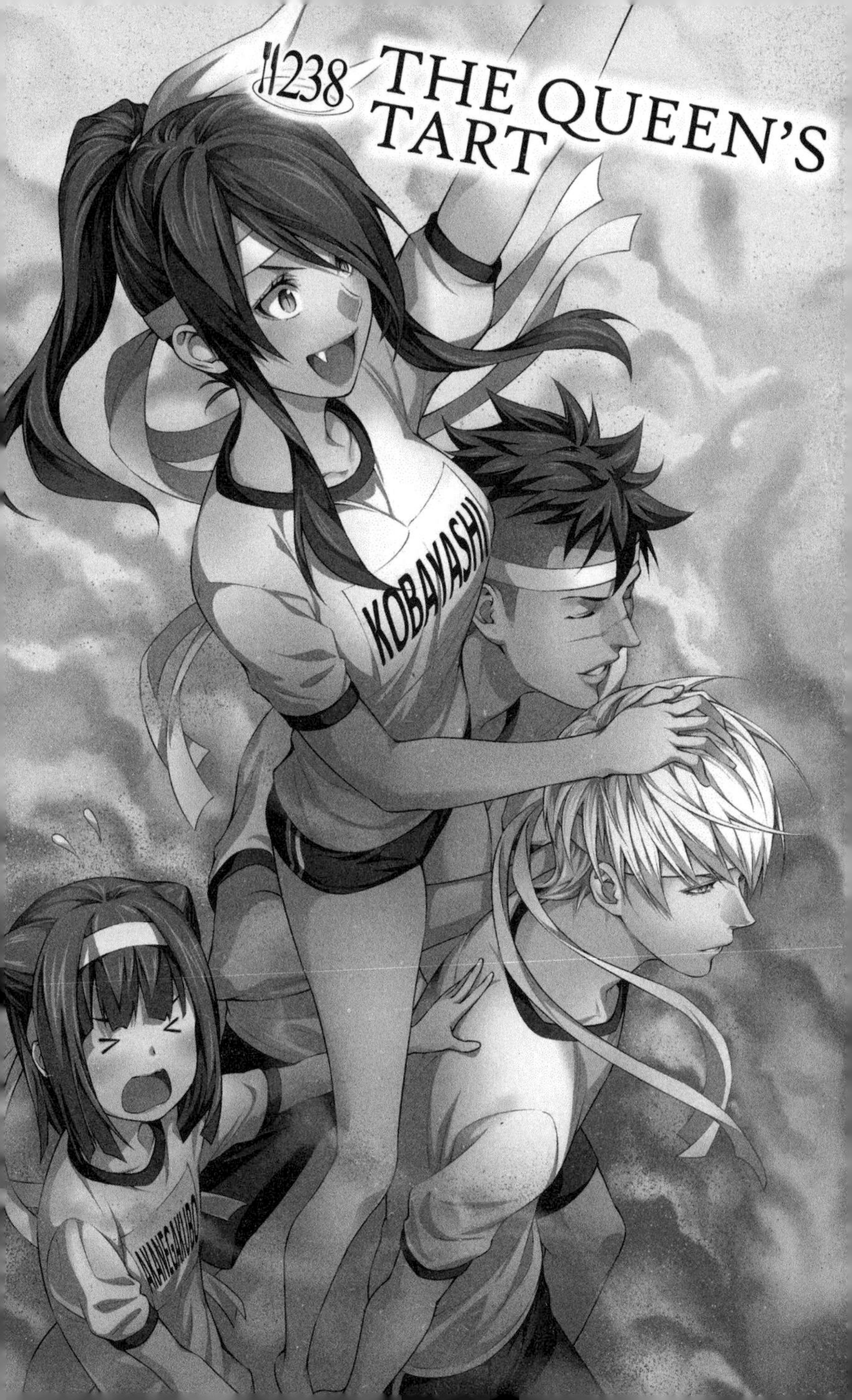

238 THE QUEEN'S TART
KOBAYASHI
AKANEGAKUBO

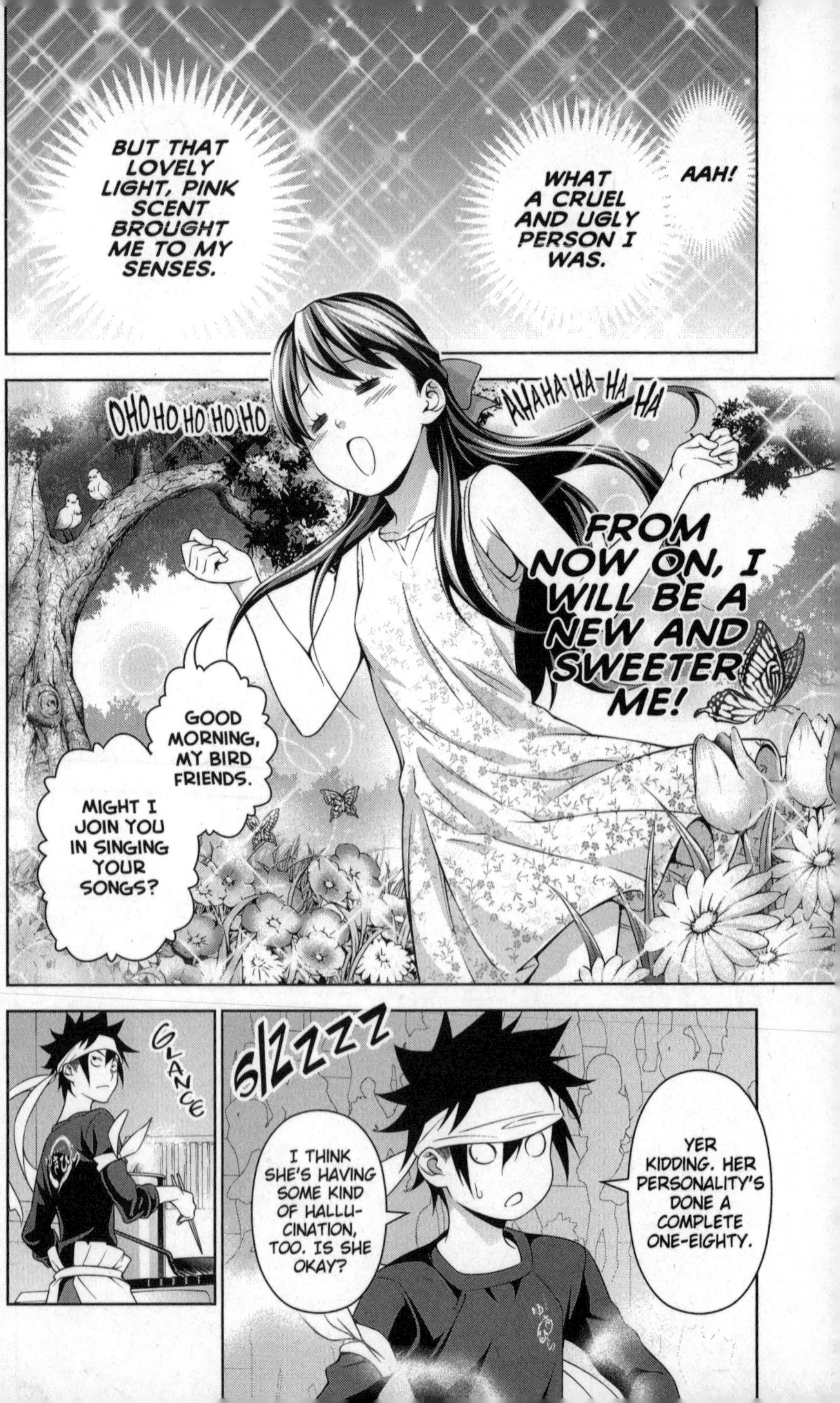
AAH!
WHAT A CRUEL AND UGLY PERSON I WAS.
BUT THAT LOVELY LIGHT, PINK SCENT BROUGHT ME TO MY SENSES.
AHAHA HA HA HA
FROM NOW ON, I WILL BE A NEW AND SWEETER ME!
OHO HO HO HO HO
GOOD MORNING, MY BIRD FRIENDS.
MIGHT I JOIN YOU IN SINGING YOUR SONGS?
SIZZZZ
YER KIDDING. HER PERSONALITY'S DONE A COMPLETE ONE-EIGHTY.
I THINK SHE'S HAVING SOME KIND OF HALLU-CINATION, TOO. IS SHE OKAY?
GLANCE

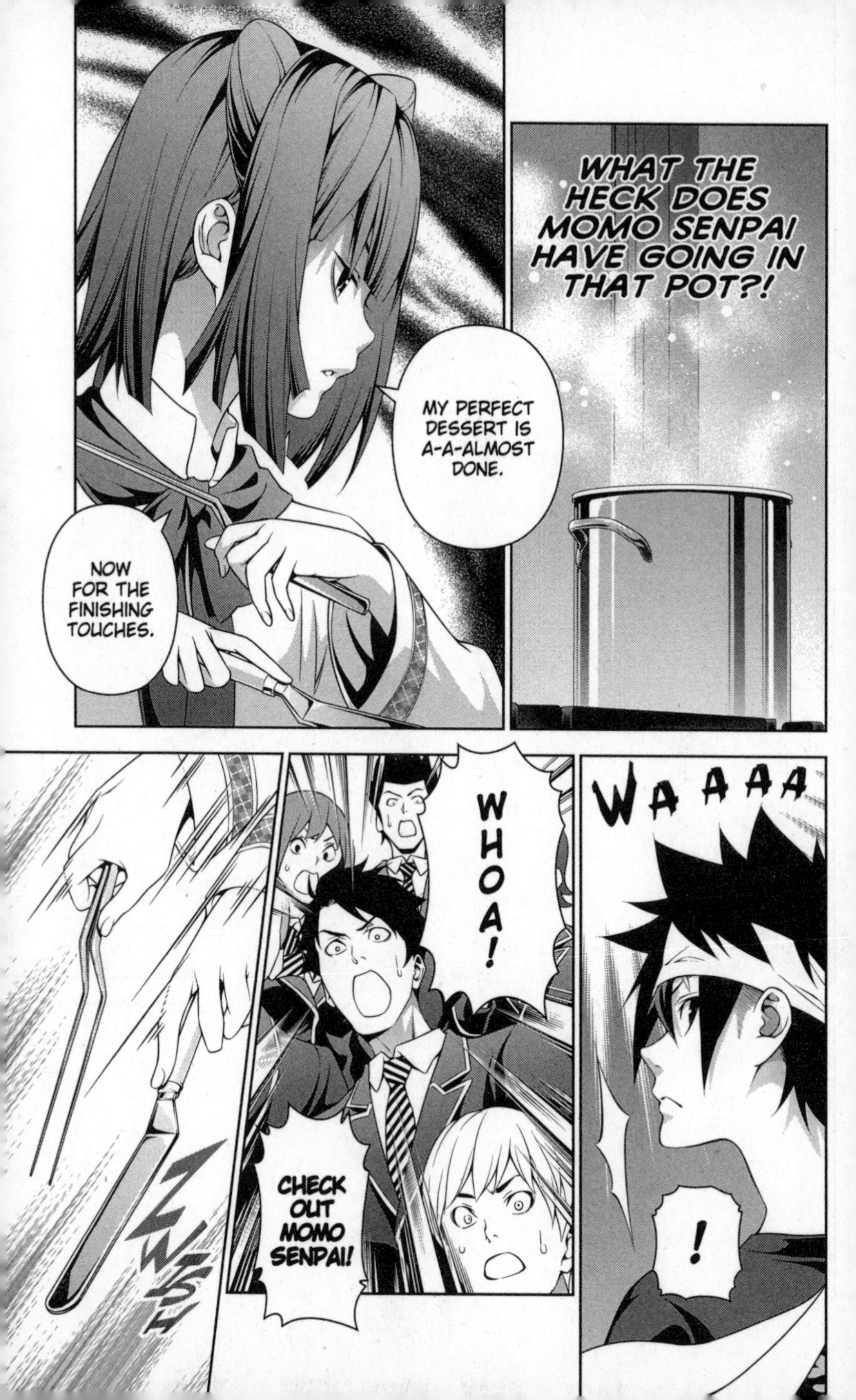
WHAT THE HECK DOES MOMO SENPAI HAVE GOING IN THAT POT?!
MY PERFECT DESSERT IS A-A-ALMOST DONE.
NOW FOR THE FINISHING TOUCHES.
WAAAA
!
WHOA!
CHECK OUT MOMO SENPAI!

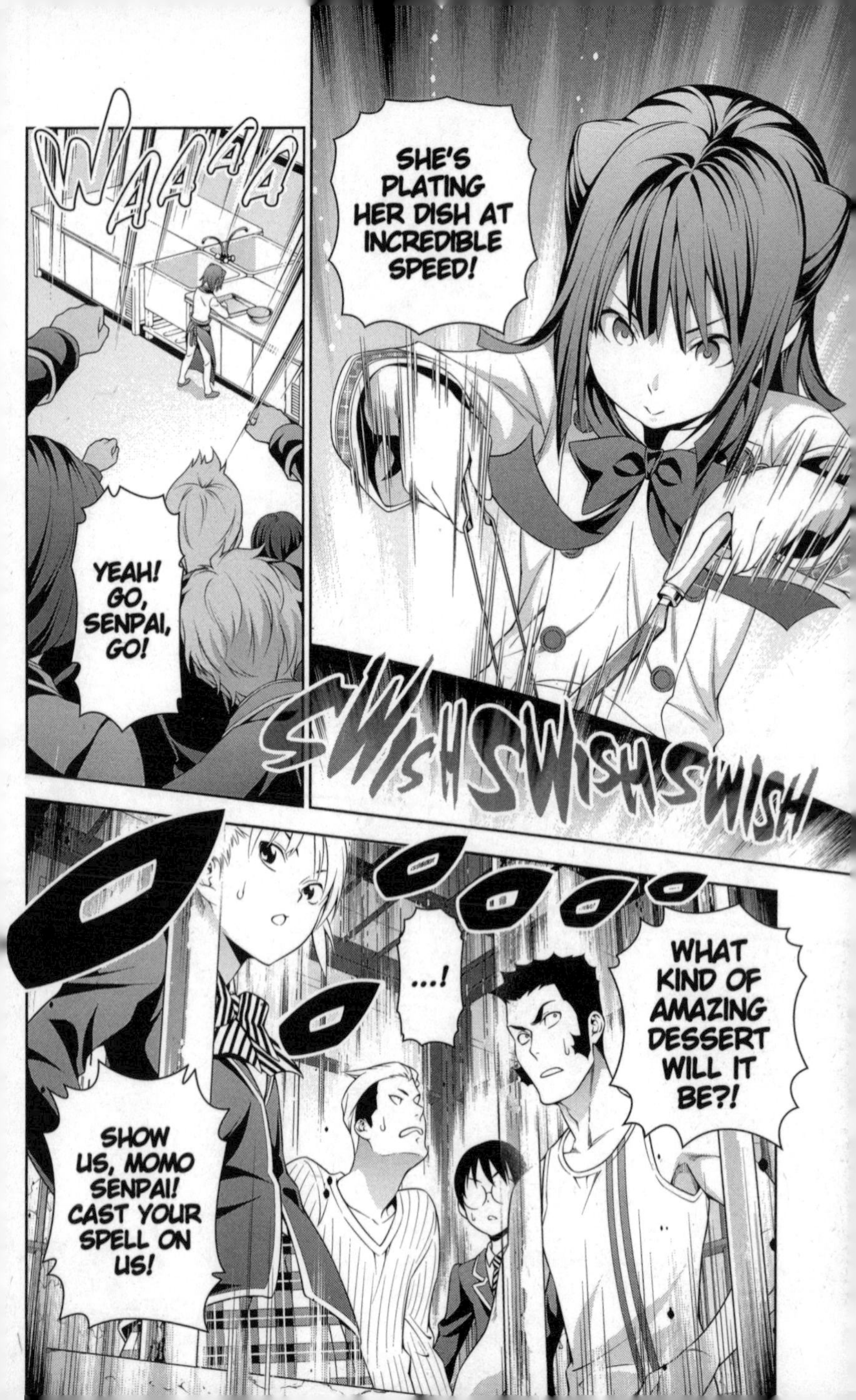
SHE'S PLATING HER DISH AT INCREDIBLE SPEED!
SWISH SWISH SWISH
WAAAAA
YEAH! GO, SENPAI, GO!
WHAT KIND OF AMAZING DESSERT WILL IT BE?!
...!
SHOW US, MOMO SENPAI! CAST YOUR SPELL ON US!

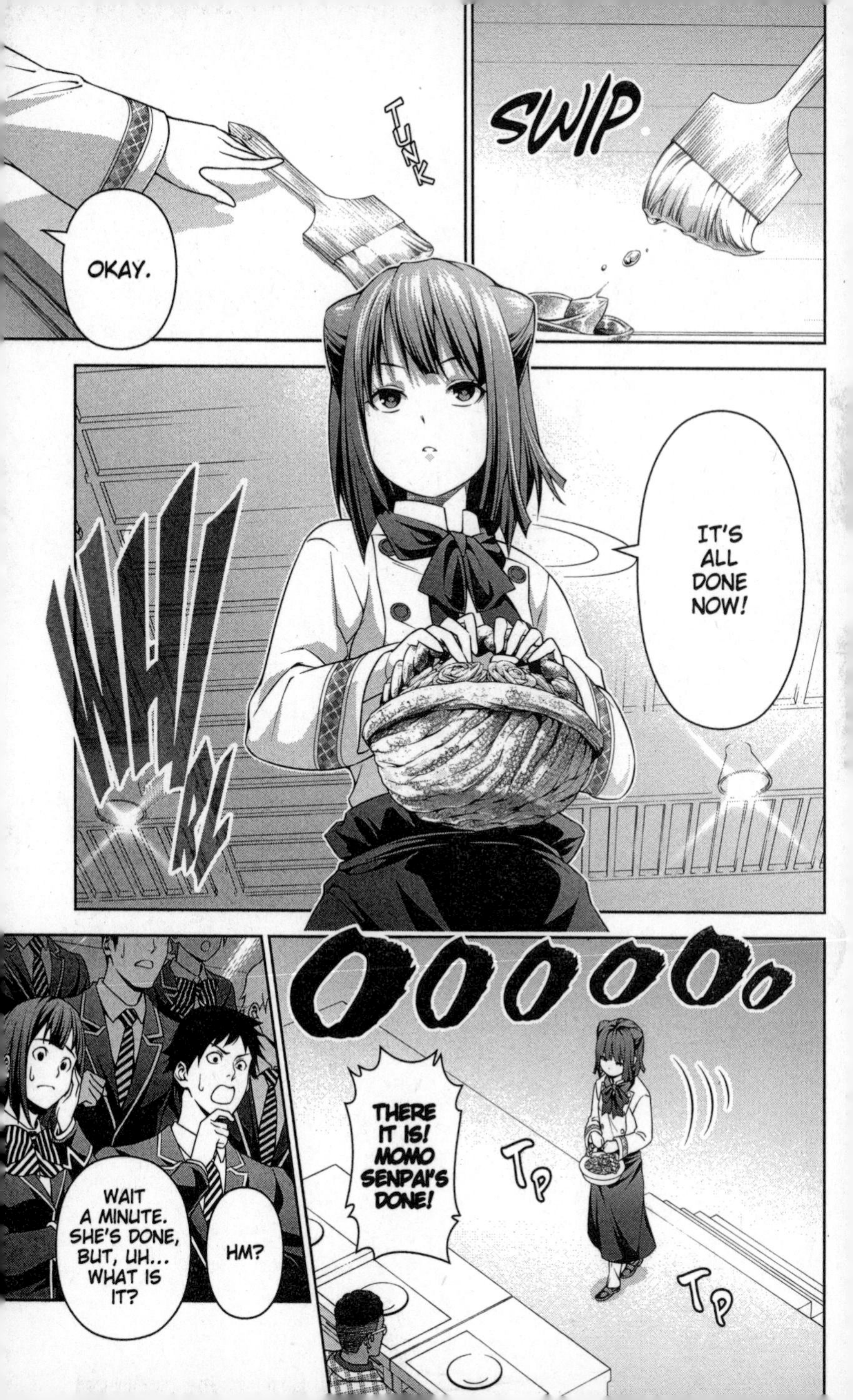
SWIP
TUNK
OKAY.
IT'S ALL DONE NOW!
OOOOOo
THERE IT IS! MOMO SENPAI'S DONE!
Tp
Tp
WAIT A MINUTE. SHE'S DONE, BUT, UH... WHAT IS IT?
HM?

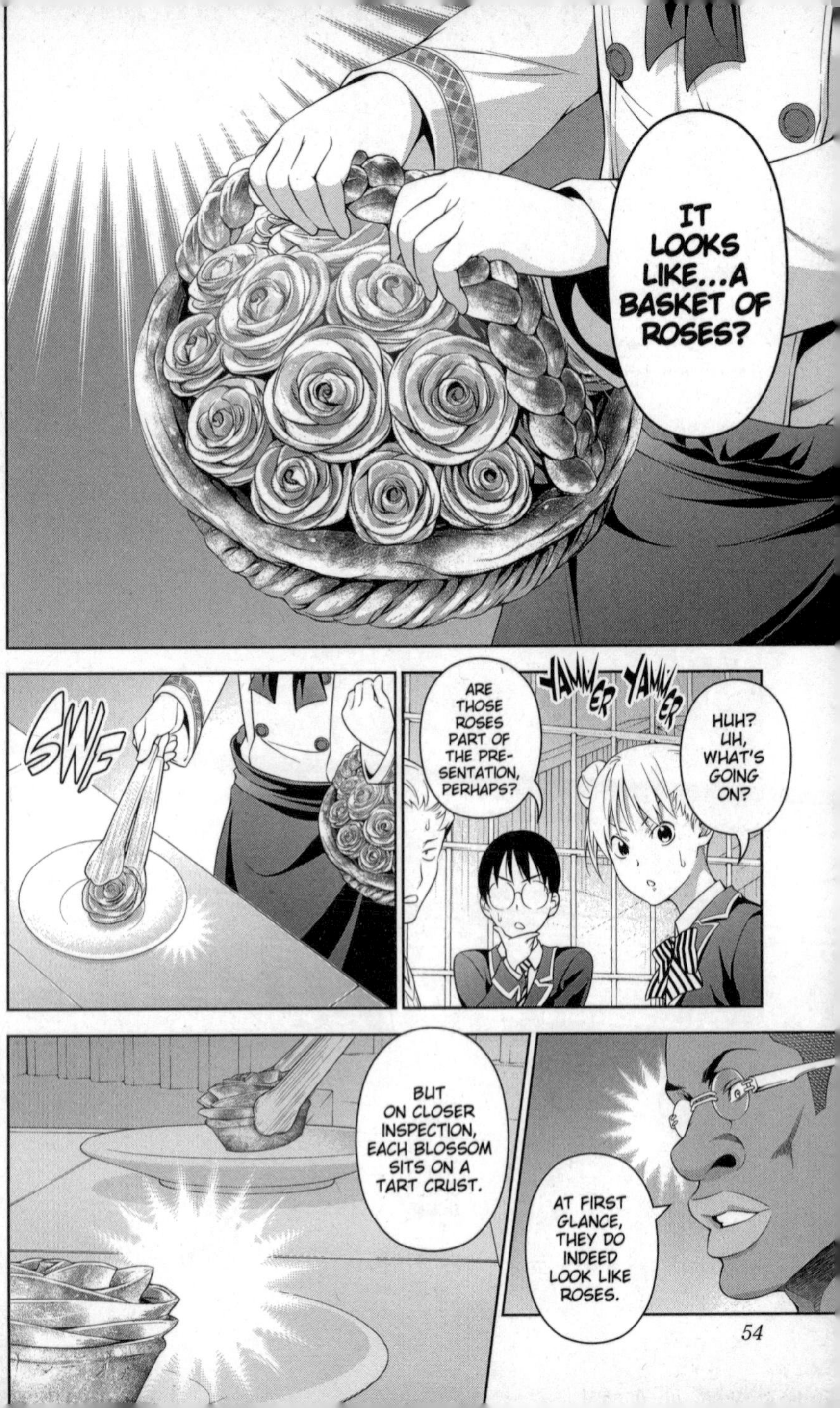
IT LOOKS LIKE...A BASKET OF ROSES?
YAMMER YAMMER
HUH? UH, WHAT'S GOING ON?
ARE THOSE ROSES PART OF THE PRESENTATION, PERHAPS?
SWF
AT FIRST GLANCE, THEY DO INDEED LOOK LIKE ROSES.
BUT ON CLOSER INSPECTION, EACH BLOSSOM SITS ON A TART CRUST.

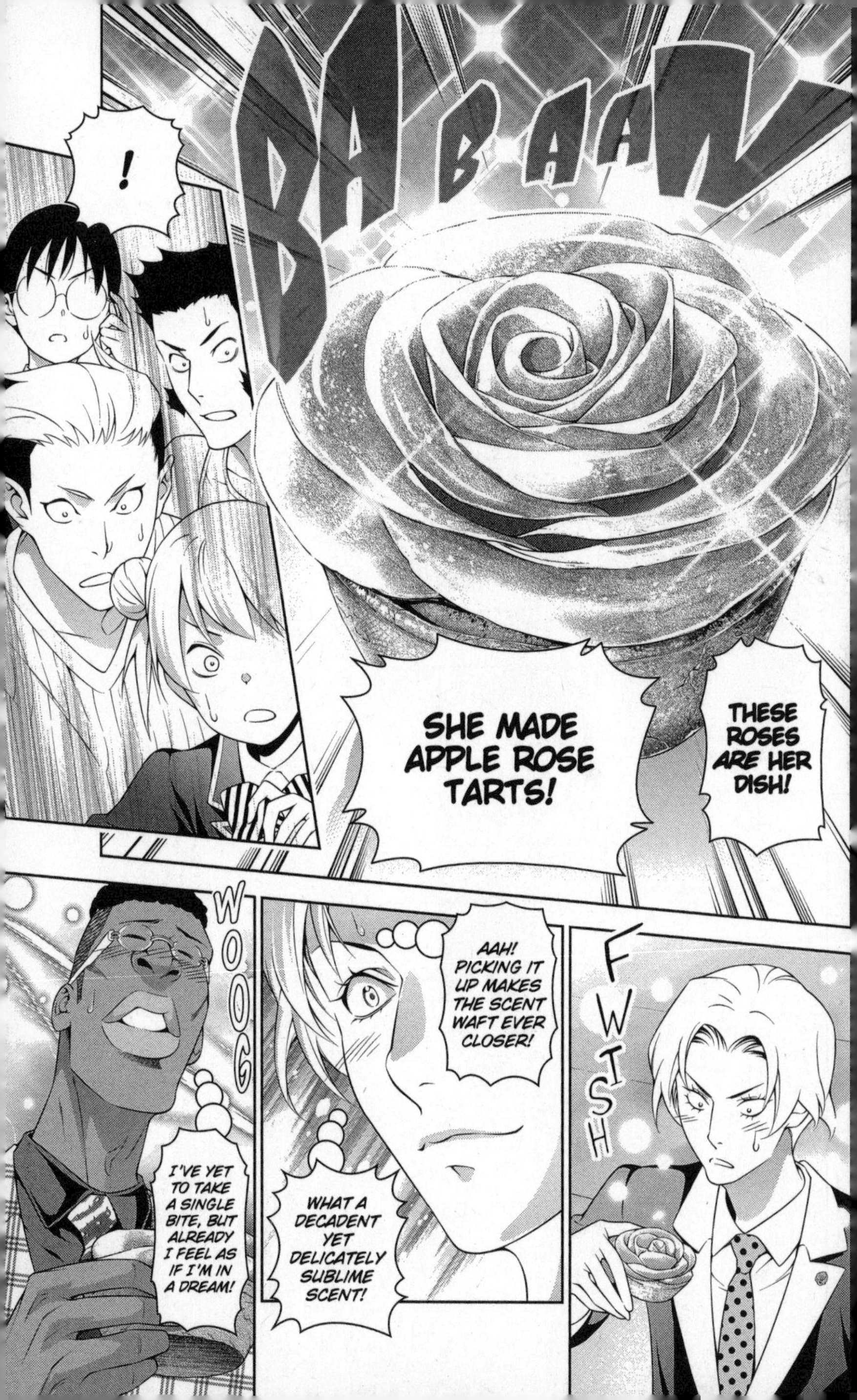
BABAAN
THESE ROSES ARE HER DISH!
SHE MADE APPLE ROSE TARTS!
!
FWISH
AAH! PICKING IT UP MAKES THE SCENT WAFT EVER CLOSER!
WHAT A DECADENT YET DELICATELY SUBLIME SCENT!
WOOG
I'VE YET TO TAKE A SINGLE BITE, BUT ALREADY I FEEL AS IF I'M IN A DREAM!

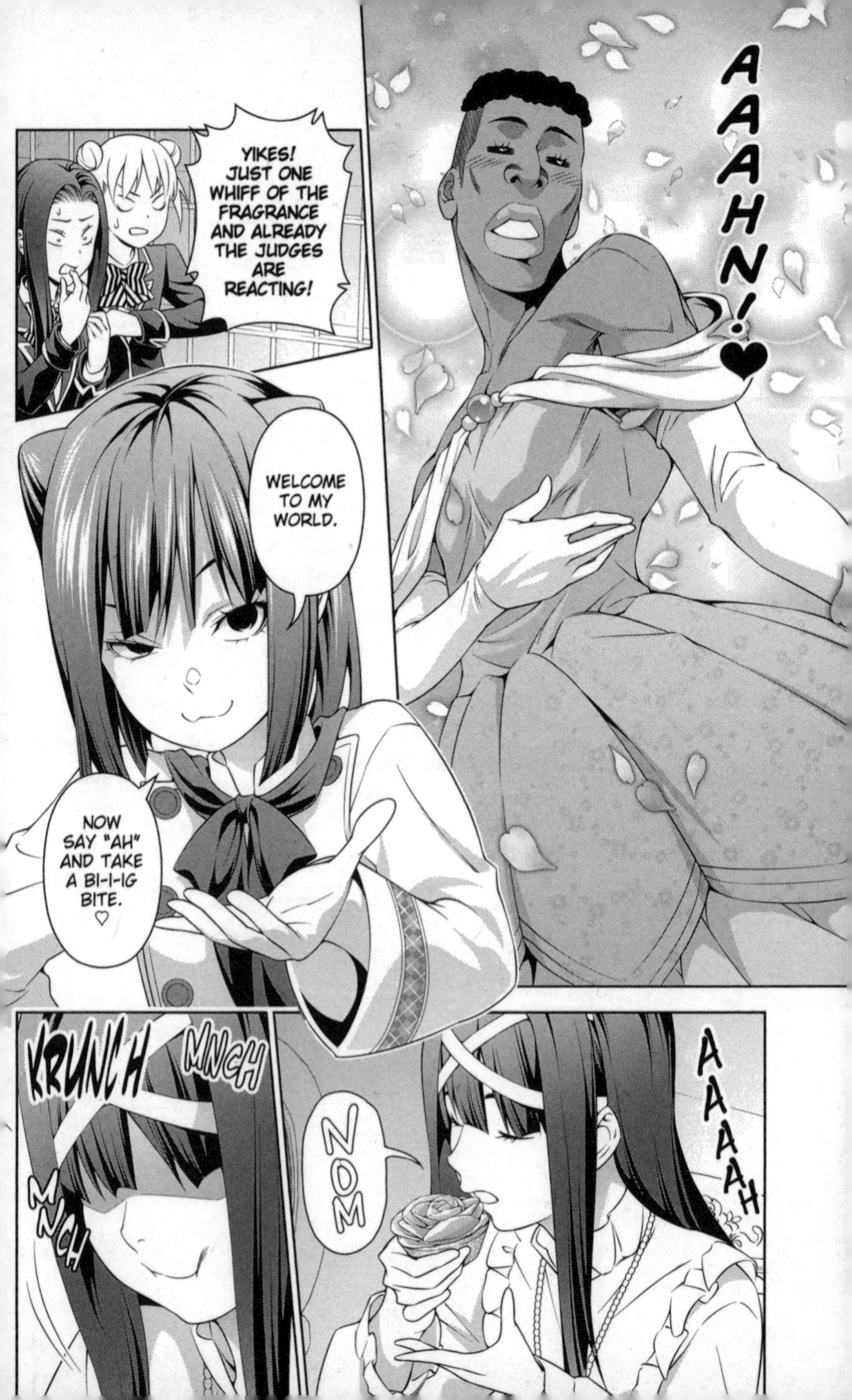
AAAHN! ♥
YIKES! JUST ONE WHIFF OF THE FRAGRANCE AND ALREADY THE JUDGES ARE REACTING!
WELCOME TO MY WORLD.
NOW SAY "AH" AND TAKE A BI-I-IG BITE. ♡
AAAAH
NOM
KRUNCH
MNCH
MNCH

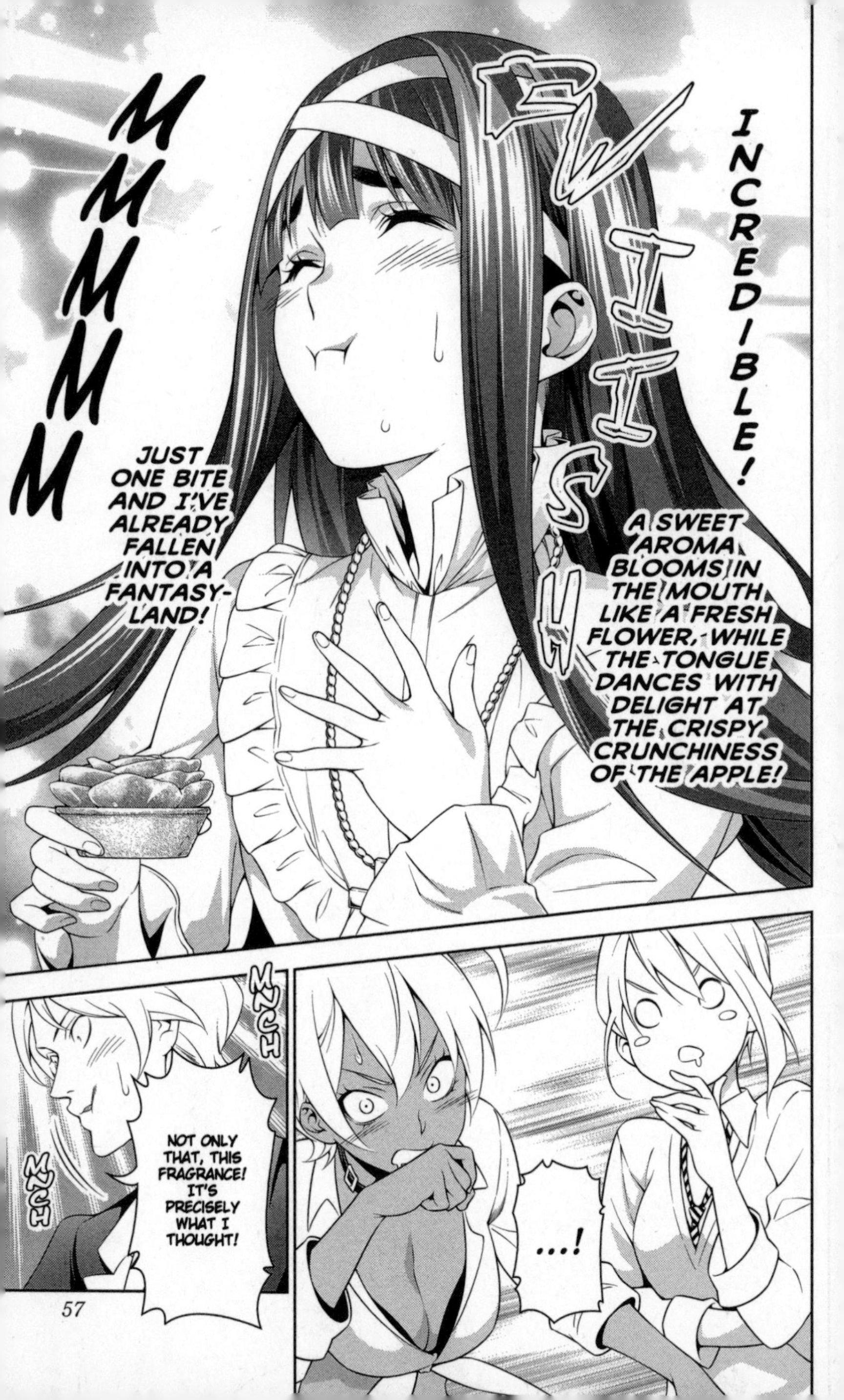
INCREDIBLE!
SWIISH
A SWEET AROMA BLOOMS IN THE MOUTH LIKE A FRESH FLOWER, WHILE THE TONGUE DANCES WITH DELIGHT AT THE CRISPY CRUNCHINESS OF THE APPLE!
MMMMMM
JUST ONE BITE AND I'VE ALREADY FALLEN INTO A FANTASY-LAND!
...!
MNCH
NOT ONLY THAT, THIS FRAGRANCE! IT'S PRECISELY WHAT I THOUGHT!
MNCH

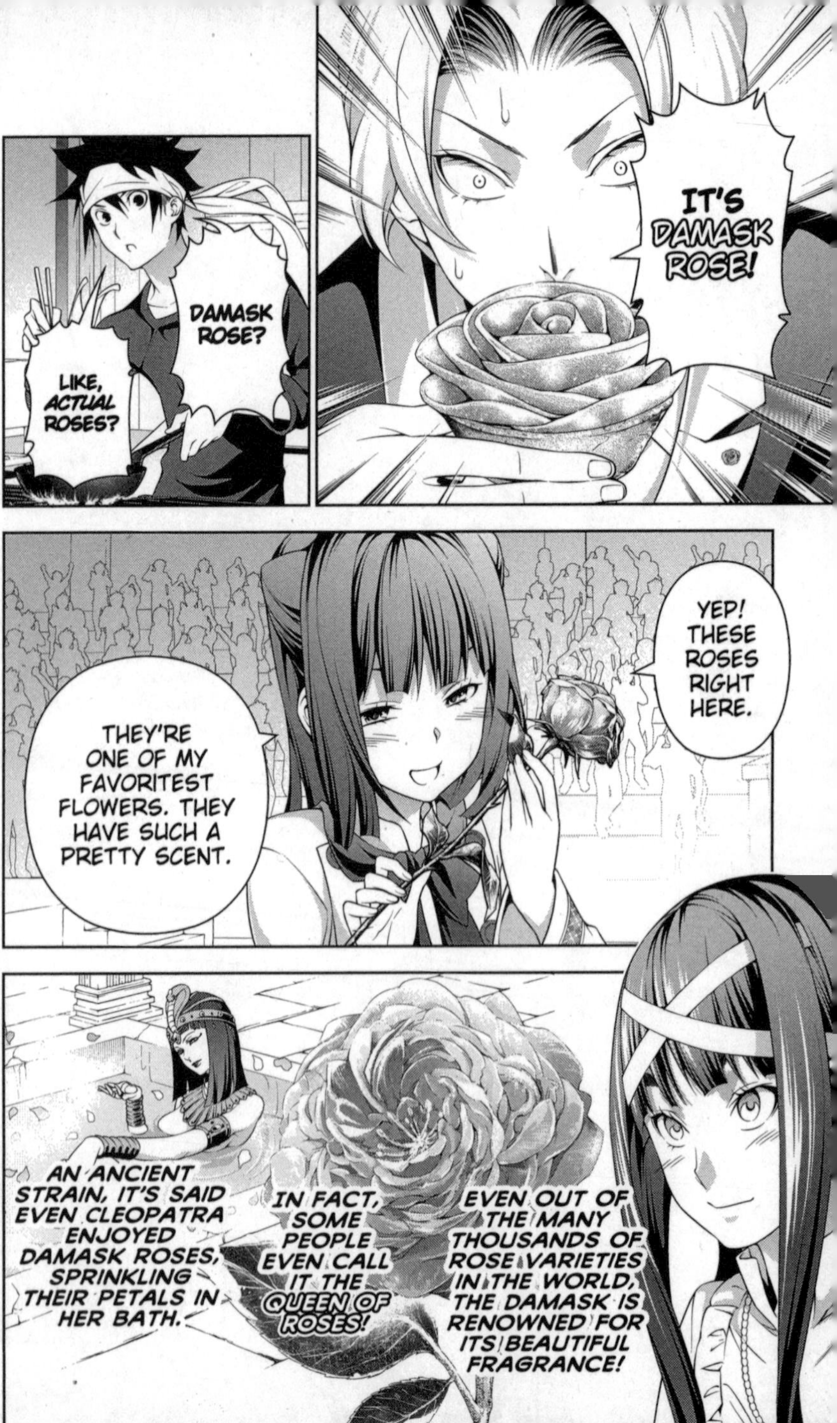
IT'S DAMASK ROSE!
DAMASK ROSE?
LIKE, ACTUAL ROSES?
YEP! THESE ROSES RIGHT HERE.
THEY'RE ONE OF MY FAVORITEST FLOWERS. THEY HAVE SUCH A PRETTY SCENT.
EVEN OUT OF THE MANY THOUSANDS OF ROSE VARIETIES IN THE WORLD, THE DAMASK IS RENOWNED FOR ITS BEAUTIFUL FRAGRANCE!
IN FACT, SOME PEOPLE EVEN CALL IT THE QUEEN OF ROSES!
AN ANCIENT STRAIN, IT'S SAID EVEN CLEOPATRA ENJOYED DAMASK ROSES, SPRINKLING THEIR PETALS IN HER BATH.

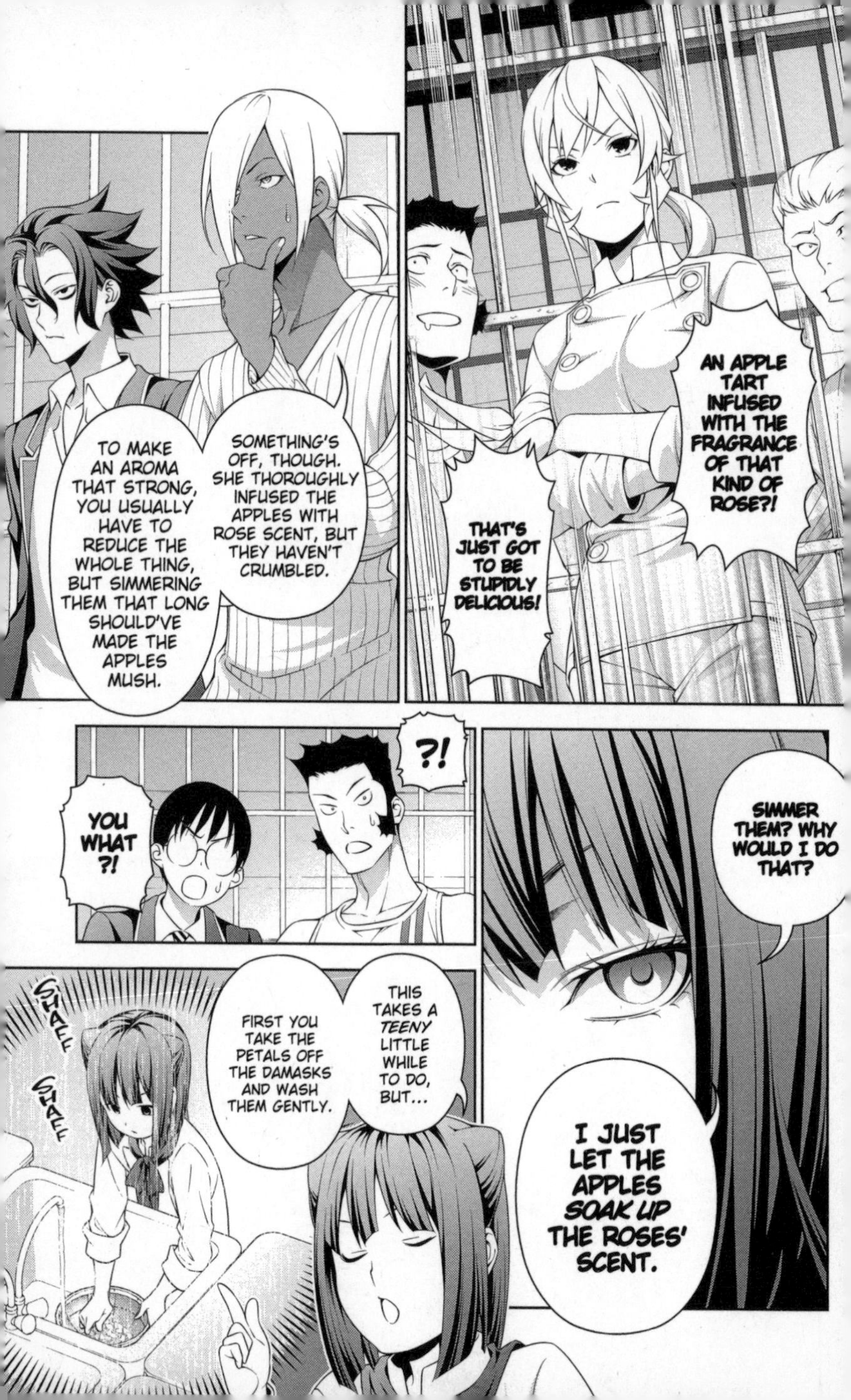
AN APPLE TART INFUSED WITH THE FRAGRANCE OF THAT KIND OF ROSE?!
THAT'S JUST GOT TO BE STUPIDLY DELICIOUS!
SOMETHING'S OFF, THOUGH. SHE THOROUGHLY INFUSED THE APPLES WITH ROSE SCENT, BUT THEY HAVEN'T CRUMBLED.
TO MAKE AN AROMA THAT STRONG, YOU USUALLY HAVE TO REDUCE THE WHOLE THING, BUT SIMMERING THEM THAT LONG SHOULD'VE MADE THE APPLES MUSH.
SIMMER THEM? WHY WOULD I DO THAT?
?!
YOU WHAT ?!
I JUST LET THE APPLES *SOAK UP* THE ROSES' SCENT.
THIS TAKES A *TEENY* LITTLE WHILE TO DO, BUT...
FIRST YOU TAKE THE PETALS OFF THE DAMASKS AND WASH THEM GENTLY.
SHAFF
SHAFF

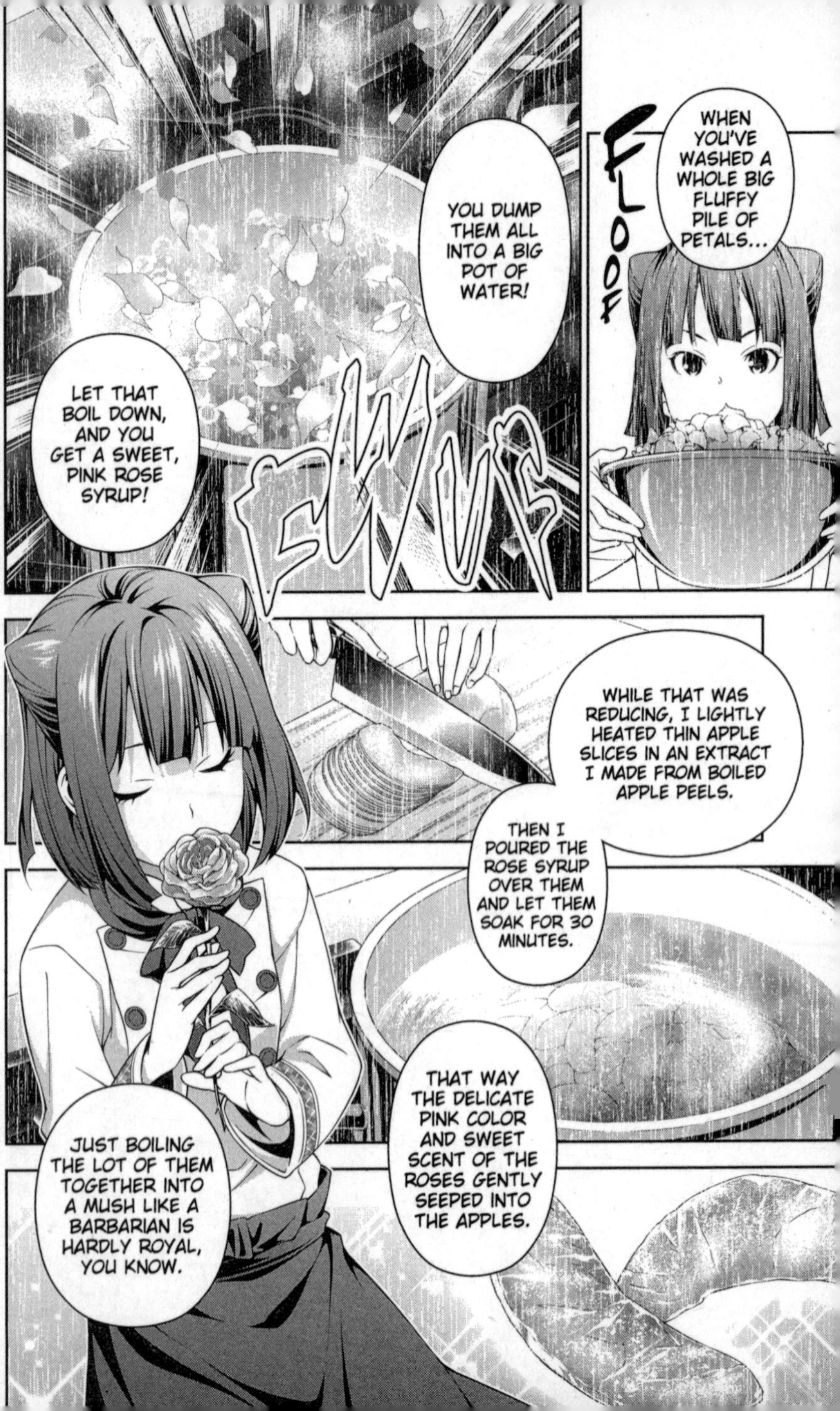
WHEN YOU'VE WASHED A WHOLE BIG FLUFFY PILE OF PETALS...
FLOOF
YOU DUMP THEM ALL INTO A BIG POT OF WATER!
LET THAT BOIL DOWN, AND YOU GET A SWEET, PINK ROSE SYRUP!
WHILE THAT WAS REDUCING, I LIGHTLY HEATED THIN APPLE SLICES IN AN EXTRACT I MADE FROM BOILED APPLE PEELS.
THEN I POURED THE ROSE SYRUP OVER THEM AND LET THEM SOAK FOR 30 MINUTES.
THAT WAY THE DELICATE PINK COLOR AND SWEET SCENT OF THE ROSES GENTLY SEEPED INTO THE APPLES.
JUST BOILING THE LOT OF THEM TOGETHER INTO A MUSH LIKE A BARBARIAN IS HARDLY ROYAL, YOU KNOW.

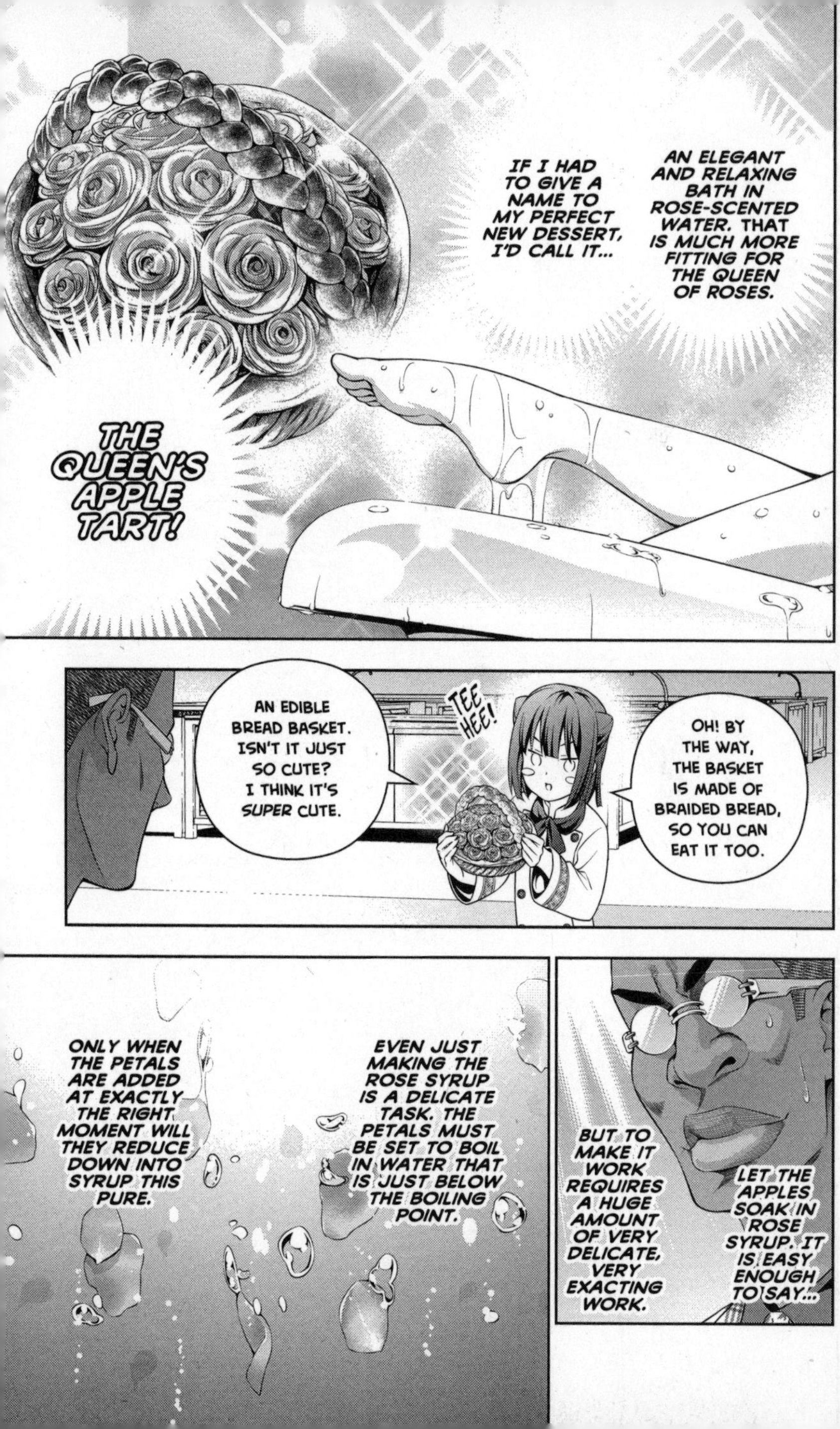
AN ELEGANT AND RELAXING BATH IN ROSE-SCENTED WATER. THAT IS MUCH MORE FITTING FOR THE QUEEN OF ROSES.
IF I HAD TO GIVE A NAME TO MY PERFECT NEW DESSERT, I'D CALL IT...
THE QUEEN'S APPLE TART!
OH! BY THE WAY, THE BASKET IS MADE OF BRAIDED BREAD, SO YOU CAN EAT IT TOO.
TEE HEE!
AN EDIBLE BREAD BASKET. ISN'T IT JUST SO CUTE? I THINK IT'S SUPER CUTE.
LET THE APPLES SOAK IN ROSE SYRUP. IT IS EASY ENOUGH TO SAY...
BUT TO MAKE IT WORK REQUIRES A HUGE AMOUNT OF VERY DELICATE, VERY EXACTING WORK.
EVEN JUST MAKING THE ROSE SYRUP IS A DELICATE TASK. THE PETALS MUST BE SET TO BOIL IN WATER THAT IS JUST BELOW THE BOILING POINT.
ONLY WHEN THE PETALS ARE ADDED AT EXACTLY THE RIGHT MOMENT WILL THEY REDUCE DOWN INTO SYRUP THIS PURE.

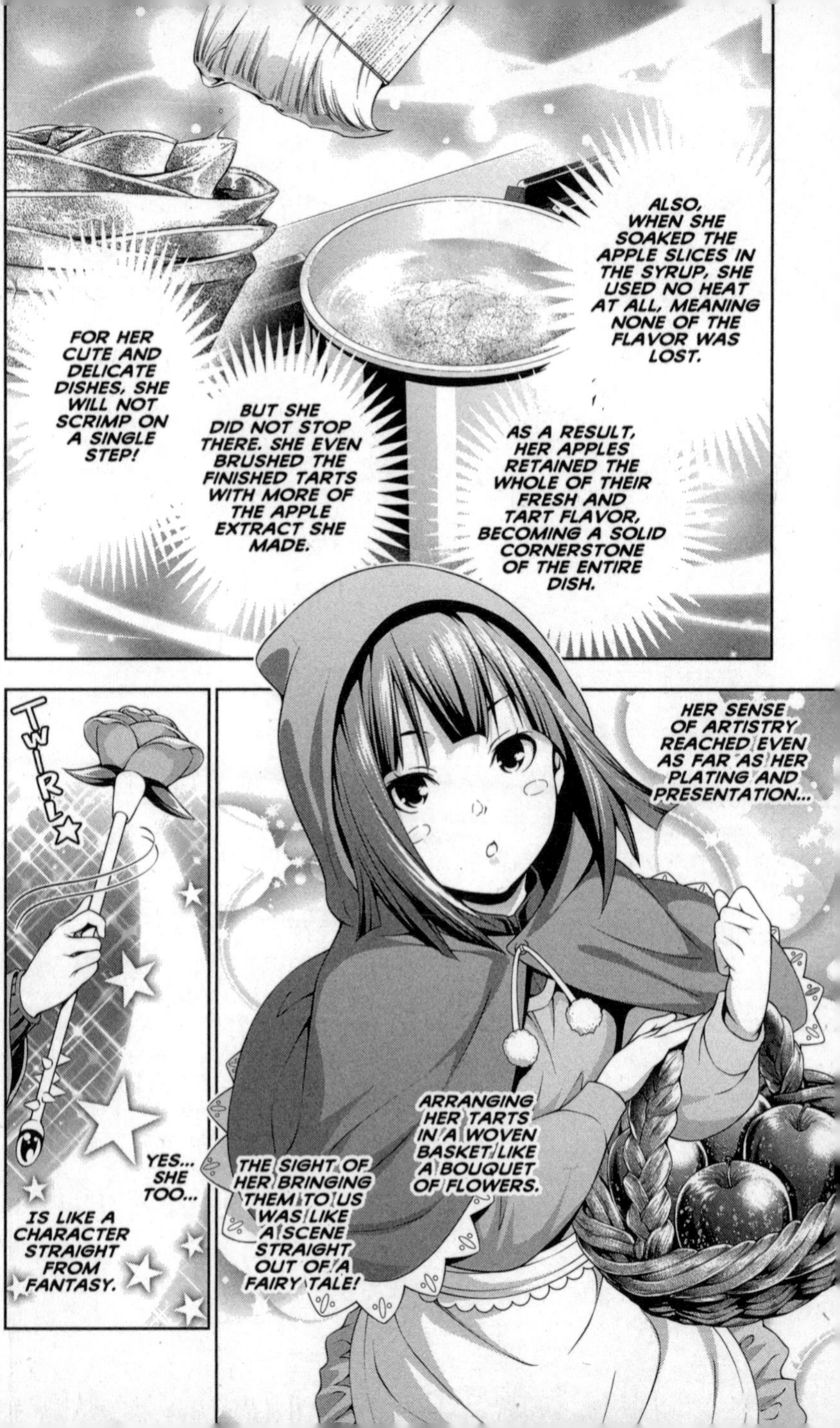
ALSO, WHEN SHE SOAKED THE APPLE SLICES IN THE SYRUP, SHE USED NO HEAT AT ALL, MEANING NONE OF THE FLAVOR WAS LOST.
AS A RESULT, HER APPLES RETAINED THE WHOLE OF THEIR FRESH AND TART FLAVOR, BECOMING A SOLID CORNERSTONE OF THE ENTIRE DISH.
BUT SHE DID NOT STOP THERE. SHE EVEN BRUSHED THE FINISHED TARTS WITH MORE OF THE APPLE EXTRACT SHE MADE.
FOR HER CUTE AND DELICATE DISHES, SHE WILL NOT SCRIMP ON A SINGLE STEP!
HER SENSE OF ARTISTRY REACHED EVEN AS FAR AS HER PLATING AND PRESENTATION...
ARRANGING HER TARTS IN A WOVEN BASKET LIKE A BOUQUET OF FLOWERS.
THE SIGHT OF HER BRINGING THEM TO US WAS LIKE A SCENE STRAIGHT OUT OF A FAIRY TALE!
TWIRL☆
YES... SHE TOO...
IS LIKE A CHARACTER STRAIGHT FROM FANTASY.

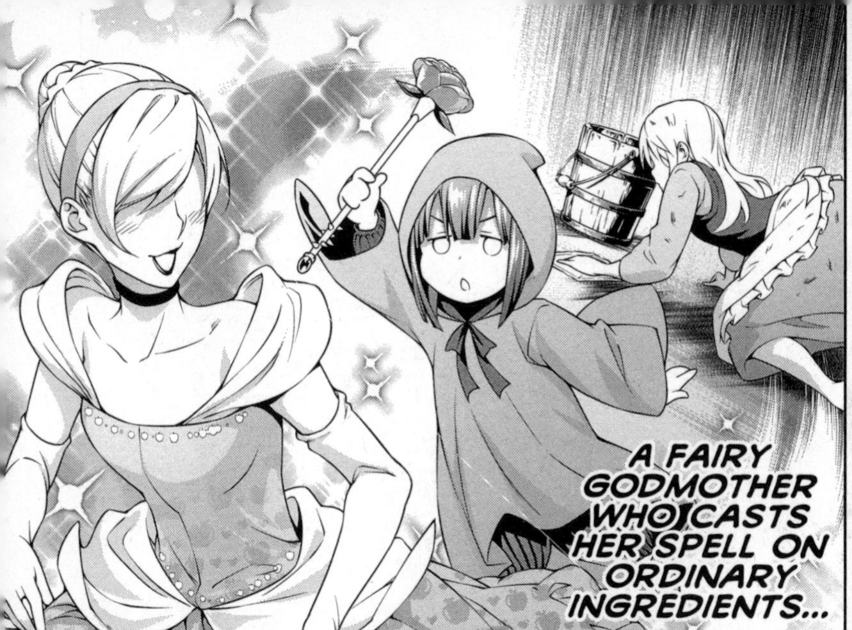
A FAIRY GODMOTHER WHO CASTS HER SPELL ON ORDINARY INGREDIENTS...
...TURNING THEM INTO BEAUTIFUL AND DELICIOUS PRINCESSES OF FOOD!

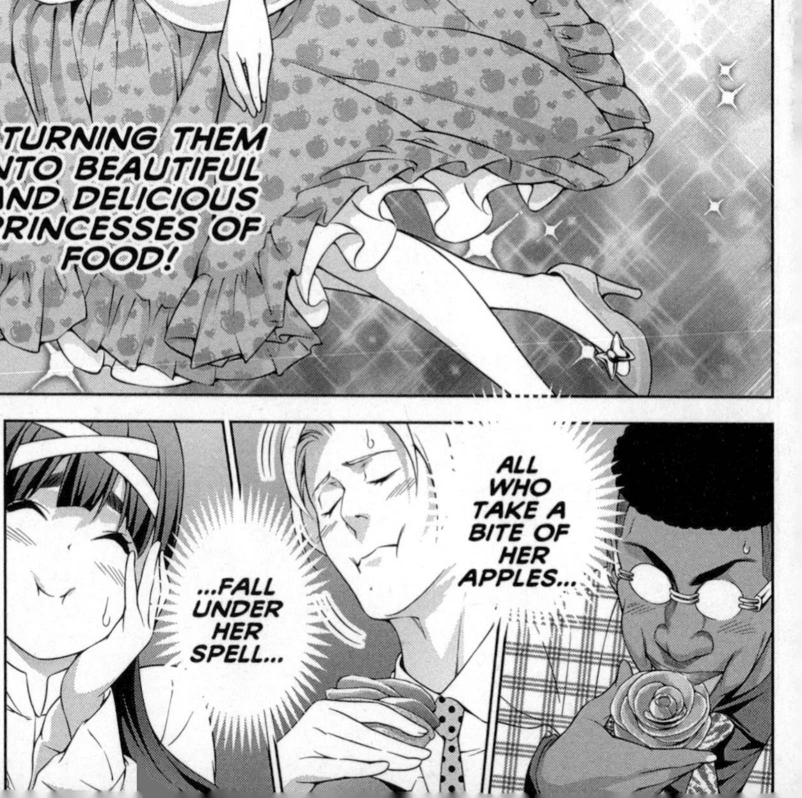
ALL WHO TAKE A BITE OF HER APPLES...
...FALL UNDER HER SPELL...

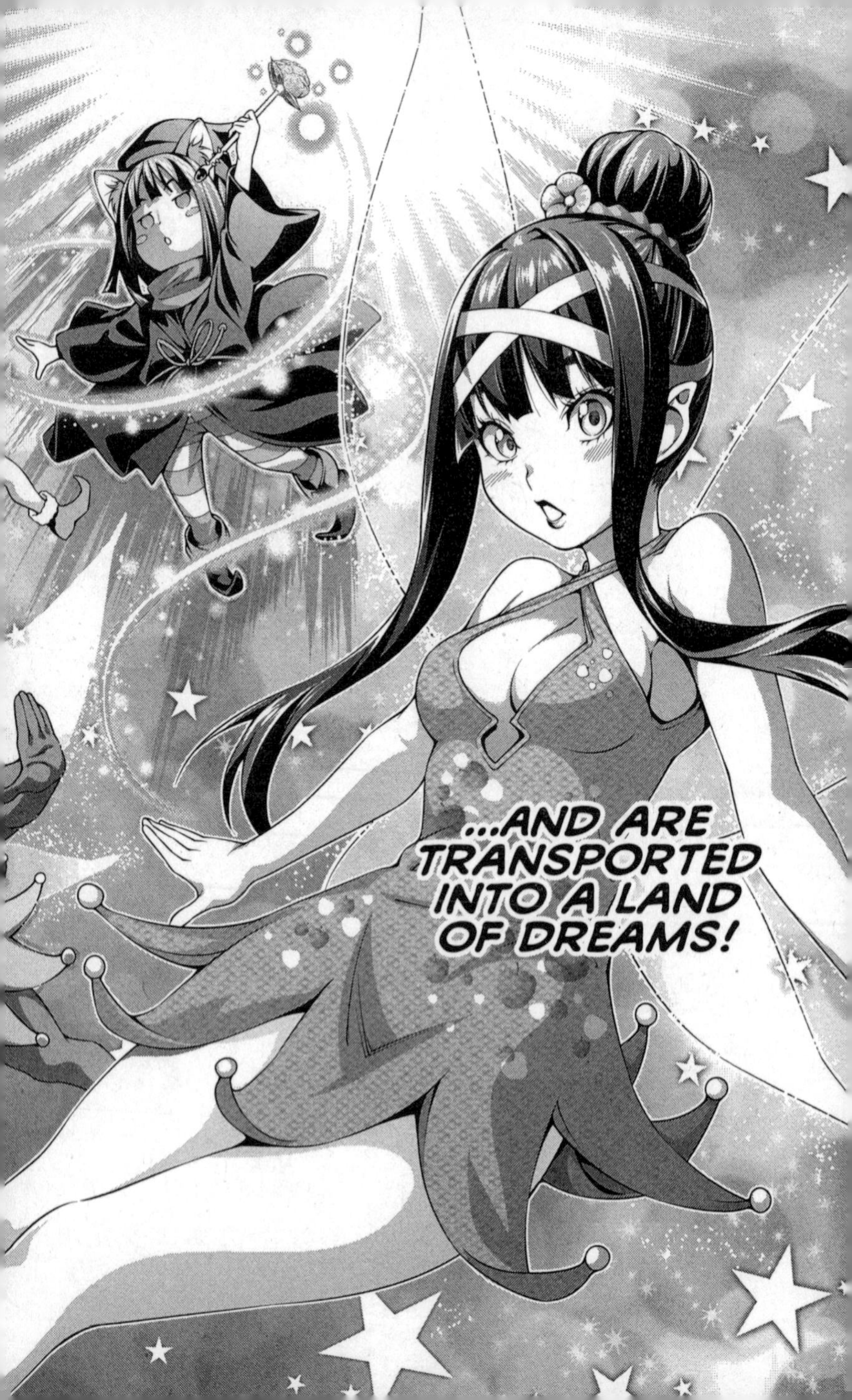
...AND ARE TRANSPORTED INTO A LAND OF DREAMS!

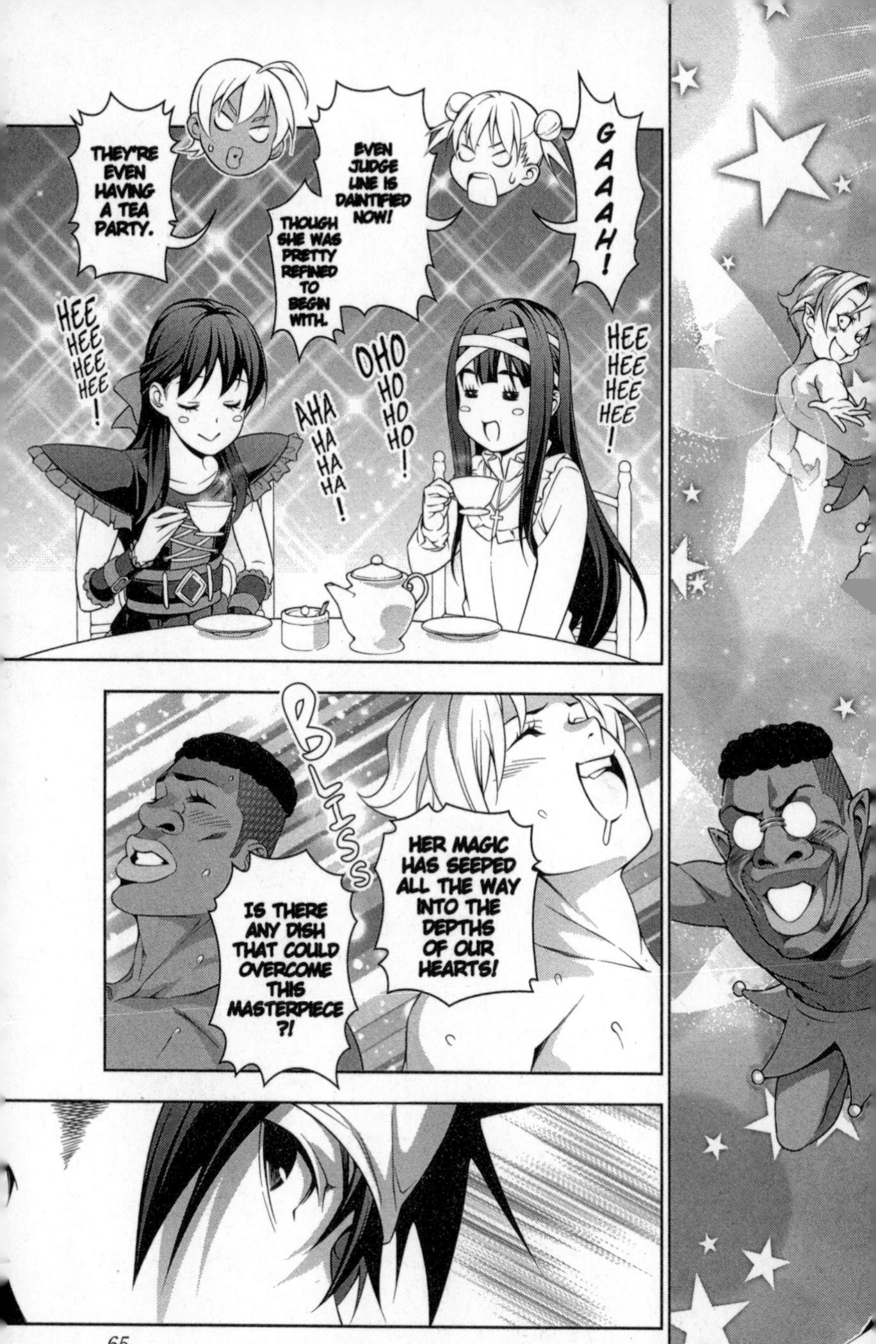
GAAAH!
EVEN JUDGE LINE IS DAINTIFIED NOW!
THEY'RE EVEN HAVING A TEA PARTY.
THOUGH SHE WAS PRETTY REFINED TO BEGIN WITH.
HEE HEE HEE HEE!
OHO HO HO HO!
AHA HA HA HA!
HEE HEE HEE HEE!
BLISS
HER MAGIC HAS SEEPED ALL THE WAY INTO THE DEPTHS OF OUR HEARTS!
IS THERE ANY DISH THAT COULD OVERCOME THIS MASTERPIECE?!

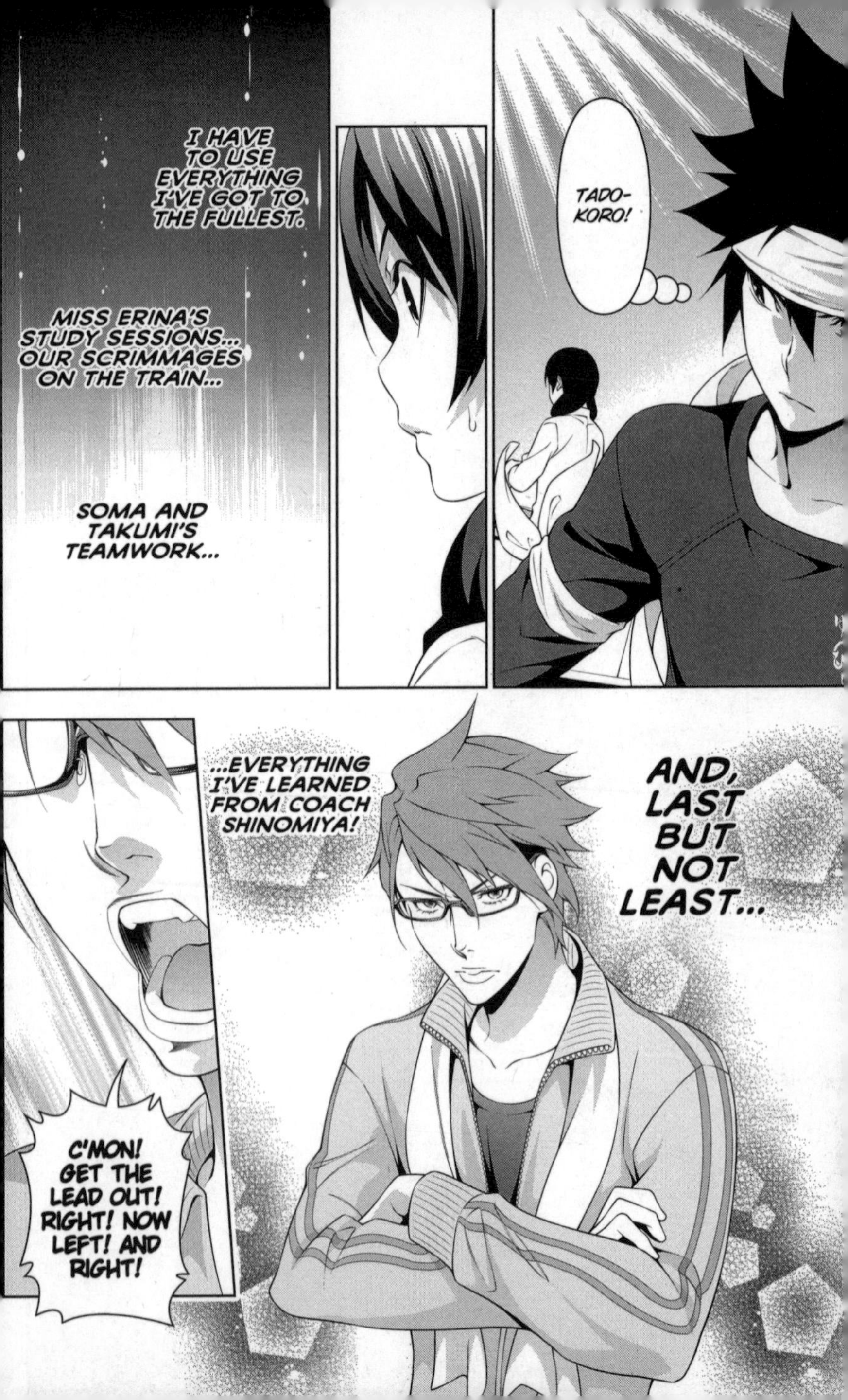
TADO-KORO!
I HAVE TO USE EVERYTHING I'VE GOT TO THE FULLEST.
MISS ERINA'S STUDY SESSIONS... OUR SCRIMMAGES ON THE TRAIN...
SOMA AND TAKUMI'S TEAMWORK...
AND, LAST BUT NOT LEAST...
...EVERYTHING I'VE LEARNED FROM COACH SHINOMIYA!
C'MON! GET THE LEAD OUT! RIGHT! NOW LEFT! AND RIGHT!

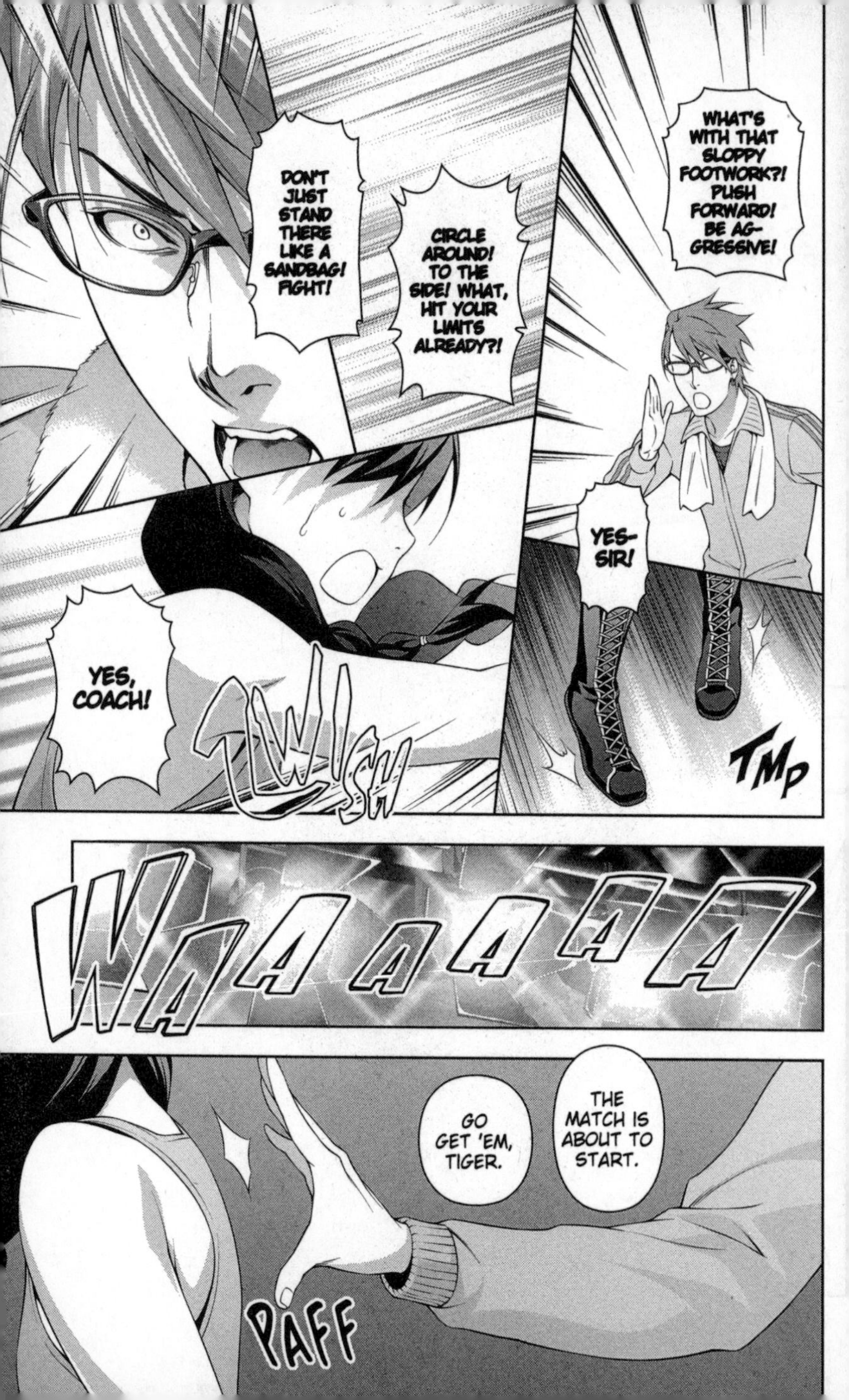
WHAT'S WITH THAT SLOPPY FOOTWORK?! PUSH FORWARD! BE AG-GRESSIVE!
CIRCLE AROUND! TO THE SIDE! WHAT, HIT YOUR LIMITS ALREADY?!
DON'T JUST STAND THERE LIKE A SANDBAG! FIGHT!
YES-SIR!
TMP
YES, COACH!
ZWISH
WAAAAAA
THE MATCH IS ABOUT TO START.
GO GET 'EM, TIGER.
PAFF

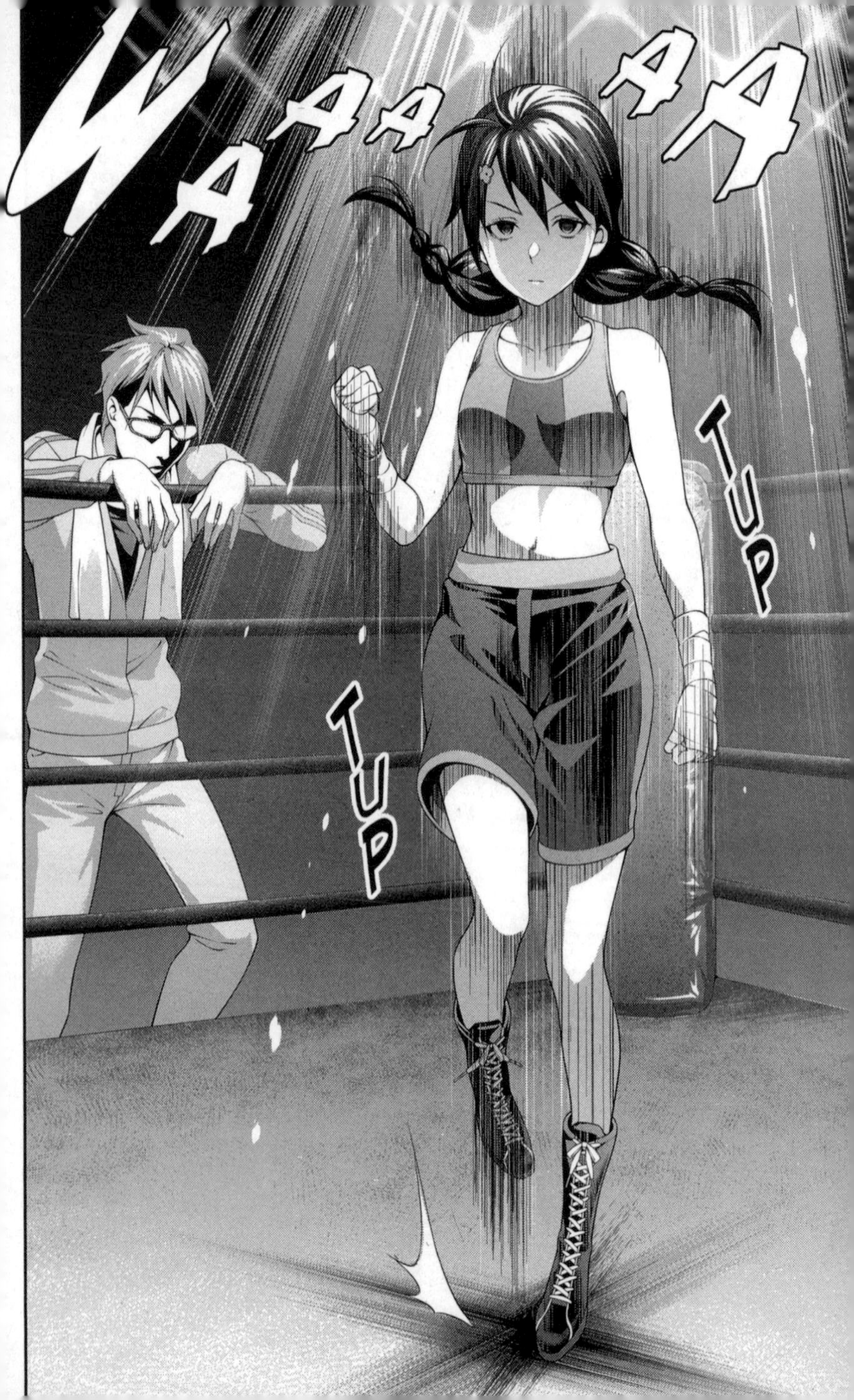
WAAAAA
TUP
TUP

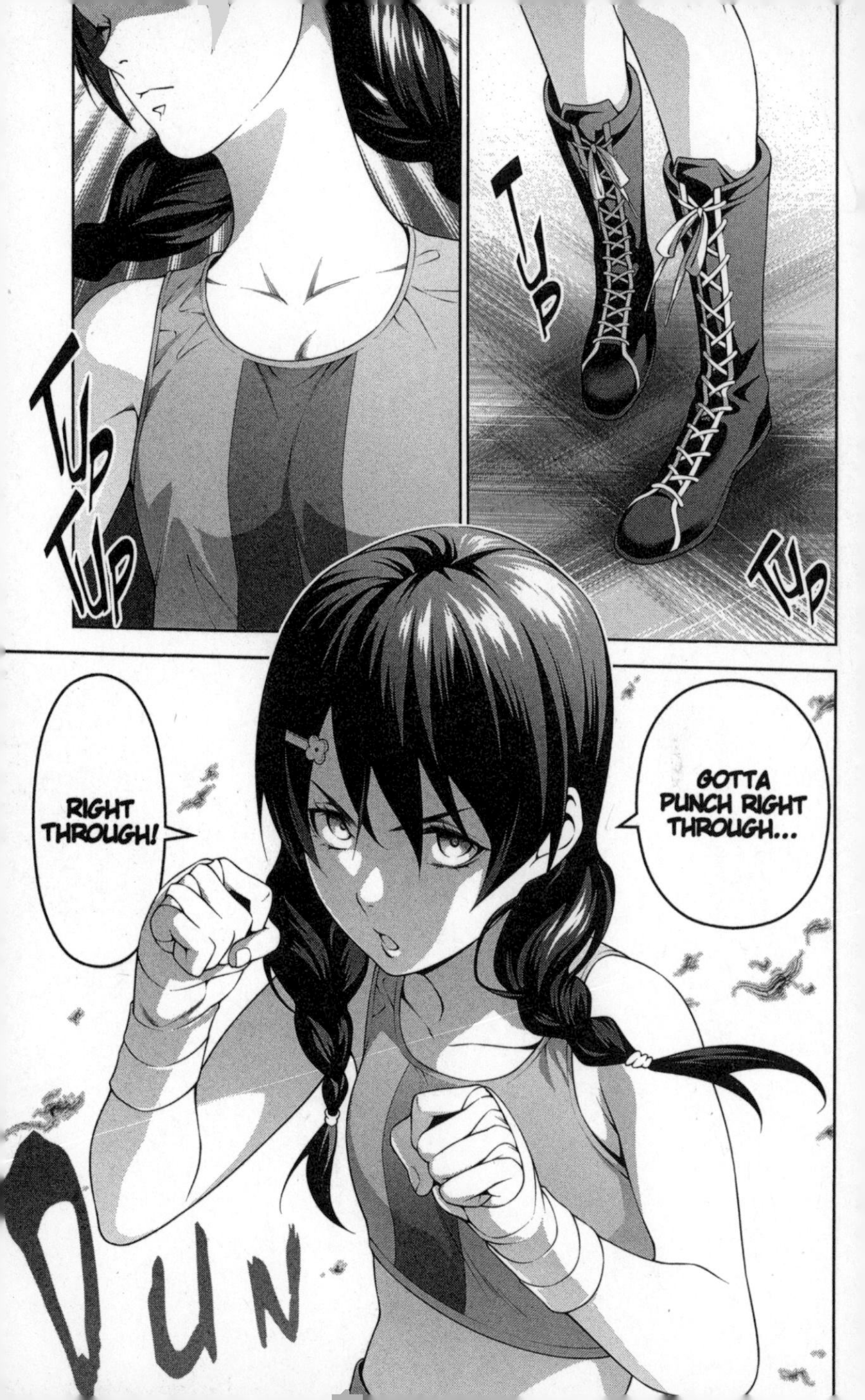
TUP
TUP
TUP TUP TUP
GOTTA PUNCH RIGHT THROUGH...
RIGHT THROUGH!
DUN

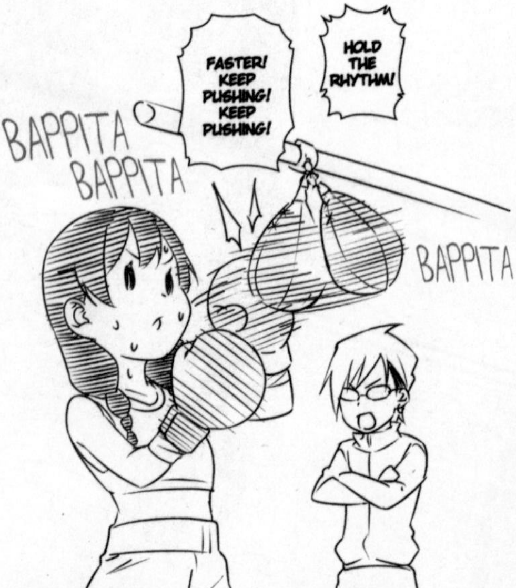
HOLD THE RHYTHM!
FASTER! KEEP PUSHING! KEEP PUSHING!
BAPPITA BAPPITA
BAPPITA

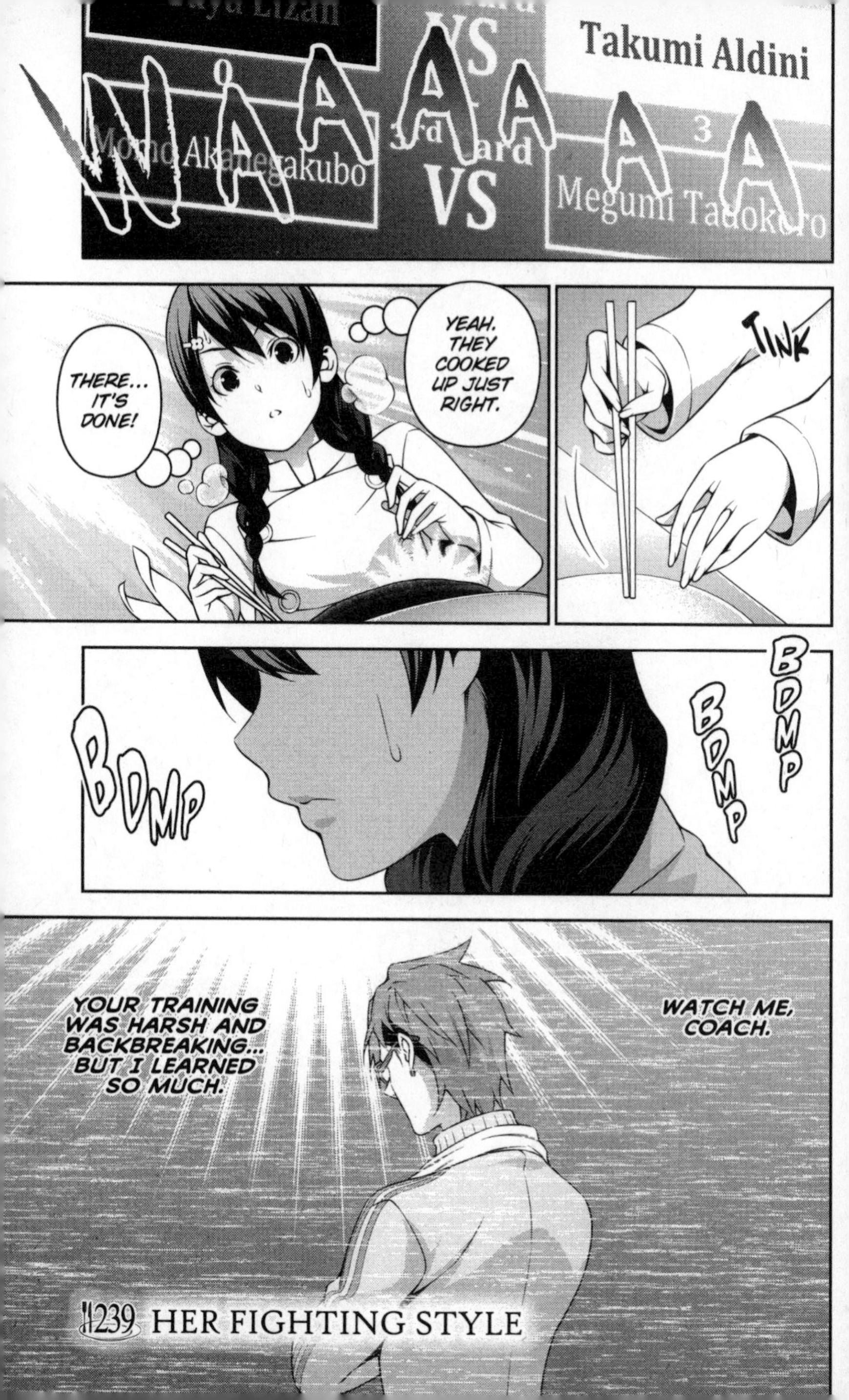
Takumi Aldini
VS
NAAAAAA
Momo Akanegakubo
VS
TINK
YEAH. THEY COOKED UP JUST RIGHT.
THERE... IT'S DONE!
BDMP
BDMP
BDMP
WATCH ME, COACH.
YOUR TRAINING WAS HARSH AND BACKBREAKING... BUT I LEARNED SO MUCH.

239 HER FIGHTING STYLE

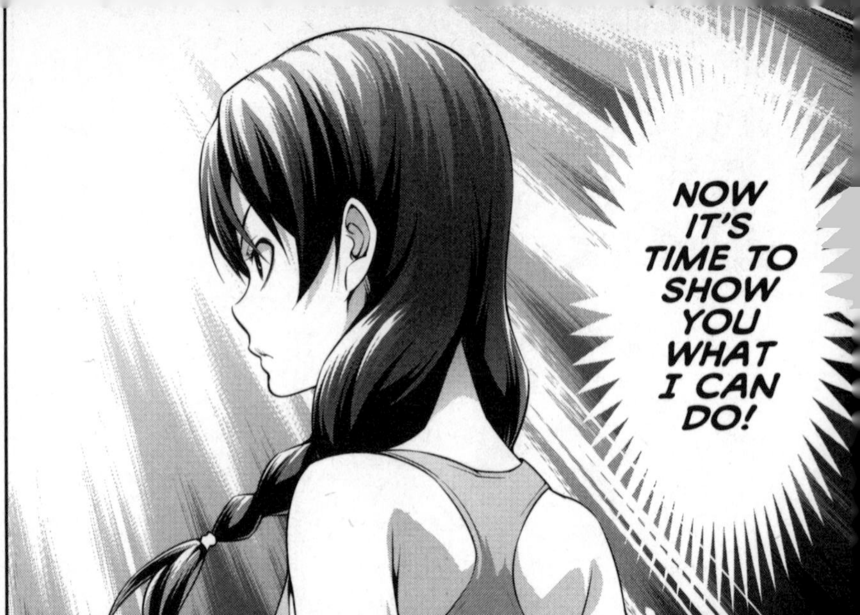
NOW IT'S TIME TO SHOW YOU WHAT I CAN DO!
239 HER FIGHTING STYLE

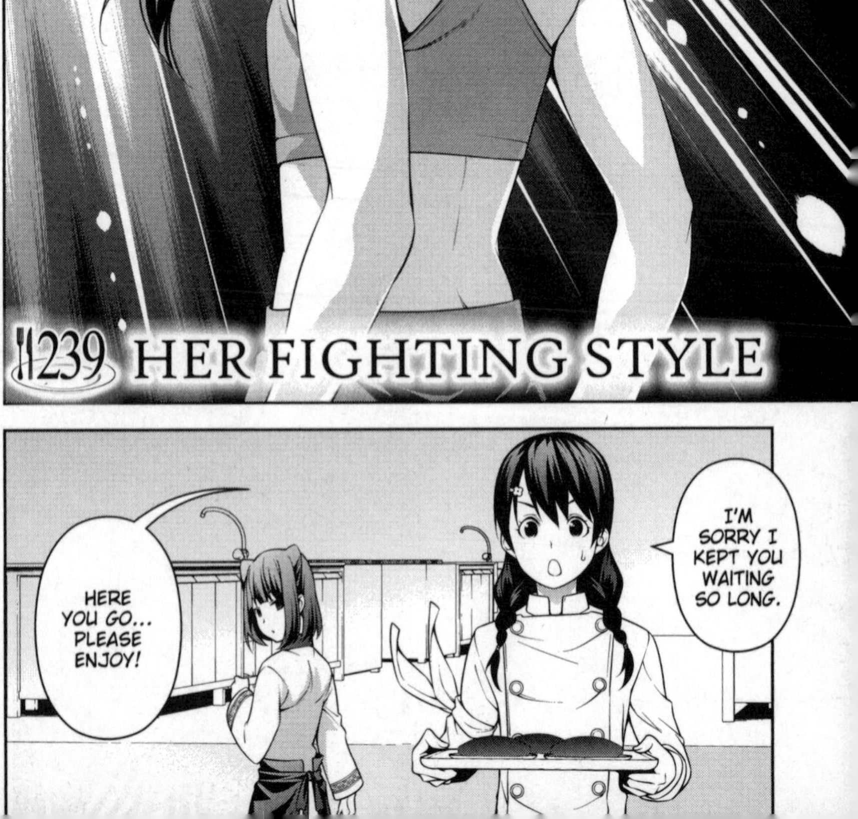
I'M SORRY I KEPT YOU WAITING SO LONG.
HERE YOU GO... PLEASE ENJOY!

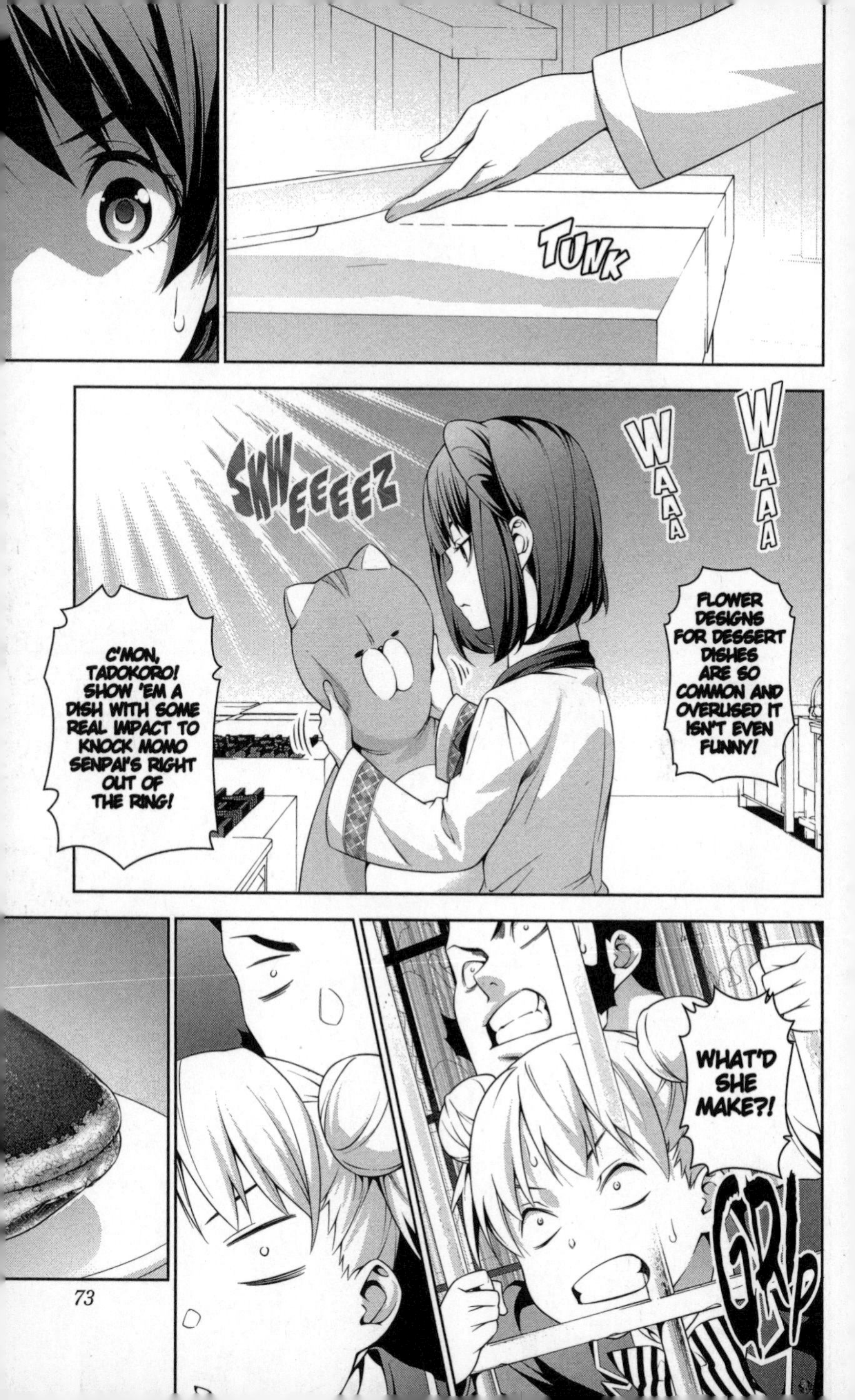
TUNK
WAAA
WAAA
SKWEEEEZ
FLOWER DESIGNS FOR DESSERT DISHES ARE SO COMMON AND OVERUSED IT ISN'T EVEN FUNNY!
C'MON, TADOKORO! SHOW 'EM A DISH WITH SOME REAL IMPACT TO KNOCK MOMO SENPAI'S RIGHT OUT OF THE RING!
WHAT'D SHE MAKE?!
GRIP

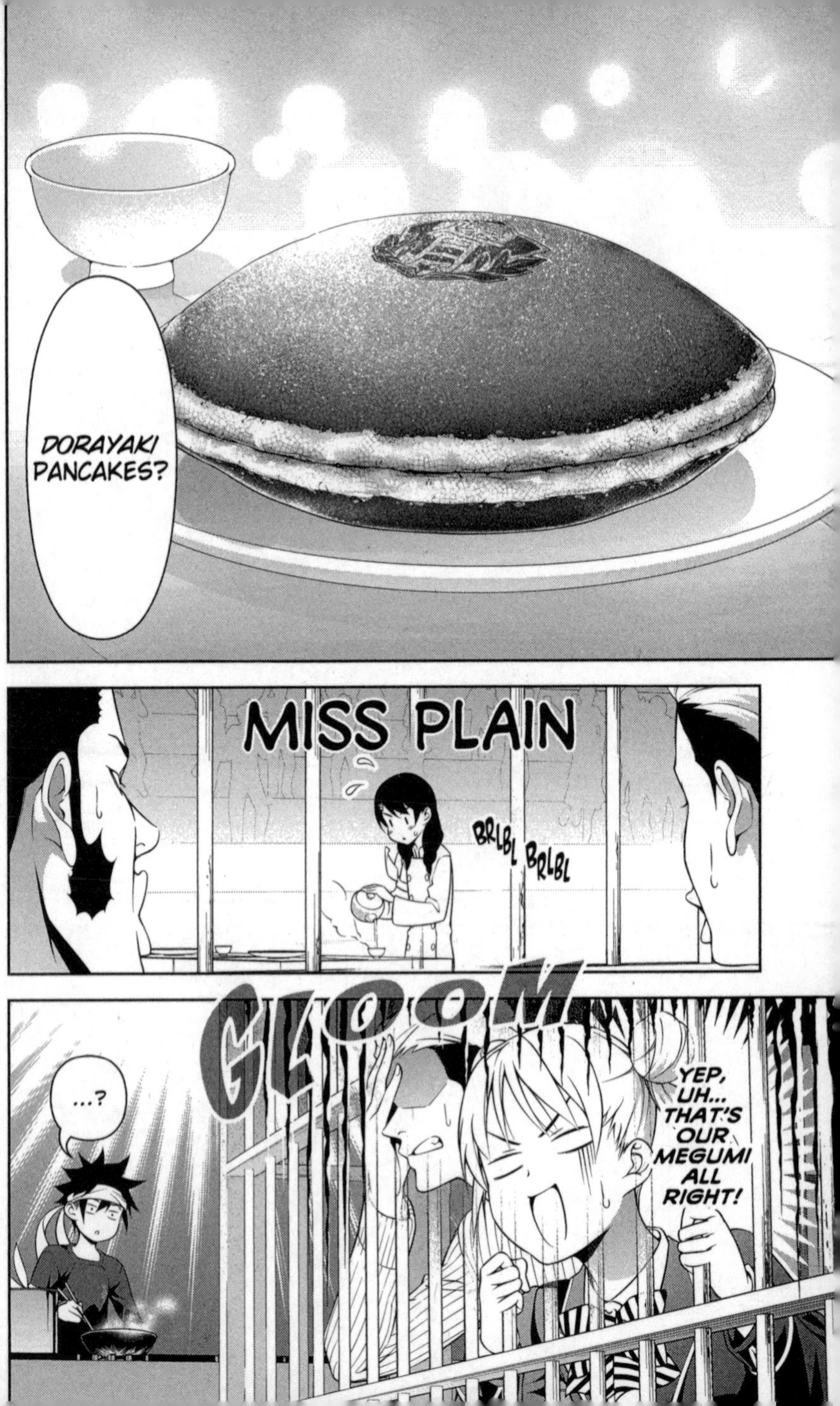
DORAYAKI PANCAKES?
MISS PLAIN
BRLBL BRLBL
GLOOOM
YEP, UH... THAT'S OUR MEGUMI ALL RIGHT!
...?

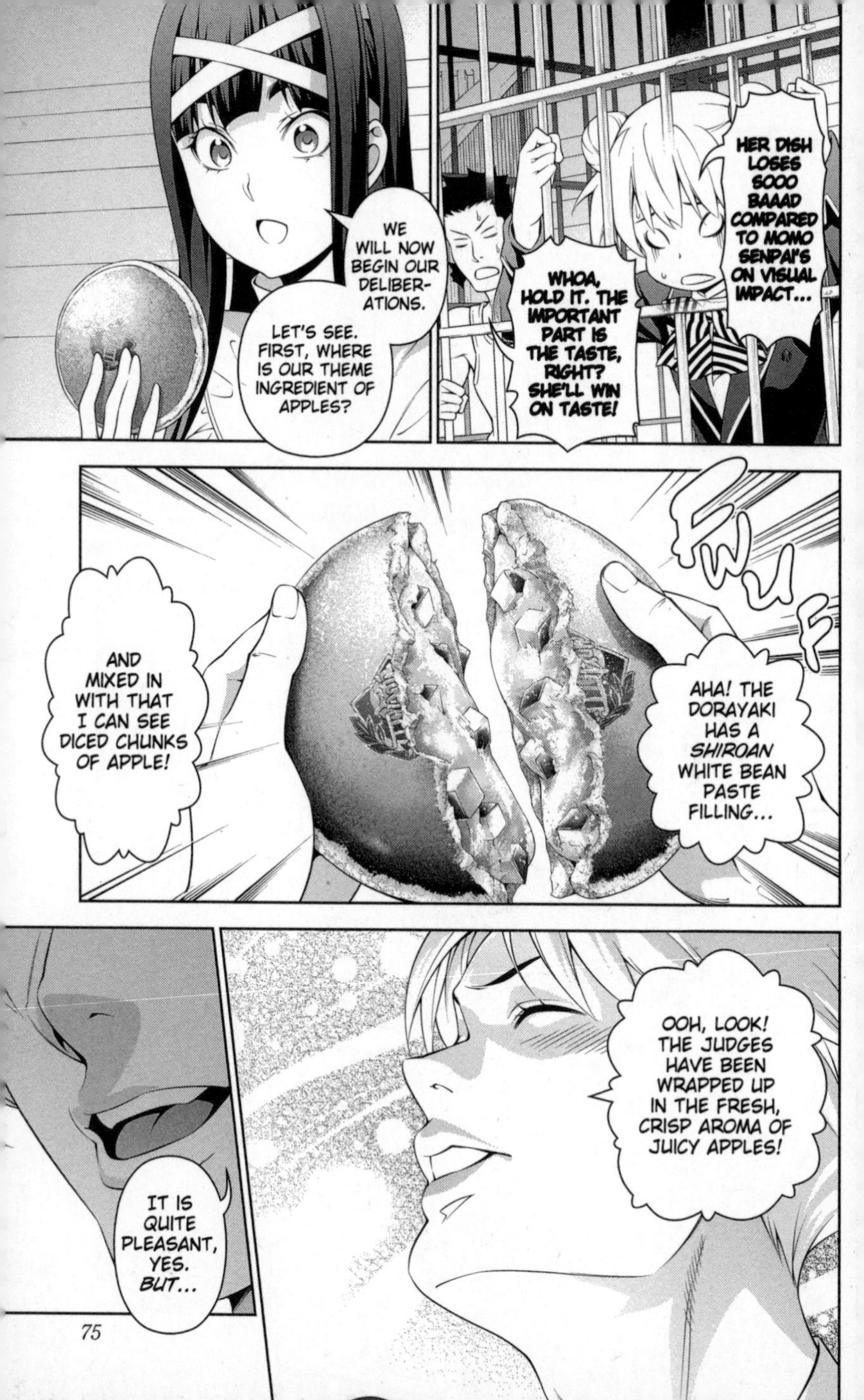
HER DISH LOSES SOOO BAAAD COMPARED TO MOMO SENPAI'S ON VISUAL IMPACT...
WHOA, HOLD IT. THE IMPORTANT PART IS THE TASTE, RIGHT? SHE'LL WIN ON TASTE!
WE WILL NOW BEGIN OUR DELIBERATIONS.
LET'S SEE. FIRST, WHERE IS OUR THEME INGREDIENT OF APPLES?
FWUF
AHA! THE DORAYAKI HAS A *SHIROAN* WHITE BEAN PASTE FILLING...
AND MIXED IN WITH THAT I CAN SEE DICED CHUNKS OF APPLE!
OOH, LOOK! THE JUDGES HAVE BEEN WRAPPED UP IN THE FRESH, CRISP AROMA OF JUICY APPLES!
IT IS QUITE PLEASANT, YES. *BUT*...

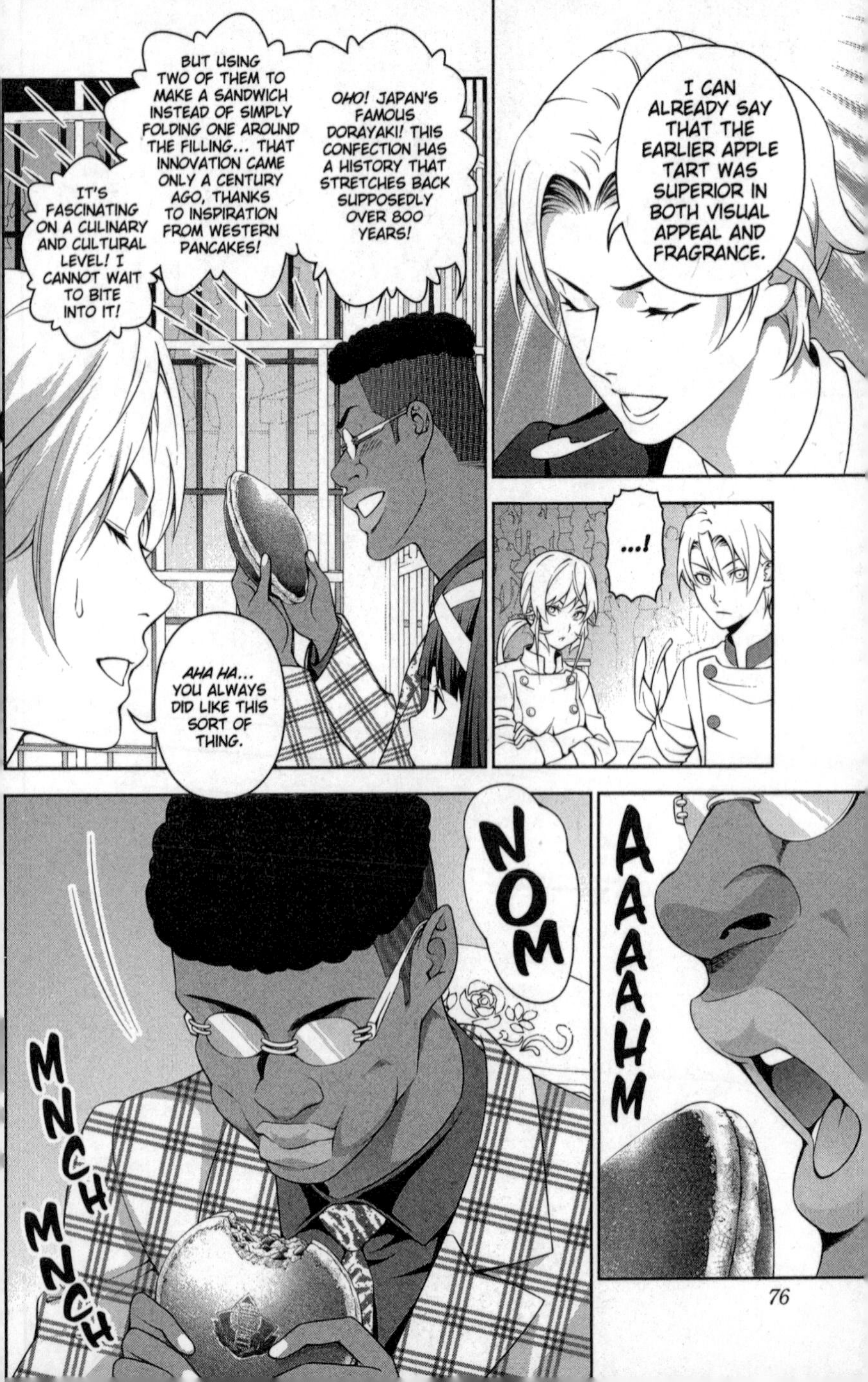
I CAN ALREADY SAY THAT THE EARLIER APPLE TART WAS SUPERIOR IN BOTH VISUAL APPEAL AND FRAGRANCE.
...!
OHO! JAPAN'S FAMOUS DORAYAKI! THIS CONFECTION HAS A HISTORY THAT STRETCHES BACK SUPPOSEDLY OVER 800 YEARS!
BUT USING TWO OF THEM TO MAKE A SANDWICH INSTEAD OF SIMPLY FOLDING ONE AROUND THE FILLING... THAT INNOVATION CAME ONLY A CENTURY AGO, THANKS TO INSPIRATION FROM WESTERN PANCAKES!
IT'S FASCINATING ON A CULINARY AND CULTURAL LEVEL! I CANNOT WAIT TO BITE INTO IT!
AHA HA... YOU ALWAYS DID LIKE THIS SORT OF THING.
AAAAHM
NOM
MNCH MNCH

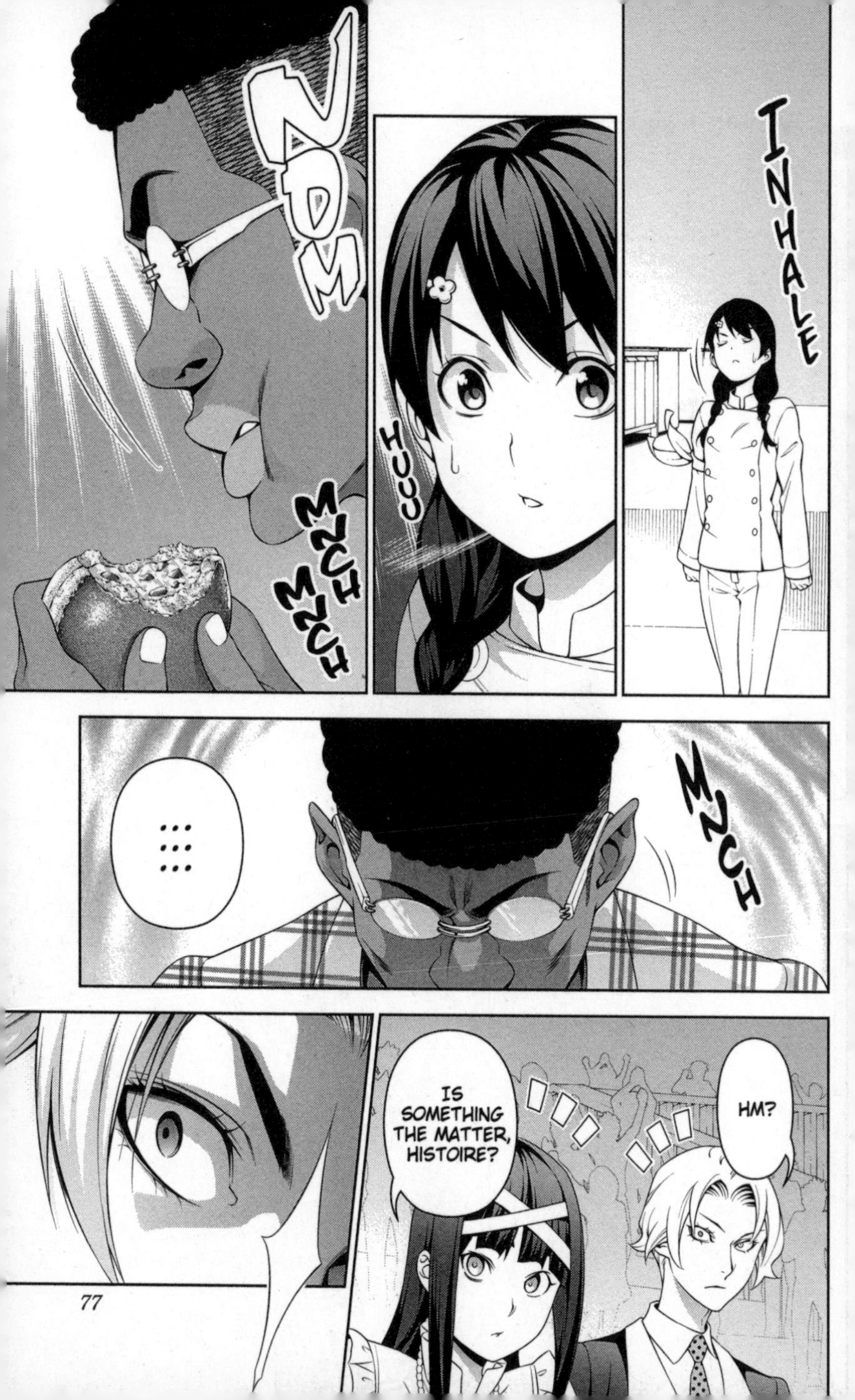
INHALE
HUUU
ZADM
MNCH MNCH
MNCH
......
HM?
IS SOMETHING THE MATTER, HISTOIRE?

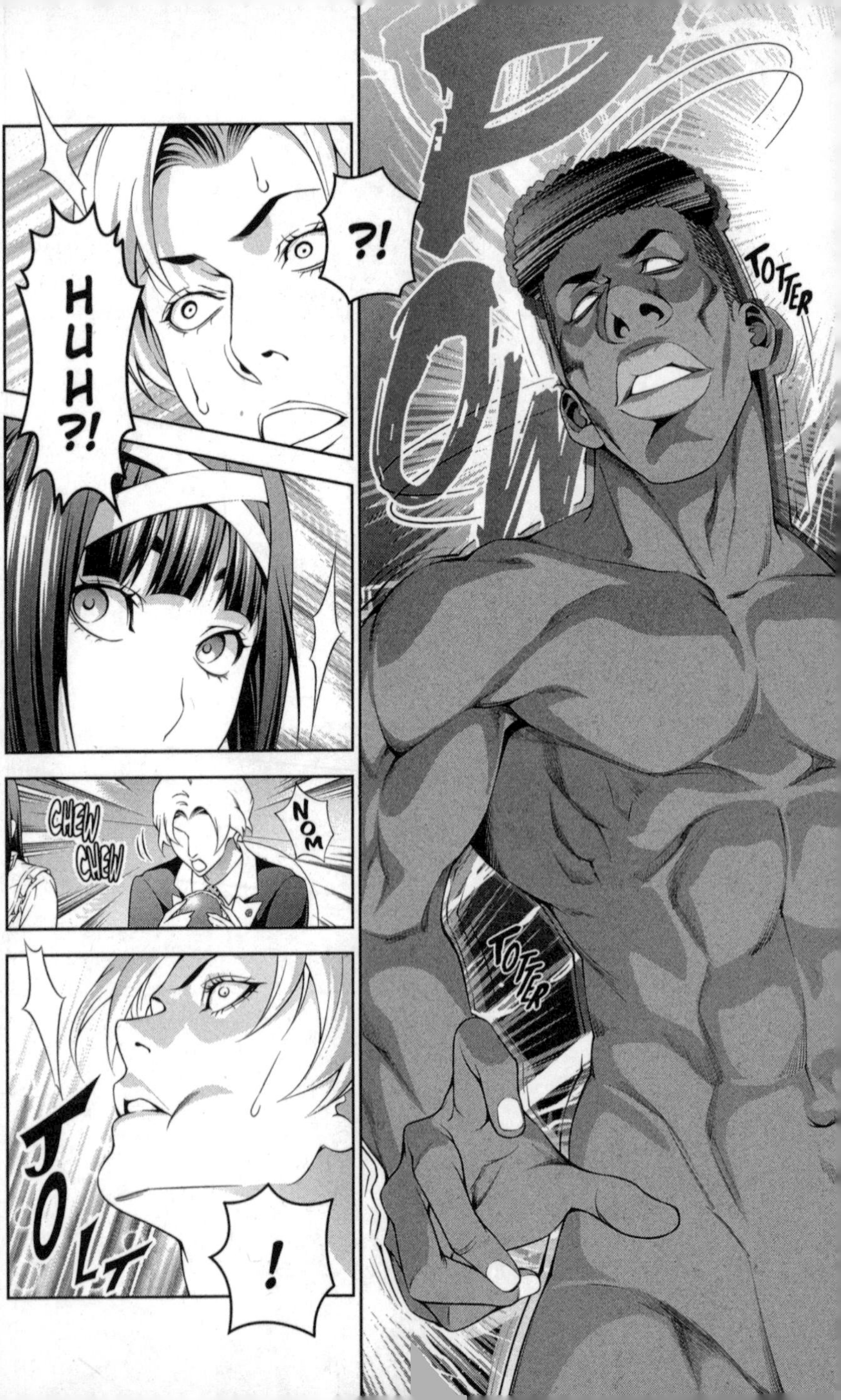

TOTTER
TOTTER
?!
HUH?!
NOM
CHEW CHEW
!
JOLT

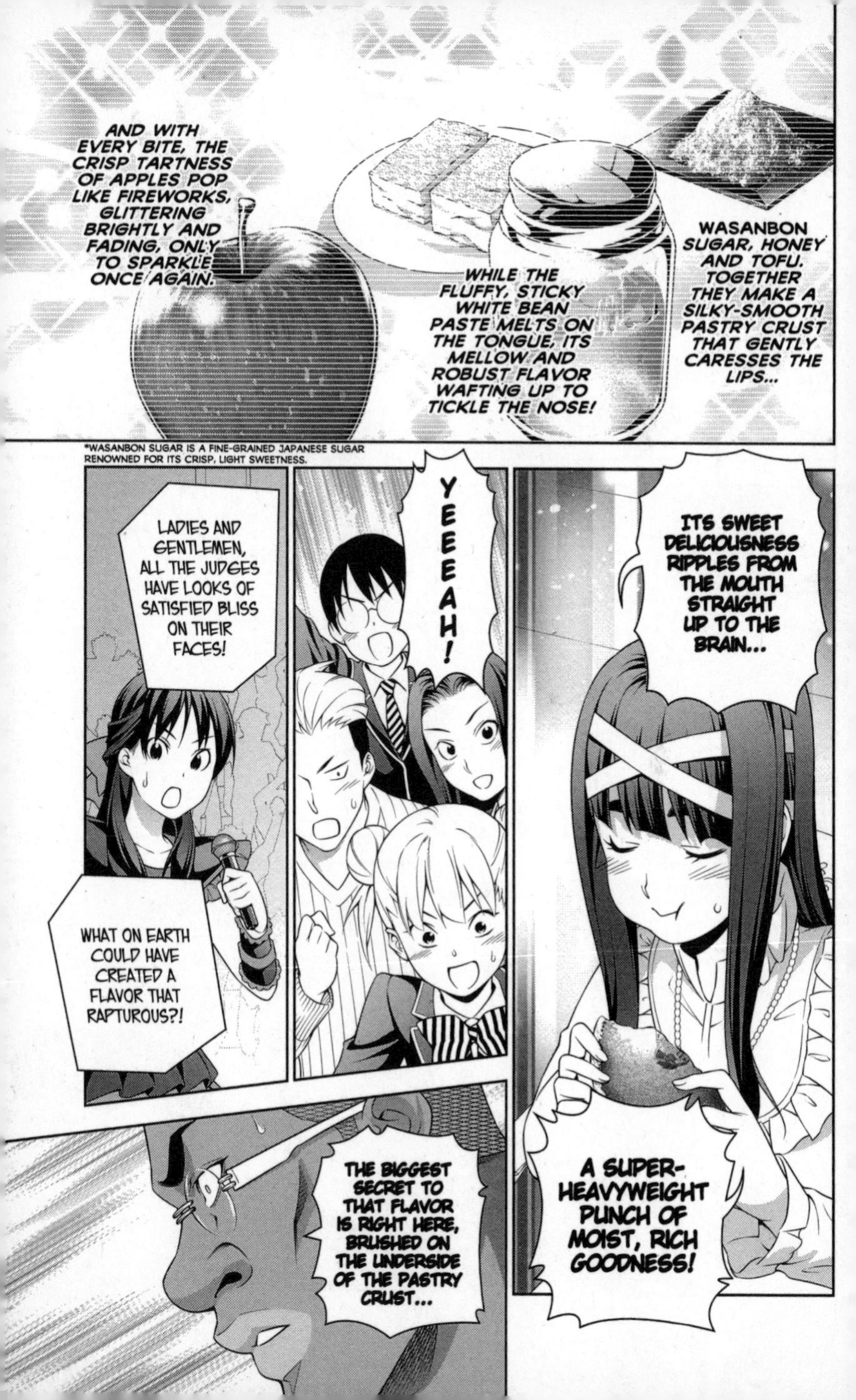
WASANBON SUGAR, HONEY AND TOFU. TOGETHER THEY MAKE A SILKY-SMOOTH PASTRY CRUST THAT GENTLY CARESSES THE LIPS...
WHILE THE FLUFFY, STICKY WHITE BEAN PASTE MELTS ON THE TONGUE, ITS MELLOW AND ROBUST FLAVOR WAFTING UP TO TICKLE THE NOSE!
AND WITH EVERY BITE, THE CRISP TARTNESS OF APPLES POP LIKE FIREWORKS, GLITTERING BRIGHTLY AND FADING, ONLY TO SPARKLE ONCE AGAIN.
*WASANBON SUGAR IS A FINE-GRAINED JAPANESE SUGAR RENOWNED FOR ITS CRISP, LIGHT SWEETNESS.
ITS SWEET DELICIOUSNESS RIPPLES FROM THE MOUTH STRAIGHT UP TO THE BRAIN...
A SUPER-HEAVYWEIGHT PUNCH OF MOIST, RICH GOODNESS!
YEEEEAH!
LADIES AND GENTLEMEN, ALL THE JUDGES HAVE LOOKS OF SATISFIED BLISS ON THEIR FACES!
WHAT ON EARTH COULD HAVE CREATED A FLAVOR THAT RAPTUROUS?!
THE BIGGEST SECRET TO THAT FLAVOR IS RIGHT HERE, BRUSHED ON THE UNDERSIDE OF THE PASTRY CRUST...

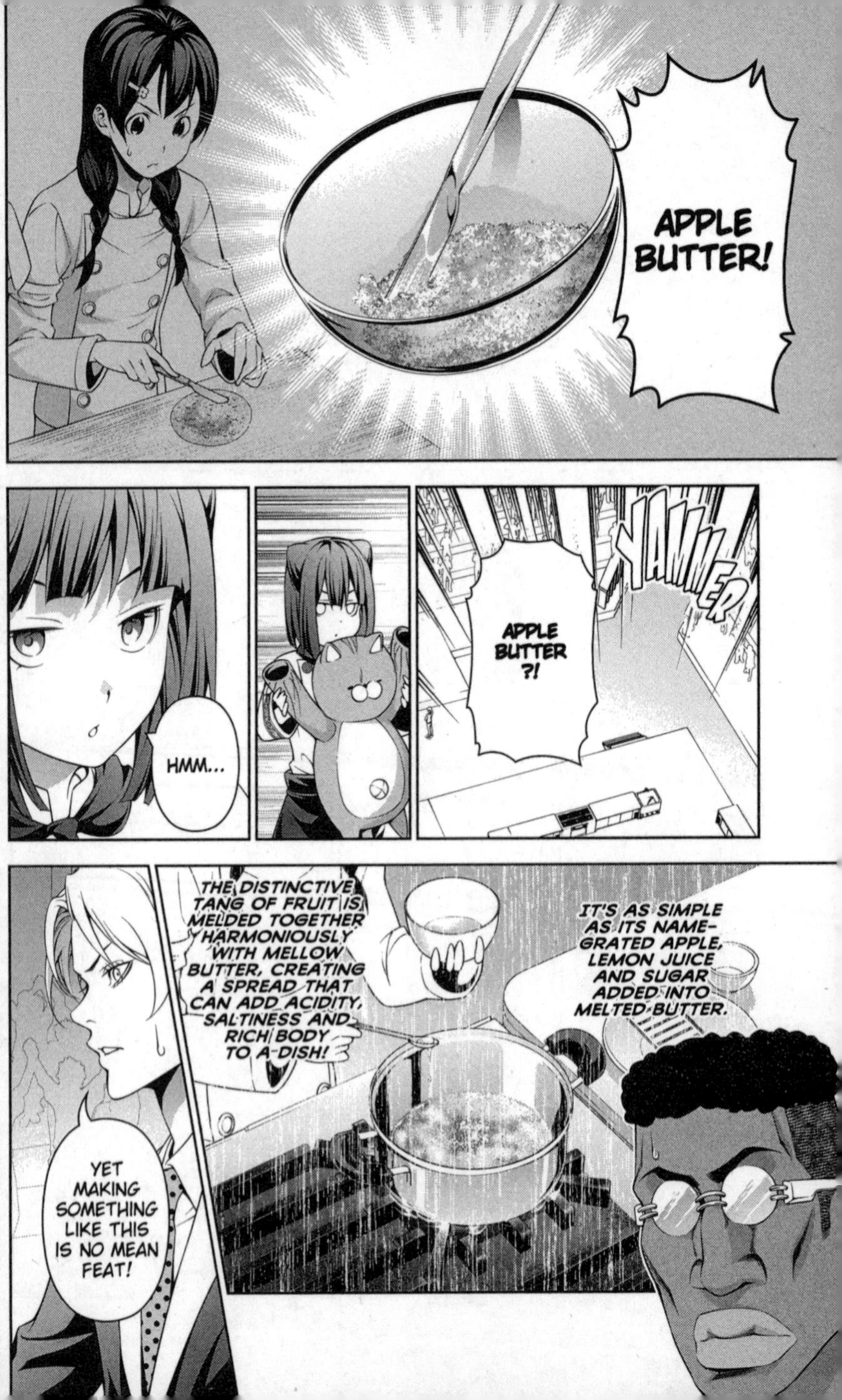

APPLE BUTTER!
YAMMER
APPLE BUTTER ?!
HMM...
IT'S AS SIMPLE AS ITS NAME- GRATED APPLE, LEMON JUICE AND SUGAR ADDED INTO MELTED BUTTER.
THE DISTINCTIVE TANG OF FRUIT IS MELDED TOGETHER HARMONIOUSLY WITH MELLOW BUTTER, CREATING A SPREAD THAT CAN ADD ACIDITY, SALTINESS AND RICH BODY TO A DISH!
YET MAKING SOMETHING LIKE THIS IS NO MEAN FEAT!

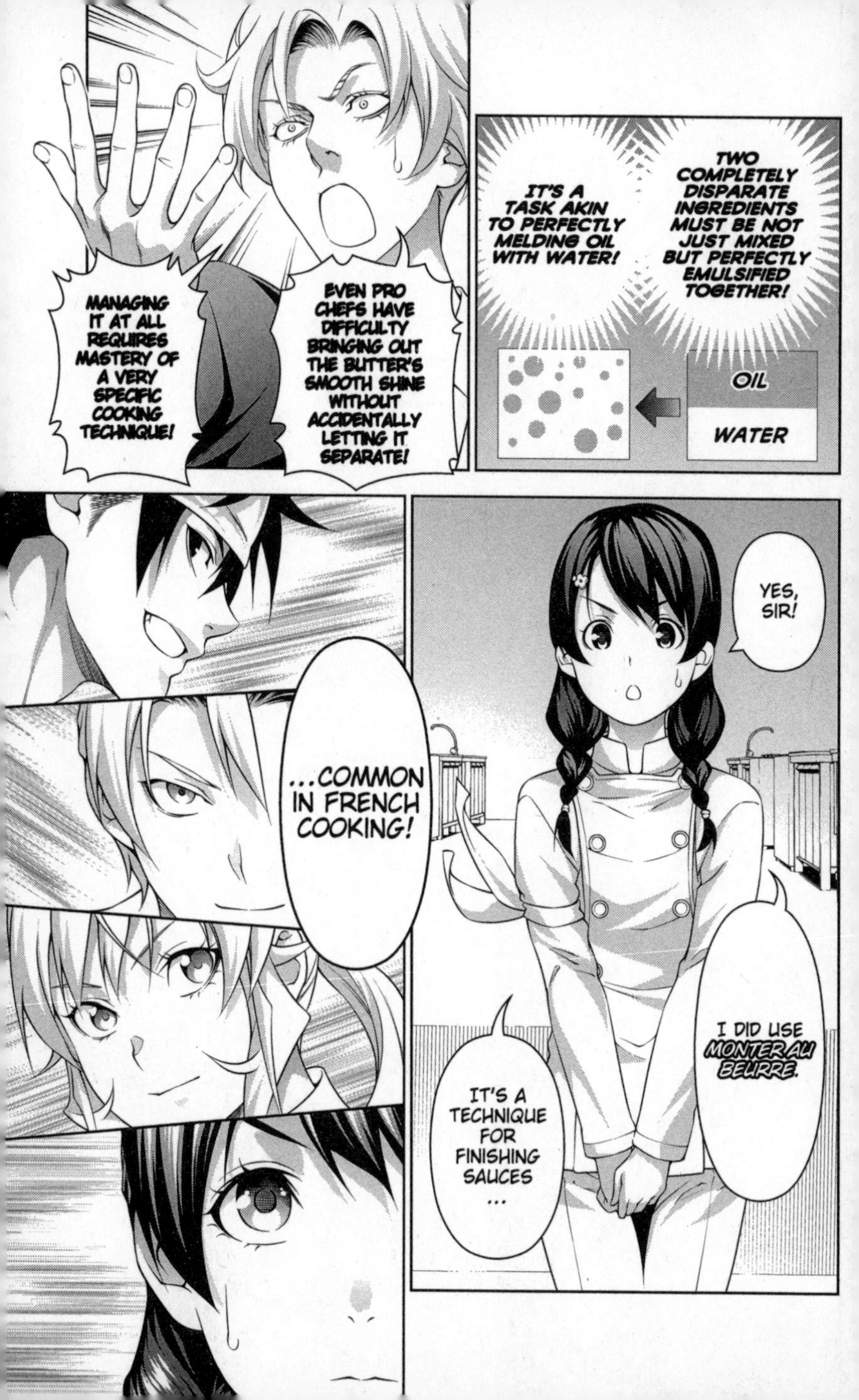
TWO COMPLETELY DISPARATE INGREDIENTS MUST BE NOT JUST MIXED BUT PERFECTLY EMULSIFIED TOGETHER!
IT'S A TASK AKIN TO PERFECTLY MELDING OIL WITH WATER!
OIL
WATER
EVEN PRO CHEFS HAVE DIFFICULTY BRINGING OUT THE BUTTER'S SMOOTH SHINE WITHOUT ACCIDENTALLY LETTING IT SEPARATE!
MANAGING IT AT ALL REQUIRES MASTERY OF A VERY SPECIFIC COOKING TECHNIQUE!
YES, SIR!
I DID USE MONTER AU BEURRE.
IT'S A TECHNIQUE FOR FINISHING SAUCES ...
...COMMON IN FRENCH COOKING!

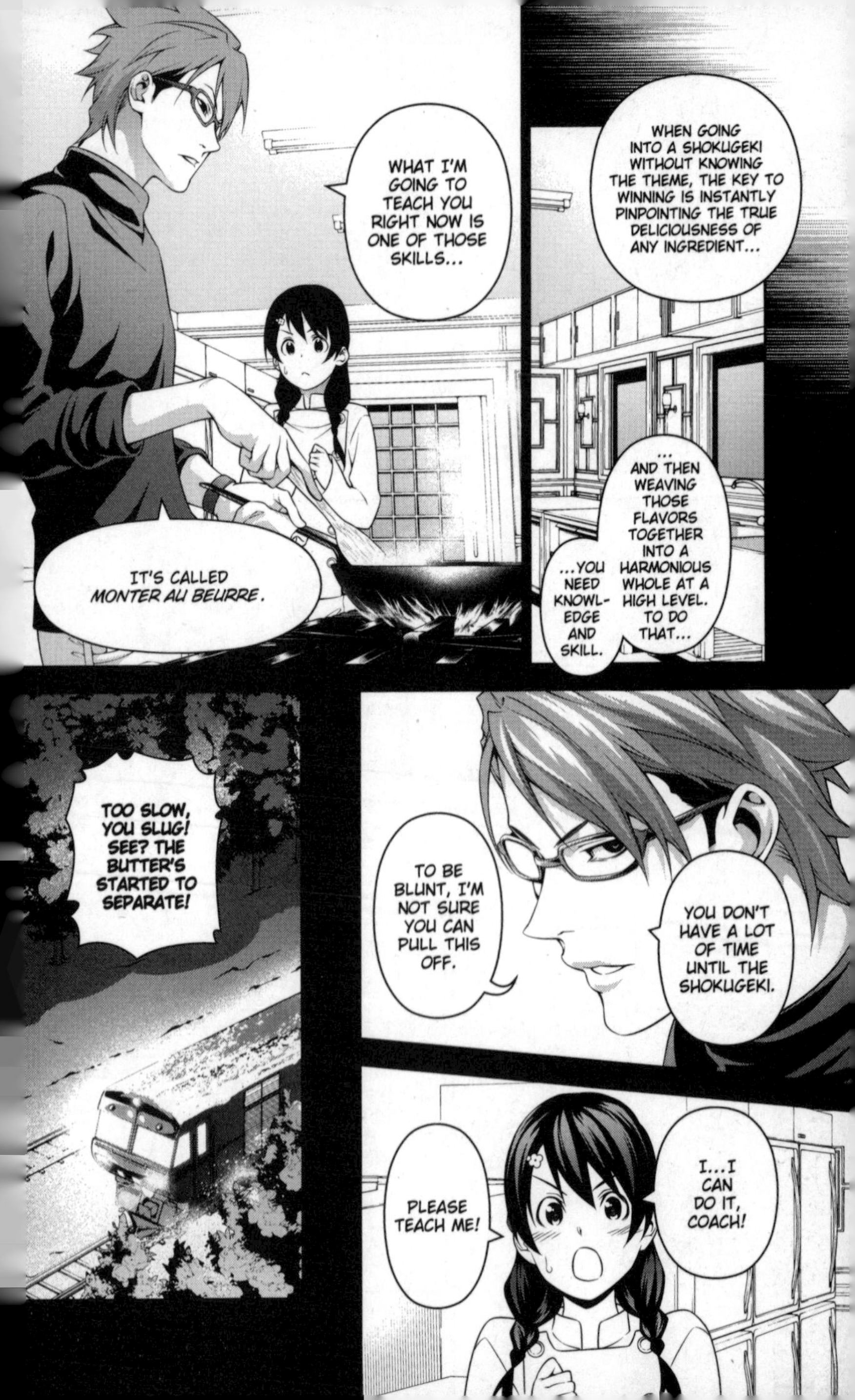

WHEN GOING INTO A SHOKUGEKI WITHOUT KNOWING THE THEME, THE KEY TO WINNING IS INSTANTLY PINPOINTING THE TRUE DELICIOUSNESS OF ANY INGREDIENT...
... AND THEN WEAVING THOSE FLAVORS TOGETHER INTO A HARMONIOUS WHOLE AT A HIGH LEVEL. TO DO THAT...
...YOU NEED KNOWL-EDGE AND SKILL.
WHAT I'M GOING TO TEACH YOU RIGHT NOW IS ONE OF THOSE SKILLS...
IT'S CALLED *MONTER AU BEURRE*.
YOU DON'T HAVE A LOT OF TIME UNTIL THE SHOKUGEKI.
TO BE BLUNT, I'M NOT SURE YOU CAN PULL THIS OFF.
I...I CAN DO IT, COACH!
PLEASE TEACH ME!
TOO SLOW, YOU SLUG! SEE? THE BUTTER'S STARTED TO SEPARATE!

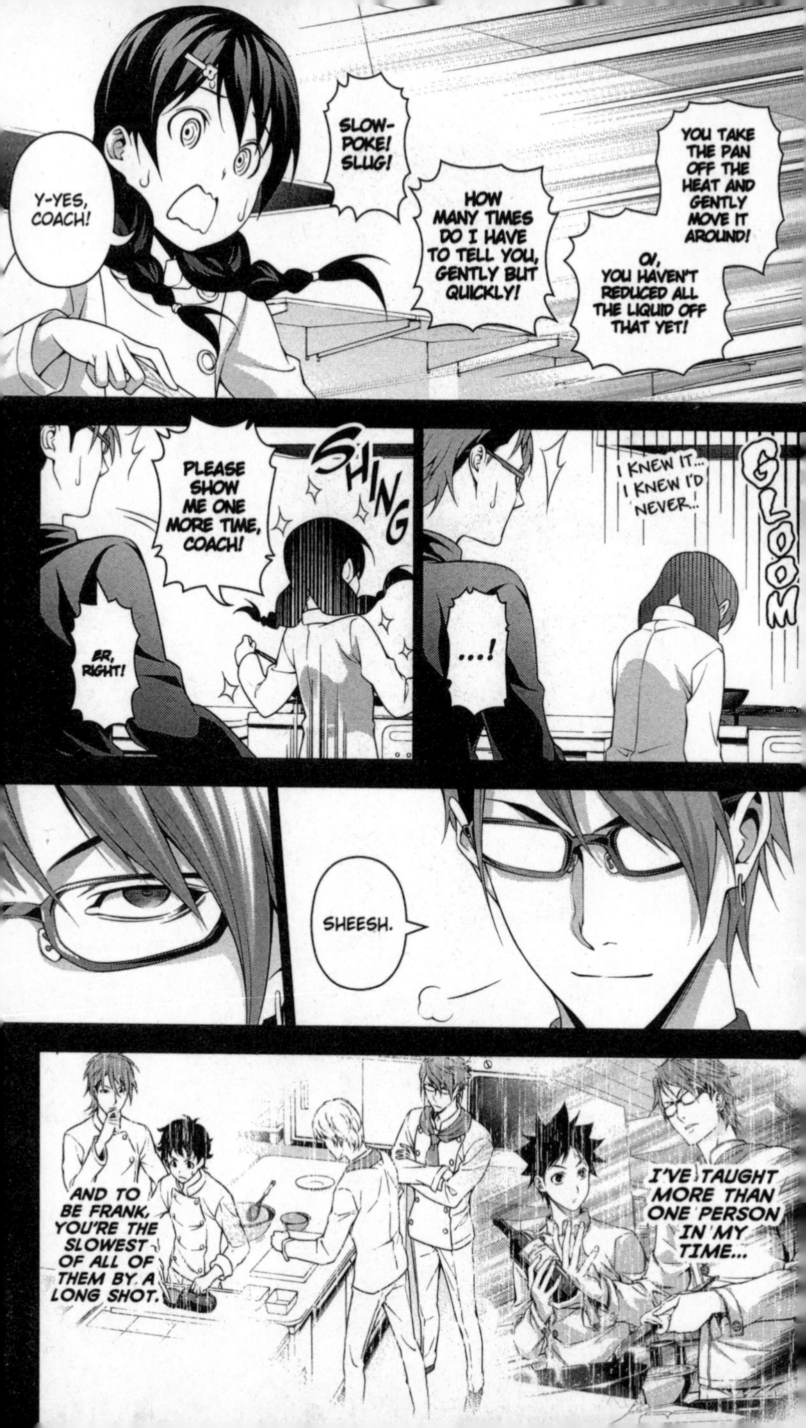
OI, YOU HAVEN'T REDUCED ALL THE LIQUID OFF THAT YET!
YOU TAKE THE PAN OFF THE HEAT AND GENTLY MOVE IT AROUND!
HOW MANY TIMES DO I HAVE TO TELL YOU, GENTLY BUT QUICKLY!
SLOW-POKE! SLUG!
Y-YES, COACH!
GLOOM
I KNEW IT... I KNEW I'D NEVER...
...!
SHING
PLEASE SHOW ME ONE MORE TIME, COACH!
ER, RIGHT!
SHEESH.
I'VE TAUGHT MORE THAN ONE PERSON IN MY TIME...
AND TO BE FRANK, YOU'RE THE SLOWEST OF ALL OF THEM BY A LONG SHOT.

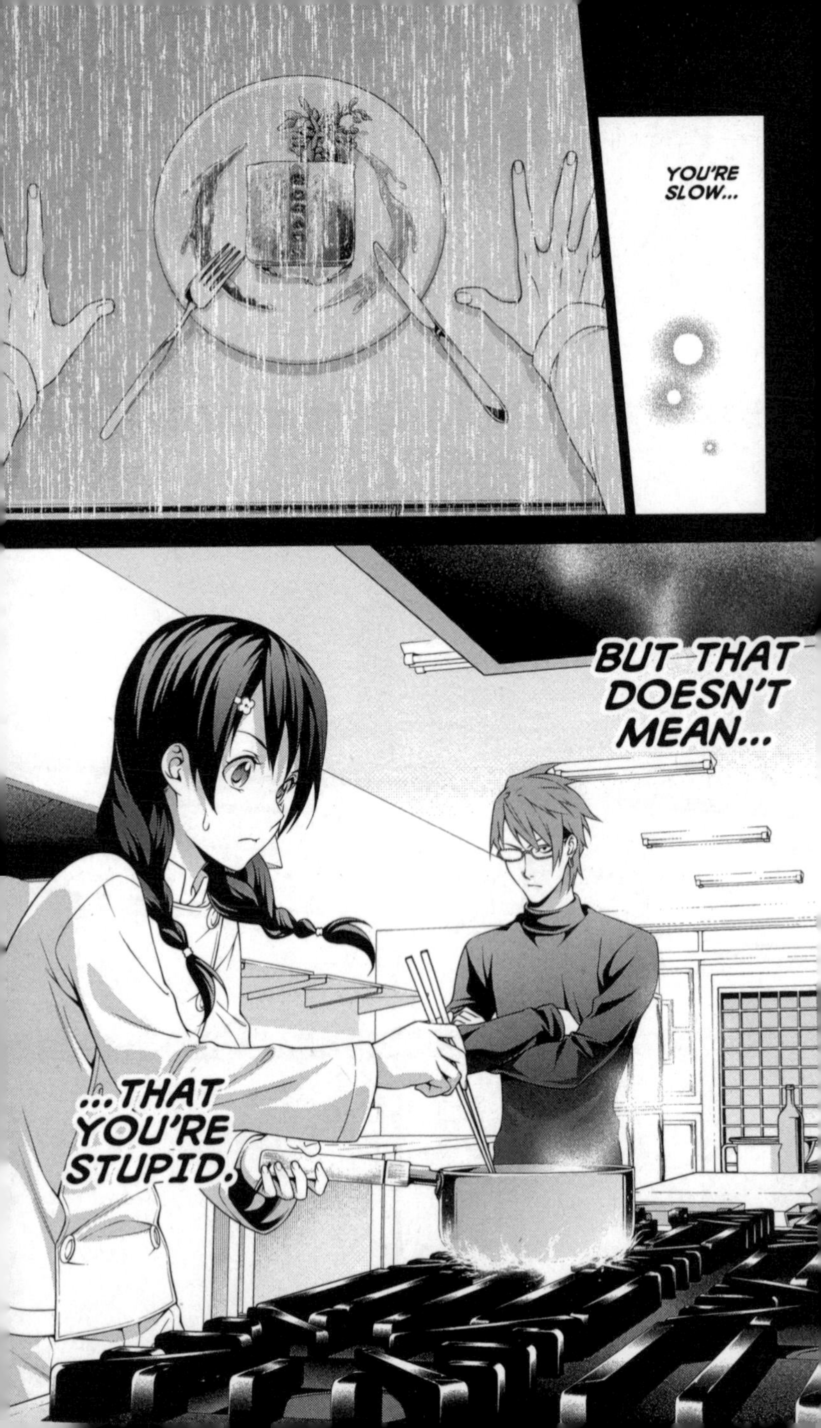
YOU'RE SLOW...
BUT THAT DOESN'T MEAN...
...THAT YOU'RE STUPID.

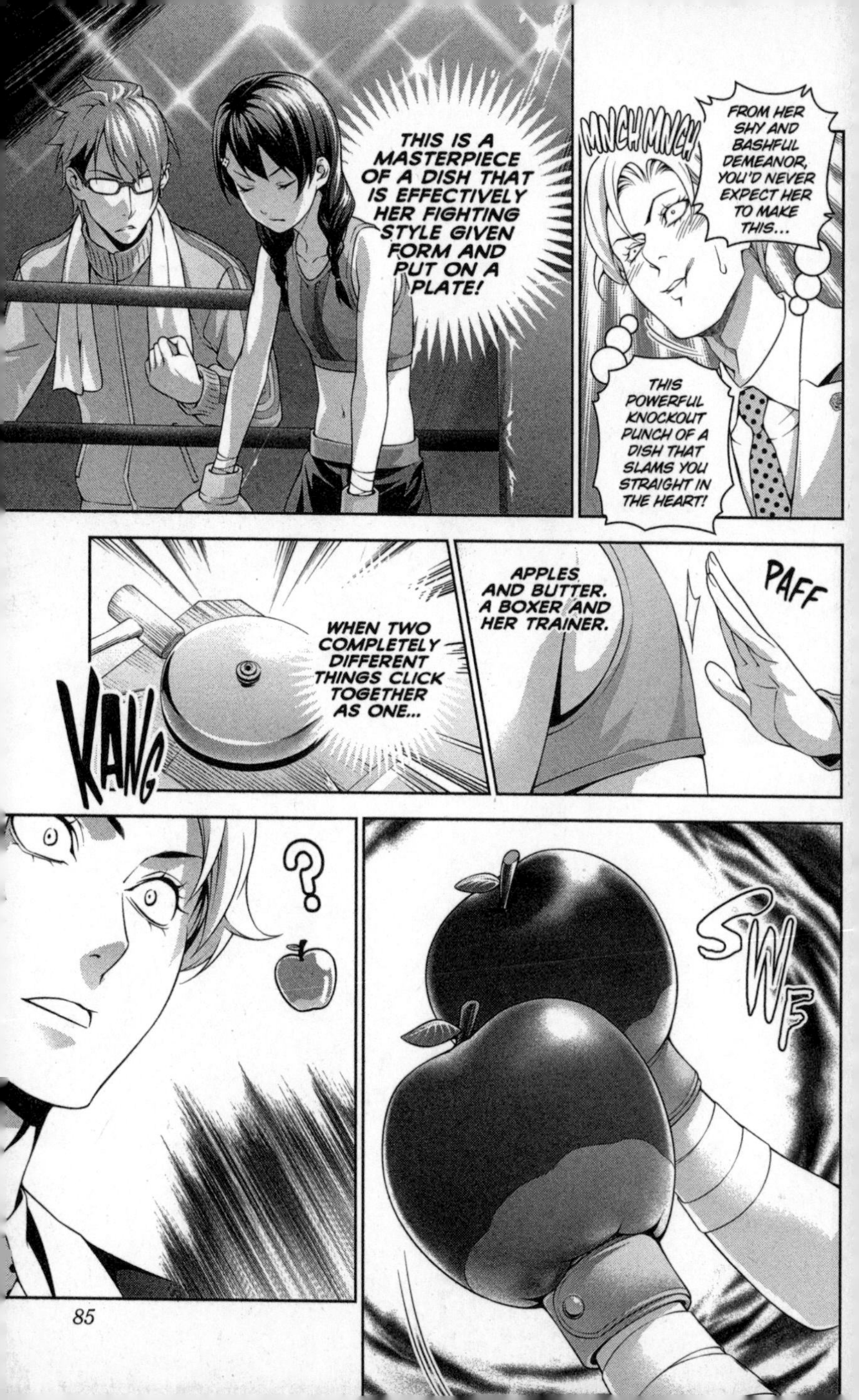
MNCH MNCH
FROM HER SHY AND BASHFUL DEMEANOR, YOU'D NEVER EXPECT HER TO MAKE THIS...
THIS POWERFUL KNOCKOUT PUNCH OF A DISH THAT SLAMS YOU STRAIGHT IN THE HEART!
THIS IS A MASTERPIECE OF A DISH THAT IS EFFECTIVELY HER FIGHTING STYLE GIVEN FORM AND PUT ON A PLATE!
APPLES AND BUTTER. A BOXER AND HER TRAINER.
PAFF
WHEN TWO COMPLETELY DIFFERENT THINGS CLICK TOGETHER AS ONE...
KANG
SWF
?

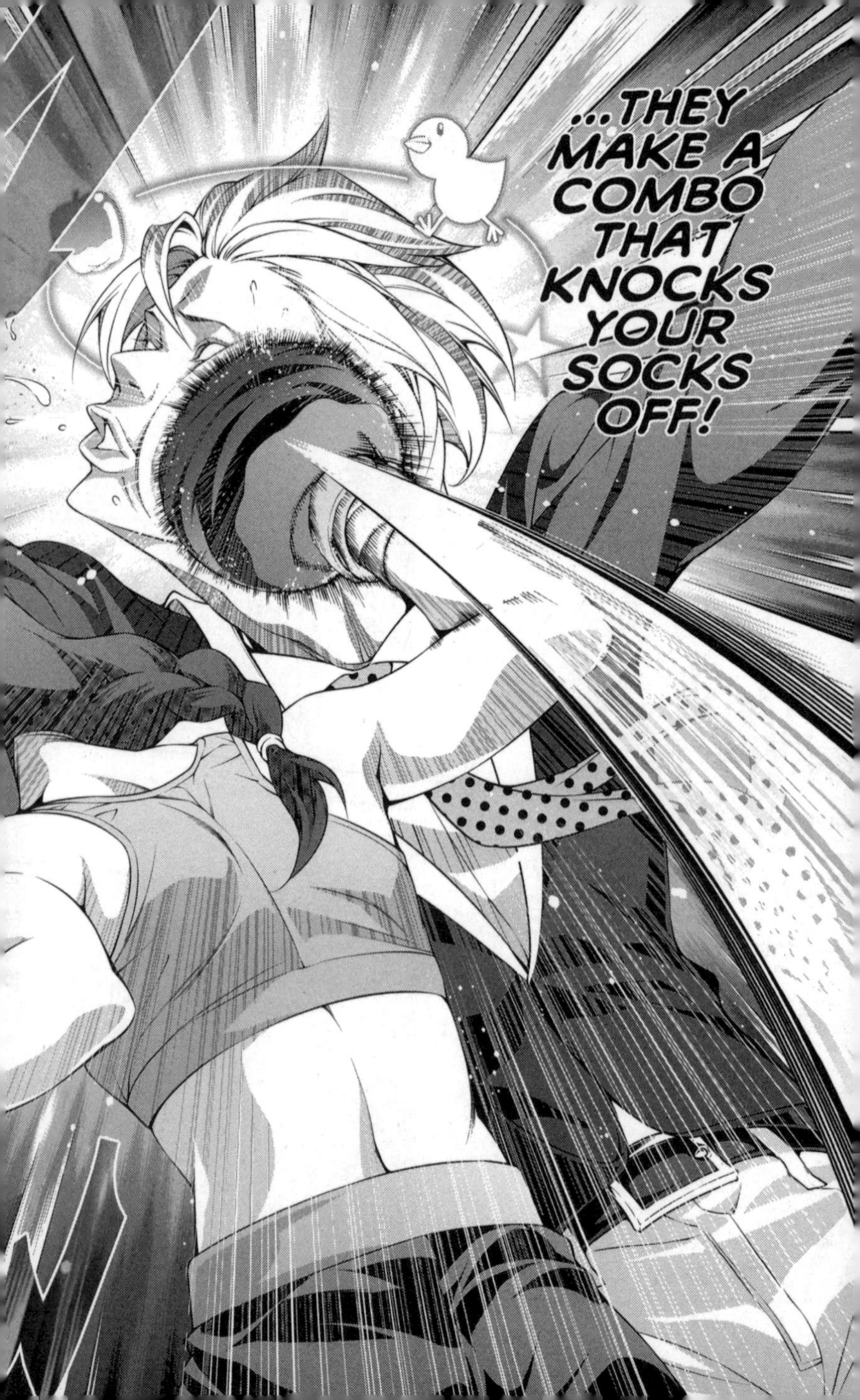
...THEY MAKE A COMBO THAT KNOCKS YOUR SOCKS OFF!

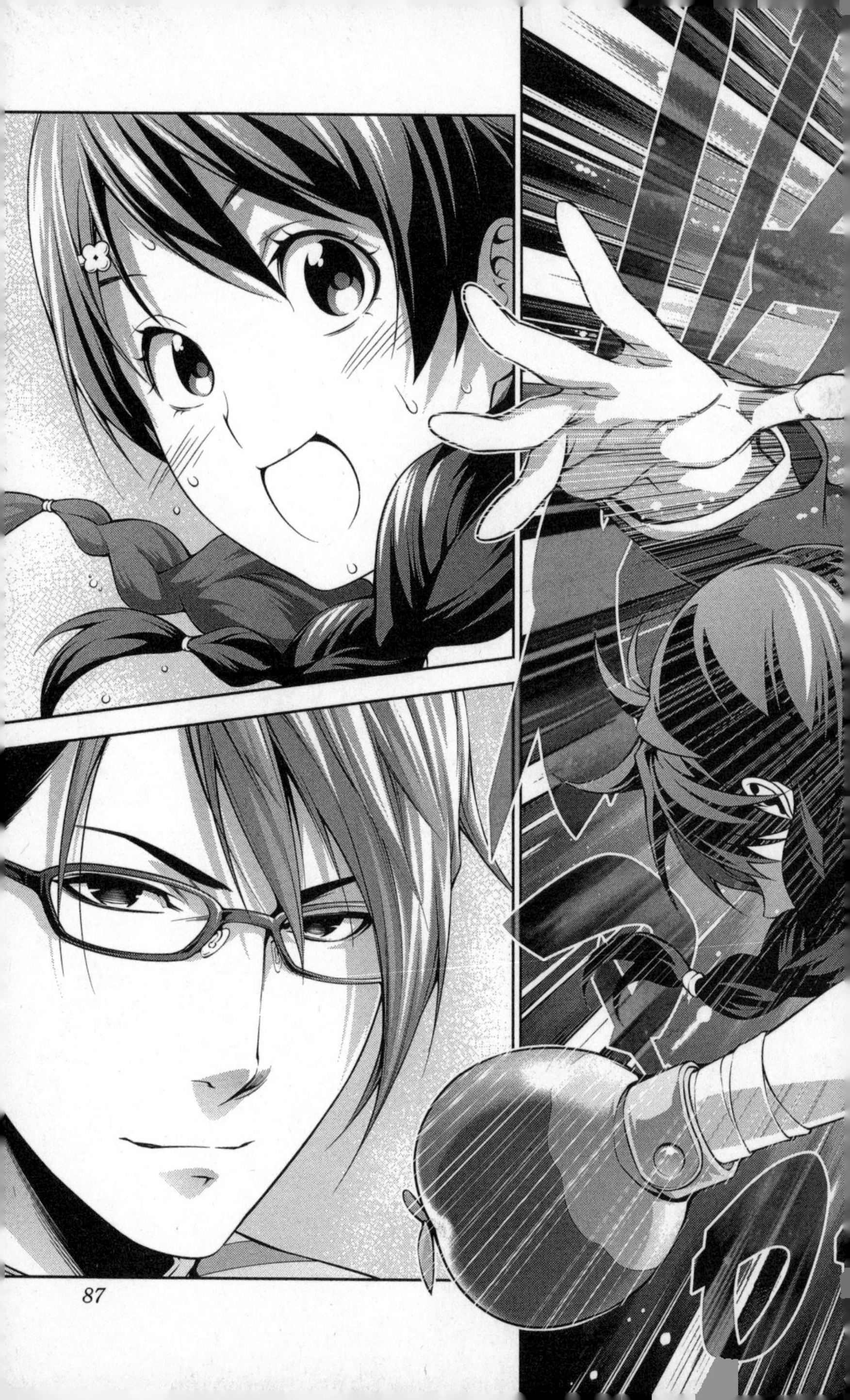

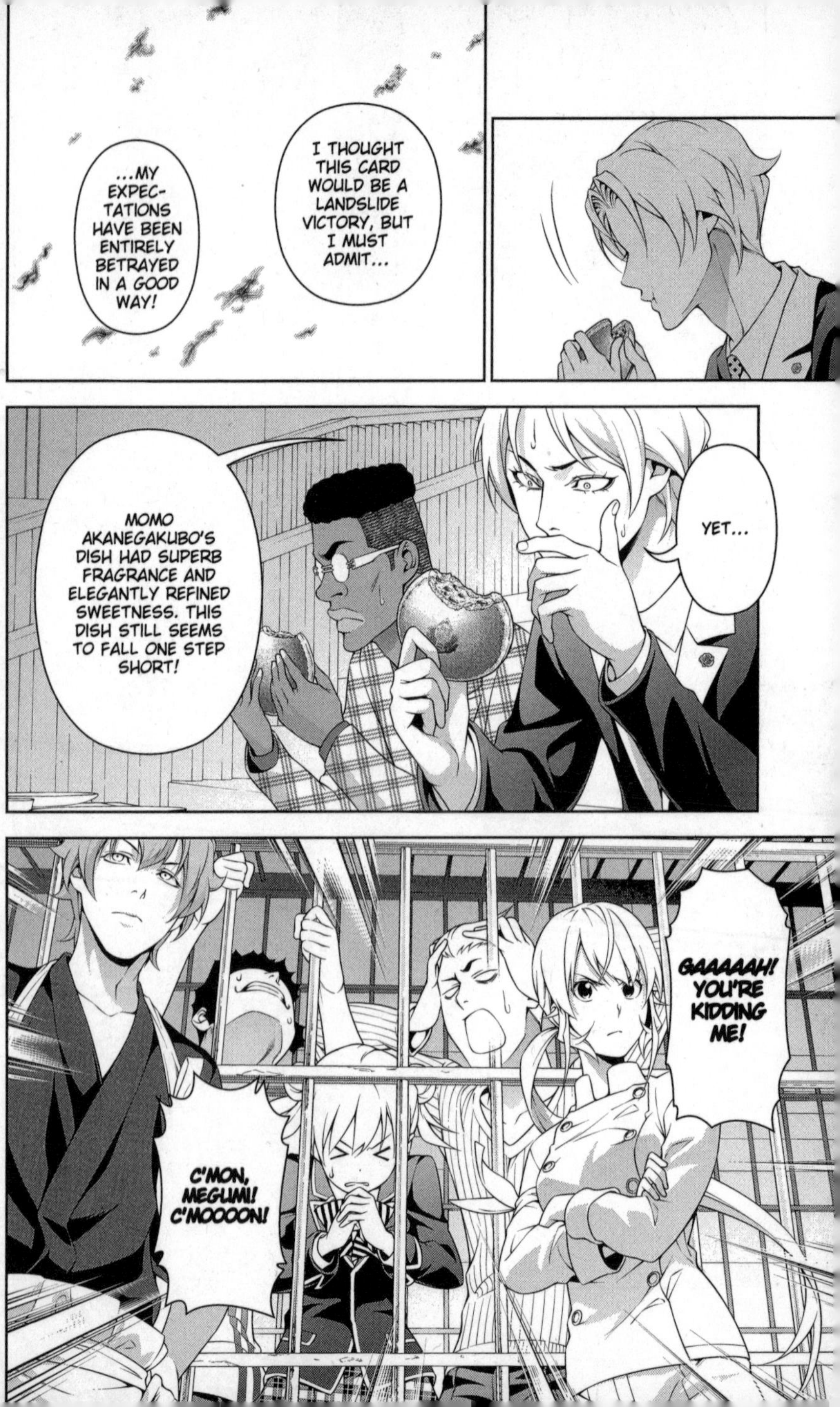
I THOUGHT THIS CARD WOULD BE A LANDSLIDE VICTORY, BUT I MUST ADMIT...
...MY EXPECTATIONS HAVE BEEN ENTIRELY BETRAYED IN A GOOD WAY!
YET...
MOMO AKANEGAKUBO'S DISH HAD SUPERB FRAGRANCE AND ELEGANTLY REFINED SWEETNESS. THIS DISH STILL SEEMS TO FALL ONE STEP SHORT!
GAAAAAH! YOU'RE KIDDING ME!
C'MON, MEGUMI! C'MOOOON!

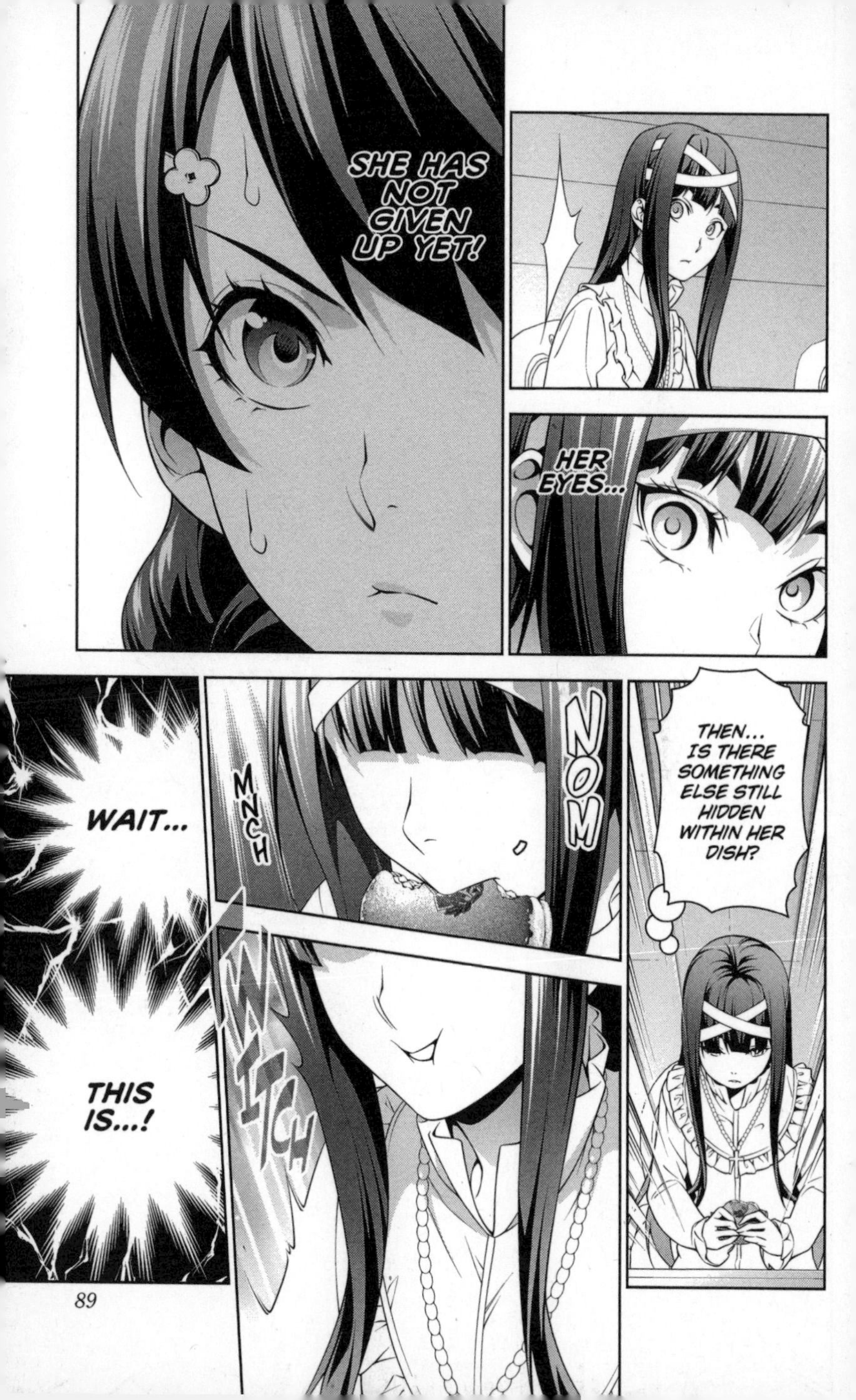
HER EYES...
SHE HAS NOT GIVEN UP YET!
THEN... IS THERE SOMETHING ELSE STILL HIDDEN WITHIN HER DISH?
NOM
MNCH
TWITCH
WAIT...
THIS IS...!

ALBERT AND SYLVETTE FROM FOOD WARS! L'ÉTOILE, CURRENTLY RUNNING IN SHONEN JUMP+.
WHEN IT COMES TO THE DUNCE CATEGORY, YOU'RE NUMBER ONE.
FACTOR IN YOUR COMMANDING LEAD IN THE RASH CATEGORY AND YOU HAVE THE TWIN CROWNS, ALBERT.
WHAT? HOW CAN YOU BE SO MEAN, MONSIEUR SHINOMIYA!
I'M SURE YOU WIN IN THE "WILLINGNESS TO TAKE ACTION" CATEGORY TOO.

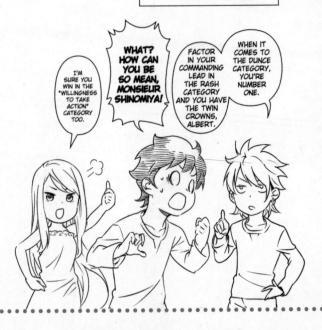

240 NOT CUTE

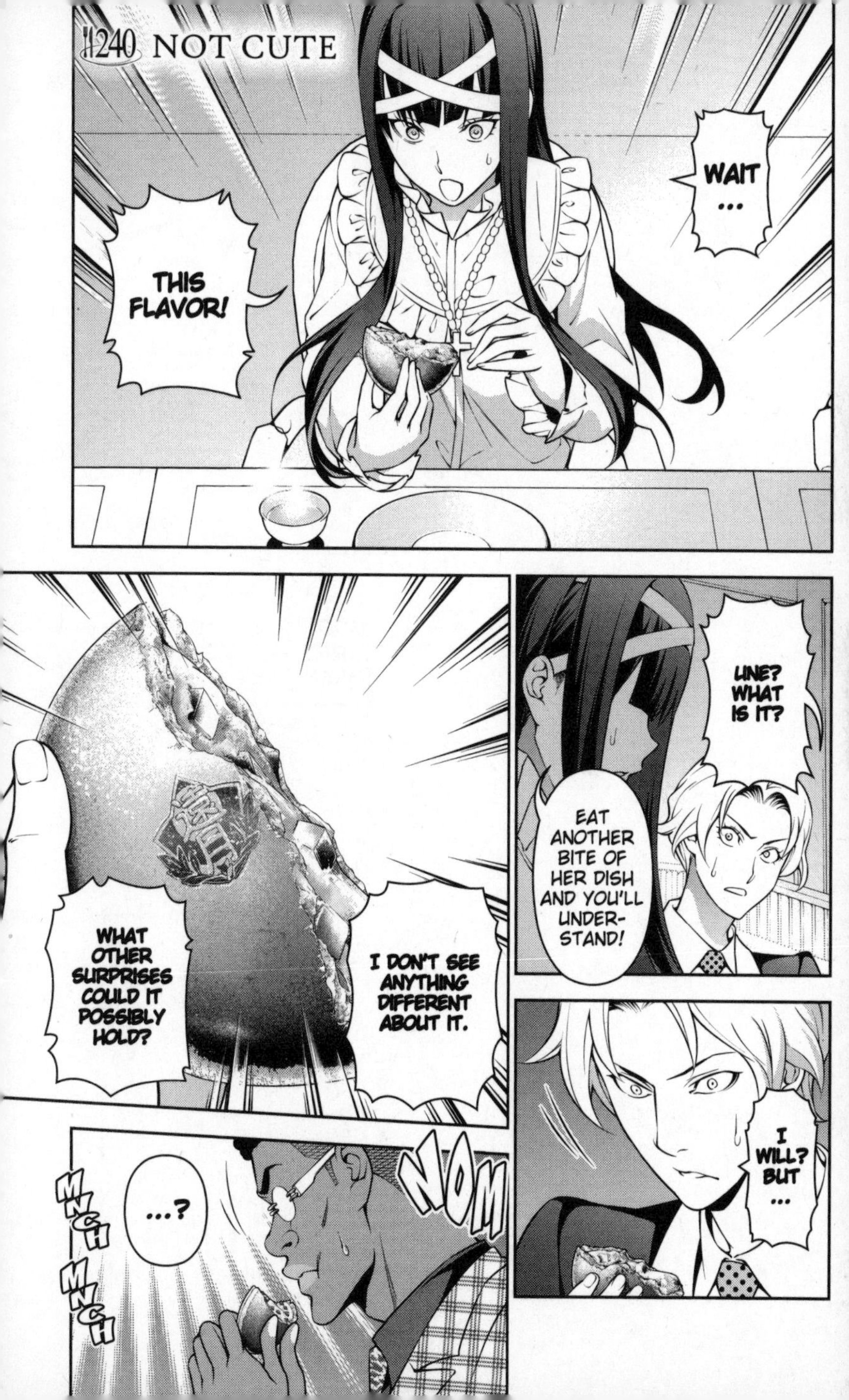
WAIT ...
THIS FLAVOR!
LINE? WHAT IS IT?
EAT ANOTHER BITE OF HER DISH AND YOU'LL UNDER-STAND!
I WILL? BUT ...
I DON'T SEE ANYTHING DIFFERENT ABOUT IT.
WHAT OTHER SURPRISES COULD IT POSSIBLY HOLD?
NOM
...?
MNCH MNCH

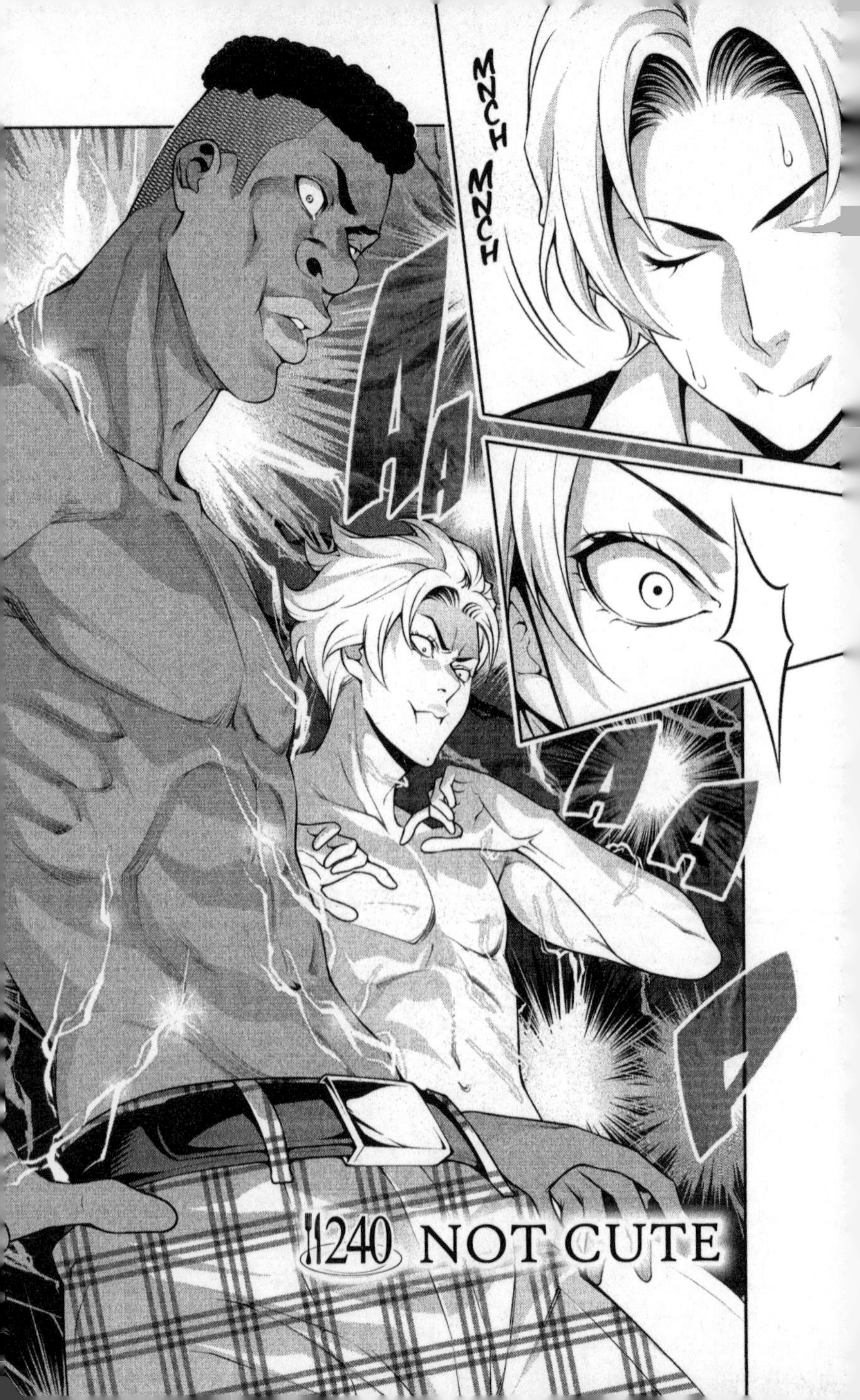
MNCH MNCH
AA
AA
A
240 NOT CUTE

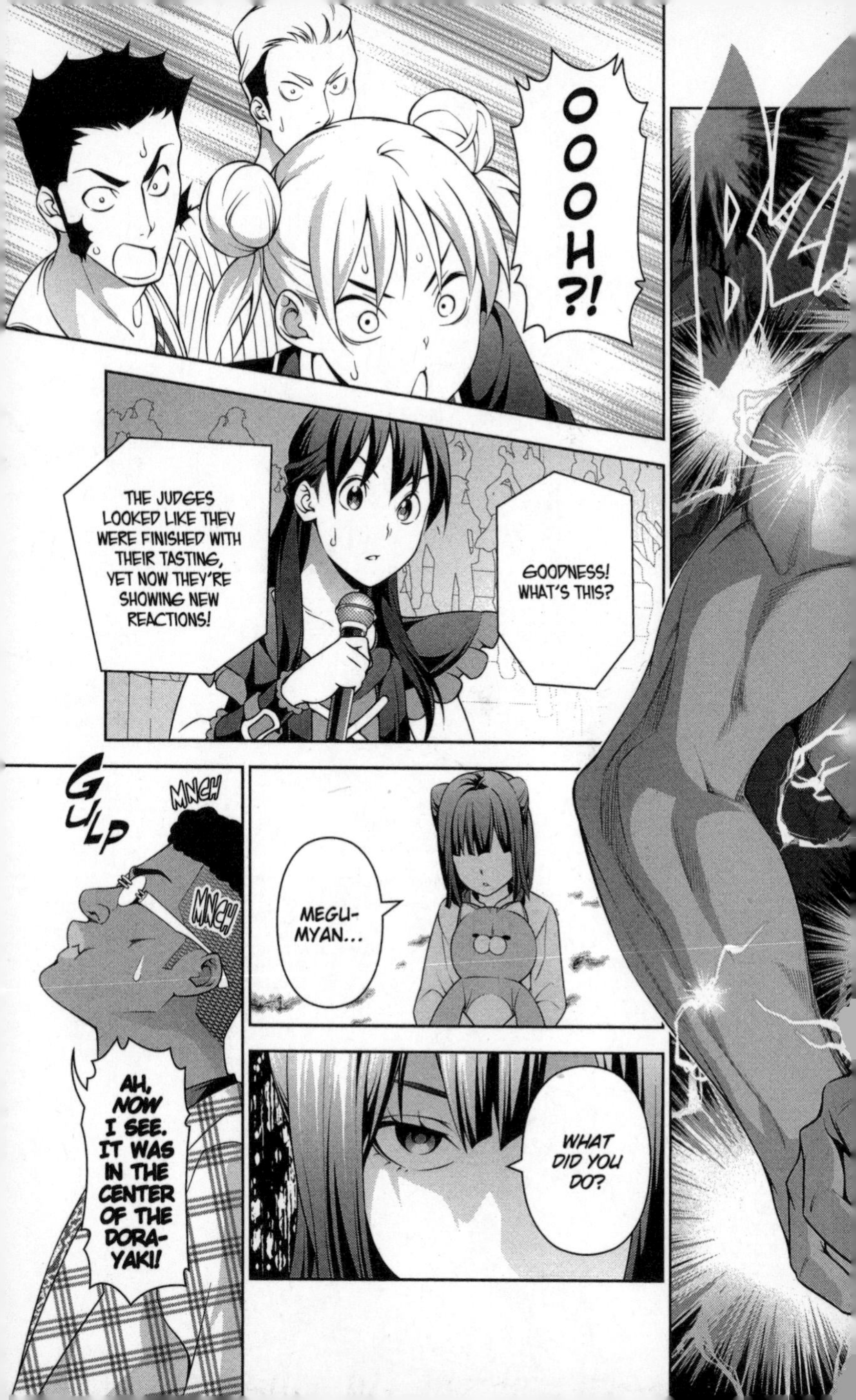
OOOOH?!
GOODNESS! WHAT'S THIS?
THE JUDGES LOOKED LIKE THEY WERE FINISHED WITH THEIR TASTING, YET NOW THEY'RE SHOWING NEW REACTIONS!
MEGU-MYAN...
WHAT DID YOU DO?
GULP
MNCH
MNCH
AH, NOW I SEE. IT WAS IN THE CENTER OF THE DORA-YAKI!

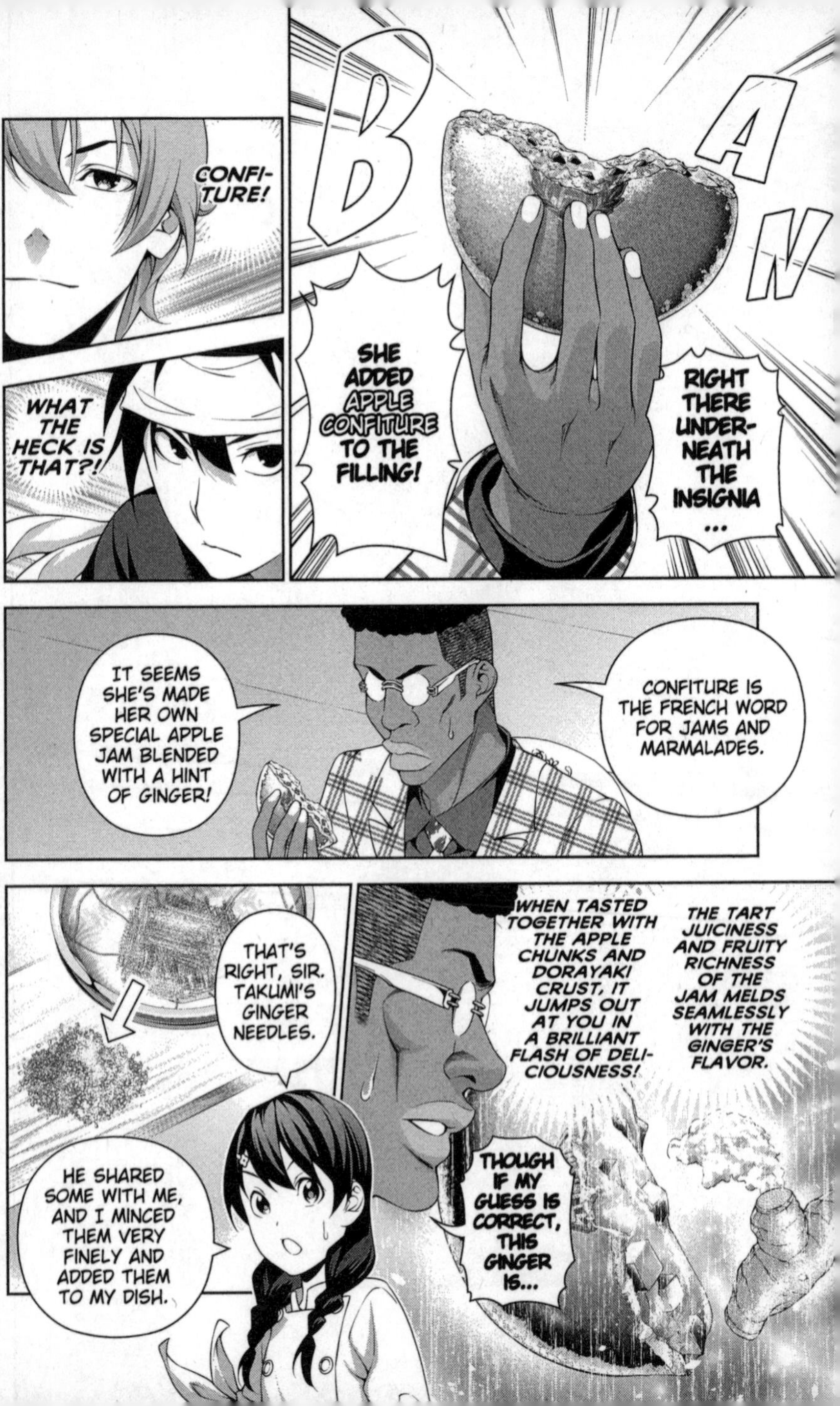
BAN
RIGHT THERE UNDER-NEATH THE INSIGNIA...
SHE ADDED APPLE CONFITURE TO THE FILLING!
CONFI-TURE!
WHAT THE HECK IS THAT?!
CONFITURE IS THE FRENCH WORD FOR JAMS AND MARMALADES.
IT SEEMS SHE'S MADE HER OWN SPECIAL APPLE JAM BLENDED WITH A HINT OF GINGER!
THE TART JUICINESS AND FRUITY RICHNESS OF THE JAM MELDS SEAMLESSLY WITH THE GINGER'S FLAVOR.
WHEN TASTED TOGETHER WITH THE APPLE CHUNKS AND DORAYAKI CRUST, IT JUMPS OUT AT YOU IN A BRILLIANT FLASH OF DELI-CIOUSNESS!
THOUGH IF MY GUESS IS CORRECT, THIS GINGER IS...
THAT'S RIGHT, SIR. TAKUMI'S GINGER NEEDLES.
HE SHARED SOME WITH ME, AND I MINCED THEM VERY FINELY AND ADDED THEM TO MY DISH.

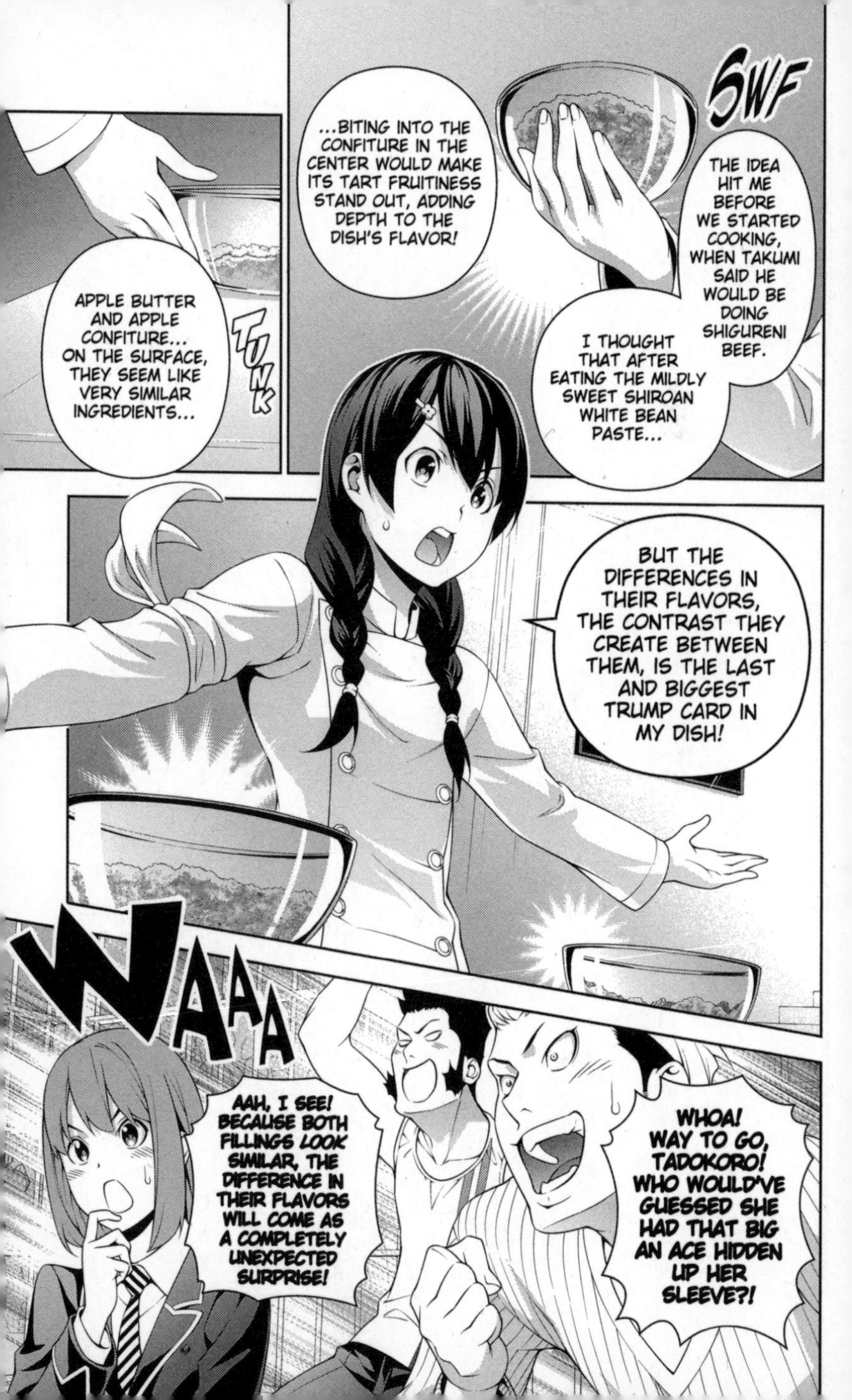
SWF
THE IDEA HIT ME BEFORE WE STARTED COOKING, WHEN TAKUMI SAID HE WOULD BE DOING SHIGURENI BEEF.
I THOUGHT THAT AFTER EATING THE MILDLY SWEET SHIROAN WHITE BEAN PASTE...
...BITING INTO THE CONFITURE IN THE CENTER WOULD MAKE ITS TART FRUITINESS STAND OUT, ADDING DEPTH TO THE DISH'S FLAVOR!
APPLE BUTTER AND APPLE CONFITURE... ON THE SURFACE, THEY SEEM LIKE VERY SIMILAR INGREDIENTS...
TUNK
BUT THE DIFFERENCES IN THEIR FLAVORS, THE CONTRAST THEY CREATE BETWEEN THEM, IS THE LAST AND BIGGEST TRUMP CARD IN MY DISH!
WAAA
WHOA! WAY TO GO, TADOKORO! WHO WOULD'VE GUESSED SHE HAD THAT BIG AN ACE HIDDEN UP HER SLEEVE?!
AAH, I SEE! BECAUSE BOTH FILLINGS *LOOK* SIMILAR, THE DIFFERENCE IN THEIR FLAVORS WILL COME AS A COMPLETELY UNEXPECTED SURPRISE!

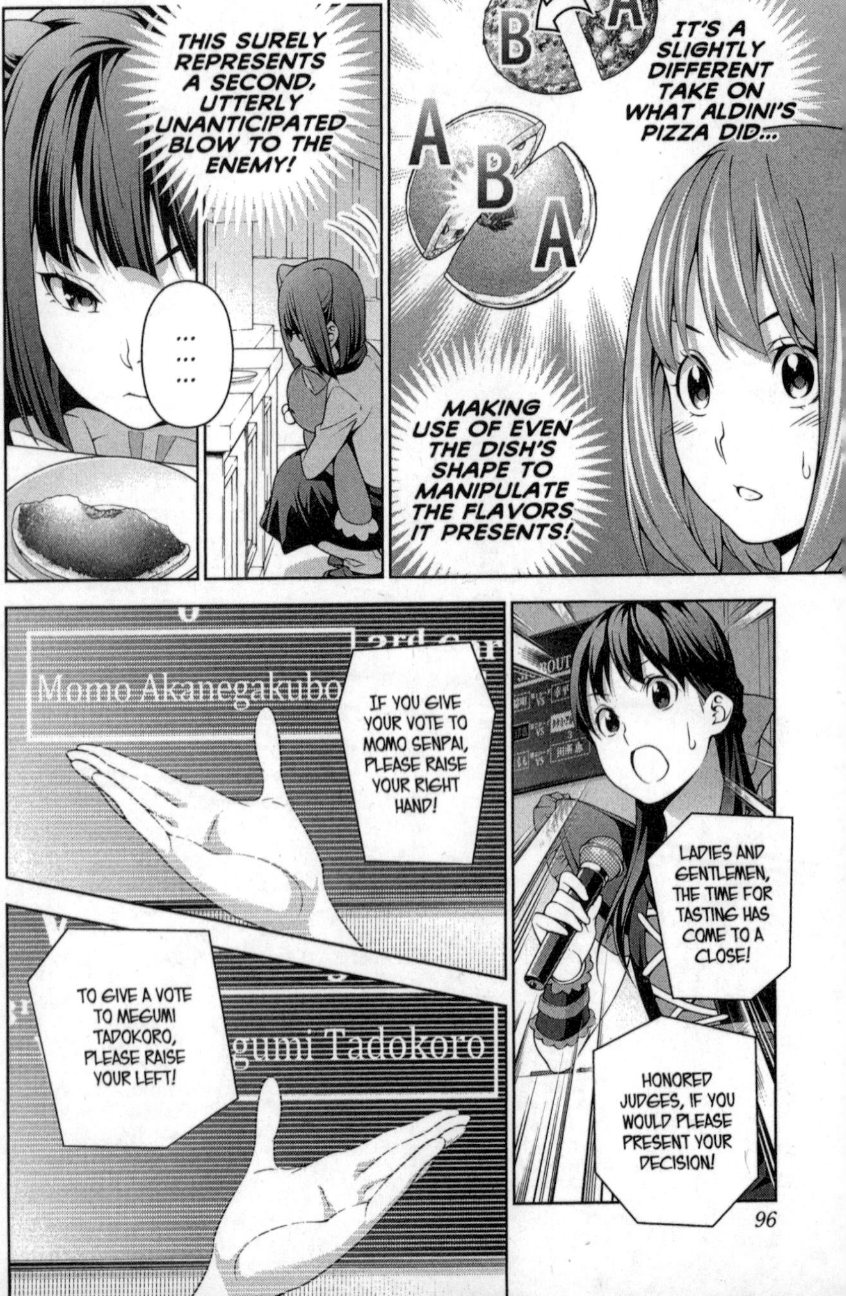
A
B
A
B
A
IT'S A SLIGHTLY DIFFERENT TAKE ON WHAT ALDINI'S PIZZA DID...
MAKING USE OF EVEN THE DISH'S SHAPE TO MANIPULATE THE FLAVORS IT PRESENTS!
THIS SURELY REPRESENTS A SECOND, UTTERLY UNANTICIPATED BLOW TO THE ENEMY!
... ...
LADIES AND GENTLEMEN, THE TIME FOR TASTING HAS COME TO A CLOSE!
HONORED JUDGES, IF YOU WOULD PLEASE PRESENT YOUR DECISION!
Momo Akanegakubo
IF YOU GIVE YOUR VOTE TO MOMO SENPAI, PLEASE RAISE YOUR RIGHT HAND!
TO GIVE A VOTE TO MEGUMI TADOKORO, PLEASE RAISE YOUR LEFT!
gumi Tadokoro

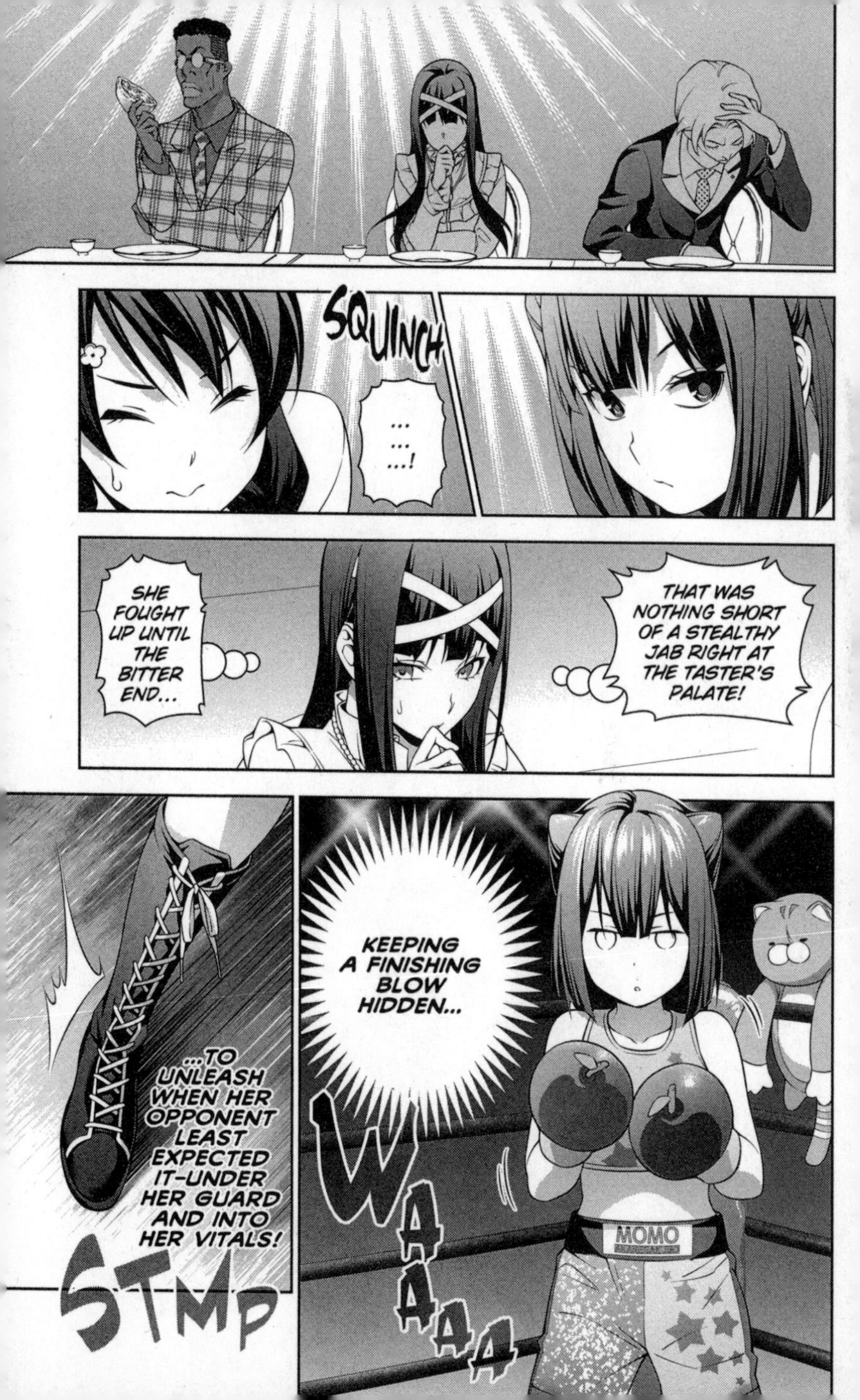
SQUINCH
... ...!
THAT WAS NOTHING SHORT OF A STEALTHY JAB RIGHT AT THE TASTER'S PALATE!
SHE FOUGHT UP UNTIL THE BITTER END...
KEEPING A FINISHING BLOW HIDDEN...
WAAAAA
MOMO
...TO UNLEASH WHEN HER OPPONENT LEAST EXPECTED IT—UNDER HER GUARD AND INTO HER VITALS!
STMP

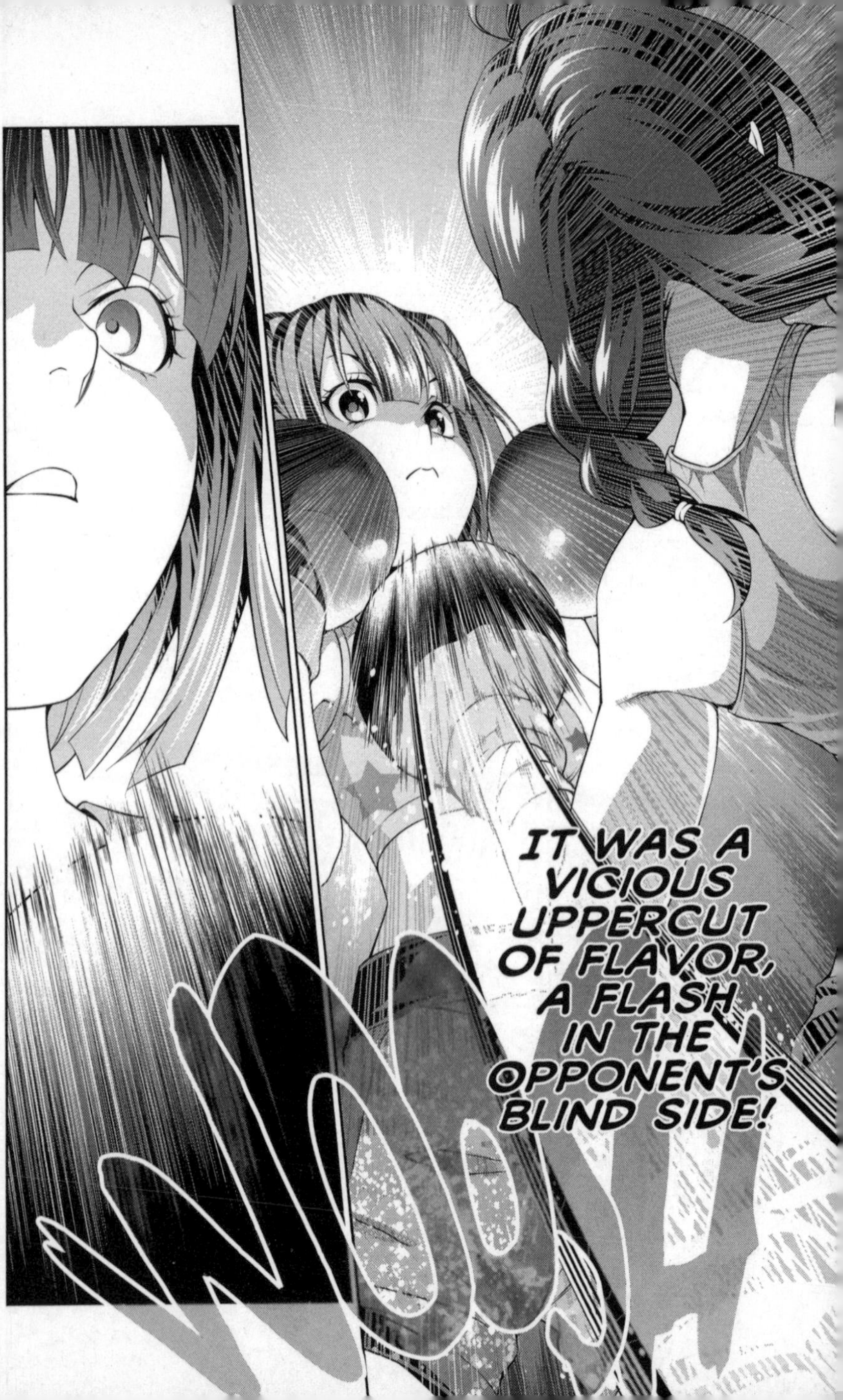
IT WAS A VICIOUS UPPERCUT OF FLAVOR, A FLASH IN THE OPPONENT'S BLIND SIDE!

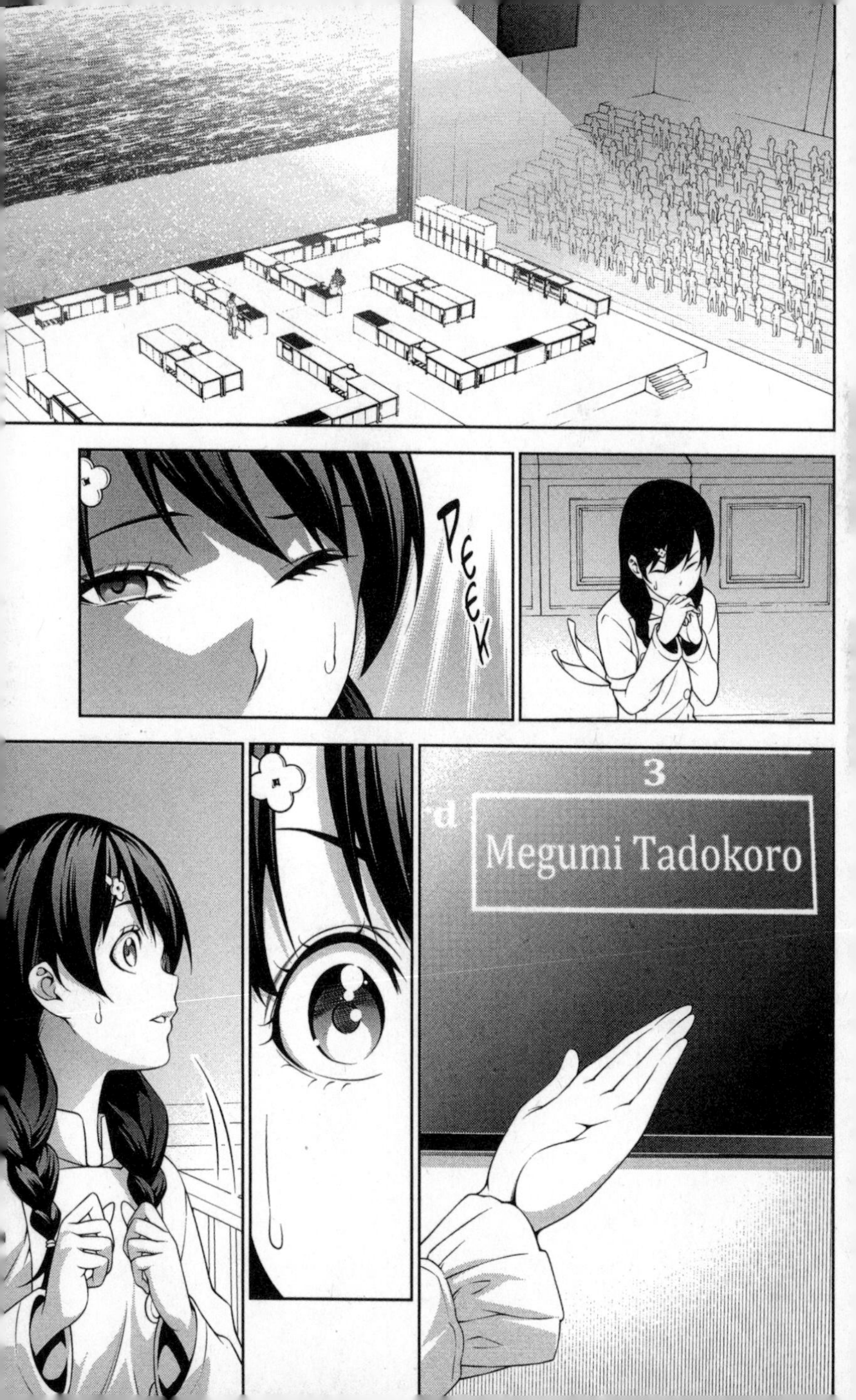
PEEK
3
Megumi Tadokoro

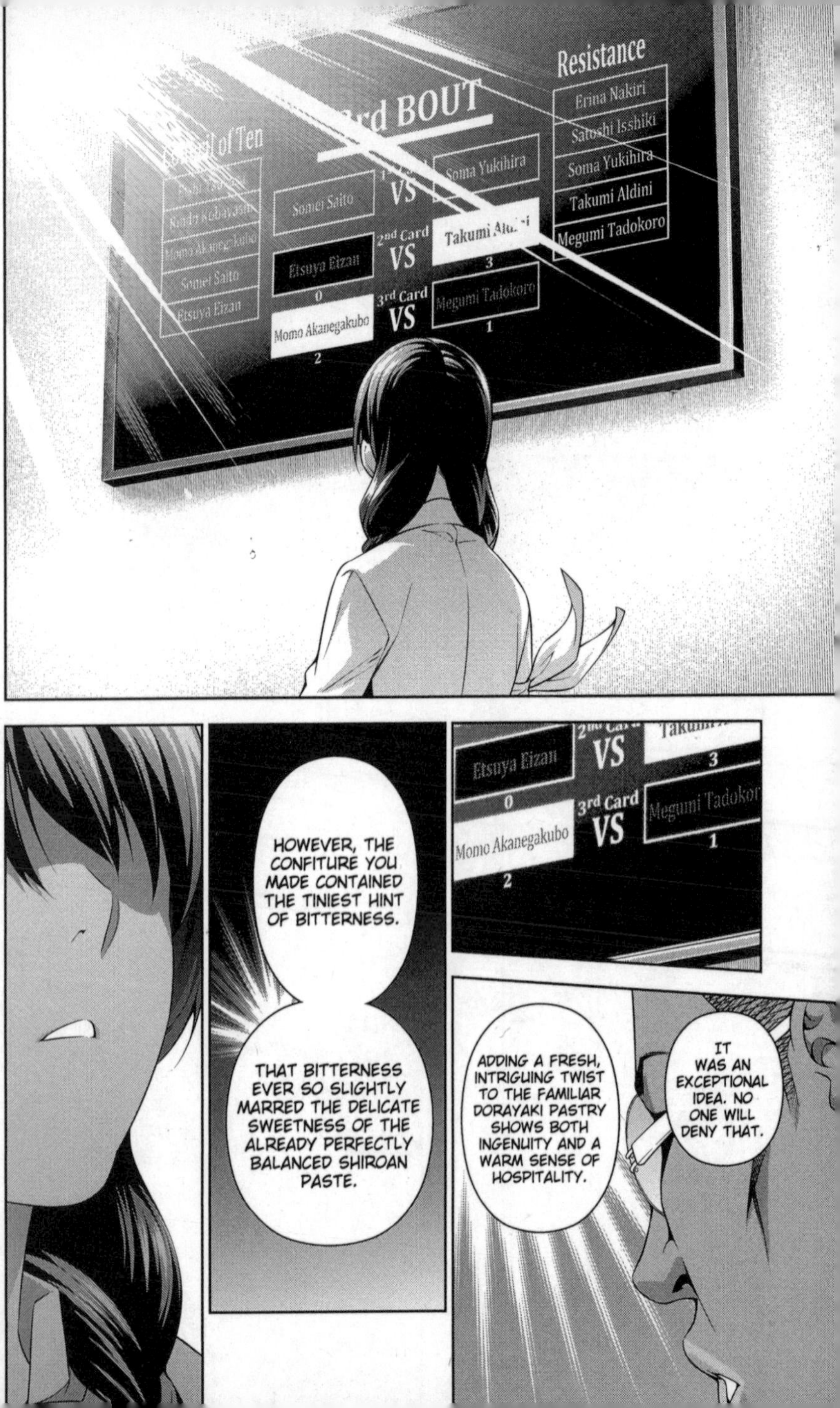

Resistance
Erina Nakiri
Satoshi Isshiki
Soma Yukihira
Takumi Aldini
Megumi Tadokoro
Soma Yukihira
VS
Somei Saito
2nd Card
VS
Etsuya Eizan
3
0
3rd Card
VS
Megumi Tadokoro
Momo Akanegakubo
1
2
Somei Saito
Etsuya Eizan
Etsuya Eizan
VS
3
0
3rd Card
VS
Momo Akanegakubo
1
2
IT WAS AN EXCEPTIONAL IDEA. NO ONE WILL DENY THAT.
ADDING A FRESH, INTRIGUING TWIST TO THE FAMILIAR DORAYAKI PASTRY SHOWS BOTH INGENUITY AND A WARM SENSE OF HOSPITALITY.
HOWEVER, THE CONFITURE YOU MADE CONTAINED THE TINIEST HINT OF BITTERNESS.
THAT BITTERNESS EVER SO SLIGHTLY MARRED THE DELICATE SWEETNESS OF THE ALREADY PERFECTLY BALANCED SHIROAN PASTE.

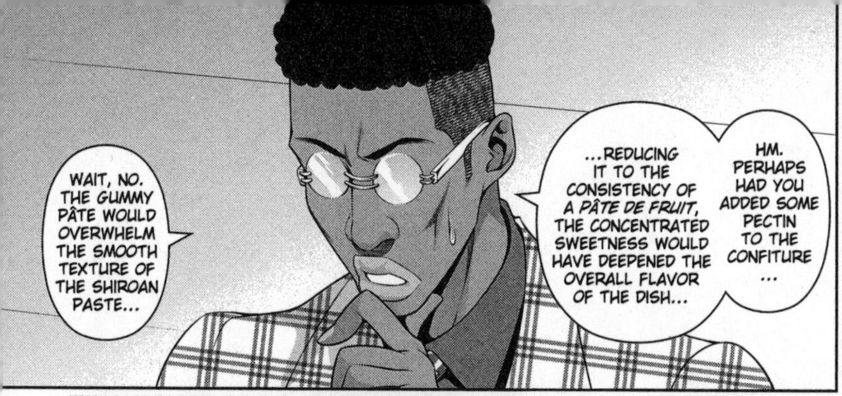
HM. PERHAPS HAD YOU ADDED SOME PECTIN TO THE CONFITURE ...
...REDUCING IT TO THE CONSISTENCY OF A *PÂTE DE FRUIT*, THE CONCENTRATED SWEETNESS WOULD HAVE DEEPENED THE OVERALL FLAVOR OF THE DISH...
WAIT, NO. THE GUMMY PÂTE WOULD OVERWHELM THE SMOOTH TEXTURE OF THE SHIROAN PASTE...

*PECTIN IS A COMPONENT FOUND IN ABUNDANCE IN APPLES AND CITRUS FRUIT. A NATURAL GELLING AGENT, IT IS USED IN A WIDE VARIETY OF FOODS.

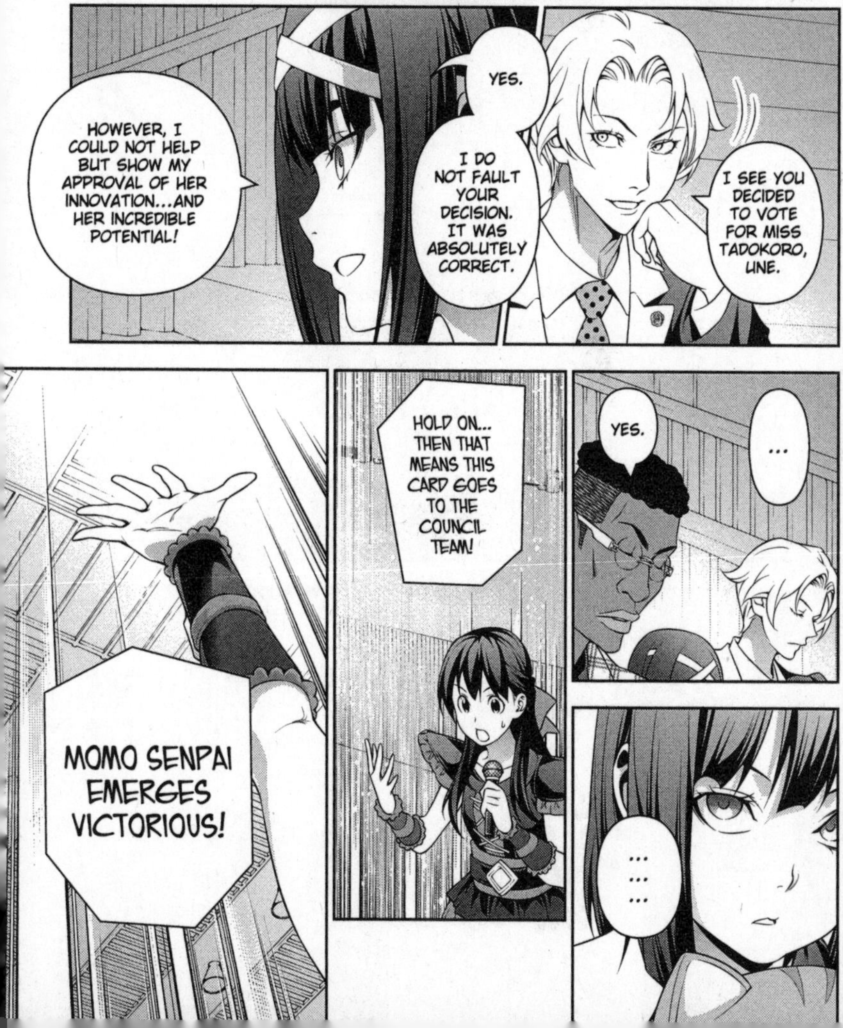
I SEE YOU DECIDED TO VOTE FOR MISS TADOKORO, UNE.
YES.
I DO NOT FAULT YOUR DECISION. IT WAS ABSOLUTELY CORRECT.
HOWEVER, I COULD NOT HELP BUT SHOW MY APPROVAL OF HER INNOVATION...AND HER INCREDIBLE POTENTIAL!
...
YES.
... ...
HOLD ON... THEN THAT MEANS THIS CARD GOES TO THE COUNCIL TEAM!
MOMO SENPAI EMERGES VICTORIOUS!

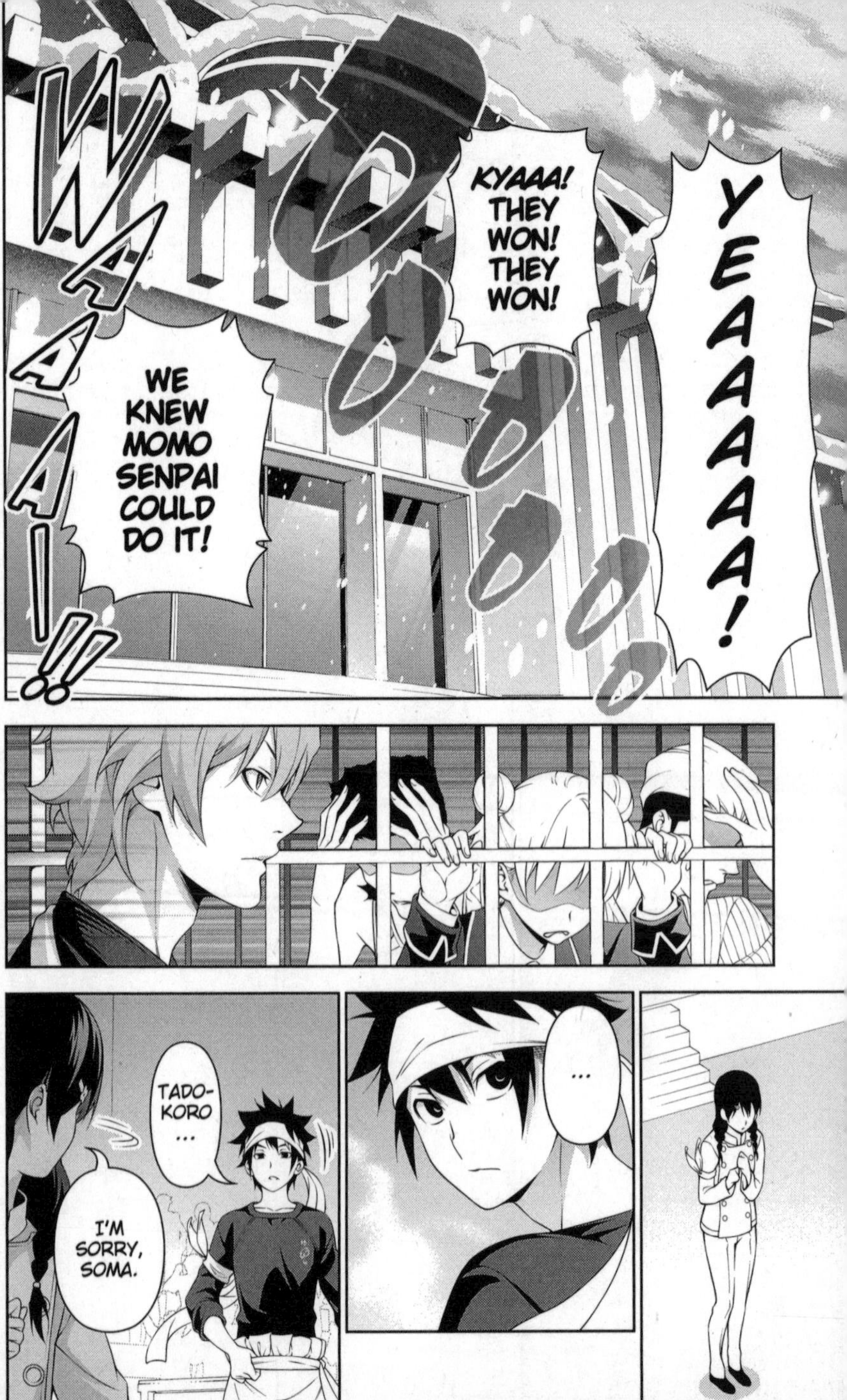
YEAAAAAA!
KYAAA! THEY WON! THEY WON!
WE KNEW MOMO SENPAI COULD DO IT!
WAAAI!!
...
TADOKORO ...
I'M SORRY, SOMA.

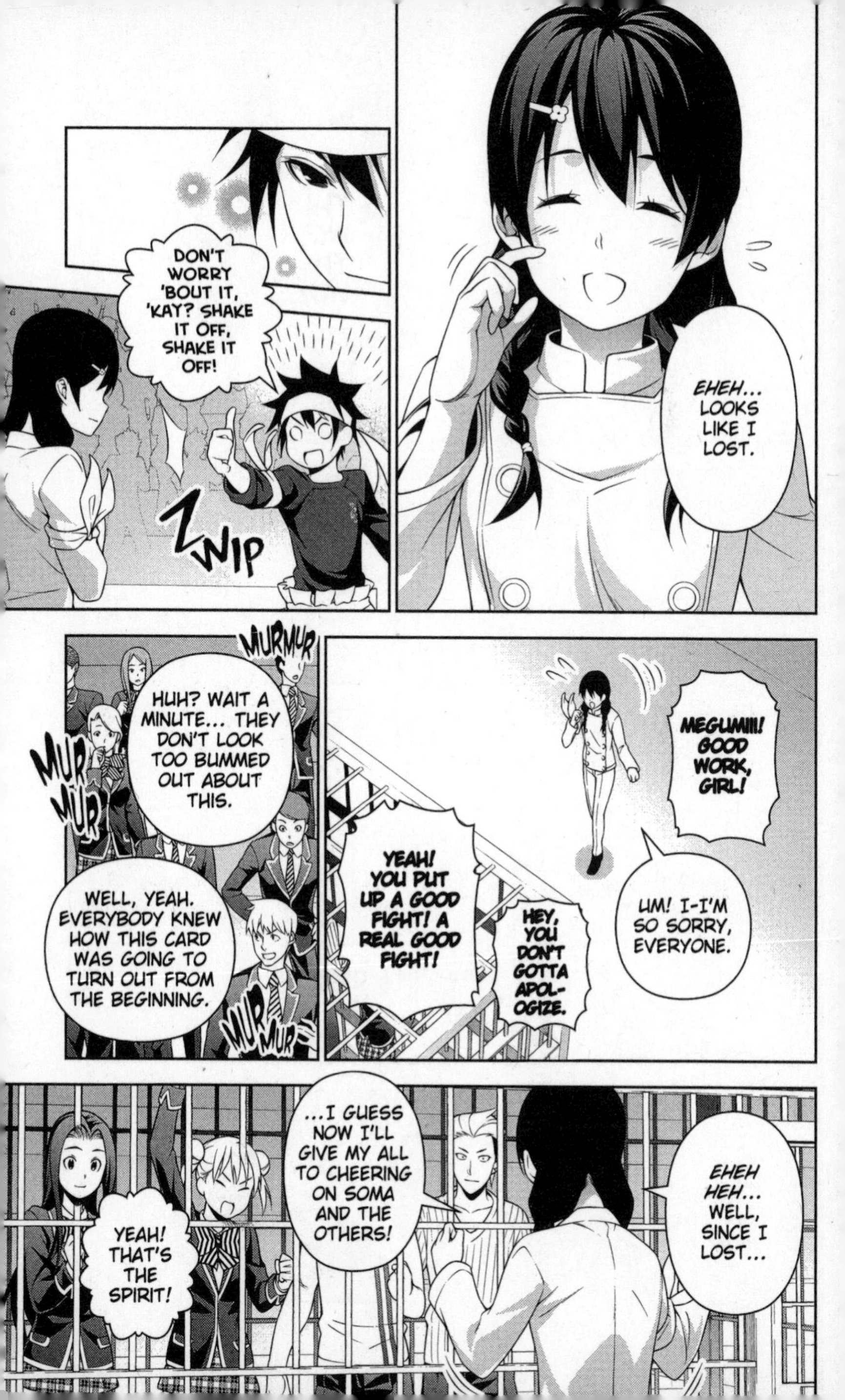
EHEH... LOOKS LIKE I LOST.
DON'T WORRY 'BOUT IT, 'KAY? SHAKE IT OFF, SHAKE IT OFF!
ZWIP
MEGUMIII! GOOD WORK, GIRL!
UM! I-I'M SO SORRY, EVERYONE.
HEY, YOU DON'T GOTTA APOL-OGIZE.
YEAH! YOU PUT UP A GOOD FIGHT! A REAL GOOD FIGHT!
MURMUR
HUH? WAIT A MINUTE... THEY DON'T LOOK TOO BUMMED OUT ABOUT THIS.
MUR MUR
WELL, YEAH. EVERYBODY KNEW HOW THIS CARD WAS GOING TO TURN OUT FROM THE BEGINNING.
MUR MUR
EHEH HEH... WELL, SINCE I LOST...
...I GUESS NOW I'LL GIVE MY ALL TO CHEERING ON SOMA AND THE OTHERS!
YEAH! THAT'S THE SPIRIT!

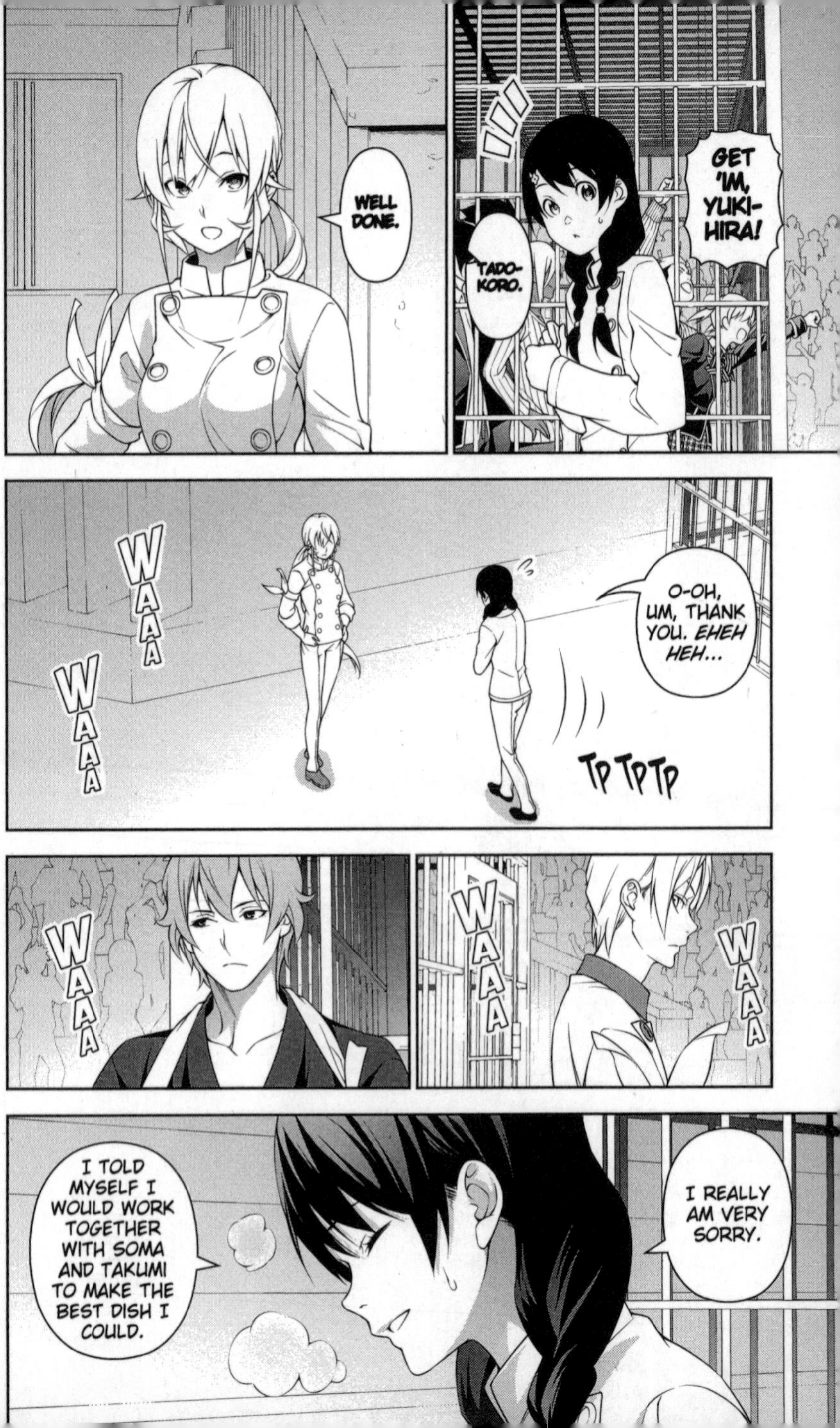
GET 'IM, YUKI-HIRA!
TADO-KORO.
WELL DONE.
O-OH, UM, THANK YOU. *EHEH HEH...*
Tp Tp Tp
WAAA
WAAA
WAAA
WAAA
WAAA
I REALLY AM VERY SORRY.
I TOLD MYSELF I WOULD WORK TOGETHER WITH SOMA AND TAKUMI TO MAKE THE BEST DISH I COULD.

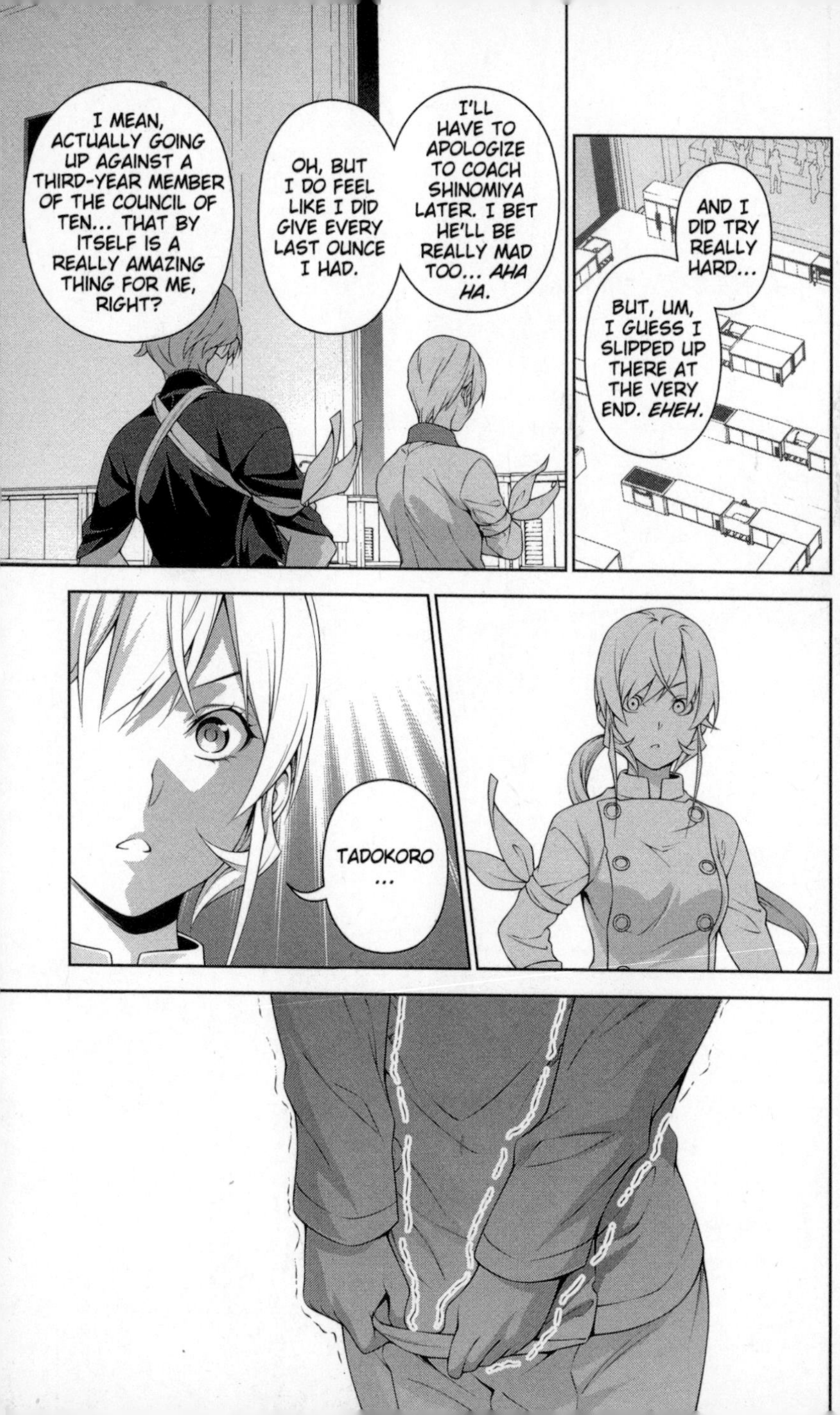
AND I DID TRY REALLY HARD...
BUT, UM, I GUESS I SLIPPED UP THERE AT THE VERY END. *EHEH.*
I'LL HAVE TO APOLOGIZE TO COACH SHINOMIYA LATER. I BET HE'LL BE REALLY MAD TOO... *AHA HA.*
OH, BUT I DO FEEL LIKE I DID GIVE EVERY LAST OUNCE I HAD.
I MEAN, ACTUALLY GOING UP AGAINST A THIRD-YEAR MEMBER OF THE COUNCIL OF TEN... THAT BY ITSELF IS A REALLY AMAZING THING FOR ME, RIGHT?
TADOKORO ...

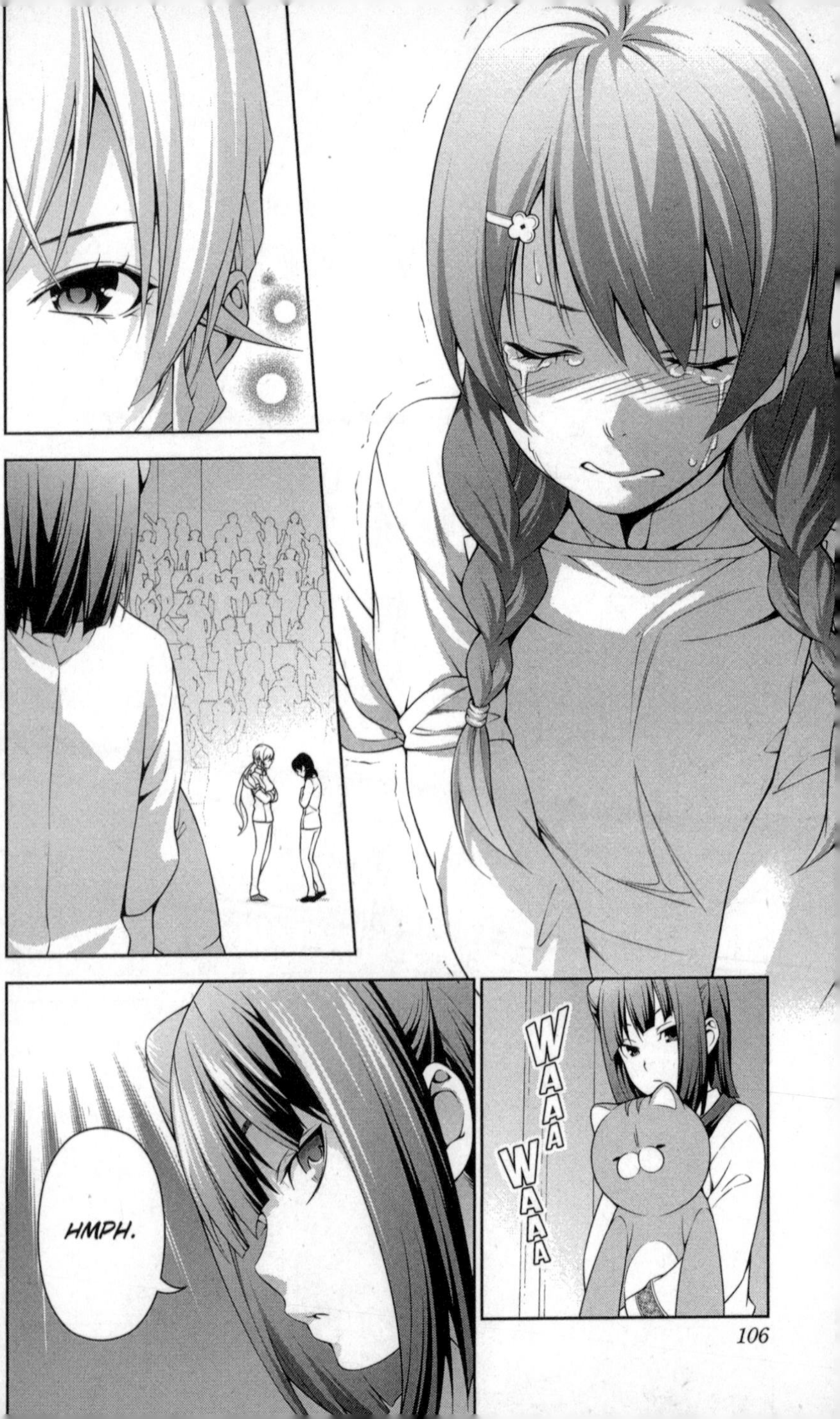
WAAA
WAAA
HMPH.

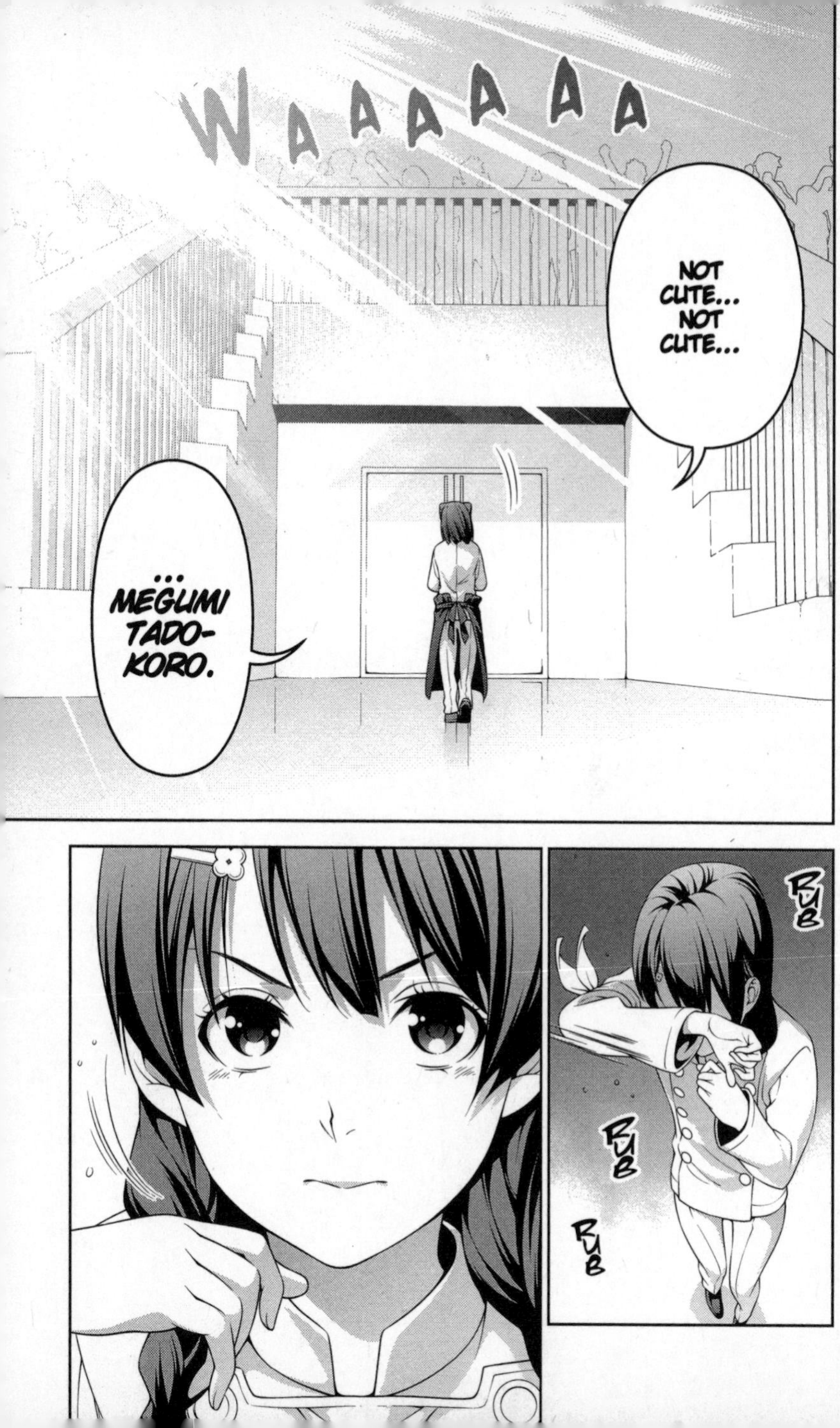
WAAAAAA
NOT CUTE... NOT CUTE...
...MEGUMI TADOKORO.
RUB
RUB
RUB

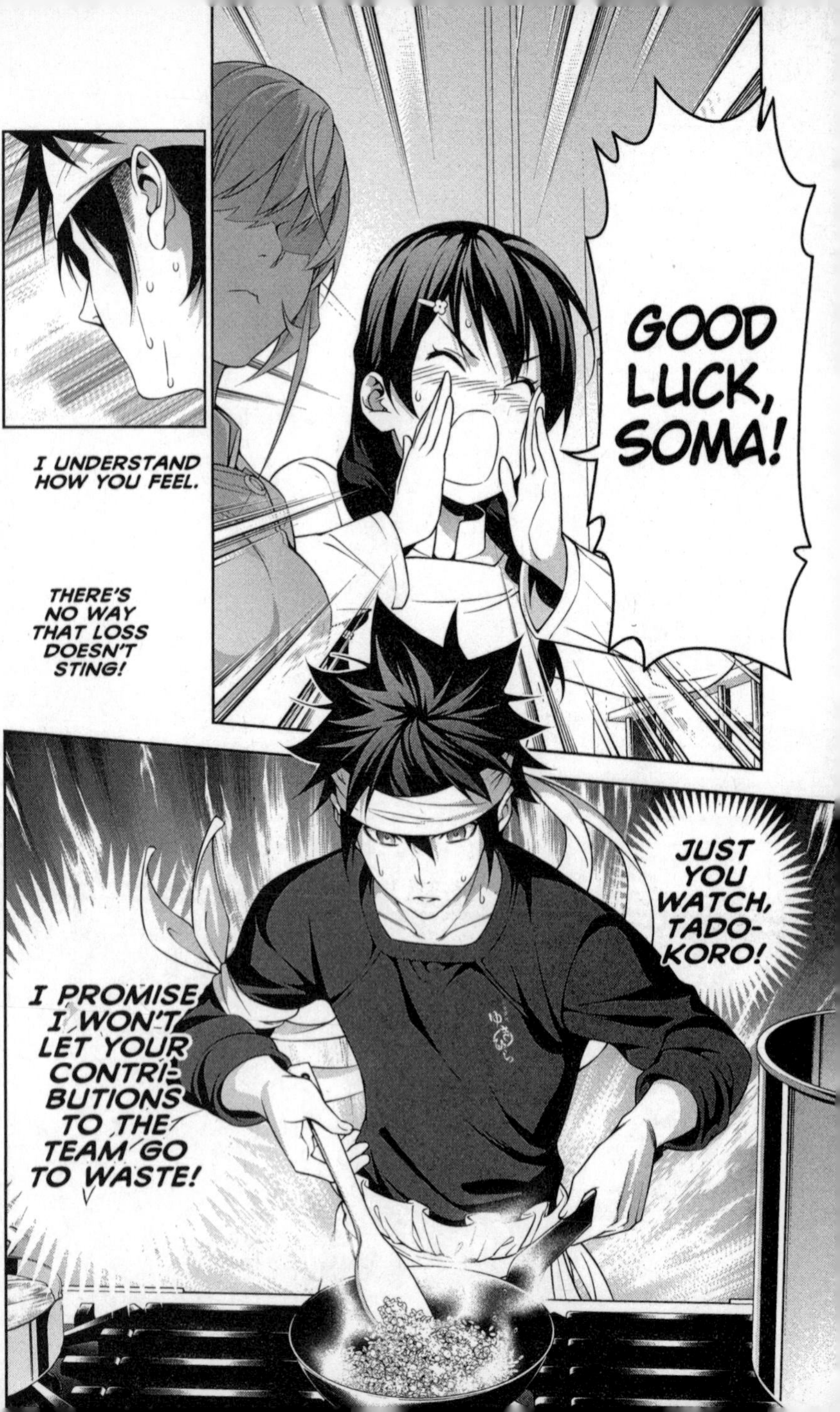
GOOD LUCK, SOMA!
I UNDERSTAND HOW YOU FEEL.
THERE'S NO WAY THAT LOSS DOESN'T STING!
JUST YOU WATCH, TADO-KORO!
I PROMISE I WON'T LET YOUR CONTRI-BUTIONS TO THE TEAM GO TO WASTE!

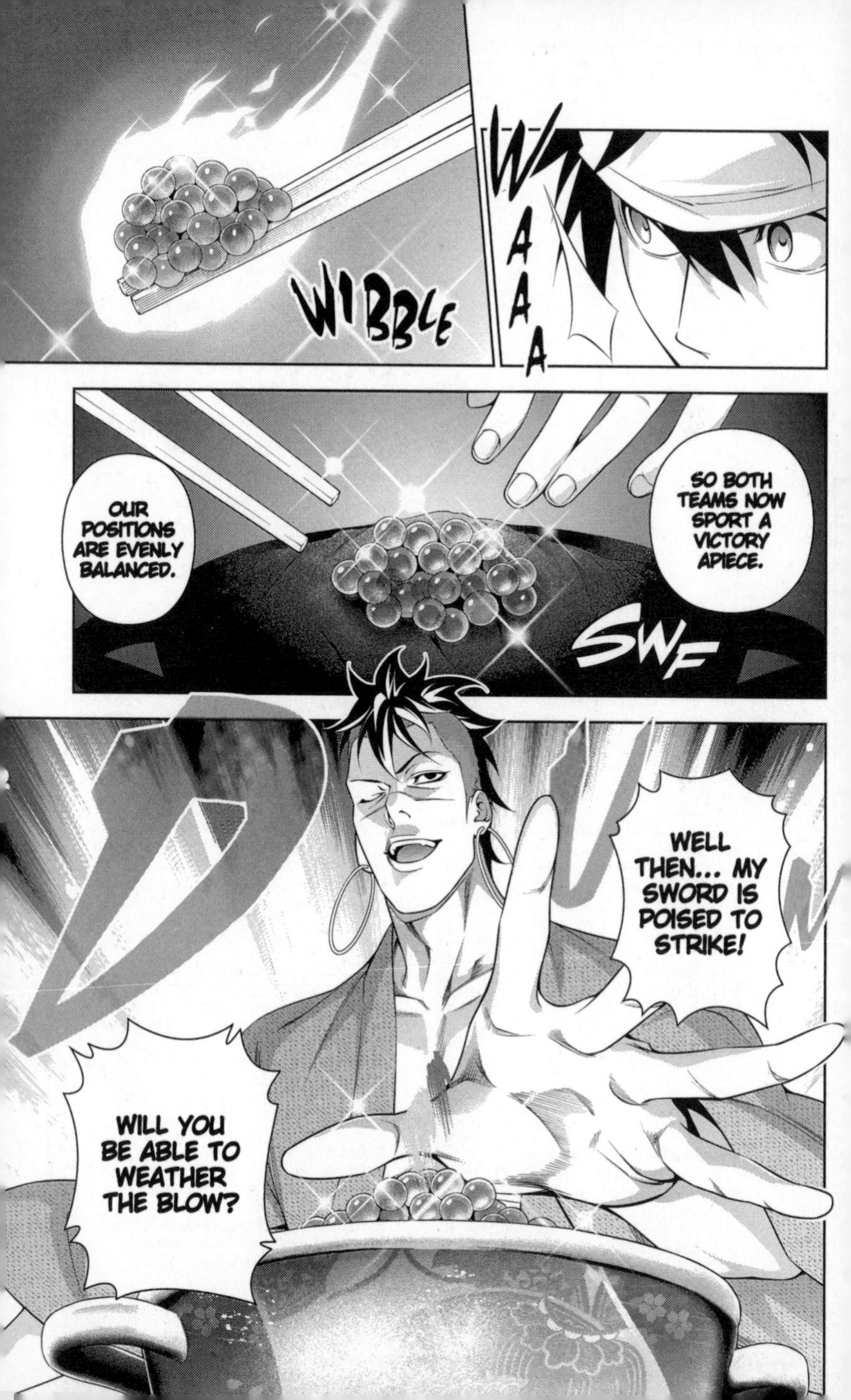
WAAAA
WIBBLE
SO BOTH TEAMS NOW SPORT A VICTORY APIECE.
OUR POSITIONS ARE EVENLY BALANCED.
SWF
WELL THEN... MY SWORD IS POISED TO STRIKE!
WILL YOU BE ABLE TO WEATHER THE BLOW?

ARTIST: YUTO TSUKUDA   RECIPE BY: YUKI MORISAKI

VOLUME 28
SPECIAL SUPPLEMENT!

PRACTICAL RECIPE #2

MEGUMI'S APPLE SHIROAN DORAYAKI

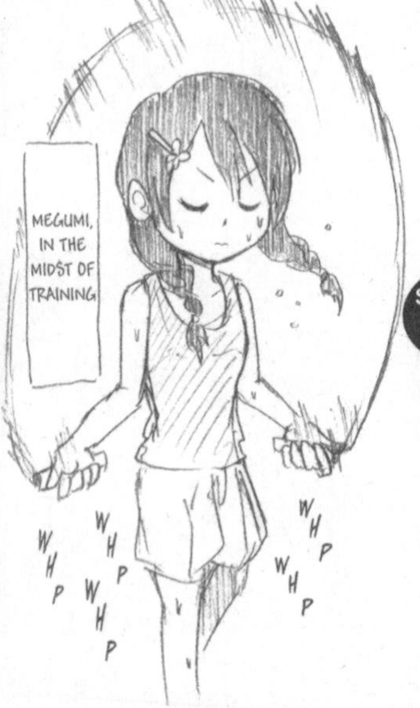

MEGUMI, IN THE MIDST OF TRAINING
WHP
WHP
WHP
WHP
WHP

SIMPLIFIED HOME VERSION

INGREDIENTS
(MAKES 6)

★PASTRY SHELL

[A]
- 150 GRAMS FLOUR
- 1 TABLESPOON BAKING POWDER
- 80 GRAMS WASANBON SUGAR (OR SUPERFINE SUGAR)

- 3 EGGS
- 1 TEASPOON SOY SAUCE
- 1 TABLESPOON HONEY
- 100 GRAMS SILKEN TOFU

★APPLE FILLING

- 150 GRAMS APPLES

[B]
- 2 TABLESPOONS SUGAR
- 1 TEASPOON LEMON JUICE

- 300 GRAMS SHIROAN SWEET BEAN PASTE
- BUTTER, APPLE JELLY

1. CRACK THE EGGS INTO A BOWL AND WHISK UNTIL FLUFFY. SPLIT THE SUGAR INTO THREE EQUAL PORTIONS. SLOWLY ADD EACH PORTION TO THE EGGS ONE BY ONE WHILE WHISKING. KEEP WHISKING UNTIL SOFT PEAKS FORM.

2. POUR THE SILKEN TOFU INTO A DIFFERENT BOWL AND BLEND WITH A HAND MIXER UNTIL SMOOTH. ADD THE SOY SAUCE AND HONEY AND MIX UNTIL FULLY COMBINED. THEN POUR THE MIXTURE INTO THE MERINGUE FROM (1) AND CAREFULLY FOLD TOGETHER.

3. SIFT (A) INTO (2) AND FOLD TOGETHER UNTIL COMBINED.

4. HEAT A TEFLON FRYING PAN OVER MEDIUM HEAT UNTIL WATER DROPLETS SIZZLE ON CONTACT. LADLE A PORTION OF THE BATTER ONTO THE FRYING PAN (APPROX. 4" IN DIAMETER) AND COOK UNTIL GOLDEN BROWN ON BOTH SIDES. REPEAT FOR THE REMAINING BATTER. (SHOULD MAKE TWELVE PANCAKES.)

5. ★MAKE THE APPLE FILLING★
QUARTER THE APPLES AND PLACE IN A POT WITH (B). BRING TO A SIMMER AND REDUCE UNTIL ALL THE LIQUID IS GONE. BLEND WITH THE SHIROAN SWEET BEAN PASTE AND THEN SPLIT INTO SIX EQUAL PORTIONS.

6. SPREAD BUTTER ON ONE SIDE OF EACH OF THE PANCAKES. PLACE A PORTION OF THE APPLE FILLING ON ONE AND THEN ADD A DOLLOP OF APPLE JELLY BEFORE SANDWICHING WITH ANOTHER PANCAKE. REPEAT FOR THE REMAINING PANCAKES AND FILLING.

241 WARRIOR'S HONOR

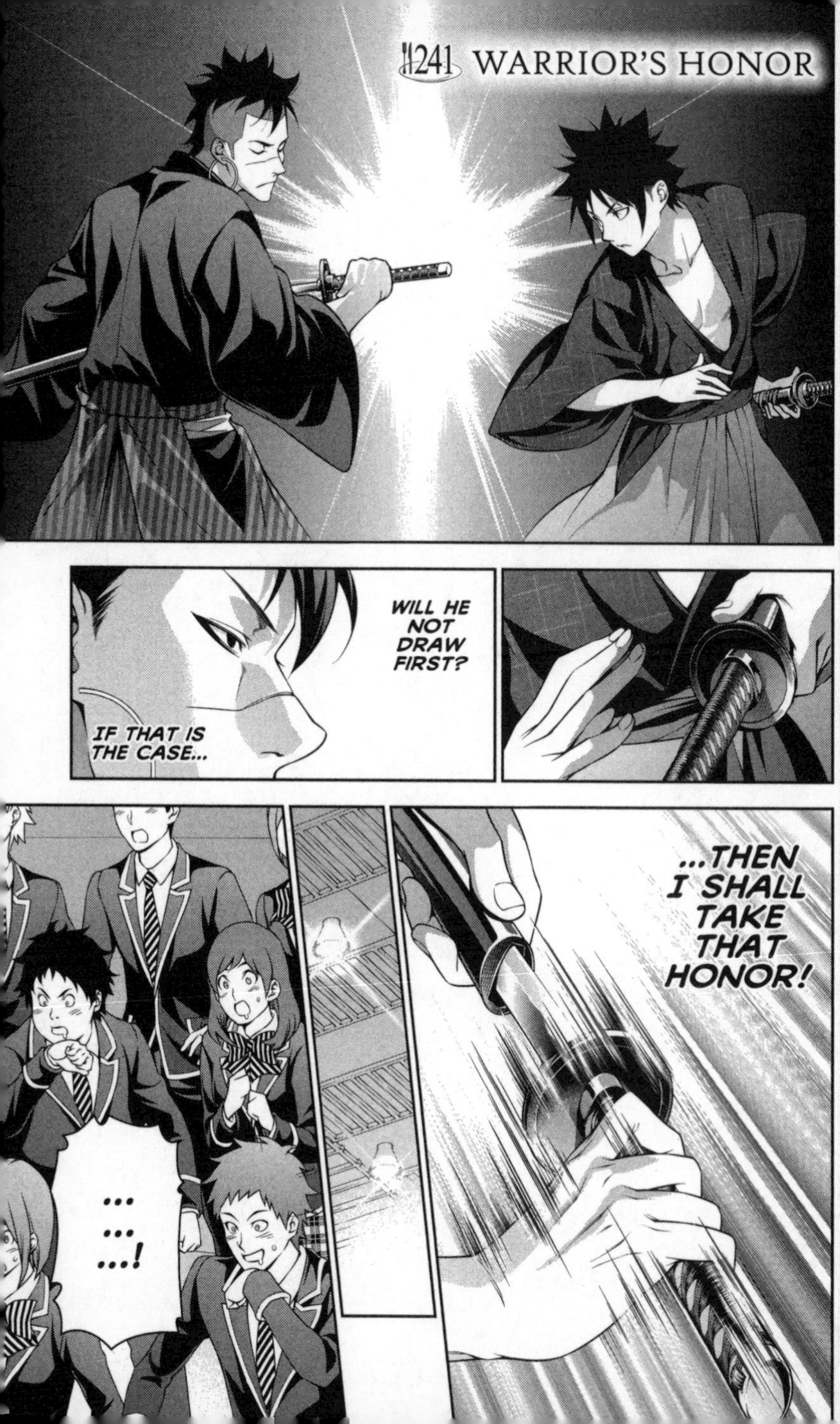
WILL HE NOT DRAW FIRST?
IF THAT IS THE CASE...
...THEN I SHALL TAKE THAT HONOR!
...
...
...!

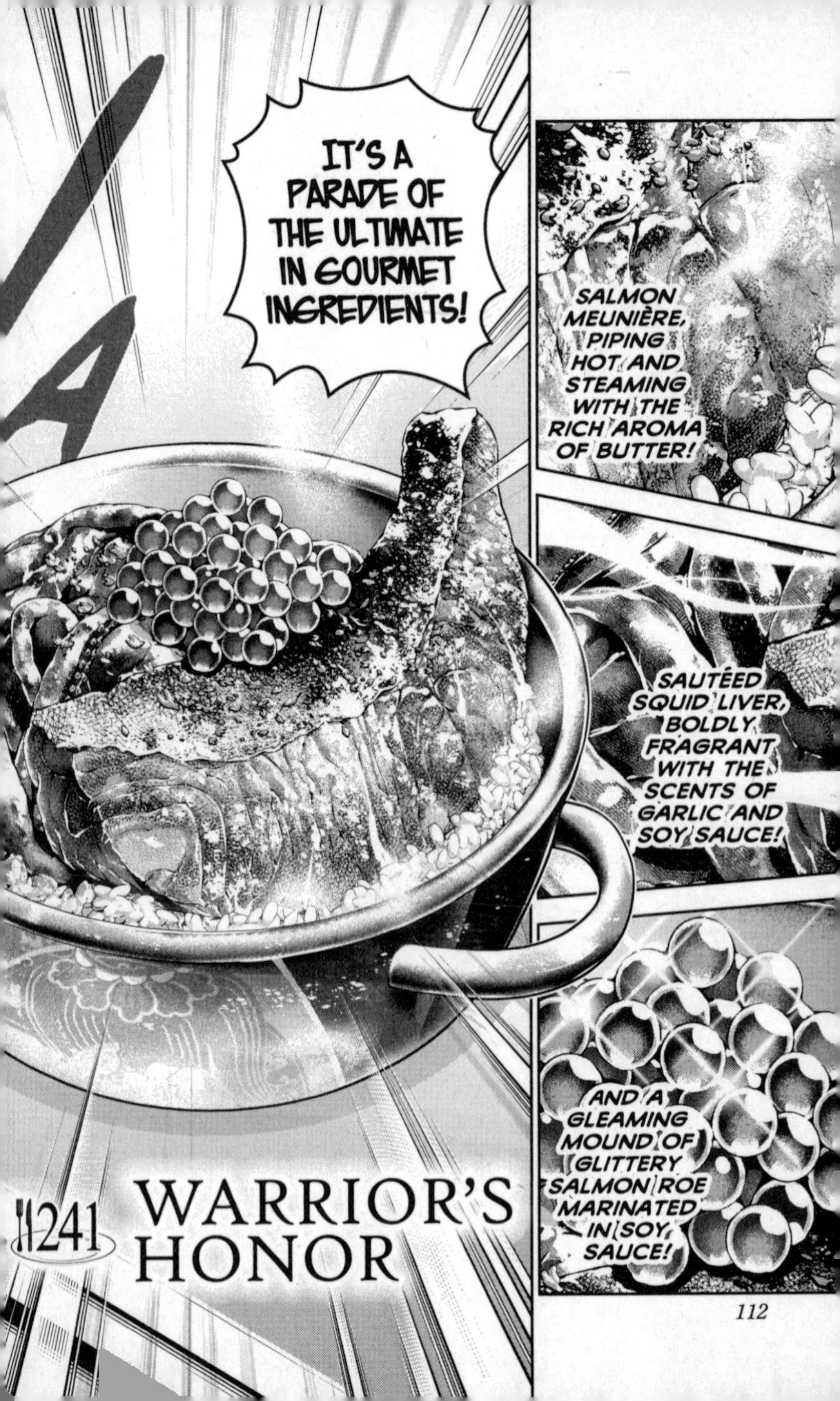
SALMON MEUNIÈRE, PIPING HOT AND STEAMING WITH THE RICH AROMA OF BUTTER!
SAUTÉED SQUID LIVER, BOLDLY FRAGRANT WITH THE SCENTS OF GARLIC AND SOY SAUCE!
AND A GLEAMING MOUND OF GLITTERY SALMON ROE MARINATED IN SOY SAUCE!
IT'S A PARADE OF THE ULTIMATE IN GOURMET INGREDIENTS!
241 WARRIOR'S HONOR

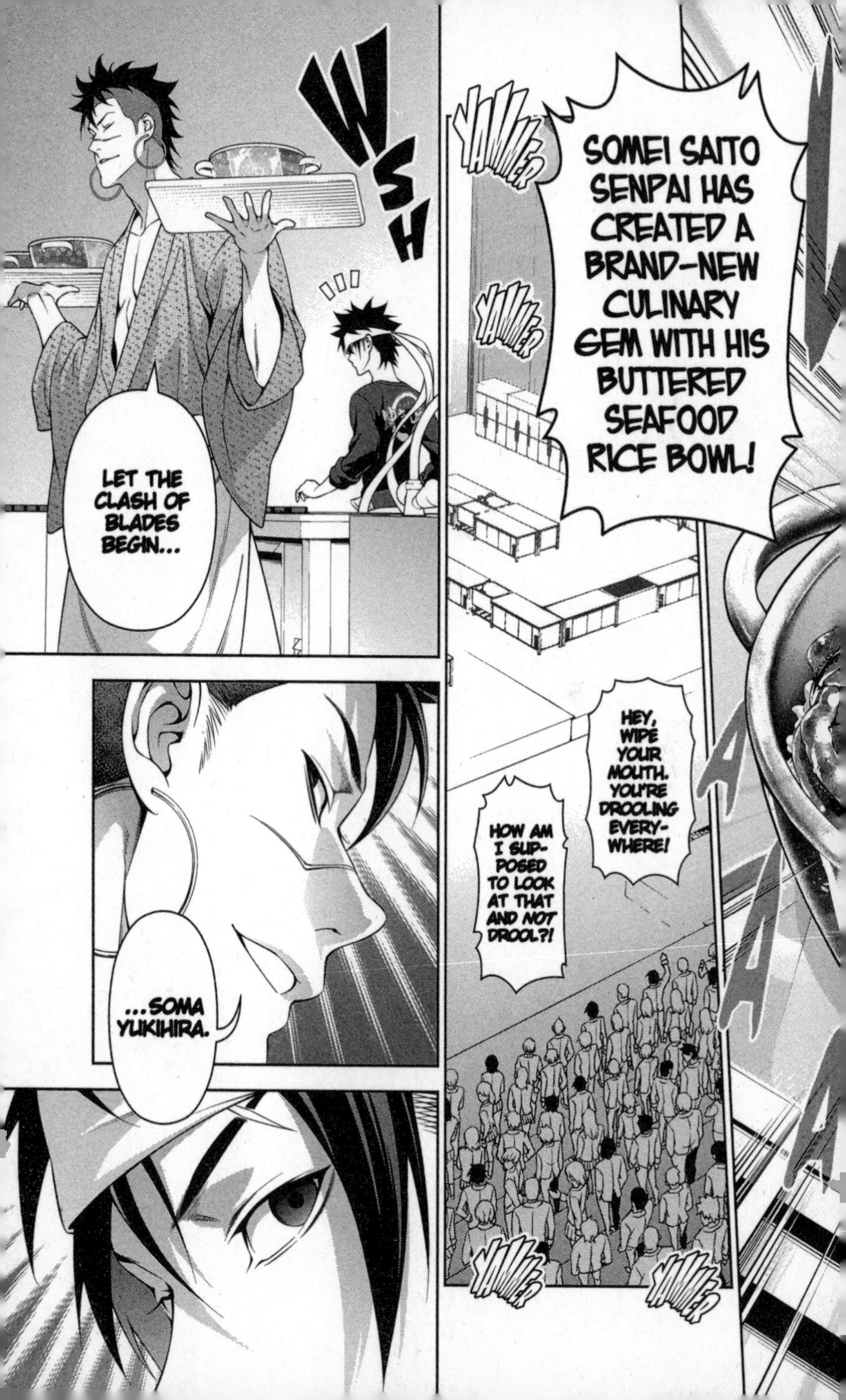
SOMEI SAITO SENPAI HAS CREATED A BRAND-NEW CULINARY GEM WITH HIS BUTTERED SEAFOOD RICE BOWL!
YAMMER
YAMMER
HEY, WIPE YOUR MOUTH. YOU'RE DROOLING EVERY-WHERE!
HOW AM I SUP-POSED TO LOOK AT THAT AND NOT DROOL?!
YAMMER
YAMMER
WSH
LET THE CLASH OF BLADES BEGIN...
...SOMA YUKIHIRA.

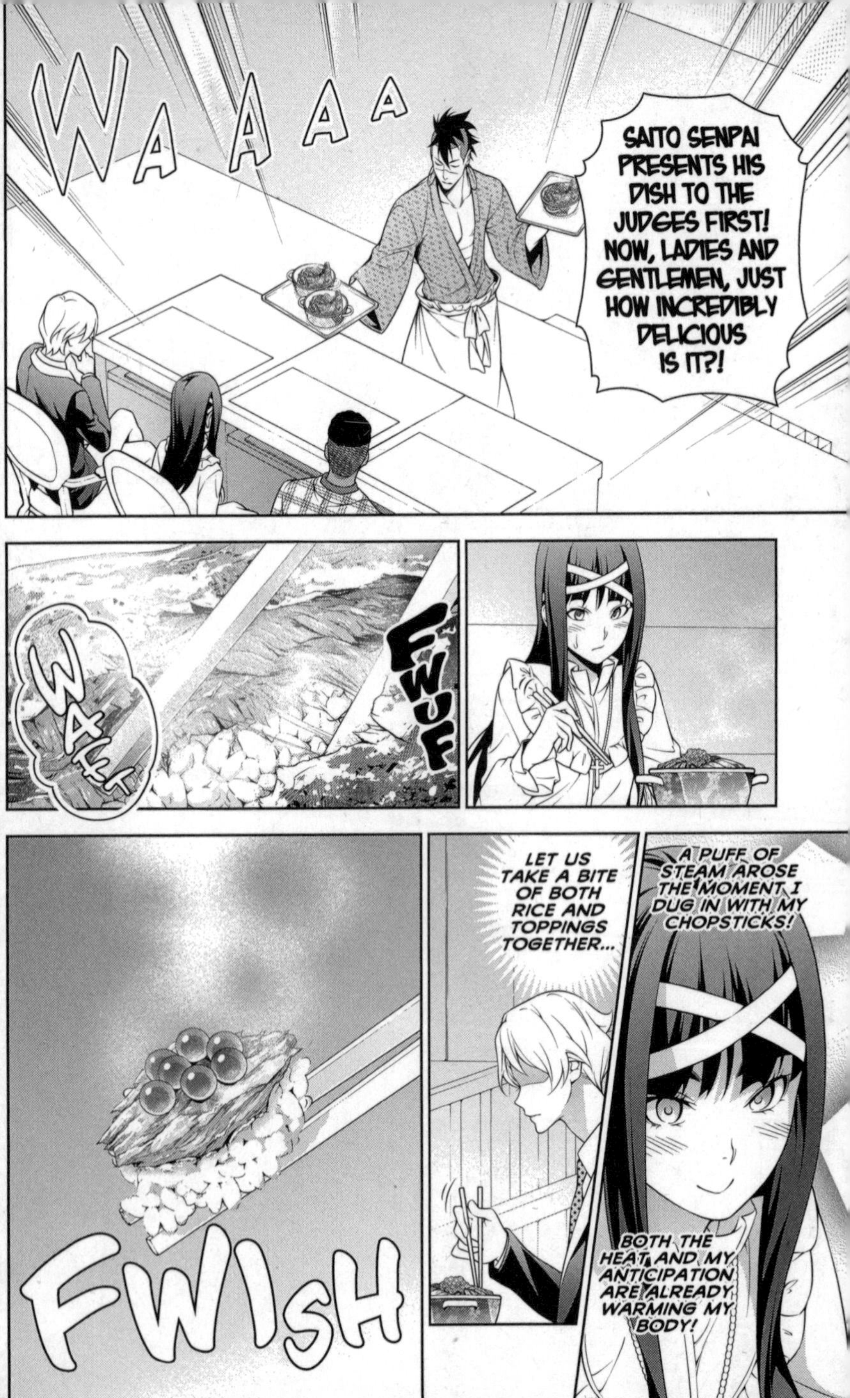
WAAAA
SAITO SENPAI PRESENTS HIS DISH TO THE JUDGES FIRST! NOW, LADIES AND GENTLEMEN, JUST HOW INCREDIBLY DELICIOUS IS IT?!
FWUF
WAFT
LET US TAKE A BITE OF BOTH RICE AND TOPPINGS TOGETHER...
A PUFF OF STEAM AROSE THE MOMENT I DUG IN WITH MY CHOPSTICKS!
BOTH THE HEAT AND MY ANTICIPATION ARE ALREADY WARMING MY BODY!
FWISH

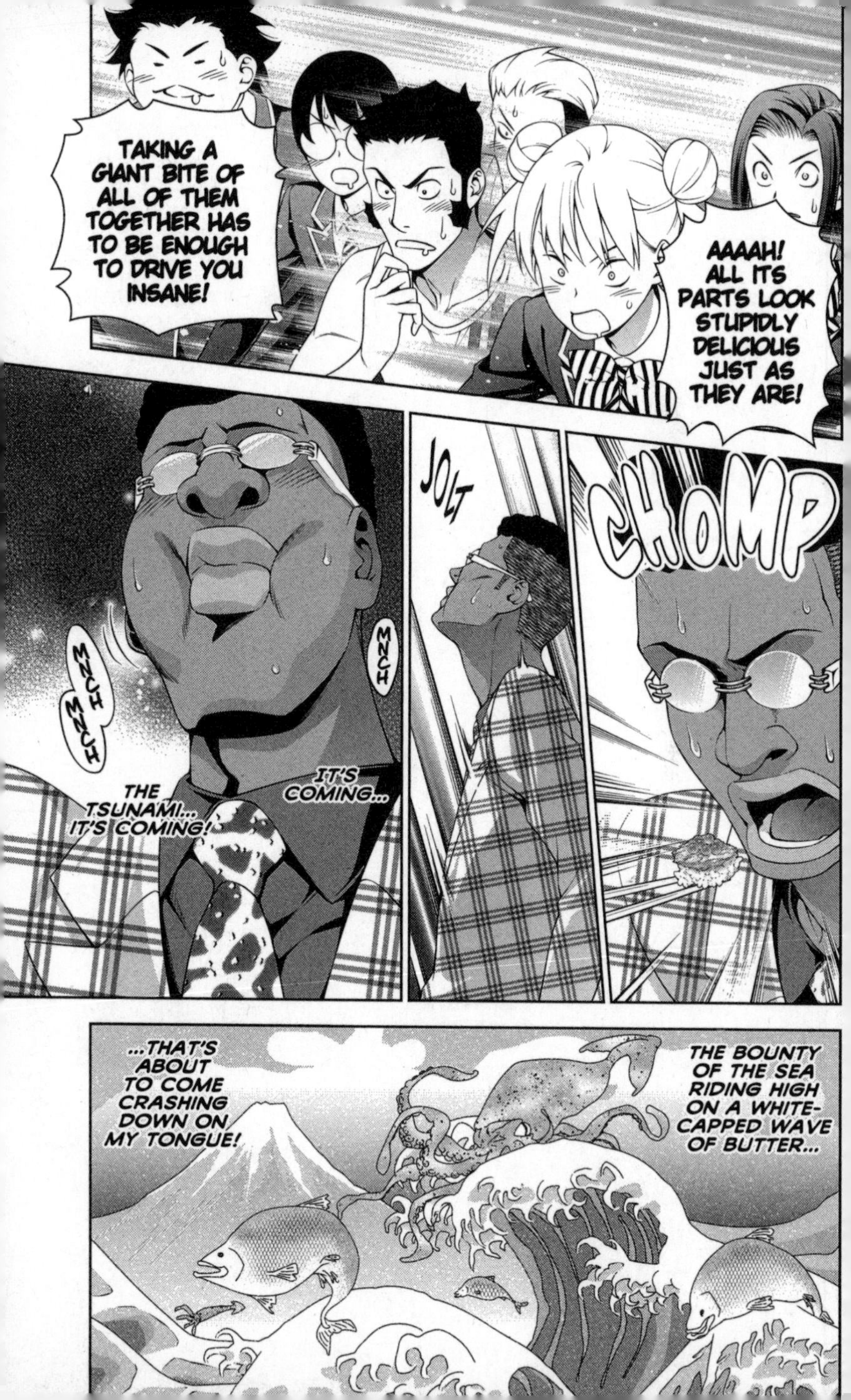
AAAAH! ALL ITS PARTS LOOK STUPIDLY DELICIOUS JUST AS THEY ARE!
TAKING A GIANT BITE OF ALL OF THEM TOGETHER HAS TO BE ENOUGH TO DRIVE YOU INSANE!
CHOMP
JOLT
MNCH
MNCH MNCH
IT'S COMING...
THE TSUNAMI... IT'S COMING!
THE BOUNTY OF THE SEA RIDING HIGH ON A WHITE-CAPPED WAVE OF BUTTER...
...THAT'S ABOUT TO COME CRASHING DOWN ON MY TONGUE!

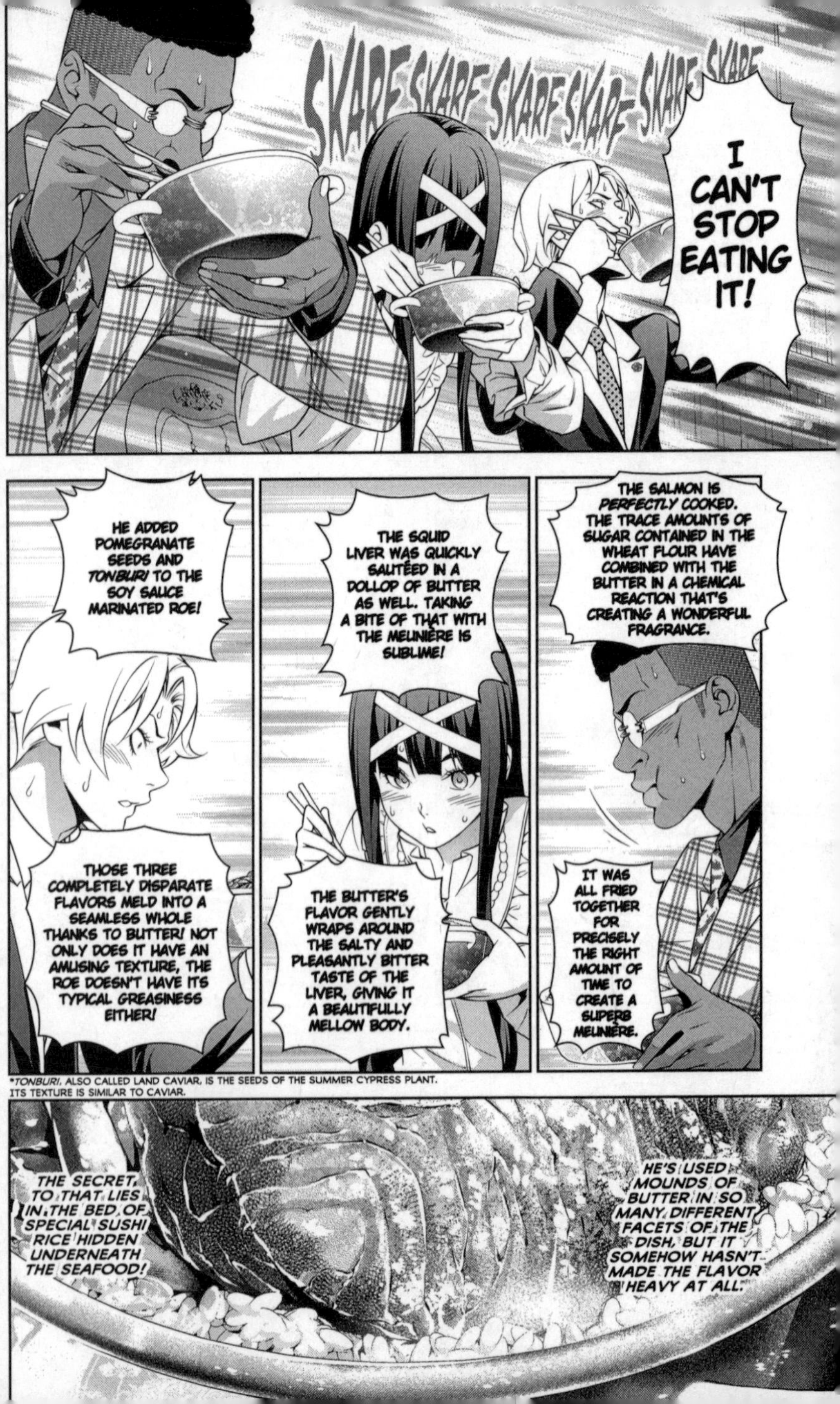
I CAN'T STOP EATING IT!
SKARF SKARF SKARF SKARF SKARF SKARF
THE SALMON IS *PERFECTLY* COOKED. THE TRACE AMOUNTS OF SUGAR CONTAINED IN THE WHEAT FLOUR HAVE COMBINED WITH THE BUTTER IN A CHEMICAL REACTION THAT'S CREATING A WONDERFUL FRAGRANCE.
IT WAS ALL FRIED TOGETHER FOR PRECISELY THE RIGHT AMOUNT OF TIME TO CREATE A SUPERB MEUNIÈRE.
THE SQUID LIVER WAS QUICKLY SAUTÉED IN A DOLLOP OF BUTTER AS WELL. TAKING A BITE OF THAT WITH THE MEUNIÈRE IS SUBLIME!
THE BUTTER'S FLAVOR GENTLY WRAPS AROUND THE SALTY AND PLEASANTLY BITTER TASTE OF THE LIVER, GIVING IT A BEAUTIFULLY MELLOW BODY.
HE ADDED POMEGRANATE SEEDS AND *TONBURI* TO THE SOY SAUCE MARINATED ROE!
THOSE THREE COMPLETELY DISPARATE FLAVORS MELD INTO A SEAMLESS WHOLE THANKS TO BUTTER! NOT ONLY DOES IT HAVE AN AMUSING TEXTURE, THE ROE DOESN'T HAVE ITS TYPICAL GREASINESS EITHER!
HE'S USED MOUNDS OF BUTTER IN SO MANY DIFFERENT FACETS OF THE DISH, BUT IT SOMEHOW HASN'T MADE THE FLAVOR HEAVY AT ALL.
THE SECRET TO THAT LIES IN THE BED OF SPECIAL SUSHI RICE HIDDEN UNDERNEATH THE SEAFOOD!

*TONBURI, ALSO CALLED LAND CAVIAR, IS THE SEEDS OF THE SUMMER CYPRESS PLANT. ITS TEXTURE IS SIMILAR TO CAVIAR.

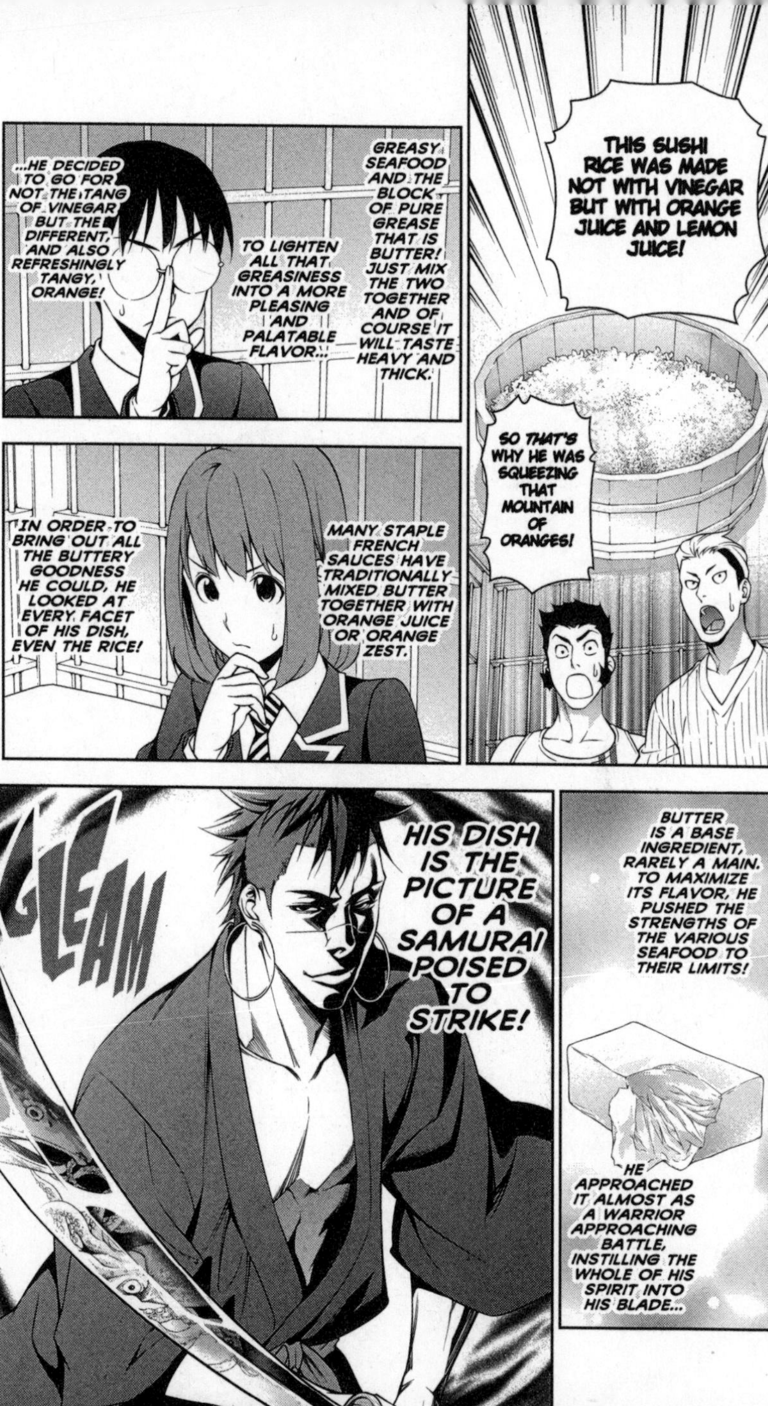
THIS SUSHI RICE WAS MADE NOT WITH VINEGAR BUT WITH ORANGE JUICE AND LEMON JUICE!
SO THAT'S WHY HE WAS SQUEEZING THAT MOUNTAIN OF ORANGES!
GREASY SEAFOOD AND THE BLOCK OF PURE GREASE THAT IS BUTTER! JUST MIX THE TWO TOGETHER AND OF COURSE IT WILL TASTE HEAVY AND THICK.
TO LIGHTEN ALL THAT GREASINESS INTO A MORE PLEASING AND PALATABLE FLAVOR...
...HE DECIDED TO GO FOR NOT THE TANG OF VINEGAR BUT THE DIFFERENT, AND ALSO REFRESHINGLY TANGY, ORANGE!
MANY STAPLE FRENCH SAUCES HAVE TRADITIONALLY MIXED BUTTER TOGETHER WITH ORANGE JUICE OR ORANGE ZEST.
IN ORDER TO BRING OUT ALL THE BUTTERY GOODNESS HE COULD, HE LOOKED AT EVERY FACET OF HIS DISH, EVEN THE RICE!
BUTTER IS A BASE INGREDIENT, RARELY A MAIN. TO MAXIMIZE ITS FLAVOR, HE PUSHED THE STRENGTHS OF THE VARIOUS SEAFOOD TO THEIR LIMITS!
HE APPROACHED IT ALMOST AS A WARRIOR APPROACHING BATTLE, INSTILLING THE WHOLE OF HIS SPIRIT INTO HIS BLADE...
HIS DISH IS THE PICTURE OF A SAMURAI POISED TO STRIKE!
GLEAM

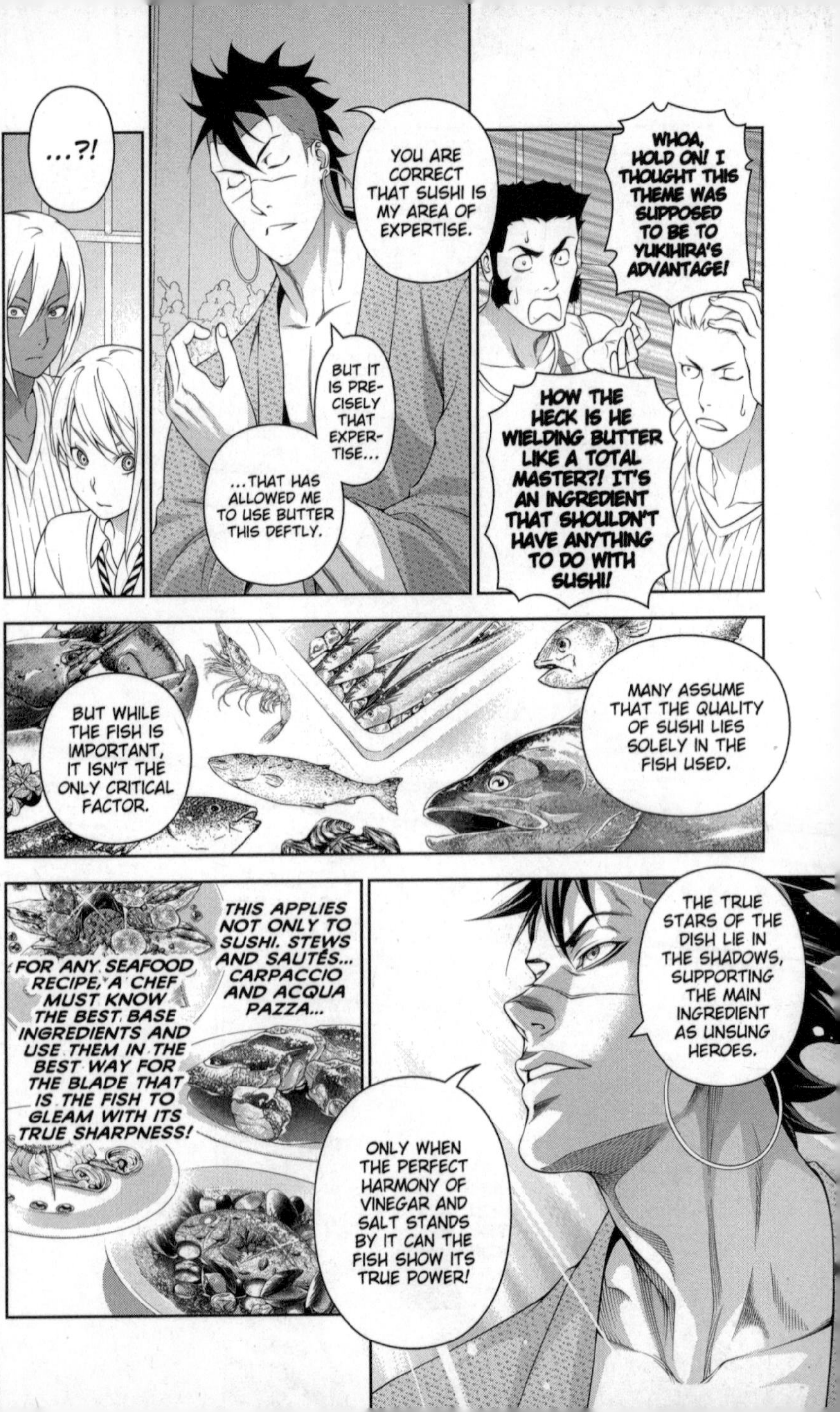
WHOA, HOLD ON! I THOUGHT THIS THEME WAS SUPPOSED TO BE TO YUKIHIRA'S ADVANTAGE!
HOW THE HECK IS HE WIELDING BUTTER LIKE A TOTAL MASTER?! IT'S AN INGREDIENT THAT SHOULDN'T HAVE ANYTHING TO DO WITH SUSHI!
YOU ARE CORRECT THAT SUSHI IS MY AREA OF EXPERTISE.
BUT IT IS PRECISELY THAT EXPERTISE...
...THAT HAS ALLOWED ME TO USE BUTTER THIS DEFTLY.
...?!
MANY ASSUME THAT THE QUALITY OF SUSHI LIES SOLELY IN THE FISH USED.
BUT WHILE THE FISH IS IMPORTANT, IT ISN'T THE ONLY CRITICAL FACTOR.
THE TRUE STARS OF THE DISH LIE IN THE SHADOWS, SUPPORTING THE MAIN INGREDIENT AS UNSUNG HEROES.
ONLY WHEN THE PERFECT HARMONY OF VINEGAR AND SALT STANDS BY IT CAN THE FISH SHOW ITS TRUE POWER!
THIS APPLIES NOT ONLY TO SUSHI. STEWS AND SAUTÉS... CARPACCIO AND ACQUA PAZZA...
FOR ANY SEAFOOD RECIPE, A CHEF MUST KNOW THE BEST BASE INGREDIENTS AND USE THEM IN THE BEST WAY FOR THE BLADE THAT IS THE FISH TO GLEAM WITH ITS TRUE SHARPNESS!

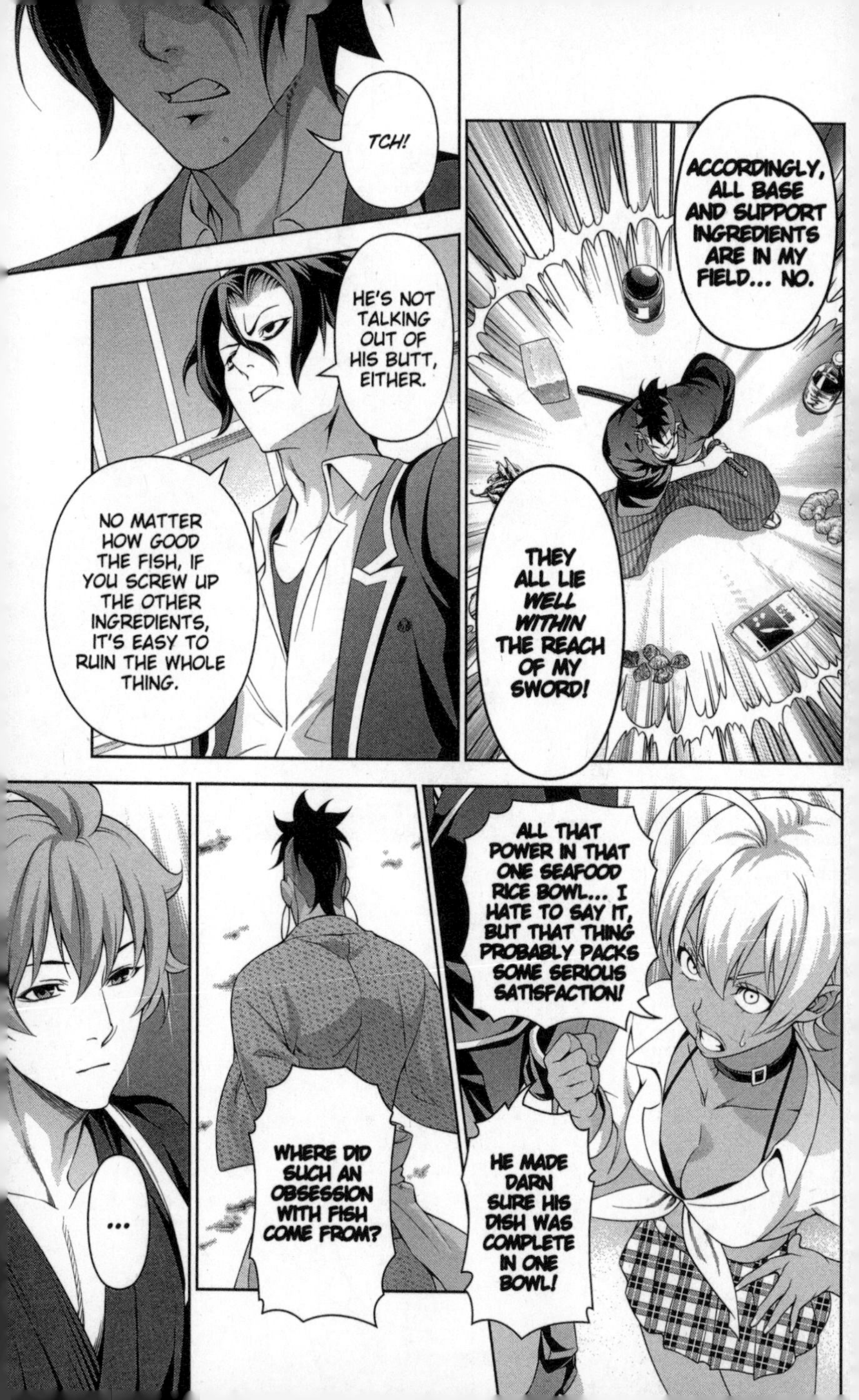
ACCORDINGLY, ALL BASE AND SUPPORT INGREDIENTS ARE IN MY FIELD... NO.
THEY ALL LIE *WELL WITHIN* THE REACH OF MY SWORD!
TCH!
HE'S NOT TALKING OUT OF HIS BUTT, EITHER.
NO MATTER HOW GOOD THE FISH, IF YOU SCREW UP THE OTHER INGREDIENTS, IT'S EASY TO RUIN THE WHOLE THING.
ALL THAT POWER IN THAT ONE SEAFOOD RICE BOWL... I HATE TO SAY IT, BUT THAT THING PROBABLY PACKS SOME SERIOUS SATISFACTION!
HE MADE DARN SURE HIS DISH WAS COMPLETE IN ONE BOWL!
WHERE DID SUCH AN OBSESSION WITH FISH COME FROM?
...

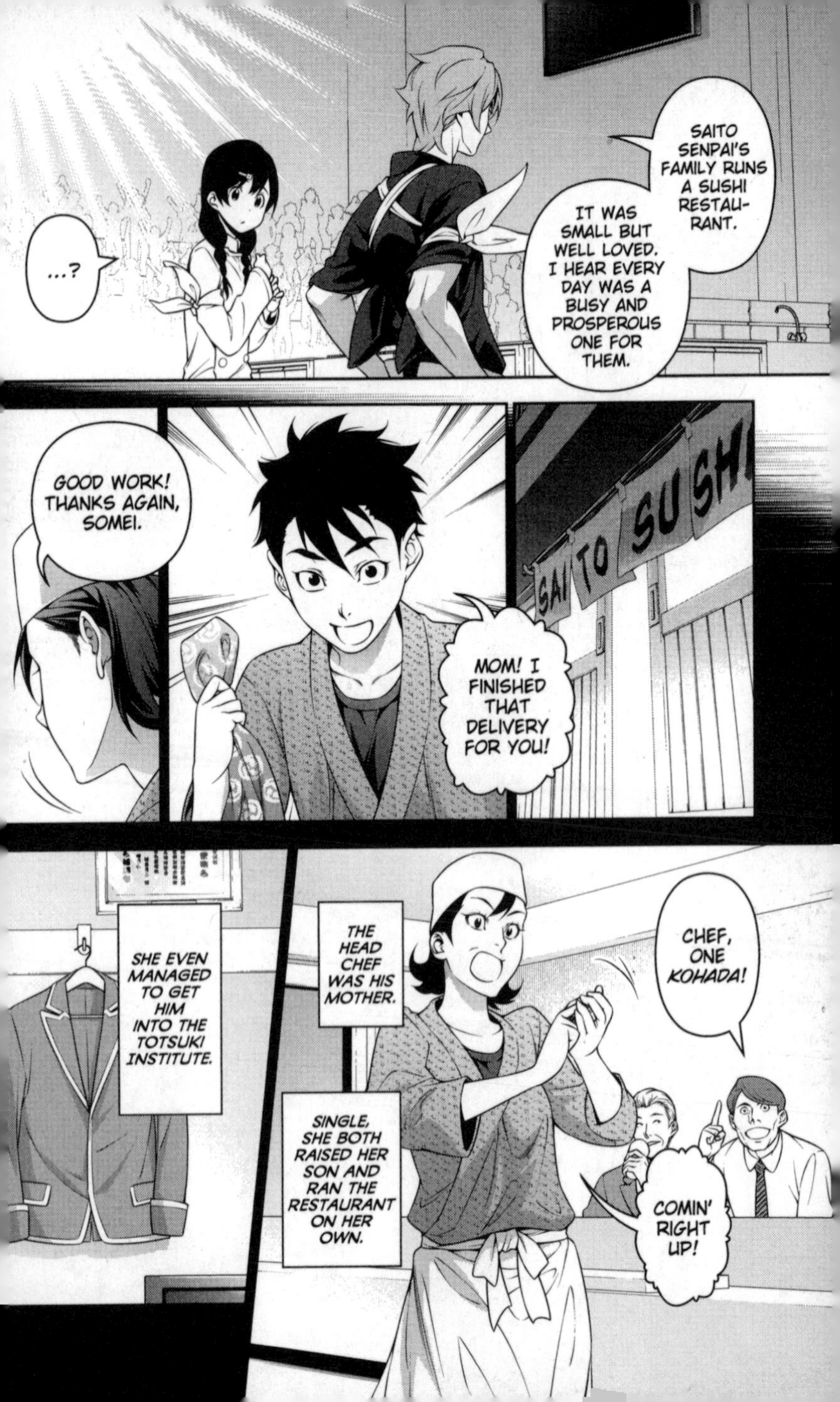
SAITO SENPAI'S FAMILY RUNS A SUSHI RESTAURANT.
IT WAS SMALL BUT WELL LOVED. I HEAR EVERY DAY WAS A BUSY AND PROSPEROUS ONE FOR THEM.
...?
SAITO SUSH
MOM! I FINISHED THAT DELIVERY FOR YOU!
GOOD WORK! THANKS AGAIN, SOMEI.
CHEF, ONE *KOHADA*!
THE HEAD CHEF WAS HIS MOTHER.
COMIN' RIGHT UP!
SINGLE, SHE BOTH RAISED HER SON AND RAN THE RESTAURANT ON HER OWN.
SHE EVEN MANAGED TO GET HIM INTO THE TOTSUKI INSTITUTE.

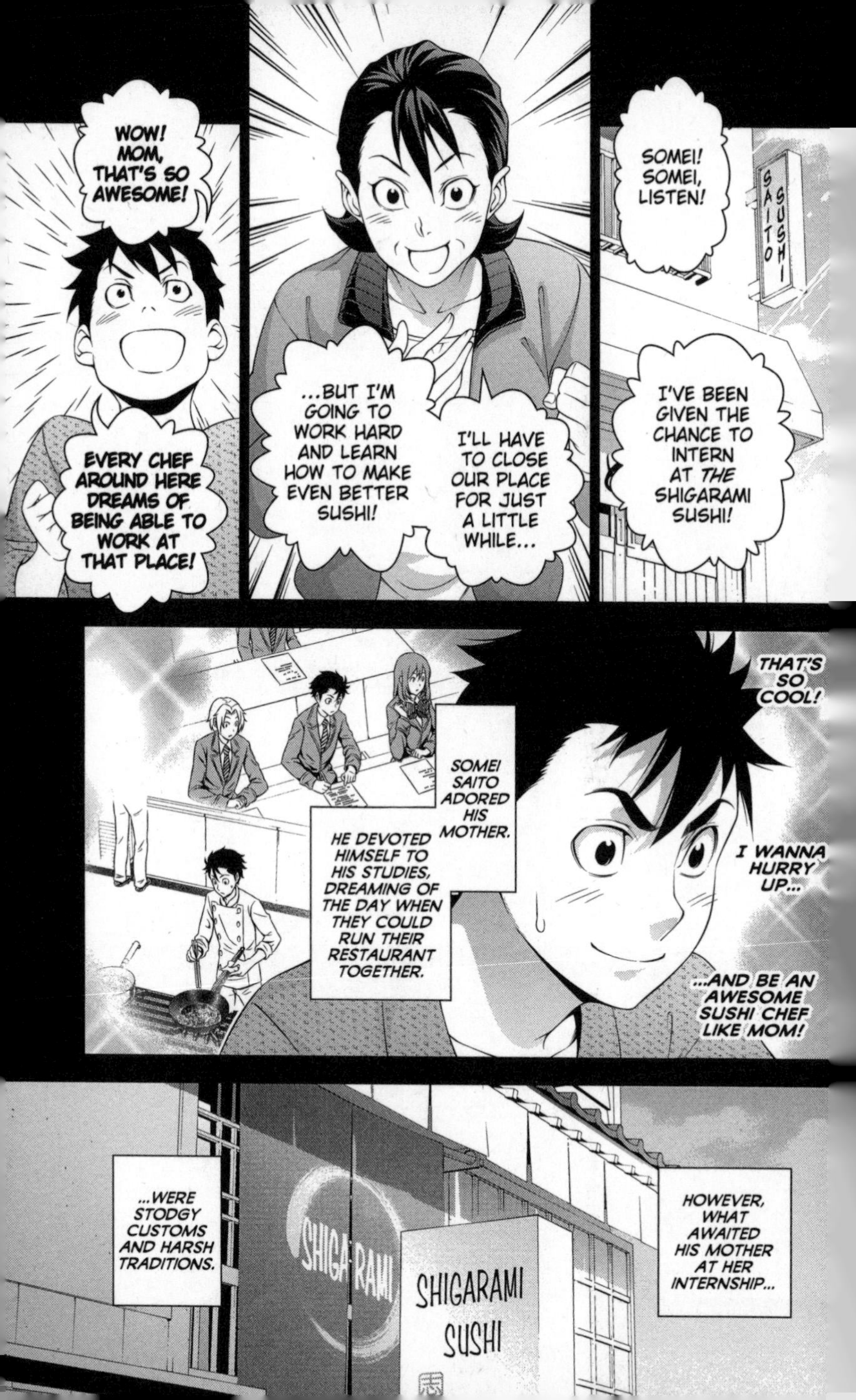
SOMEI! SOMEI, LISTEN!
SAITO SUSHI
I'VE BEEN GIVEN THE CHANCE TO INTERN AT THE SHIGARAMI SUSHI!
I'LL HAVE TO CLOSE OUR PLACE FOR JUST A LITTLE WHILE...
...BUT I'M GOING TO WORK HARD AND LEARN HOW TO MAKE EVEN BETTER SUSHI!
WOW! MOM, THAT'S SO AWESOME!
EVERY CHEF AROUND HERE DREAMS OF BEING ABLE TO WORK AT THAT PLACE!
THAT'S SO COOL!
I WANNA HURRY UP...
...AND BE AN AWESOME SUSHI CHEF LIKE MOM!
SOMEI SAITO ADORED HIS MOTHER.
HE DEVOTED HIMSELF TO HIS STUDIES, DREAMING OF THE DAY WHEN THEY COULD RUN THEIR RESTAURANT TOGETHER.
HOWEVER, WHAT AWAITED HIS MOTHER AT HER INTERNSHIP...
SHIGARAMI SUSHI
SHIGARAMI
...WERE STODGY CUSTOMS AND HARSH TRADITIONS.

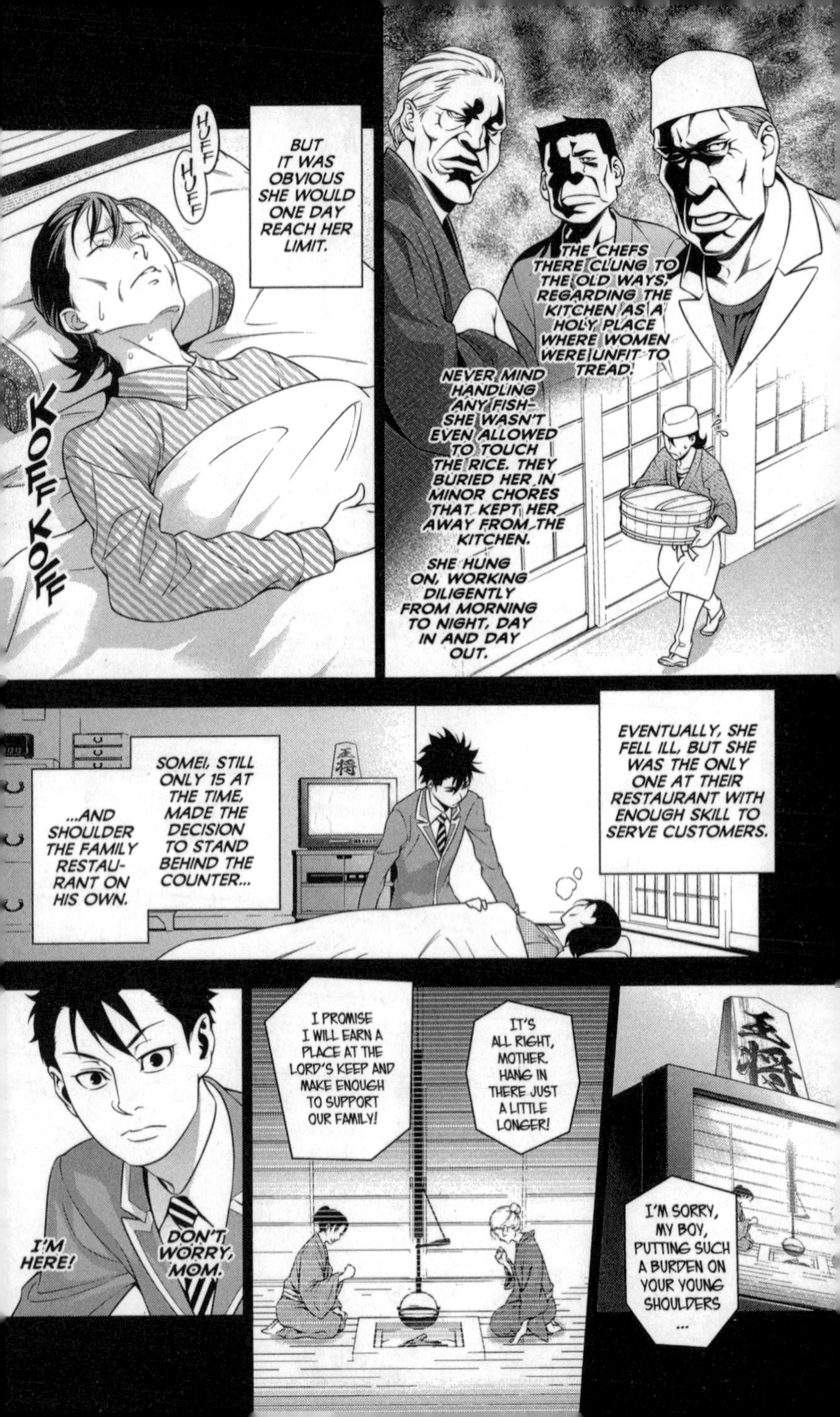
THE CHEFS THERE CLUNG TO THE OLD WAYS, REGARDING THE KITCHEN AS A HOLY PLACE WHERE WOMEN WERE UNFIT TO TREAD.
NEVER MIND HANDLING ANY FISH-SHE WASN'T EVEN ALLOWED TO TOUCH THE RICE. THEY BURIED HER IN MINOR CHORES THAT KEPT HER AWAY FROM THE KITCHEN.
SHE HUNG ON, WORKING DILIGENTLY FROM MORNING TO NIGHT, DAY IN AND DAY OUT.
BUT IT WAS OBVIOUS SHE WOULD ONE DAY REACH HER LIMIT.
HUFF HUFF
KOFF KOFF
EVENTUALLY, SHE FELL ILL, BUT SHE WAS THE ONLY ONE AT THEIR RESTAURANT WITH ENOUGH SKILL TO SERVE CUSTOMERS.
SOMEI, STILL ONLY 15 AT THE TIME, MADE THE DECISION TO STAND BEHIND THE COUNTER...
...AND SHOULDER THE FAMILY RESTAU-RANT ON HIS OWN.
I'M SORRY, MY BOY, PUTTING SUCH A BURDEN ON YOUR YOUNG SHOULDERS...
IT'S ALL RIGHT, MOTHER. HANG IN THERE JUST A LITTLE LONGER!
I PROMISE I WILL EARN A PLACE AT THE LORD'S KEEP AND MAKE ENOUGH TO SUPPORT OUR FAMILY!
DON'T WORRY, MOM.
I'M HERE!

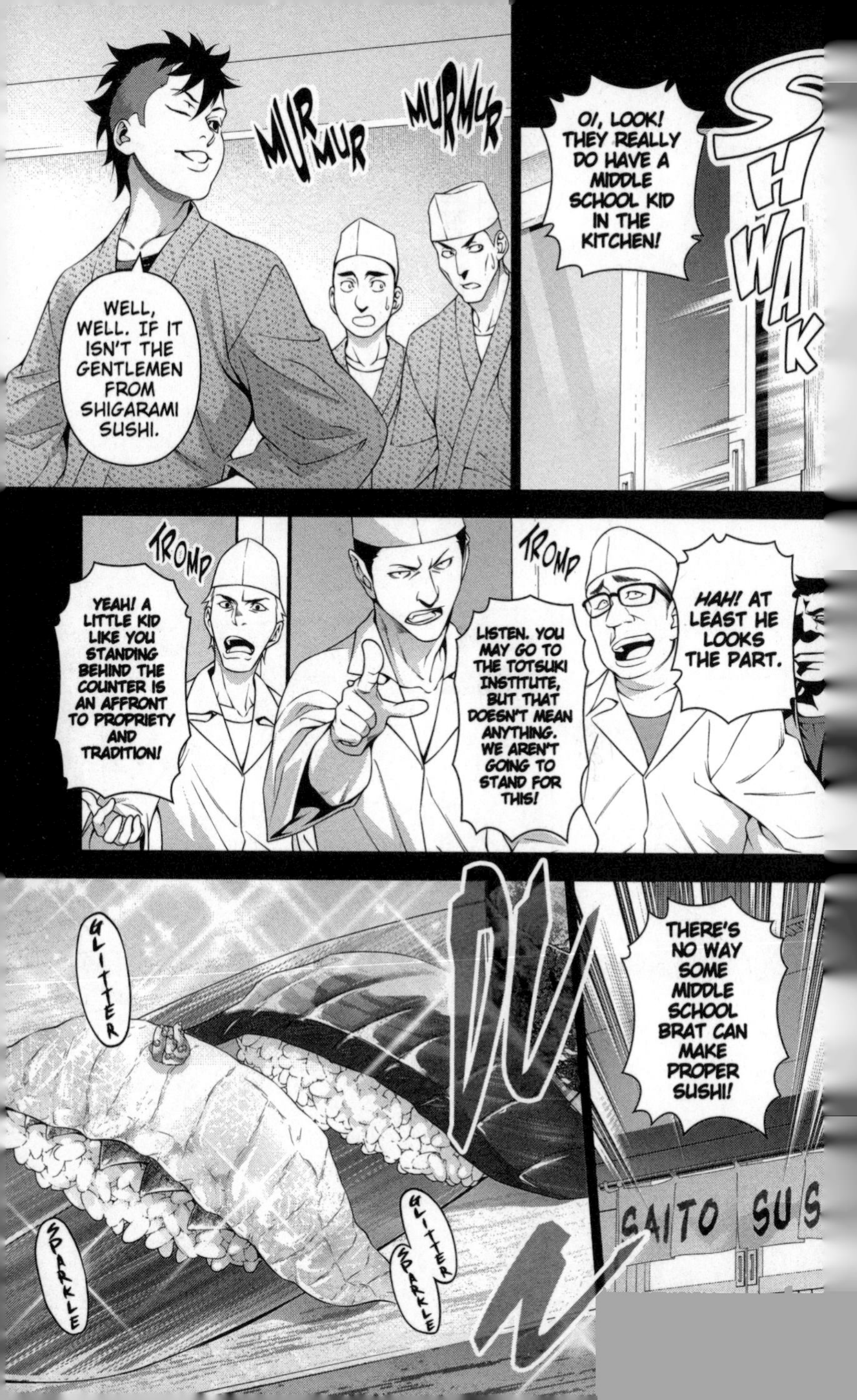
SHWAK
OI, LOOK! THEY REALLY DO HAVE A MIDDLE SCHOOL KID IN THE KITCHEN!
MURMUR
MURMUR
WELL, WELL. IF IT ISN'T THE GENTLEMEN FROM SHIGARAMI SUSHI.
HAH! AT LEAST HE LOOKS THE PART.
TROMP
LISTEN. YOU MAY GO TO THE TOTSUKI INSTITUTE, BUT THAT DOESN'T MEAN ANYTHING. WE AREN'T GOING TO STAND FOR THIS!
TROMP
YEAH! A LITTLE KID LIKE YOU STANDING BEHIND THE COUNTER IS AN AFFRONT TO PROPRIETY AND TRADITION!
THERE'S NO WAY SOME MIDDLE SCHOOL BRAT CAN MAKE PROPER SUSHI!
SAITO SUS
GLITTER
SPARKLE
GLITTER
SPARKLE

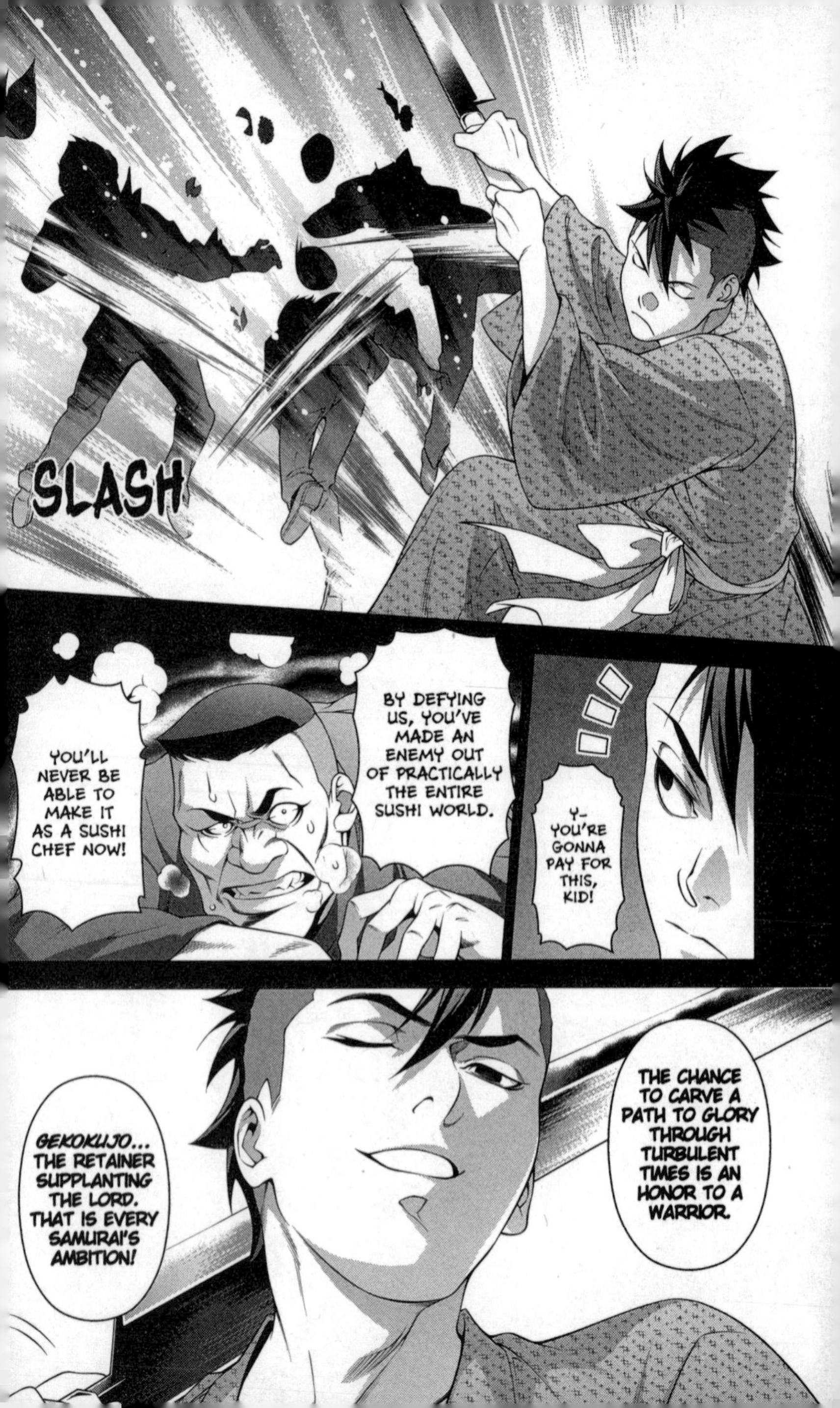
SLASH
BY DEFYING US, YOU'VE MADE AN ENEMY OUT OF PRACTICALLY THE ENTIRE SUSHI WORLD.
YOU'LL NEVER BE ABLE TO MAKE IT AS A SUSHI CHEF NOW!
Y- YOU'RE GONNA PAY FOR THIS, KID!
THE CHANCE TO CARVE A PATH TO GLORY THROUGH TURBULENT TIMES IS AN HONOR TO A WARRIOR.
GEKOKUJO... THE RETAINER SUPPLANTING THE LORD. THAT IS EVERY SAMURAI'S AMBITION!

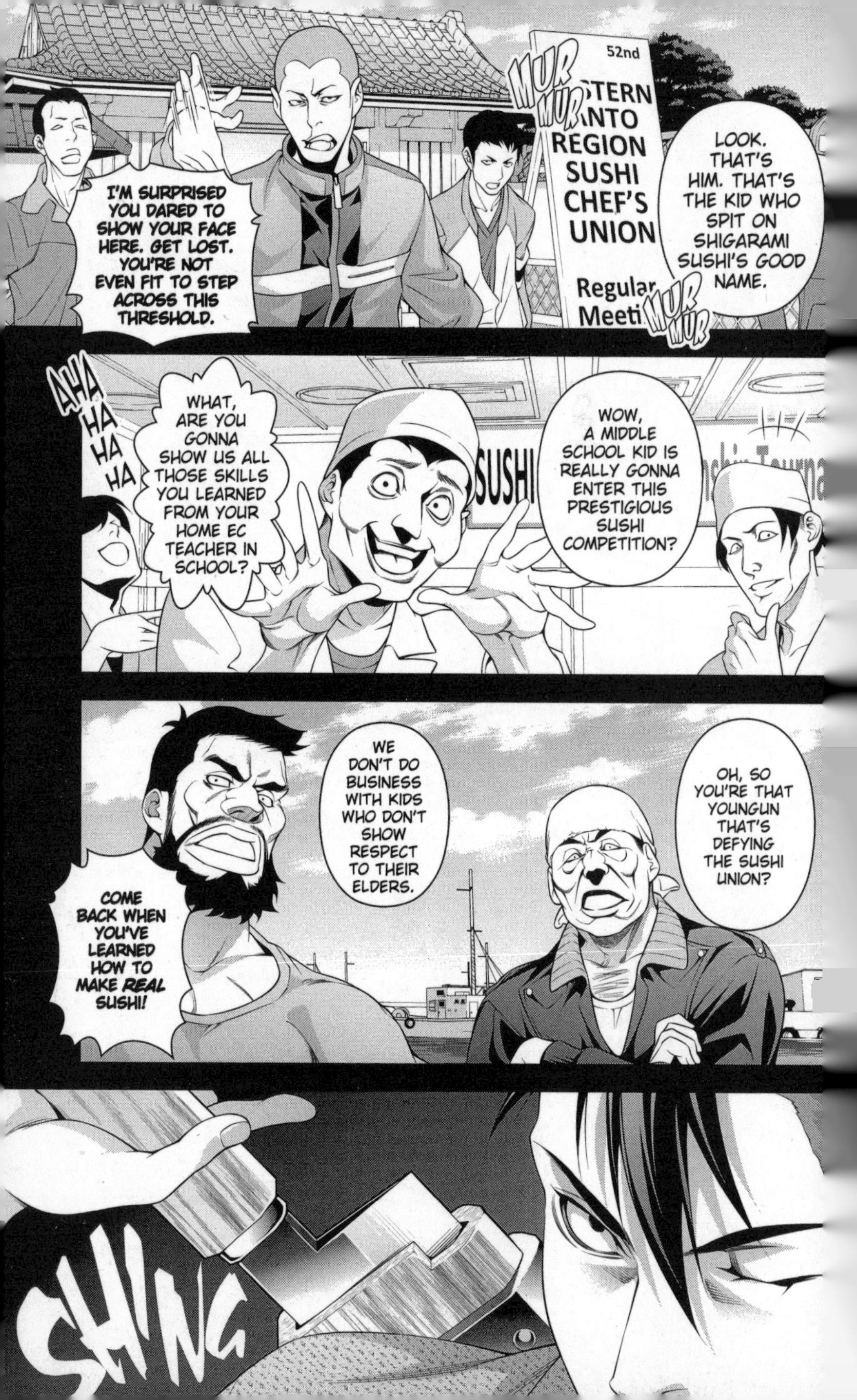
LOOK. THAT'S HIM. THAT'S THE KID WHO SPIT ON SHIGARAMI SUSHI'S GOOD NAME.
MUR MUR
52nd
STERN
NTO
REGION
SUSHI
CHEF'S
UNION
Regular
Meeti
MUR MUR
I'M SURPRISED YOU DARED TO SHOW YOUR FACE HERE. GET LOST. YOU'RE NOT EVEN FIT TO STEP ACROSS THIS THRESHOLD.
WOW, A MIDDLE SCHOOL KID IS REALLY GONNA ENTER THIS PRESTIGIOUS SUSHI COMPETITION?
SUSHI
WHAT, ARE YOU GONNA SHOW US ALL THOSE SKILLS YOU LEARNED FROM YOUR HOME EC TEACHER IN SCHOOL?
AHA HA HA HA
OH, SO YOU'RE THAT YOUNGUN THAT'S DEFYING THE SUSHI UNION?
WE DON'T DO BUSINESS WITH KIDS WHO DON'T SHOW RESPECT TO THEIR ELDERS.
COME BACK WHEN YOU'VE LEARNED HOW TO MAKE *REAL* SUSHI!
SHING

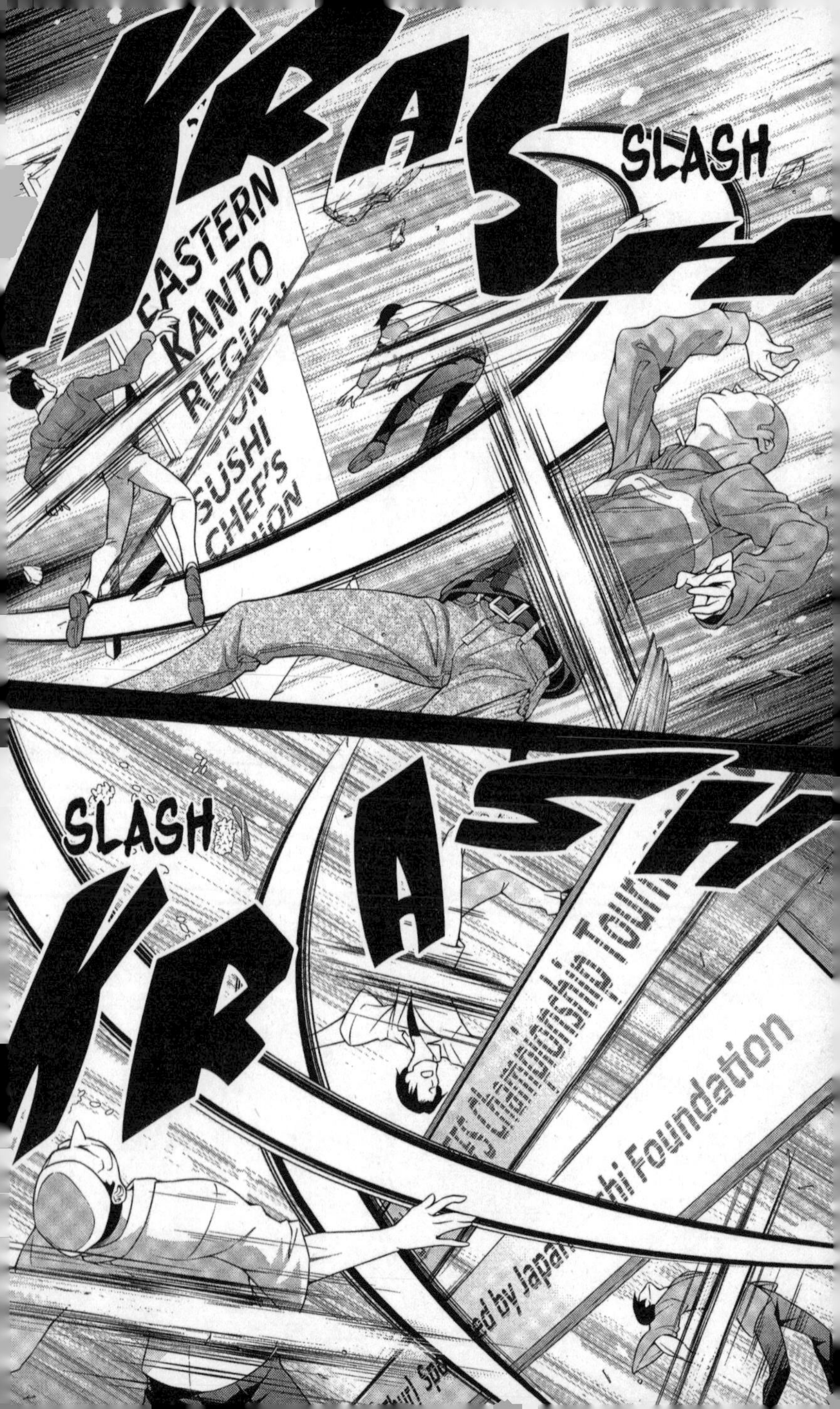
KRASH
SLASH
EASTERN
KANTO
SUSHI
CHEF'S
KRASH
SLASH
Championship Tourn
Foundation

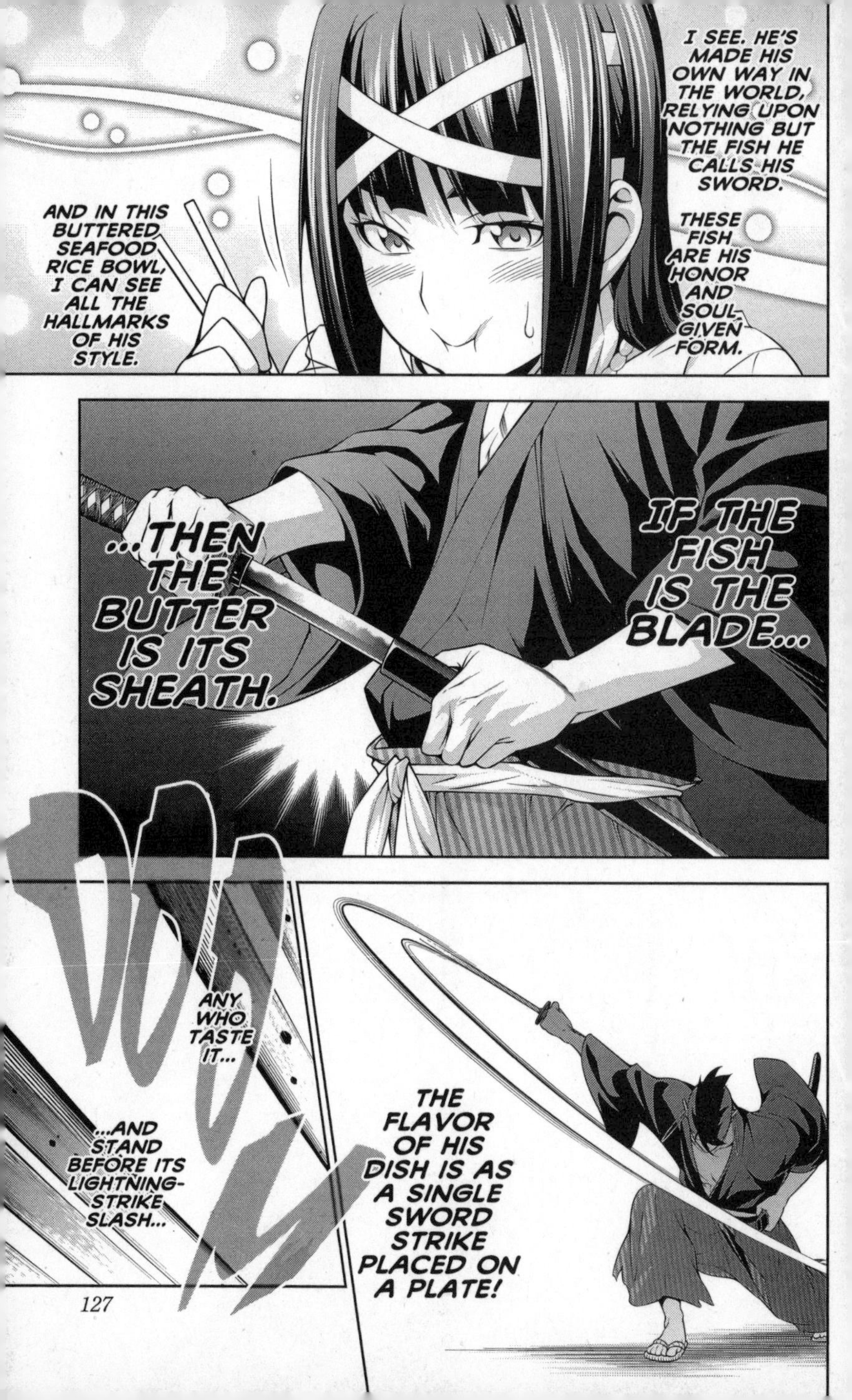
I SEE. HE'S MADE HIS OWN WAY IN THE WORLD, RELYING UPON NOTHING BUT THE FISH HE CALLS HIS SWORD.
THESE FISH ARE HIS HONOR AND SOUL GIVEN FORM.
AND IN THIS BUTTERED SEAFOOD RICE BOWL, I CAN SEE ALL THE HALLMARKS OF HIS STYLE.
IF THE FISH IS THE BLADE...
...THEN THE BUTTER IS ITS SHEATH.
THE FLAVOR OF HIS DISH IS AS A SINGLE SWORD STRIKE PLACED ON A PLATE!
ANY WHO TASTE IT...
...AND STAND BEFORE ITS LIGHTNING-STRIKE SLASH...

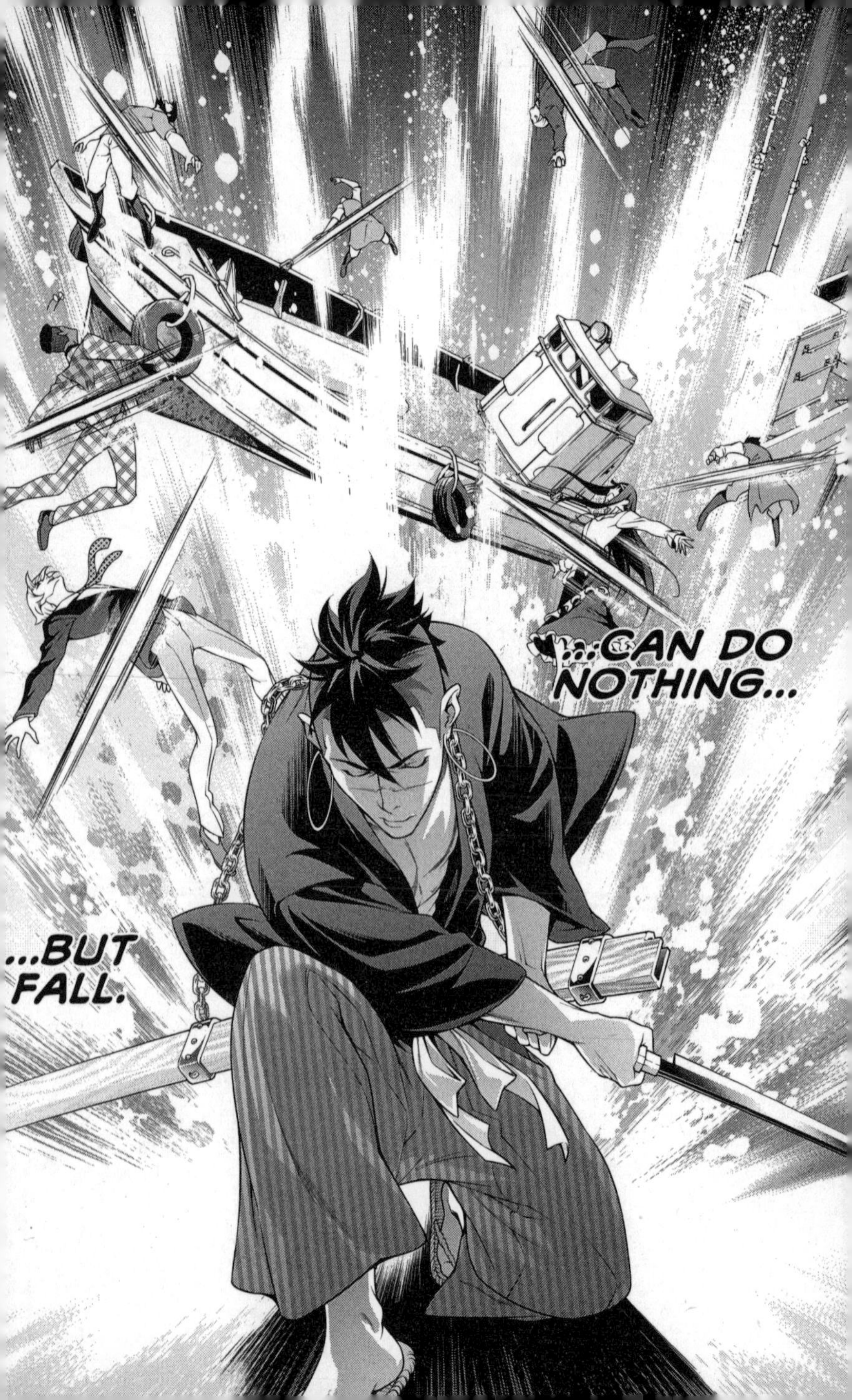
...CAN DO NOTHING...
...BUT FALL.

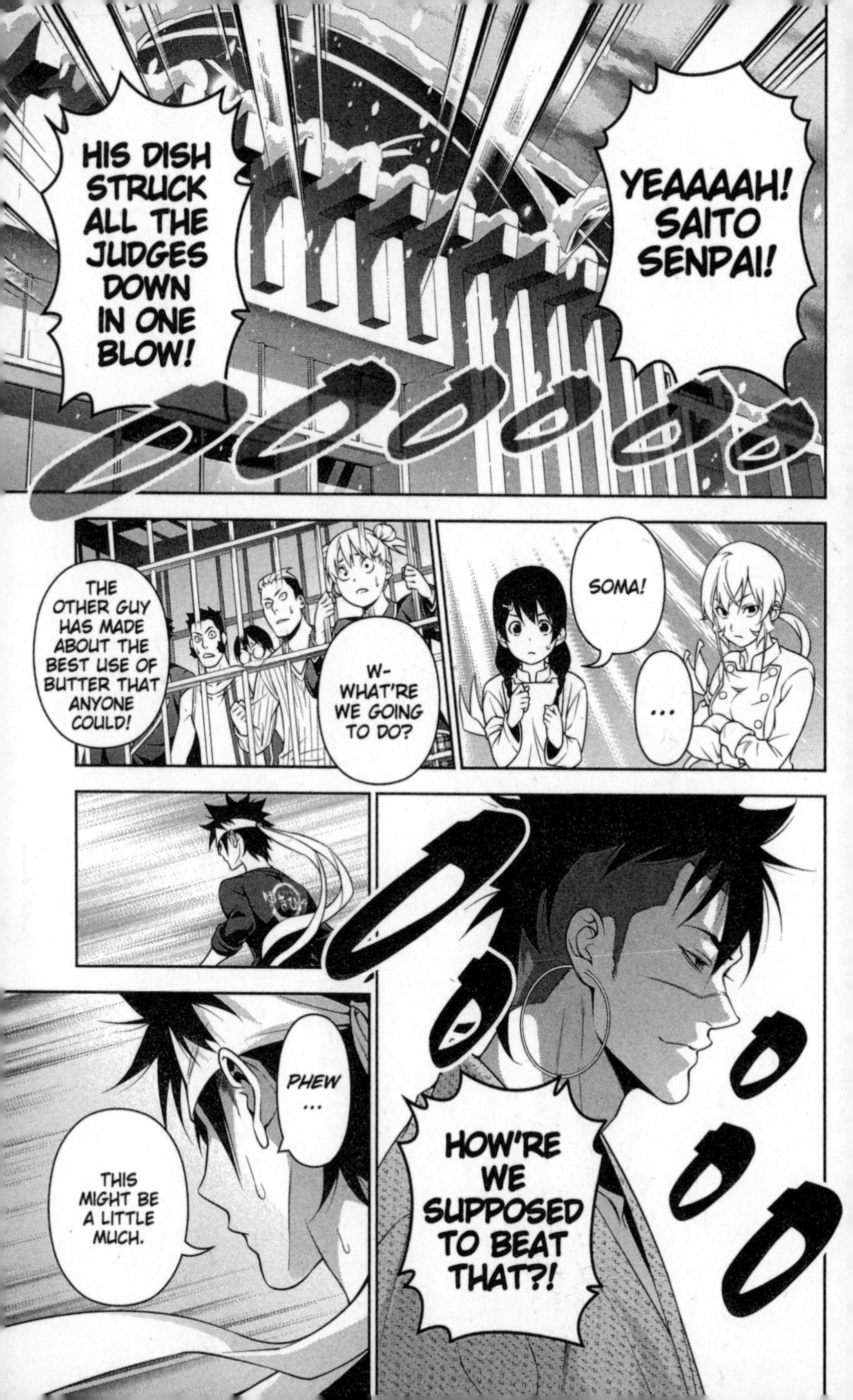
YEAAAAH! SAITO SENPAI!
HIS DISH STRUCK ALL THE JUDGES DOWN IN ONE BLOW!
SOMA!
...
W-WHAT'RE WE GOING TO DO?
THE OTHER GUY HAS MADE ABOUT THE BEST USE OF BUTTER THAT ANYONE COULD!
HOW'RE WE SUPPOSED TO BEAT THAT?!
PHEW...
THIS MIGHT BE A LITTLE MUCH.

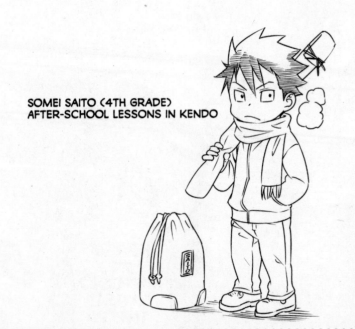

SOMEI SAITO (4TH GRADE)
AFTER-SCHOOL LESSONS IN KENDO

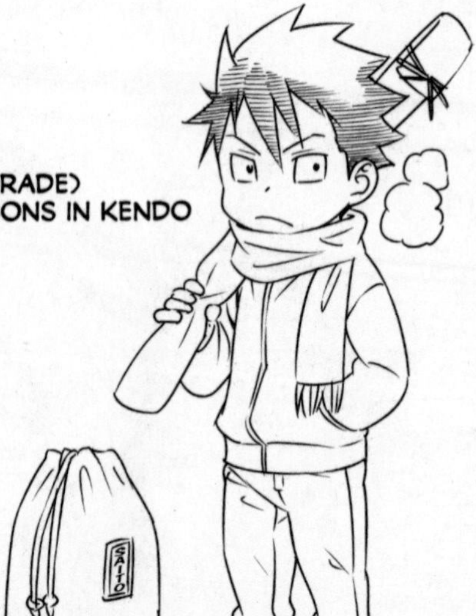
SAITO

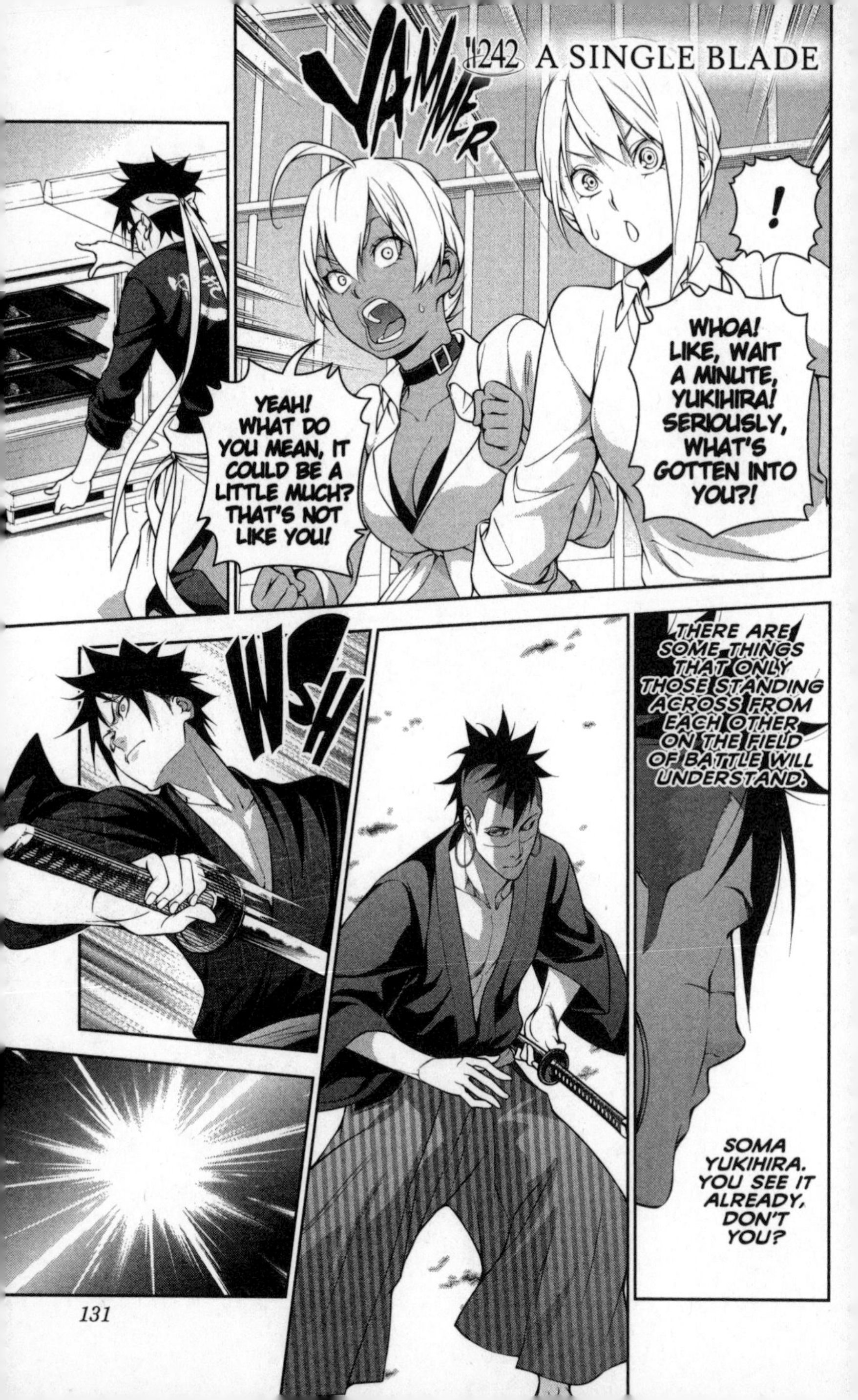

242 A SINGLE BLADE
JAMMER
!
WHOA! LIKE, WAIT A MINUTE, YUKIHIRA! SERIOUSLY, WHAT'S GOTTEN INTO YOU?!
YEAH! WHAT DO YOU MEAN, IT COULD BE A LITTLE MUCH? THAT'S NOT LIKE YOU!
THERE ARE SOME THINGS THAT ONLY THOSE STANDING ACROSS FROM EACH OTHER ON THE FIELD OF BATTLE WILL UNDERSTAND.
SOMA YUKIHIRA. YOU SEE IT ALREADY, DON'T YOU?
WSH

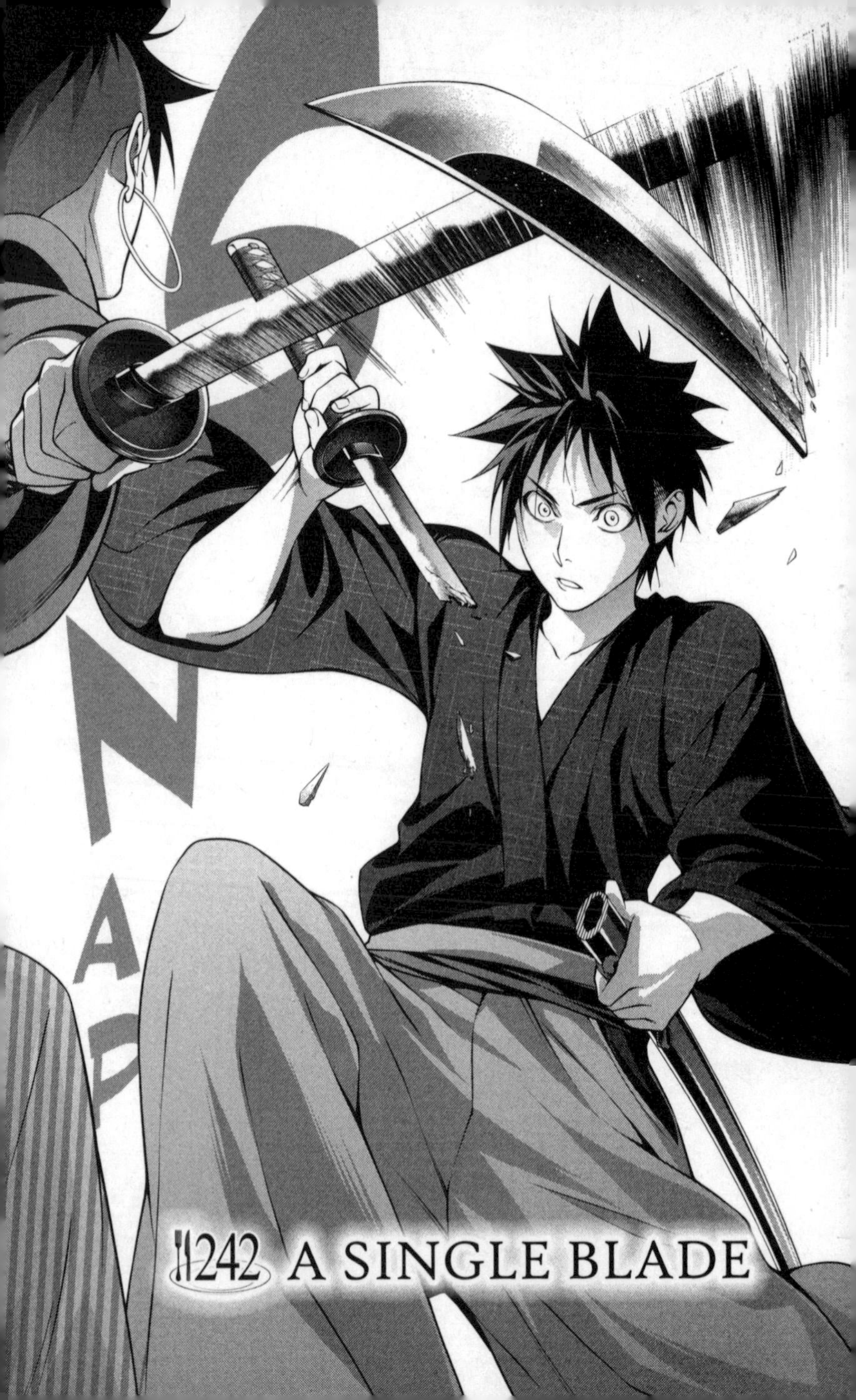

242 A SINGLE BLADE

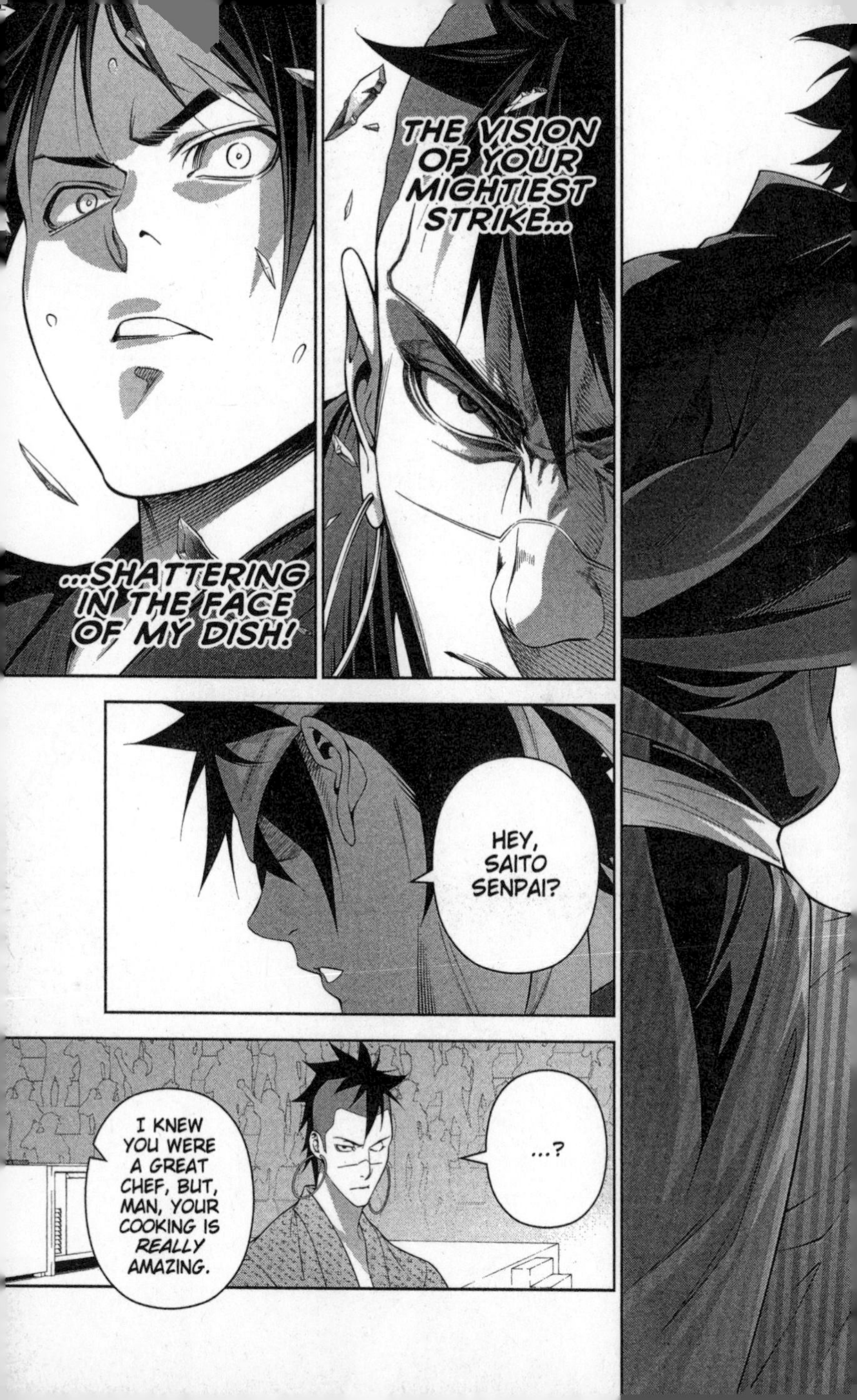
THE VISION OF YOUR MIGHTIEST STRIKE...
...SHATTERING IN THE FACE OF MY DISH!
HEY, SAITO SENPAI?
...?
I KNEW YOU WERE A GREAT CHEF, BUT, MAN, YOUR COOKING IS *REALLY* AMAZING.

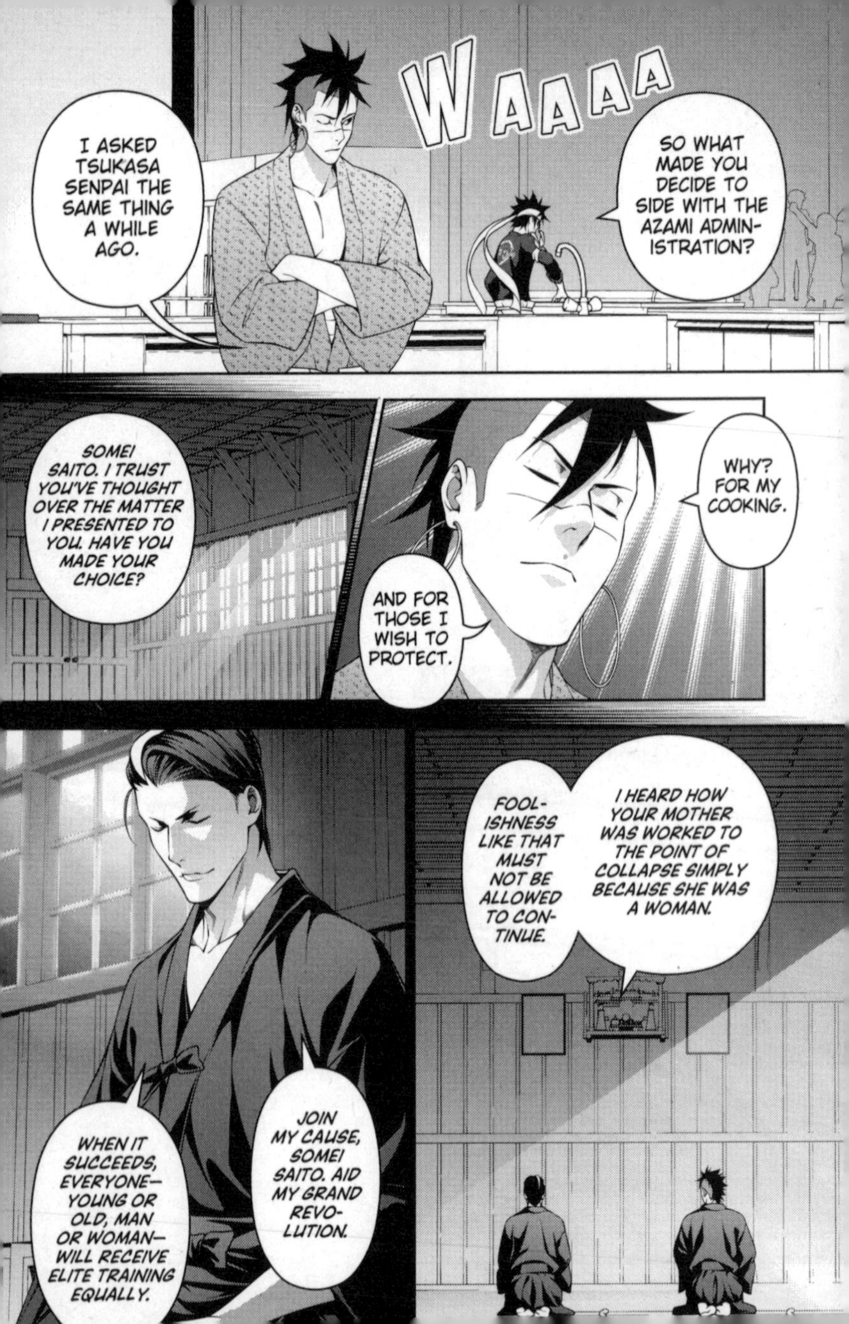
SO WHAT MADE YOU DECIDE TO SIDE WITH THE AZAMI ADMINISTRATION?
WAAAA
I ASKED TSUKASA SENPAI THE SAME THING A WHILE AGO.
WHY? FOR MY COOKING.
AND FOR THOSE I WISH TO PROTECT.
SOMEI SAITO. I TRUST YOU'VE THOUGHT OVER THE MATTER I PRESENTED TO YOU. HAVE YOU MADE YOUR CHOICE?
I HEARD HOW YOUR MOTHER WAS WORKED TO THE POINT OF COLLAPSE SIMPLY BECAUSE SHE WAS A WOMAN.
FOOLISHNESS LIKE THAT MUST NOT BE ALLOWED TO CONTINUE.
JOIN MY CAUSE, SOMEI SAITO. AID MY GRAND REVOLUTION.
WHEN IT SUCCEEDS, EVERYONE—YOUNG OR OLD, MAN OR WOMAN—WILL RECEIVE ELITE TRAINING EQUALLY.

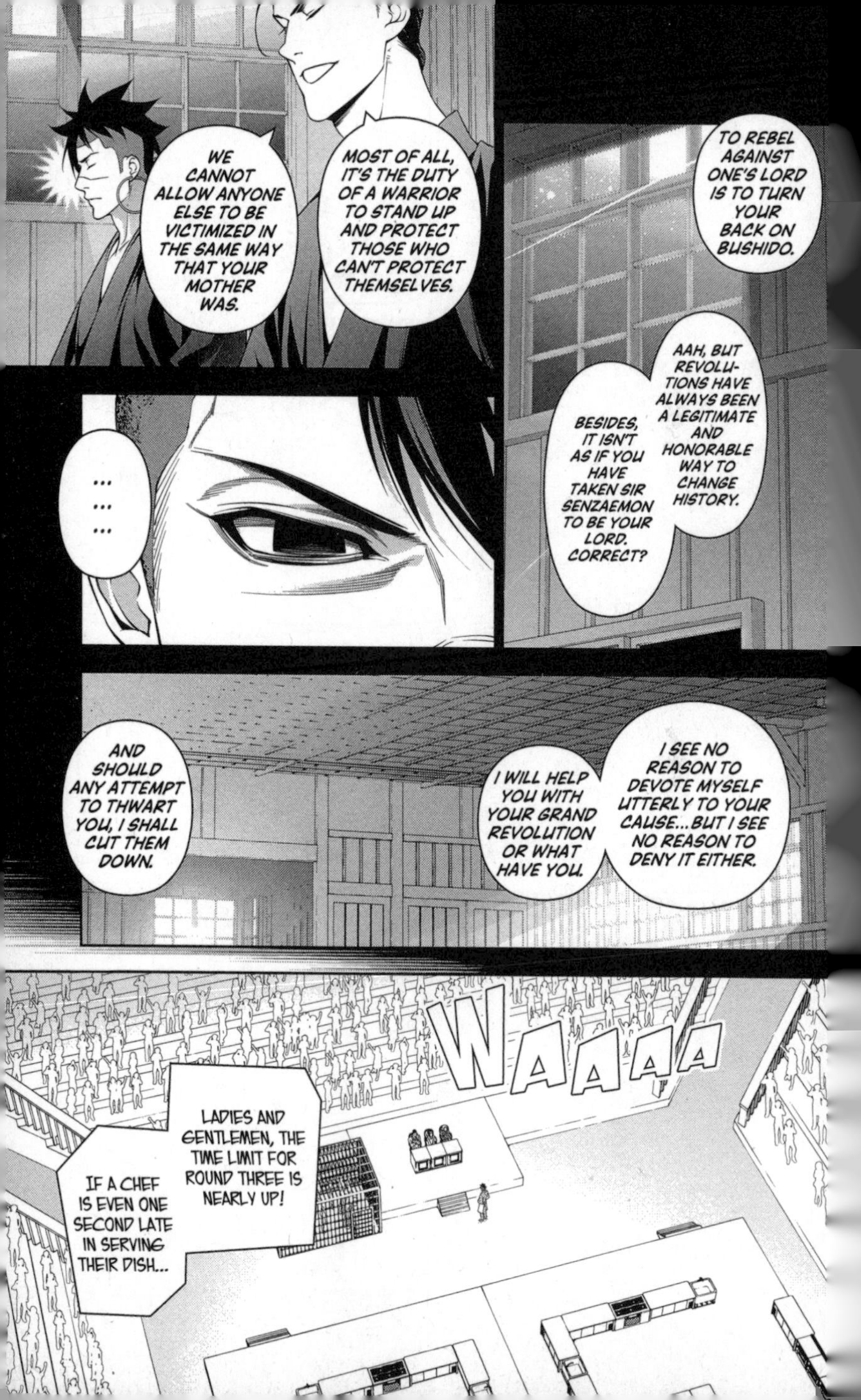
MOST OF ALL, IT'S THE DUTY OF A WARRIOR TO STAND UP AND PROTECT THOSE WHO CAN'T PROTECT THEMSELVES.
WE CANNOT ALLOW ANYONE ELSE TO BE VICTIMIZED IN THE SAME WAY THAT YOUR MOTHER WAS.
TO REBEL AGAINST ONE'S LORD IS TO TURN YOUR BACK ON BUSHIDO.
AAH, BUT REVOLUTIONS HAVE ALWAYS BEEN A LEGITIMATE AND HONORABLE WAY TO CHANGE HISTORY.
BESIDES, IT ISN'T AS IF YOU HAVE TAKEN SIR SENZAEMON TO BE YOUR LORD. CORRECT?
... ...
I SEE NO REASON TO DEVOTE MYSELF UTTERLY TO YOUR CAUSE...BUT I SEE NO REASON TO DENY IT EITHER.
I WILL HELP YOU WITH YOUR GRAND REVOLUTION OR WHAT HAVE YOU.
AND SHOULD ANY ATTEMPT TO THWART YOU, I SHALL CUT THEM DOWN.
WAAAA
LADIES AND GENTLEMEN, THE TIME LIMIT FOR ROUND THREE IS NEARLY UP!
IF A CHEF IS EVEN ONE SECOND LATE IN SERVING THEIR DISH...

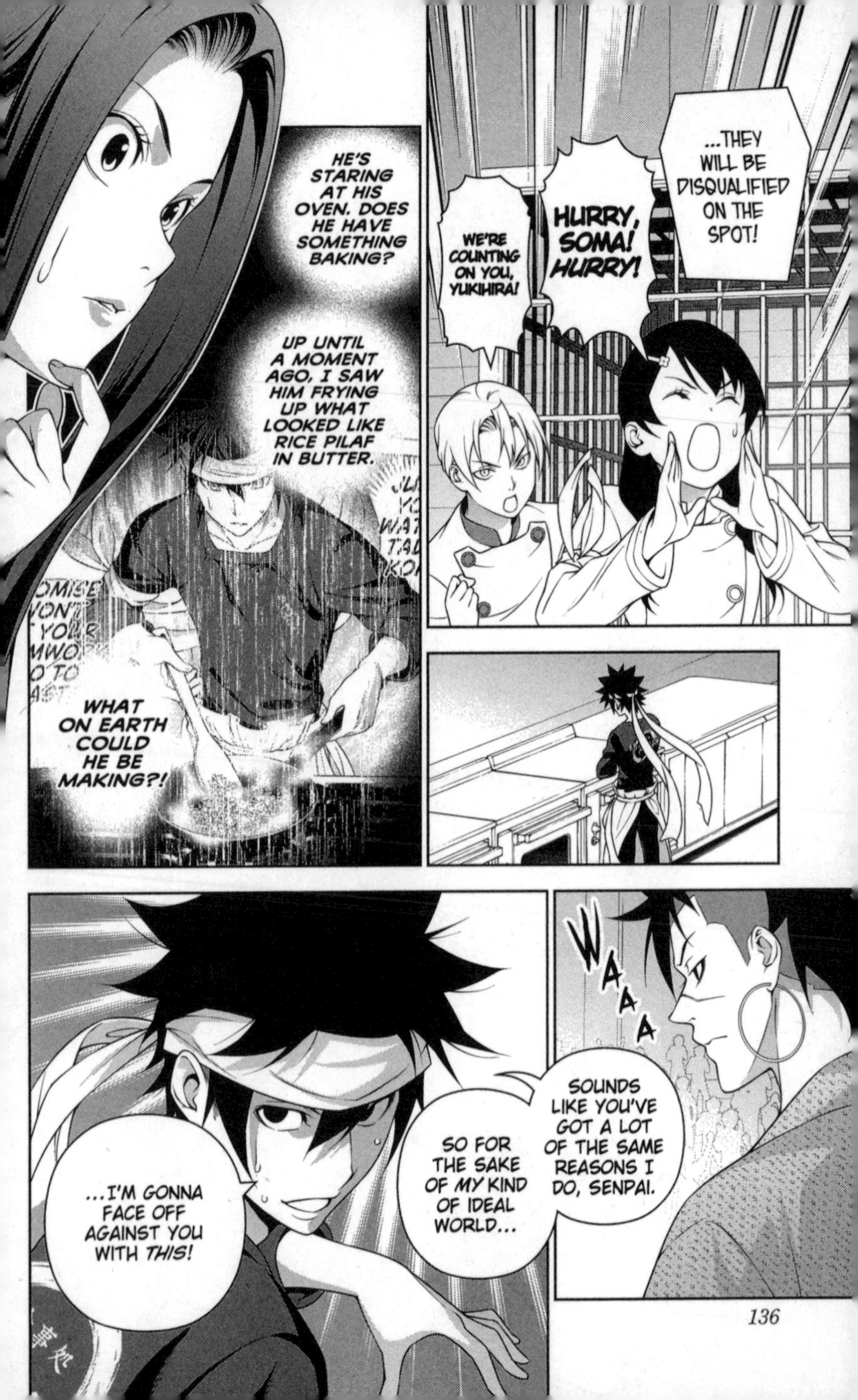
...THEY WILL BE DISQUALIFIED ON THE SPOT!
HURRY, SOMA! HURRY!
WE'RE COUNTING ON YOU, YUKIHIRA!
HE'S STARING AT HIS OVEN. DOES HE HAVE SOMETHING BAKING?
UP UNTIL A MOMENT AGO, I SAW HIM FRYING UP WHAT LOOKED LIKE RICE PILAF IN BUTTER.
WHAT ON EARTH COULD HE BE MAKING?!
WAAAA
SOUNDS LIKE YOU'VE GOT A LOT OF THE SAME REASONS I DO, SENPAI.
SO FOR THE SAKE OF MY KIND OF IDEAL WORLD...
...I'M GONNA FACE OFF AGAINST YOU WITH THIS!

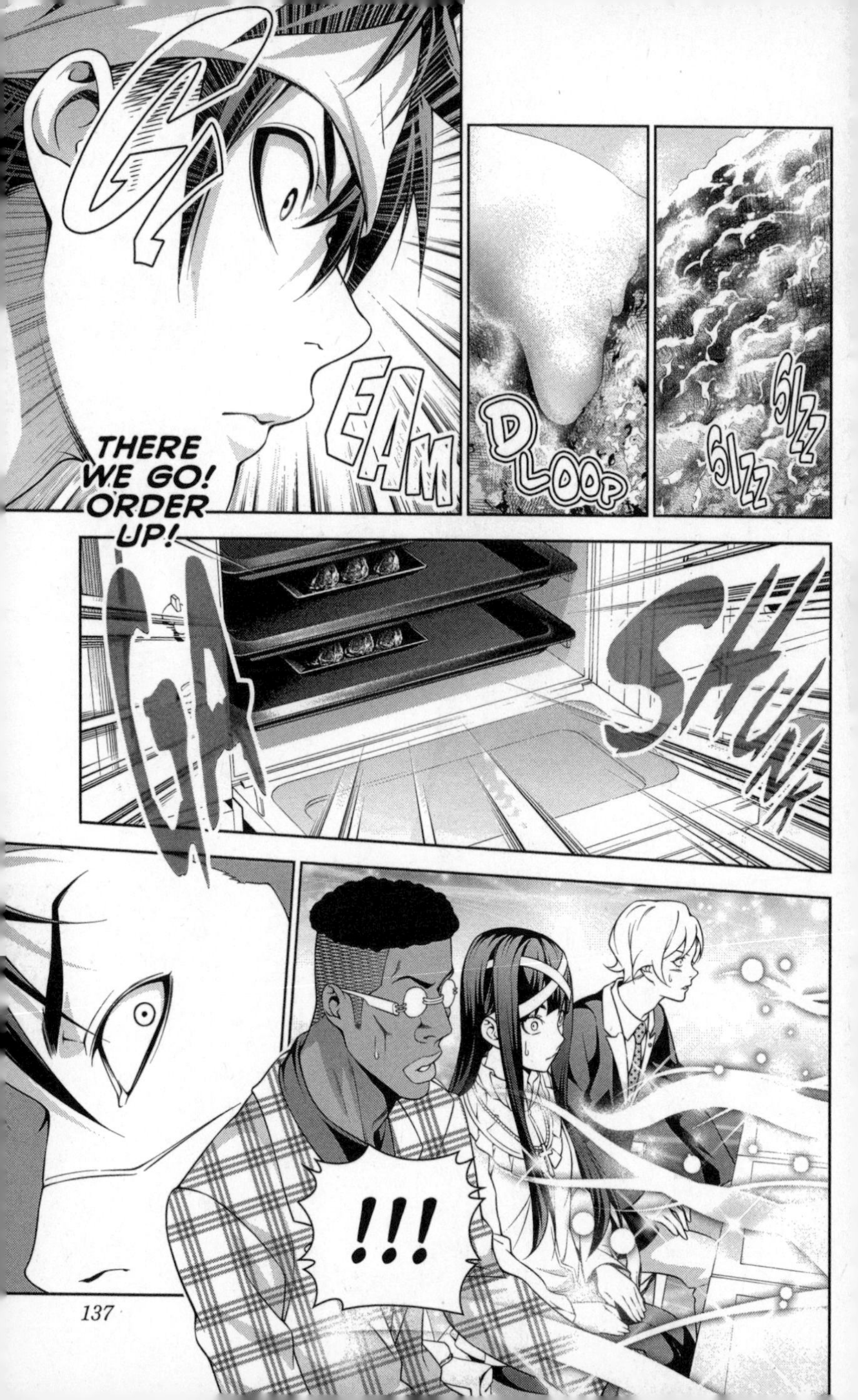
SIZZ
SIZZ
DLOOP
EAM
THERE WE GO! ORDER UP!
SHUNK
!!!

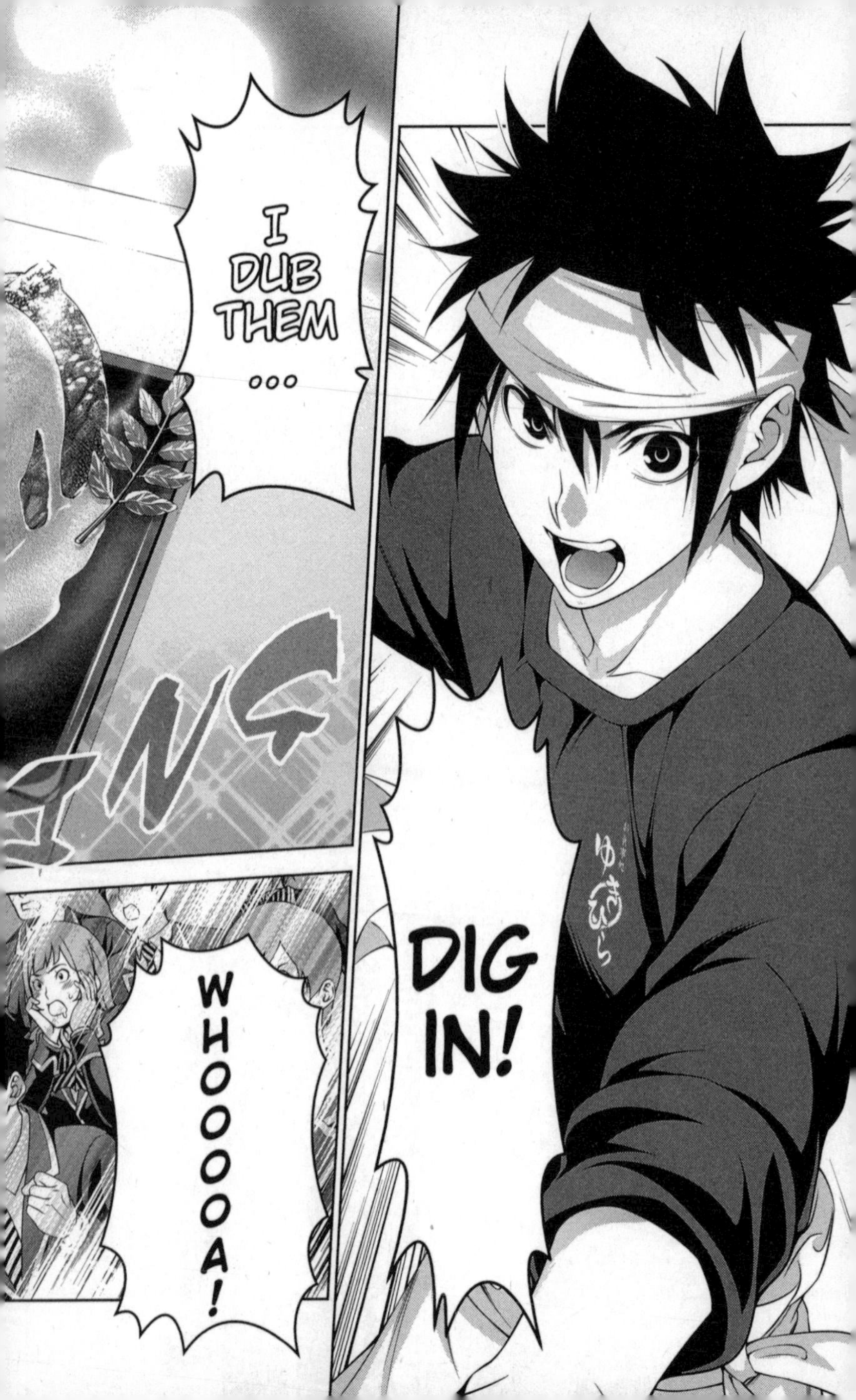
DIG IN!
I DUB THEM...
WHOOOOOA!

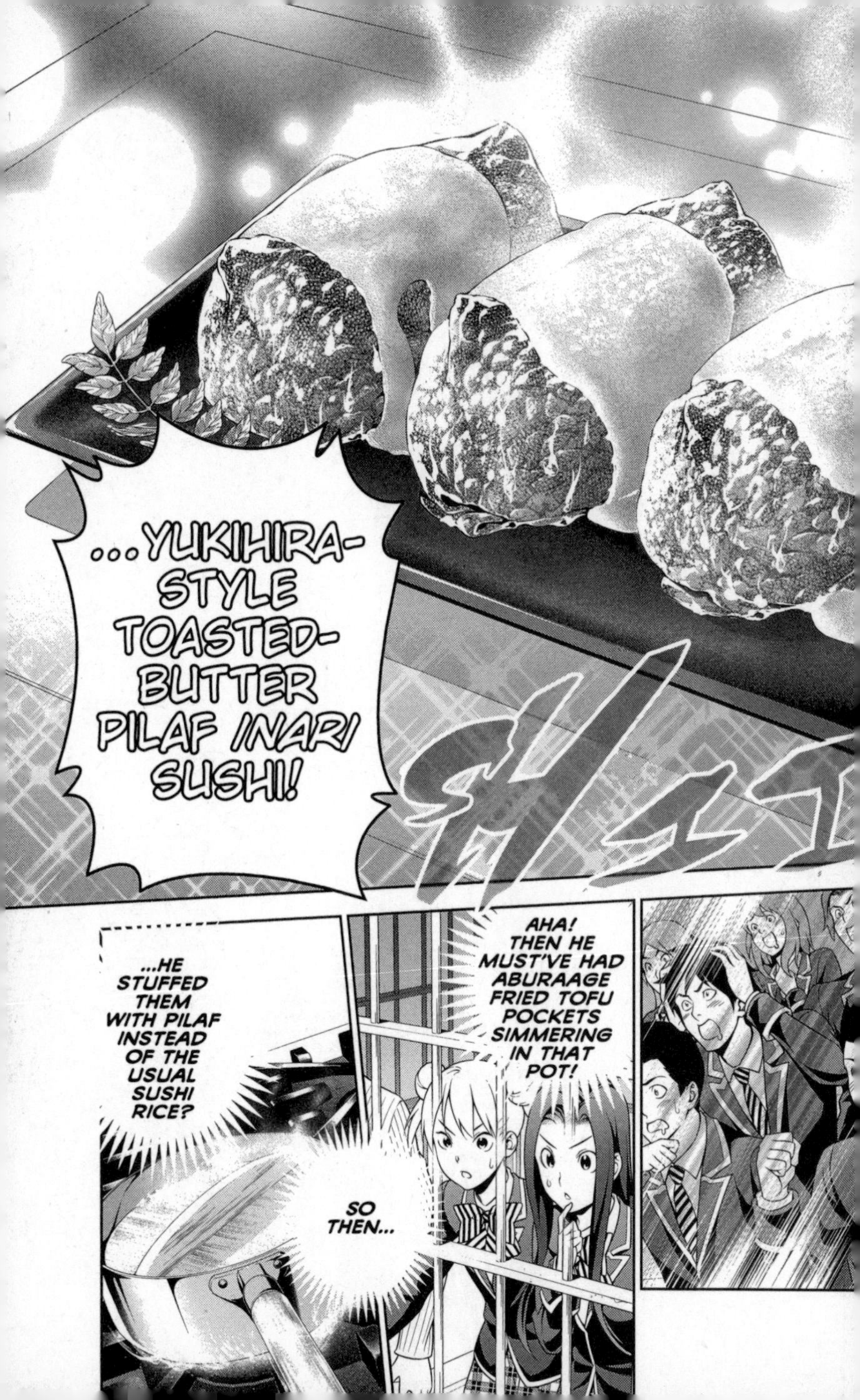
...YUKIHIRA-STYLE TOASTED-BUTTER PILAF INARI SUSHI!
AHA! THEN HE MUST'VE HAD ABURAAGE FRIED TOFU POCKETS SIMMERING IN THAT POT!
SO THEN...
...HE STUFFED THEM WITH PILAF INSTEAD OF THE USUAL SUSHI RICE?

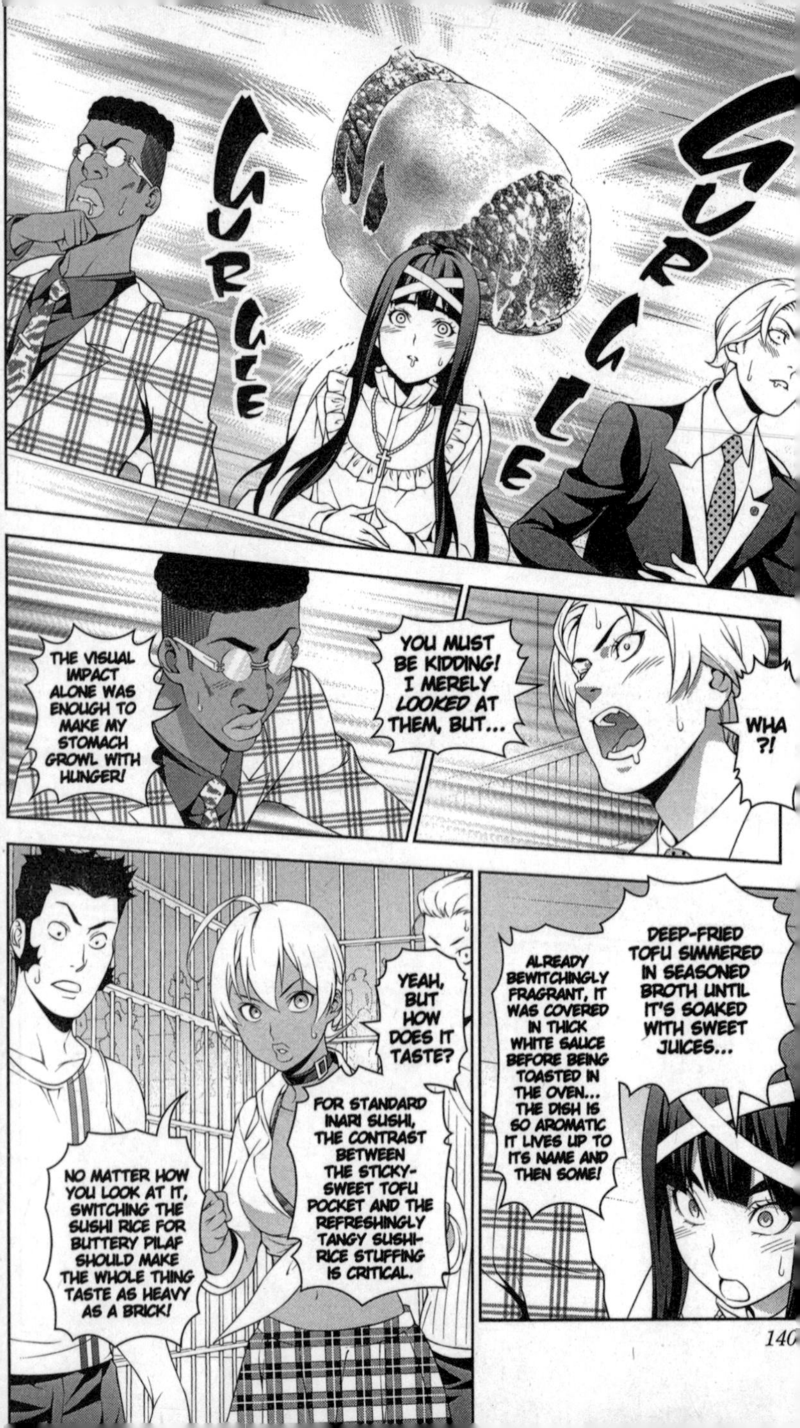
GURGLE
GURGLE
WHA?!
YOU MUST BE KIDDING! I MERELY *LOOKED* AT THEM, BUT...
THE VISUAL IMPACT ALONE WAS ENOUGH TO MAKE MY STOMACH GROWL WITH HUNGER!
DEEP-FRIED TOFU SIMMERED IN SEASONED BROTH UNTIL IT'S SOAKED WITH SWEET JUICES...
ALREADY BEWITCHINGLY FRAGRANT, IT WAS COVERED IN THICK WHITE SAUCE BEFORE BEING TOASTED IN THE OVEN... THE DISH IS SO AROMATIC IT LIVES UP TO ITS NAME AND THEN SOME!
YEAH, BUT HOW DOES IT TASTE?
FOR STANDARD INARI SUSHI, THE CONTRAST BETWEEN THE STICKY-SWEET TOFU POCKET AND THE REFRESHINGLY TANGY SUSHI-RICE STUFFING IS CRITICAL.
NO MATTER HOW YOU LOOK AT IT, SWITCHING THE SUSHI RICE FOR BUTTERY PILAF SHOULD MAKE THE WHOLE THING TASTE AS HEAVY AS A BRICK!

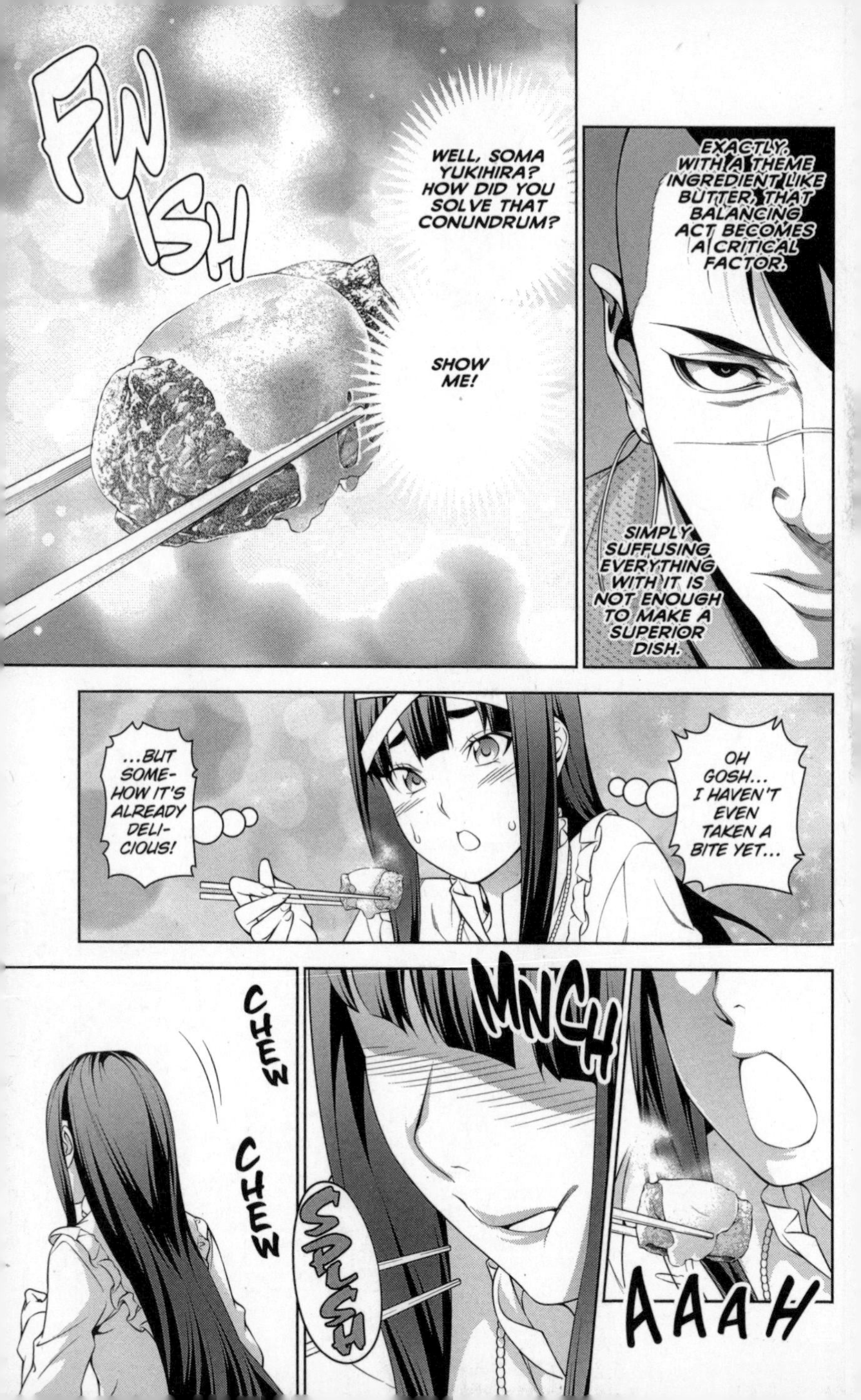
EXACTLY. WITH A THEME INGREDIENT LIKE BUTTER, THAT BALANCING ACT BECOMES A CRITICAL FACTOR.
SIMPLY SUFFUSING EVERYTHING WITH IT IS NOT ENOUGH TO MAKE A SUPERIOR DISH.
FWISH
WELL, SOMA YUKIHIRA? HOW DID YOU SOLVE THAT CONUNDRUM?
SHOW ME!
OH GOSH... I HAVEN'T EVEN TAKEN A BITE YET...
...BUT SOME-HOW IT'S ALREADY DELI-CIOUS!
AAAH
MNCH
CHEW
CHEW
CHEW

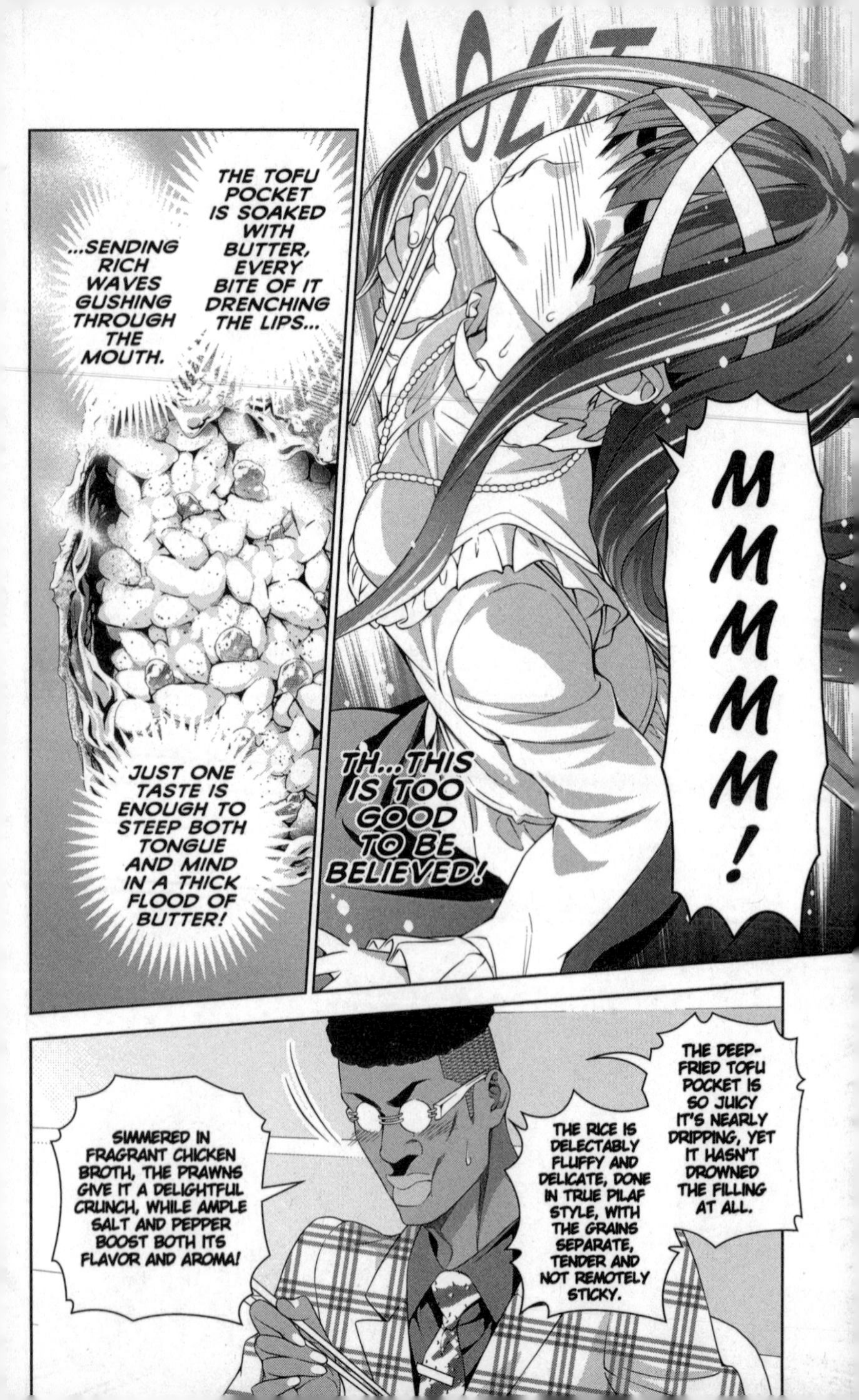
MMMMMM!
TH... THIS IS TOO GOOD TO BE BELIEVED!
THE TOFU POCKET IS SOAKED WITH BUTTER, EVERY BITE OF IT DRENCHING THE LIPS...
...SENDING RICH WAVES GUSHING THROUGH THE MOUTH.
JUST ONE TASTE IS ENOUGH TO STEEP BOTH TONGUE AND MIND IN A THICK FLOOD OF BUTTER!
THE DEEP-FRIED TOFU POCKET IS SO JUICY IT'S NEARLY DRIPPING, YET IT HASN'T DROWNED THE FILLING AT ALL.
THE RICE IS DELECTABLY FLUFFY AND DELICATE, DONE IN TRUE PILAF STYLE, WITH THE GRAINS SEPARATE, TENDER AND NOT REMOTELY STICKY.
SIMMERED IN FRAGRANT CHICKEN BROTH, THE PRAWNS GIVE IT A DELIGHTFUL CRUNCH, WHILE AMPLE SALT AND PEPPER BOOST BOTH ITS FLAVOR AND AROMA!

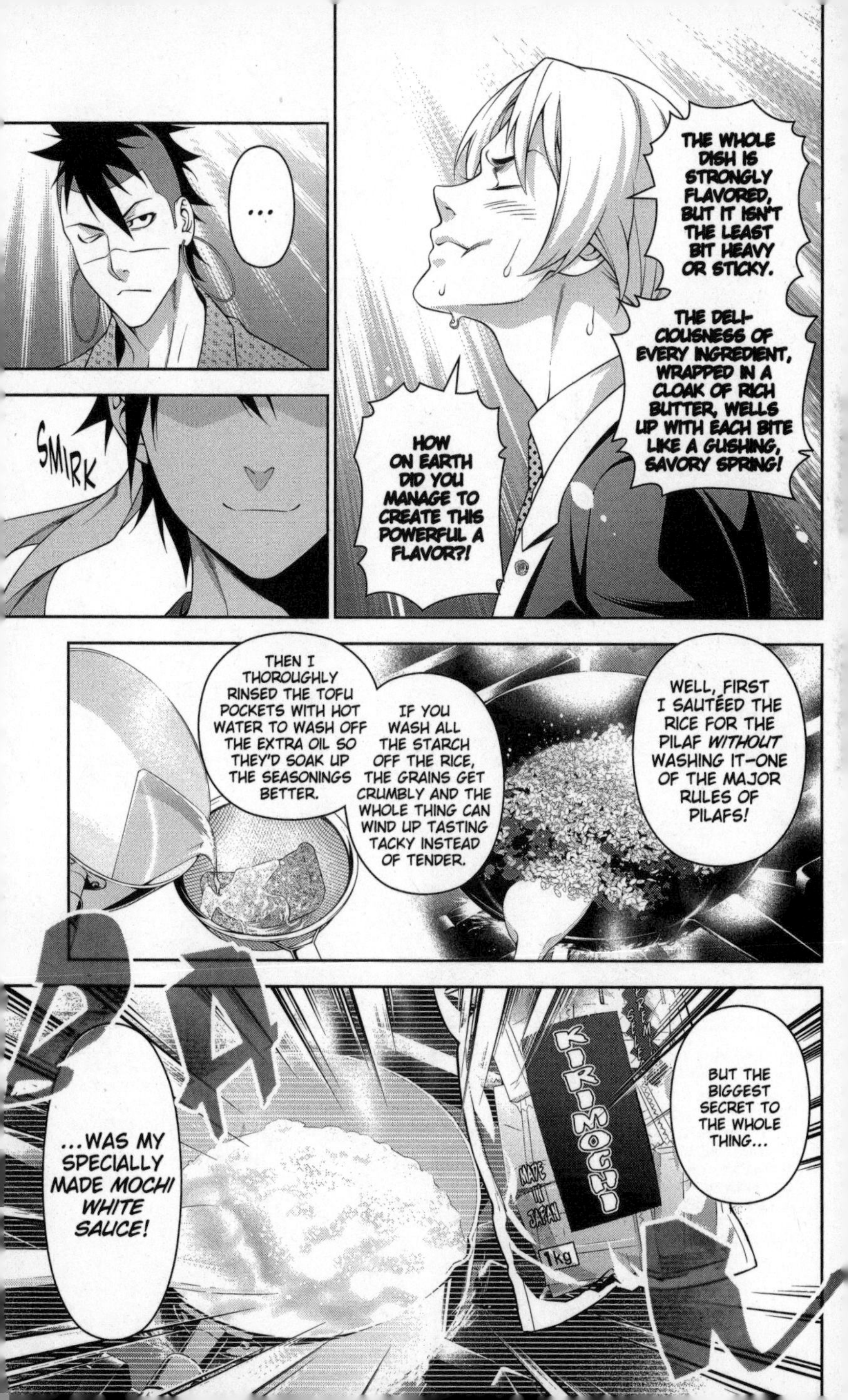
THE WHOLE DISH IS STRONGLY FLAVORED, BUT IT ISN'T THE LEAST BIT HEAVY OR STICKY.
THE DELI-CIOUSNESS OF EVERY INGREDIENT, WRAPPED IN A CLOAK OF RICH BUTTER, WELLS UP WITH EACH BITE LIKE A GUSHING, SAVORY SPRING!
HOW ON EARTH DID YOU MANAGE TO CREATE THIS POWERFUL A FLAVOR?!
...
SMIRK
WELL, FIRST I SAUTÉED THE RICE FOR THE PILAF *WITHOUT* WASHING IT—ONE OF THE MAJOR RULES OF PILAFS!
IF YOU WASH ALL THE STARCH OFF THE RICE, THE GRAINS GET CRUMBLY AND THE WHOLE THING CAN WIND UP TASTING TACKY INSTEAD OF TENDER.
THEN I THOROUGHLY RINSED THE TOFU POCKETS WITH HOT WATER TO WASH OFF THE EXTRA OIL SO THEY'D SOAK UP THE SEASONINGS BETTER.
BUT THE BIGGEST SECRET TO THE WHOLE THING...
KIRIMOCHI
MADE IN JAPAN
1kg
...WAS MY SPECIALLY MADE *MOCHI* WHITE SAUCE!

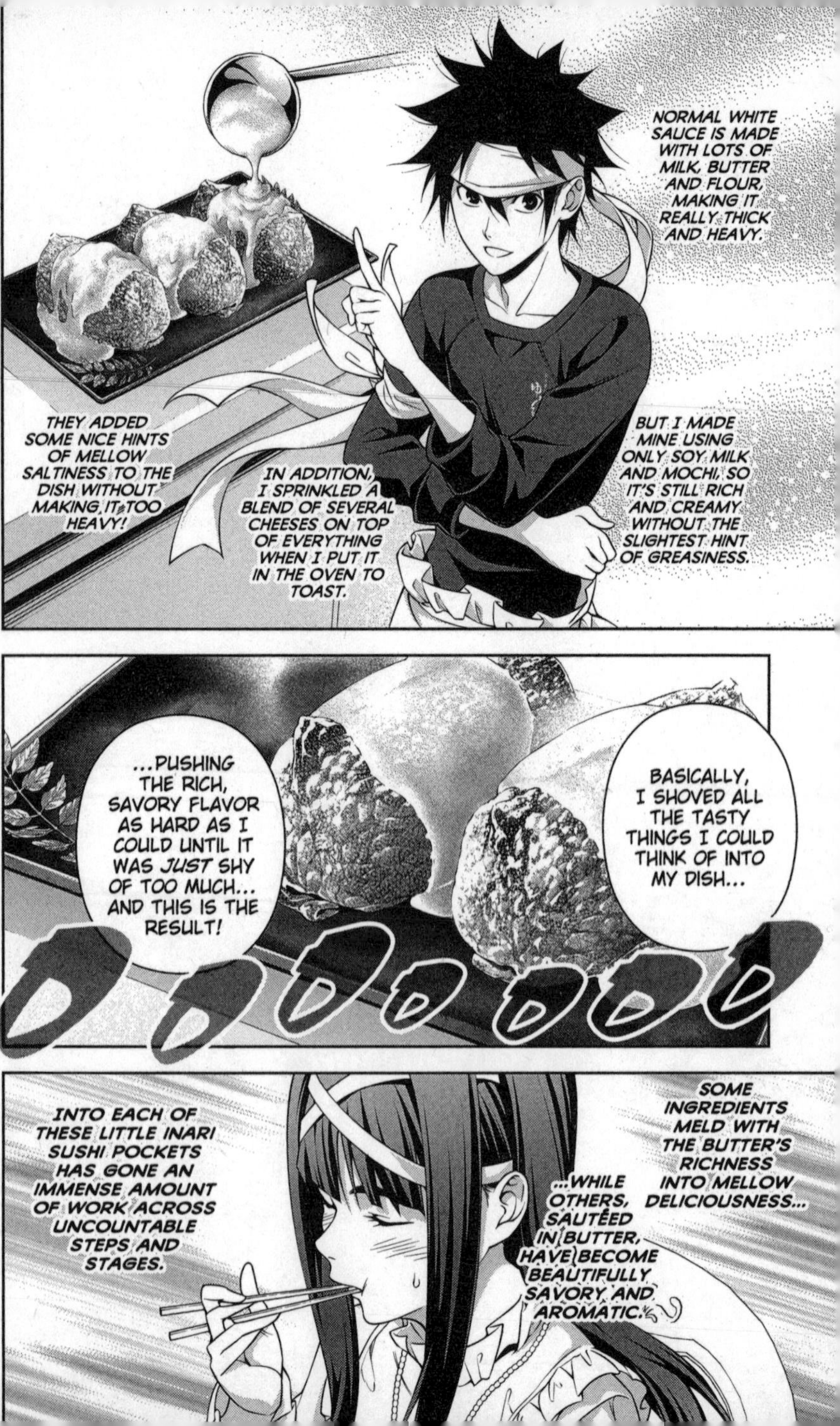
NORMAL WHITE SAUCE IS MADE WITH LOTS OF MILK, BUTTER AND FLOUR, MAKING IT REALLY THICK AND HEAVY.
BUT I MADE MINE USING ONLY SOY MILK AND MOCHI, SO IT'S STILL RICH AND CREAMY WITHOUT THE SLIGHTEST HINT OF GREASINESS.
IN ADDITION, I SPRINKLED A BLEND OF SEVERAL CHEESES ON TOP OF EVERYTHING WHEN I PUT IT IN THE OVEN TO TOAST.
THEY ADDED SOME NICE HINTS OF MELLOW SALTINESS TO THE DISH WITHOUT MAKING IT TOO HEAVY!
BASICALLY, I SHOVED ALL THE TASTY THINGS I COULD THINK OF INTO MY DISH...
...PUSHING THE RICH, SAVORY FLAVOR AS HARD AS I COULD UNTIL IT WAS *JUST* SHY OF TOO MUCH... AND THIS IS THE RESULT!
SOME INGREDIENTS MELD WITH THE BUTTER'S RICHNESS INTO MELLOW DELICIOUSNESS...
...WHILE OTHERS, SAUTÉED IN BUTTER, HAVE BECOME BEAUTIFULLY SAVORY AND AROMATIC.
INTO EACH OF THESE LITTLE INARI SUSHI POCKETS HAS GONE AN IMMENSE AMOUNT OF WORK ACROSS UNCOUNTABLE STEPS AND STAGES.

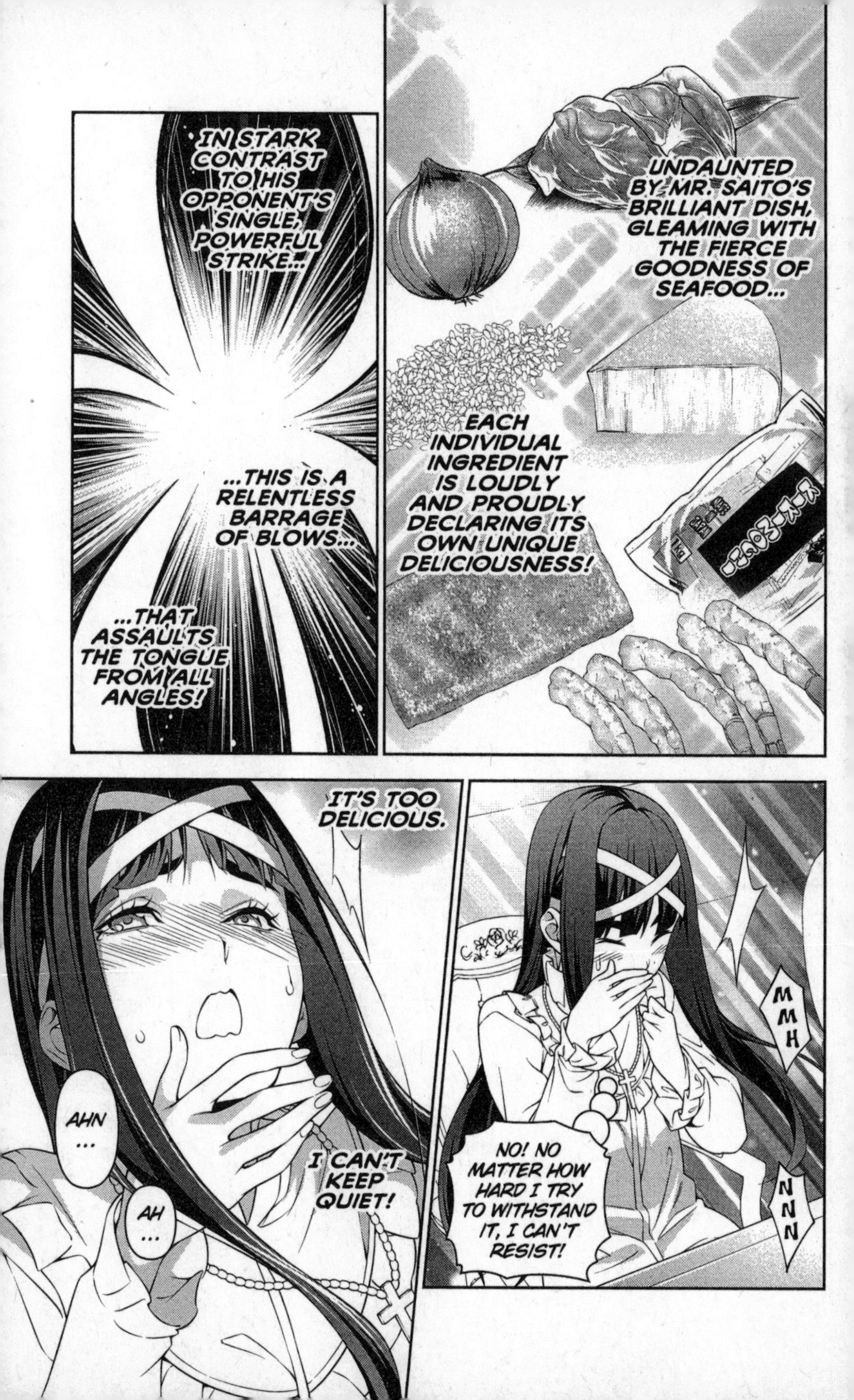
UNDAUNTED BY MR. SAITO'S BRILLIANT DISH, GLEAMING WITH THE FIERCE GOODNESS OF SEAFOOD...
EACH INDIVIDUAL INGREDIENT IS LOUDLY AND PROUDLY DECLARING ITS OWN UNIQUE DELICIOUSNESS!
IN STARK CONTRAST TO HIS OPPONENT'S SINGLE, POWERFUL STRIKE...
...THIS IS A RELENTLESS BARRAGE OF BLOWS...
...THAT ASSAULTS THE TONGUE FROM ALL ANGLES!
MMH
NO! NO MATTER HOW HARD I TRY TO WITHSTAND IT, I CAN'T RESIST!
NNN
IT'S TOO DELICIOUS.
I CAN'T KEEP QUIET!
AHN...
AH...

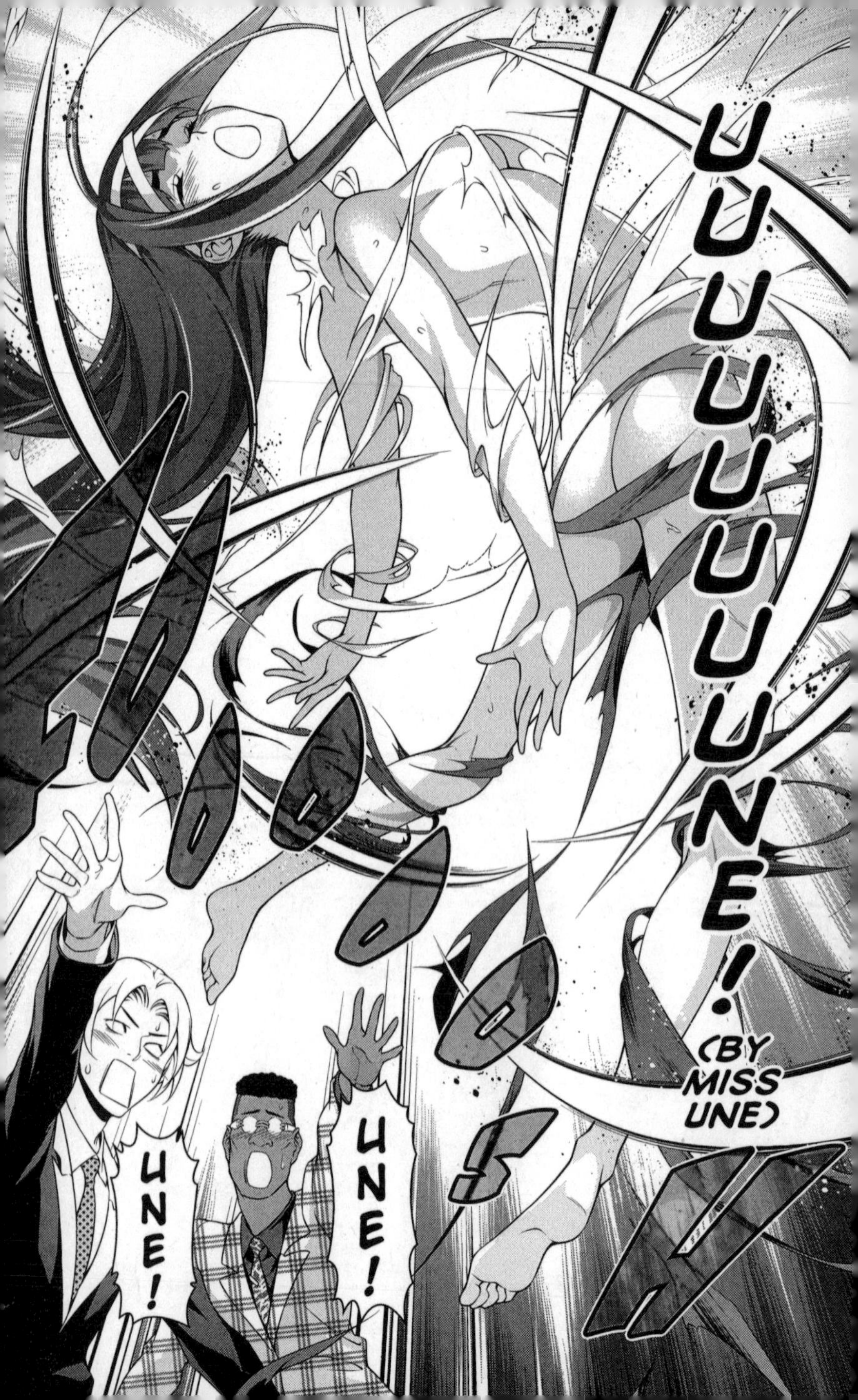
UUUUUUUUNE!
(BY MISS UNE)
UNE!
UNE!

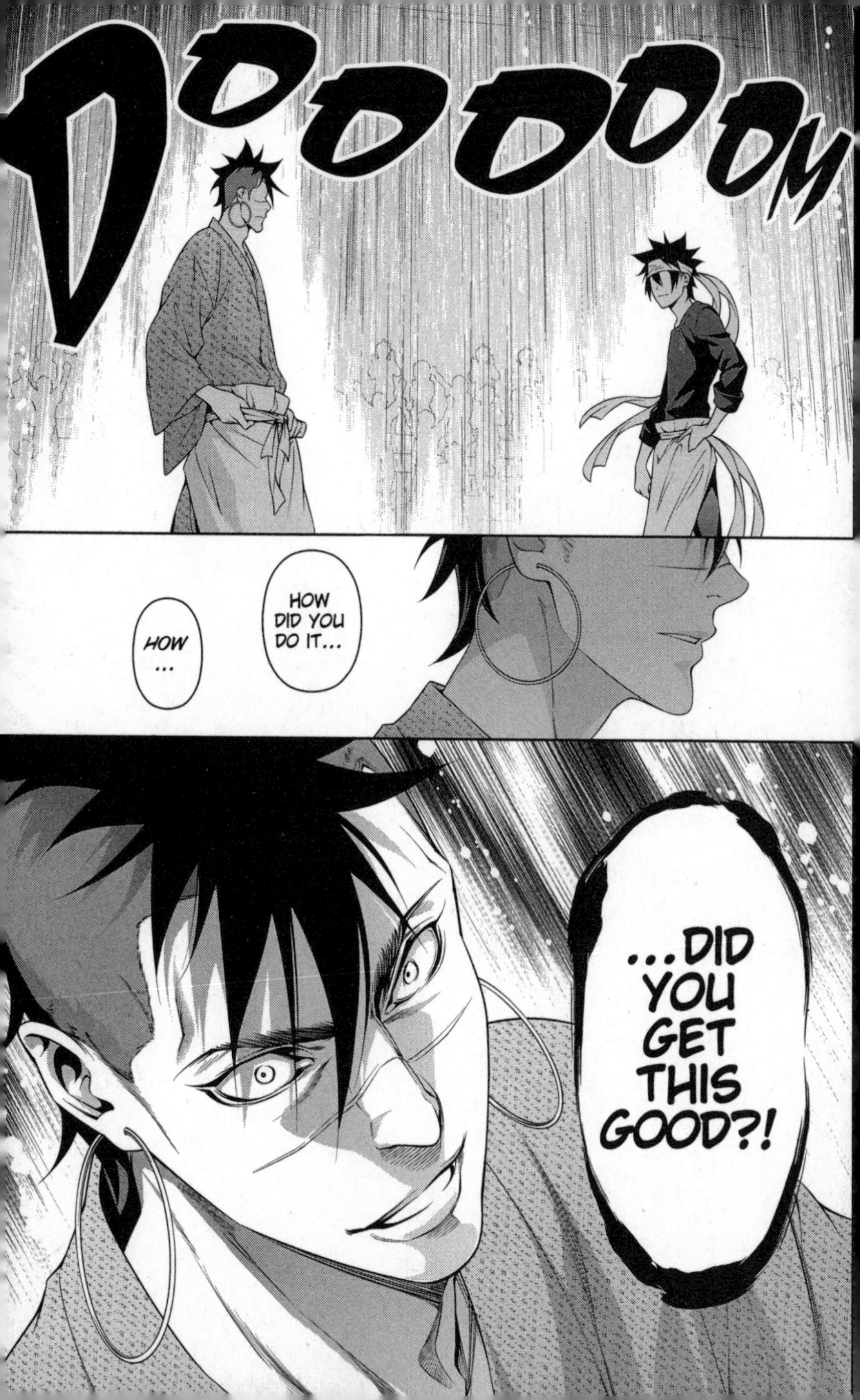
DOOOOOM
HOW DID YOU DO IT...
HOW ...
...DID YOU GET THIS GOOD?!

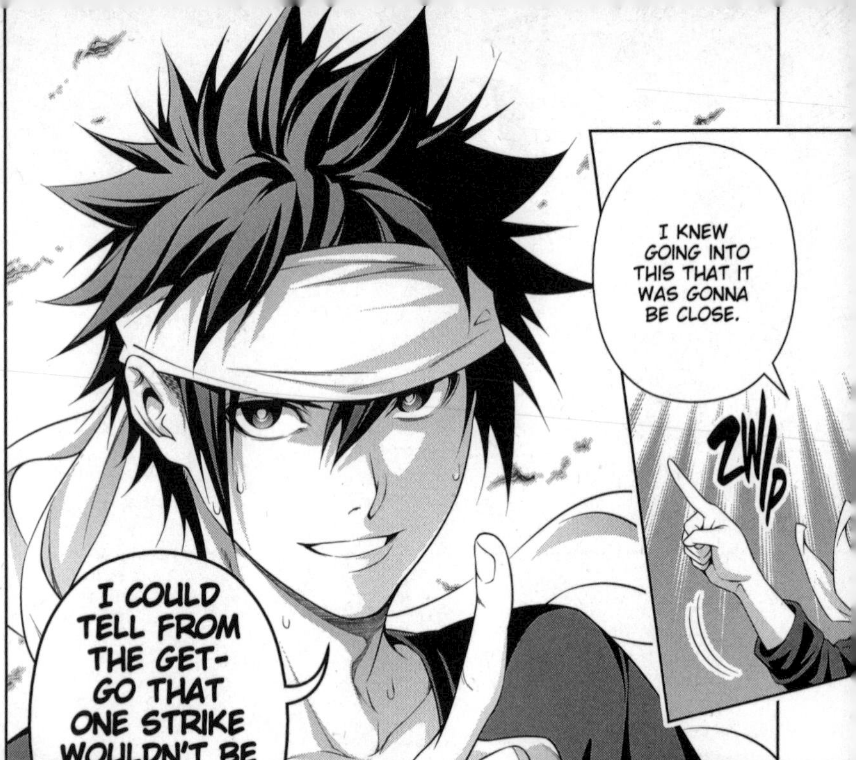
I KNEW GOING INTO THIS THAT IT WAS GONNA BE CLOSE.
ZWIP
I COULD TELL FROM THE GET-GO THAT ONE STRIKE WOULDN'T BE ENOUGH TO BEAT YOU, SENPAI.

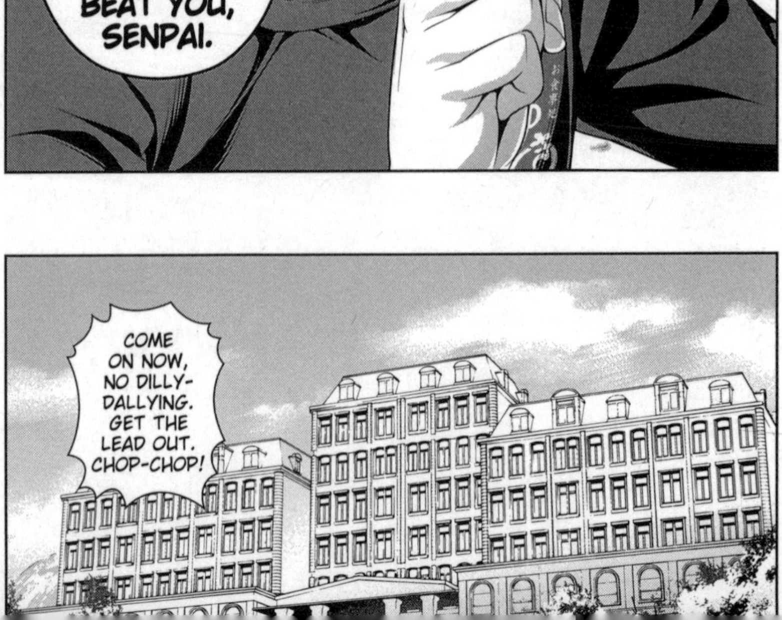
COME ON NOW, NO DILLY-DALLYING. GET THE LEAD OUT. CHOP-CHOP!

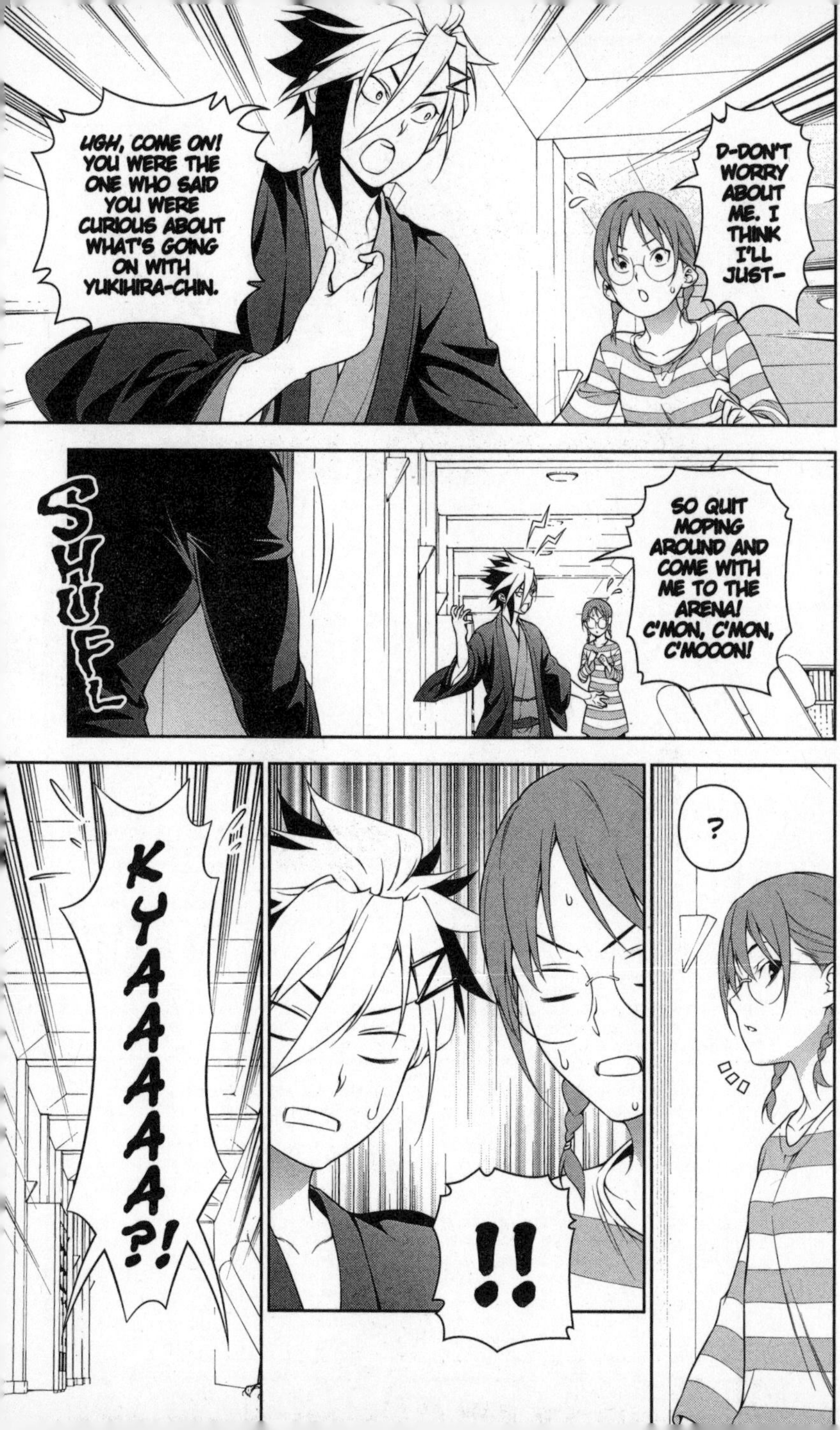
D-DON'T WORRY ABOUT ME. I THINK I'LL JUST-
UGH, COME ON! YOU WERE THE ONE WHO SAID YOU WERE CURIOUS ABOUT WHAT'S GOING ON WITH YUKIHIRA-CHIN.
SO QUIT MOPING AROUND AND COME WITH ME TO THE ARENA! C'MON, C'MON, C'MOOON!
SHUFL
?
!!
KYAAAAAAA?!

ARTIST: YUTO TSUKUDA RECIPE BY: YUKI MORISAKI

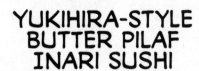

VOLUME 28
SPECIAL SUPPLEMENT!

PRACTICAL RECIPE #3

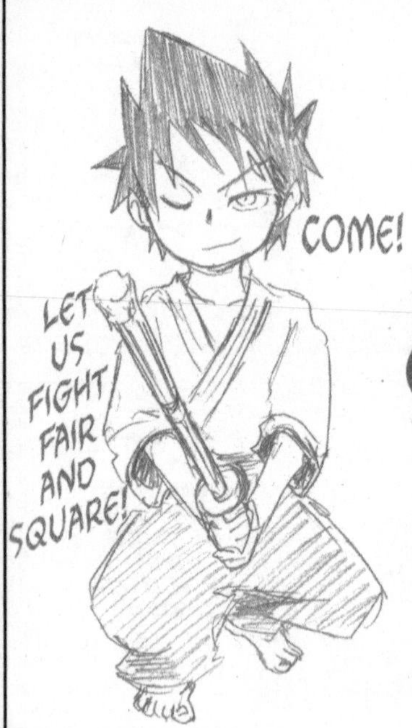
COME!
LET US FIGHT FAIR AND SQUARE!

YUKIHIRA-STYLE BUTTER PILAF INARI SUSHI

SIMPLIFIED HOME VERSION

● INGREDIENTS ●
(MAKES 12)

★ PILAF

- 300 GRAMS UNCOOKED RICE
- 1 CHICKEN THIGH
- 150 GRAMS SEAFOOD MIX
- 1/4 ONION
- 2 TABLESPOONS BUTTER, DIVIDED

[A]
- 1 TEASPOON GRANULATED CONSOMMÉ
- 2/3 TEASPOON SALT
- 400 CC WATER
- BLACK PEPPER

★ INARI SUSHI POCKETS

- 6 INARI-AGE TOFU POCKETS

[B]
- 4 TABLESPOONS EACH SOY SAUCE, SUGAR, MIRIN
- 300 CC DASHI STOCK

★ MOCHI WHITE SAUCE

- 2 BLOCKS KIRI MOCHI
- 400 CC SOY MILK
- BLACK PEPPER

1. **★MAKE THE PILAF★**
DEFROST THE SEAFOOD MIX. CUT THE CHICKEN THIGH INTO 1 CM CUBES. MINCE THE ONION.

2. HEAT 1 TABLESPOON OF BUTTER IN A FRYING PAN AND SAUTÉ THE ONIONS. ONCE THEY ARE TRANSLUCENT, ADD THE SEAFOOD MIX AND CHICKEN AND THEN SAUTÉ. ADD THE UNCOOKED RICE AND MIX UNTIL EVERYTHING IS THOROUGHLY COATED IN BUTTER.

3. MIX (A) TOGETHER, POUR OVER (2) AND BRING TO A BOIL. REDUCE THE HEAT TO LOW AND COVER, LETTING IT SIMMER FOR 15 MINUTES. THEN TURN THE HEAT OFF COMPLETELY AND LET STEAM FOR ANOTHER 10 MINUTES. ADD THE OTHER TABLESPOON OF BUTTER AND MIX TOGETHER.

4. WHILE THE PILAF IS STEAMING, MAKE THE INARI SUSHI POCKETS. RINSE THE INARI-AGE TOFU WITH HOT WATER TO REMOVE MUCH OF THE OIL, AND THEN CUT EACH IN HALF AND OPEN THE POCKETS. PUT THE POCKETS AND (B) IN A POT AND BRING TO A BOIL. LET REDUCE FOR 15 MINUTES OR UNTIL ALL THE LIQUID IS GONE.

5. DIVIDE THE PILAF FROM (3) INTO 12 EQUAL PORTIONS. FORM INTO ROUGH BALLS AND STUFF EACH INTO AN INARI-AGE POCKET. FOLD THE OPEN END OF THE POCKET OVER AND PLATE FACEDOWN.

6. **★MAKE THE APPLE FILLING★**
CHOP THE KIRI-MOCHI BLOCKS INTO SMALL PIECES. PUT IN A POT OVER MEDIUM HEAT AND POUR IN THE SOY MILK. COOK UNTIL THE MOCHI HAS COMPLETELY MELTED INTO THE SOY MILK, STIRRING FREQUENTLY. SEASON TO TASTE WITH BLACK PEPPER.

7. DRIZZLE (6) OVER (5) AND TOP GENEROUSLY WITH PIZZA CHEESE. PLACE UNDER THE BROILER FOR 10 MINUTES OR UNTIL THE CHEESE IS MELTED AND GOLDEN BROWN. DONE!

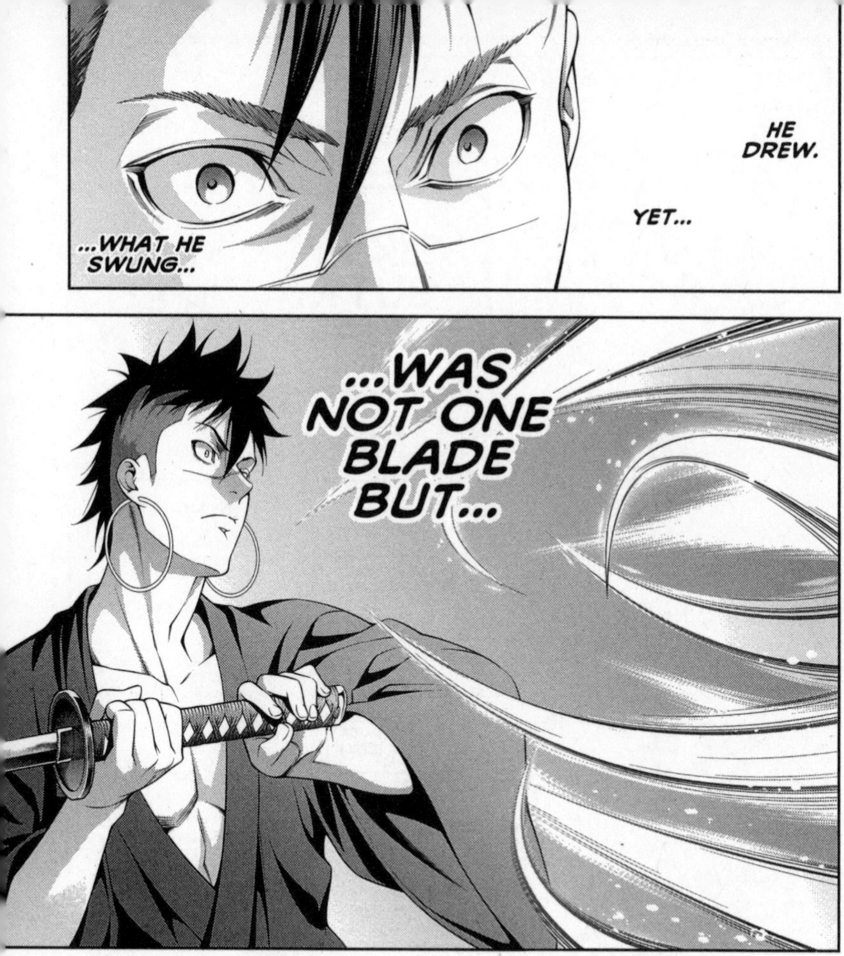
HE DREW.
YET...
...WHAT HE SWUNG...
...WAS NOT ONE BLADE BUT...

243 FIRST-YEAR KID

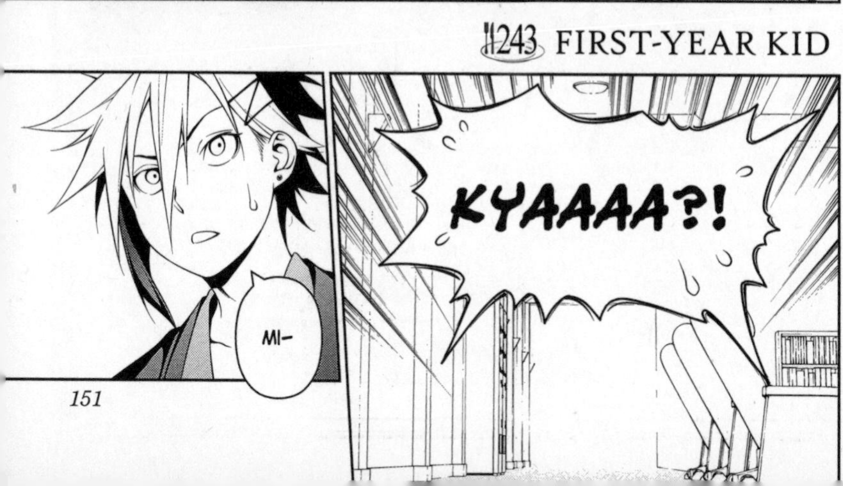
KYAAAA?!
MI-

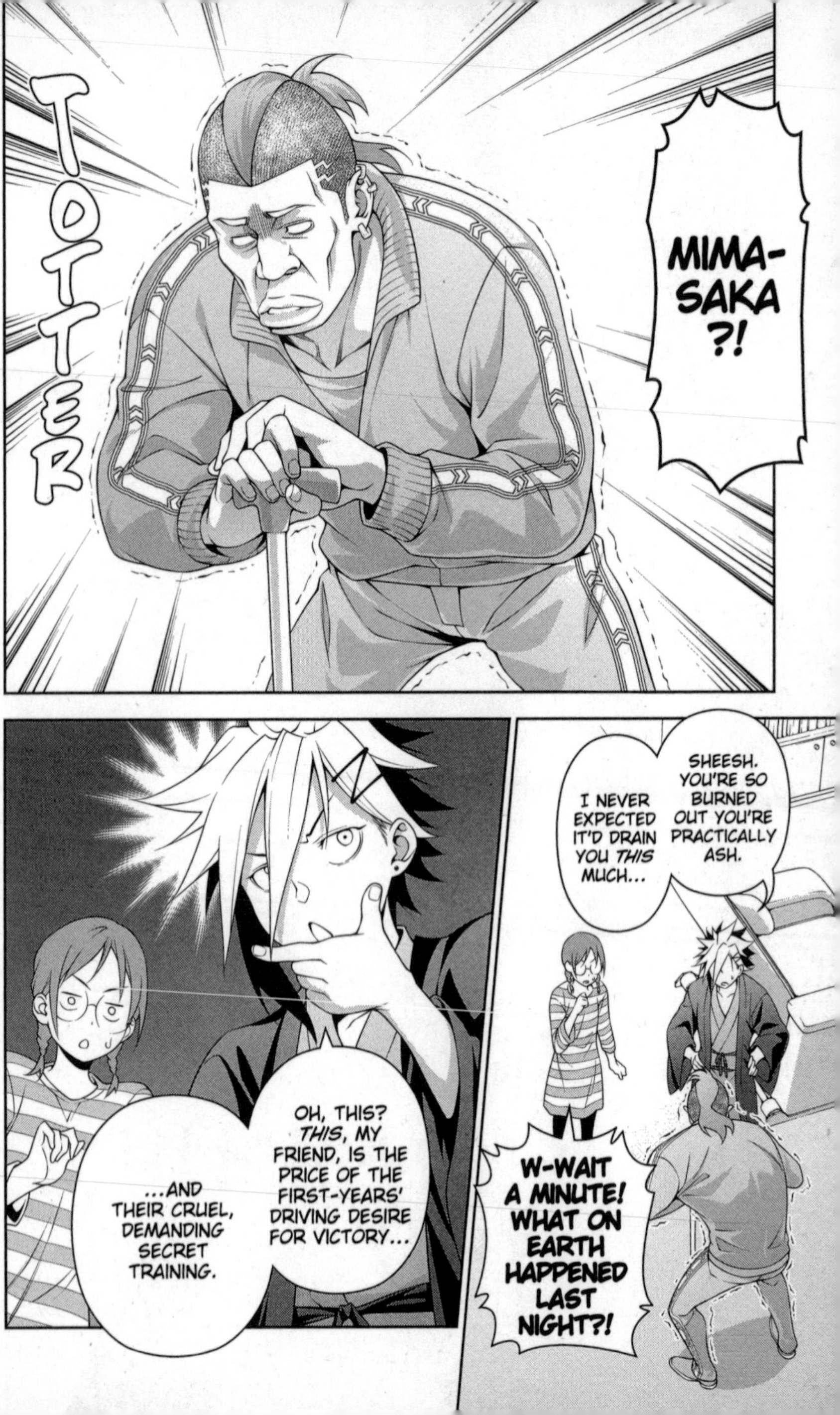
MIMA-SAKA?!
TOTTER
SHEESH. YOU'RE SO BURNED OUT YOU'RE PRACTICALLY ASH.
I NEVER EXPECTED IT'D DRAIN YOU *THIS* MUCH...
W-WAIT A MINUTE! WHAT ON EARTH HAPPENED LAST NIGHT?!
OH, THIS? *THIS*, MY FRIEND, IS THE PRICE OF THE FIRST-YEARS' DRIVING DESIRE FOR VICTORY...
...AND THEIR CRUEL, DEMANDING SECRET TRAINING.

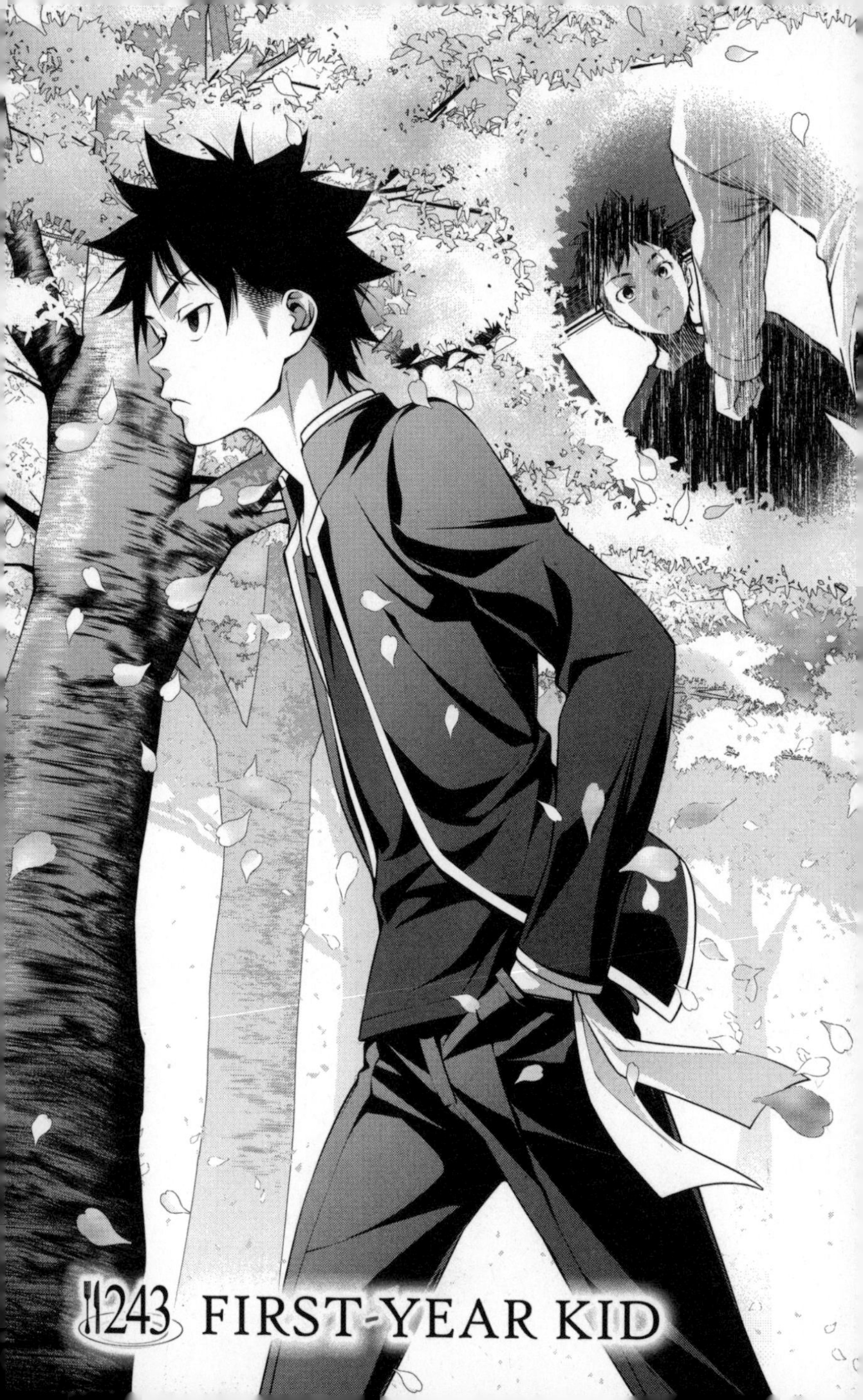

243 FIRST-YEAR KID

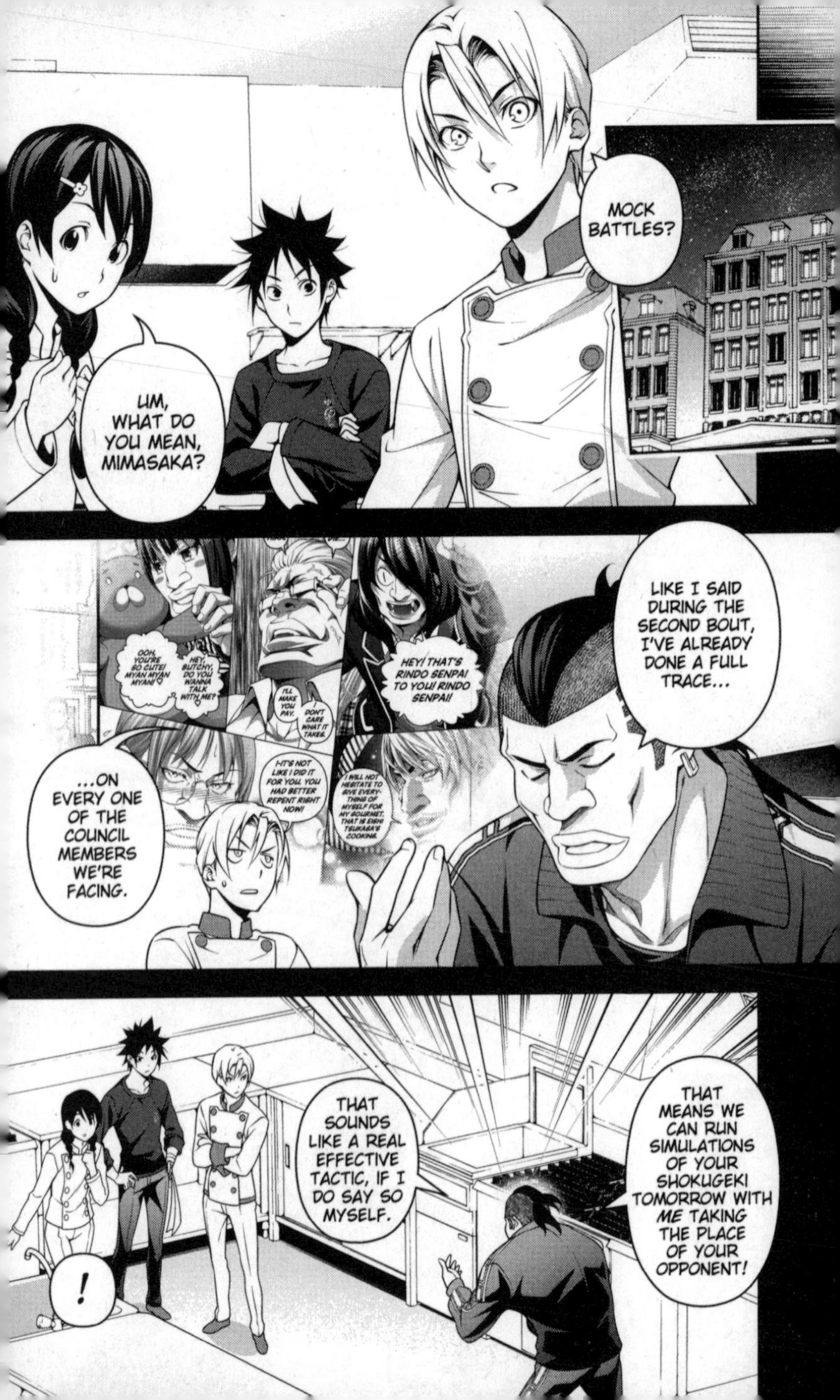
MOCK BATTLES?
UM, WHAT DO YOU MEAN, MIMASAKA?
LIKE I SAID DURING THE SECOND BOUT, I'VE ALREADY DONE A FULL TRACE...
HEY! THAT'S RINDO SENPAI TO YOU! RINDO SENPAI!
I'LL MAKE YOU PAY.
I DON'T CARE WHAT IT TAKES.
HEY, BUTCHY, DO YOU WANNA TALK WITH ME? ♡
OOH, YOU'RE SO CUTE! MYAN MYAN MYAN! ♡
I WILL NOT HESITATE TO GIVE EVERYTHING OF MYSELF FOR MY GOURMET. THAT IS EISHI TSUKASA'S COOKING.
I-IT'S NOT LIKE I DID IT FOR YOU. YOU HAD BETTER REPENT RIGHT NOW!
...ON EVERY ONE OF THE COUNCIL MEMBERS WE'RE FACING.
THAT MEANS WE CAN RUN SIMULATIONS OF YOUR SHOKUGEKI TOMORROW WITH *ME* TAKING THE PLACE OF YOUR OPPONENT!
THAT SOUNDS LIKE A REAL EFFECTIVE TACTIC, IF I DO SAY SO MYSELF.
!

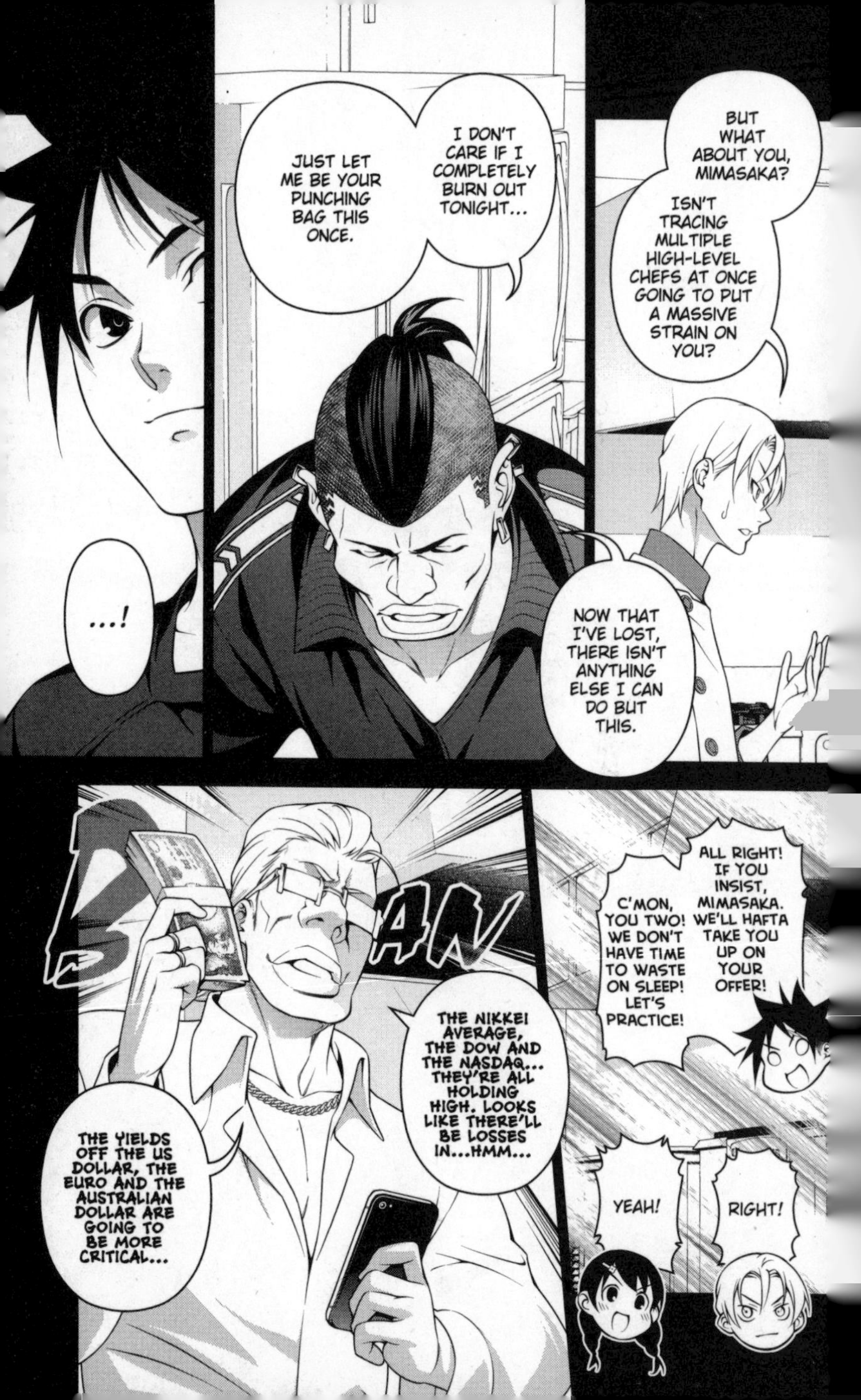
BUT WHAT ABOUT YOU, MIMASAKA?
ISN'T TRACING MULTIPLE HIGH-LEVEL CHEFS AT ONCE GOING TO PUT A MASSIVE STRAIN ON YOU?
I DON'T CARE IF I COMPLETELY BURN OUT TONIGHT...
JUST LET ME BE YOUR PUNCHING BAG THIS ONCE.
NOW THAT I'VE LOST, THERE ISN'T ANYTHING ELSE I CAN DO BUT THIS.
...!
ALL RIGHT! IF YOU INSIST, MIMASAKA. WE'LL HAFTA TAKE YOU UP ON YOUR OFFER!
C'MON, YOU TWO! WE DON'T HAVE TIME TO WASTE ON SLEEP! LET'S PRACTICE!
RIGHT!
YEAH!
THE NIKKEI AVERAGE, THE DOW AND THE NASDAQ... THEY'RE ALL HOLDING HIGH. LOOKS LIKE THERE'LL BE LOSSES IN...HMM...
THE YIELDS OFF THE US DOLLAR, THE EURO AND THE AUSTRALIAN DOLLAR ARE GOING TO BE MORE CRITICAL...

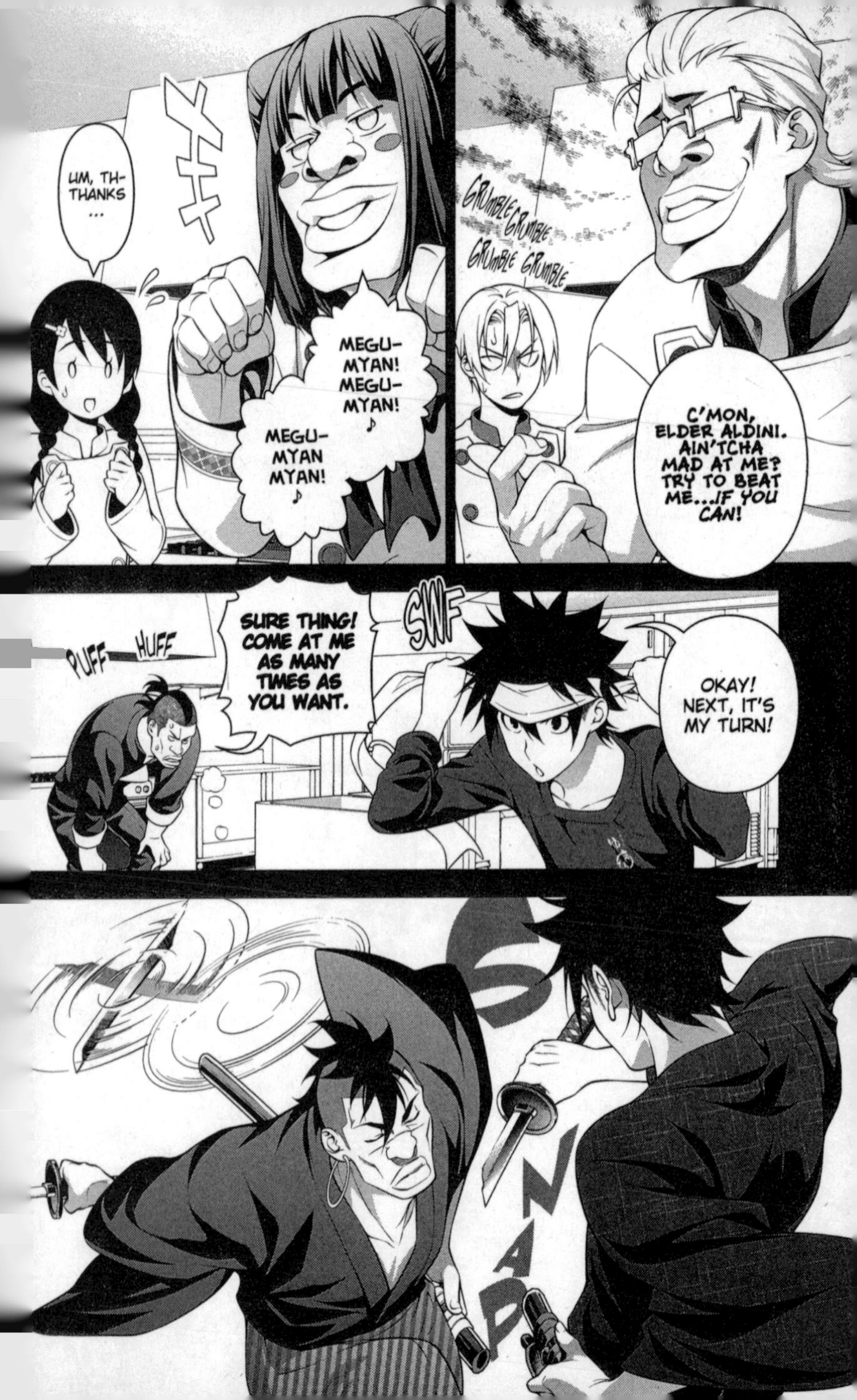
GRUMBLE GRUMBLE
GRUMBLE GRUMBLE
C'MON, ELDER ALDINI. AIN'TCHA MAD AT ME? TRY TO BEAT ME...IF YOU CAN!
MEGU-MYAN! MEGU-MYAN! ♪
MEGU-MYAN MYAN! ♪
UM, TH-THANKS...
OKAY! NEXT, IT'S MY TURN!
SWF
SURE THING! COME AT ME AS MANY TIMES AS YOU WANT.
PUFF HUFF
NAP

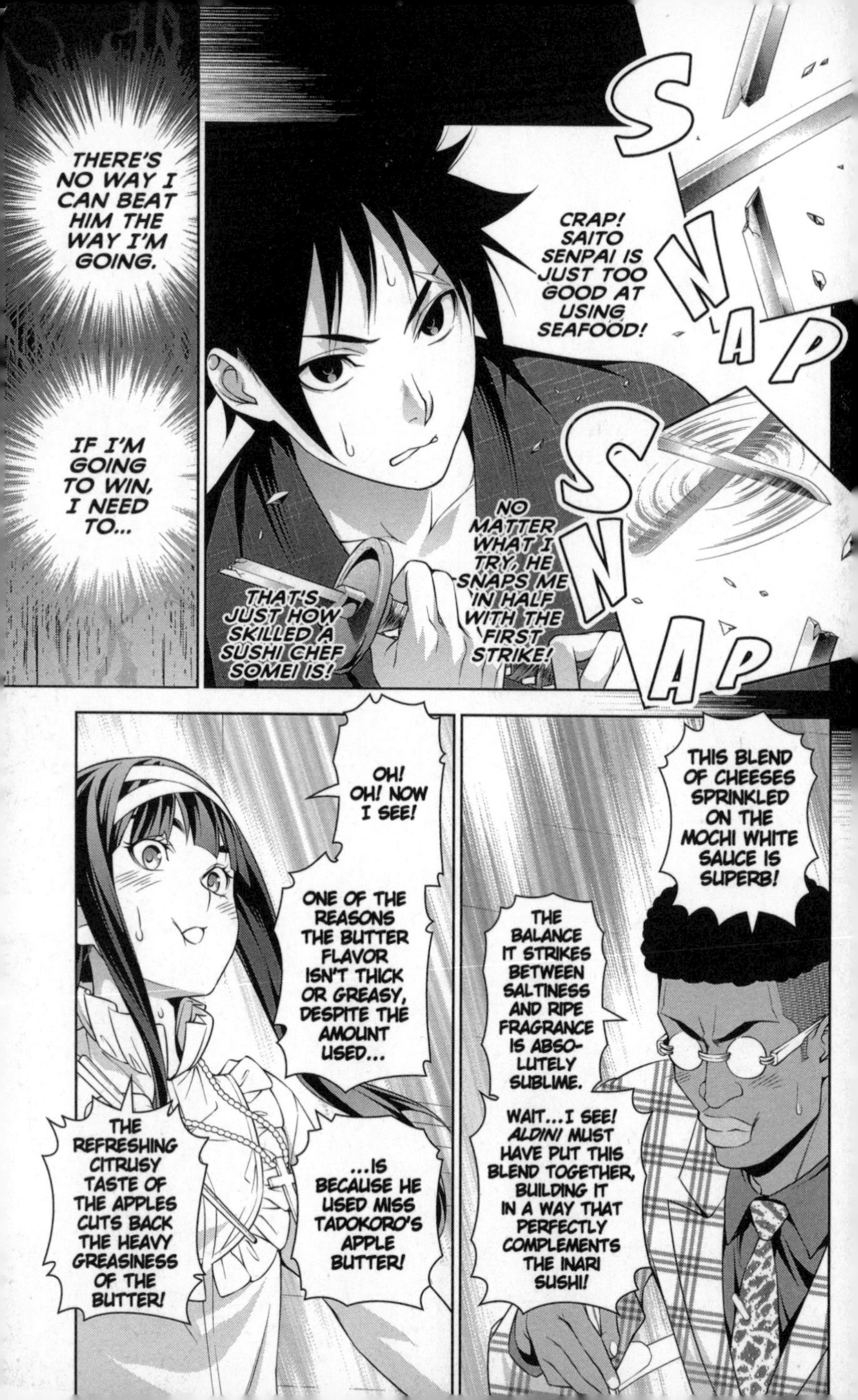
SNAP
CRAP! SAITO SENPAI IS JUST TOO GOOD AT USING SEAFOOD!
SNAP
NO MATTER WHAT I TRY, HE SNAPS ME IN HALF WITH THE FIRST STRIKE!
THAT'S JUST HOW SKILLED A SUSHI CHEF SOMEI IS!
THERE'S NO WAY I CAN BEAT HIM THE WAY I'M GOING.
IF I'M GOING TO WIN, I NEED TO...
THIS BLEND OF CHEESES SPRINKLED ON THE MOCHI WHITE SAUCE IS SUPERB!
THE BALANCE IT STRIKES BETWEEN SALTINESS AND RIPE FRAGRANCE IS ABSO-LUTELY SUBLIME.
WAIT...I SEE! *ALDINI* MUST HAVE PUT THIS BLEND TOGETHER, BUILDING IT IN A WAY THAT PERFECTLY COMPLEMENTS THE INARI SUSHI!
OH! OH! NOW I SEE!
ONE OF THE REASONS THE BUTTER FLAVOR ISN'T THICK OR GREASY, DESPITE THE AMOUNT USED...
...IS BECAUSE HE USED MISS TADOKORO'S APPLE BUTTER!
THE REFRESHING CITRUSY TASTE OF THE APPLES CUTS BACK THE HEAVY GREASINESS OF THE BUTTER!

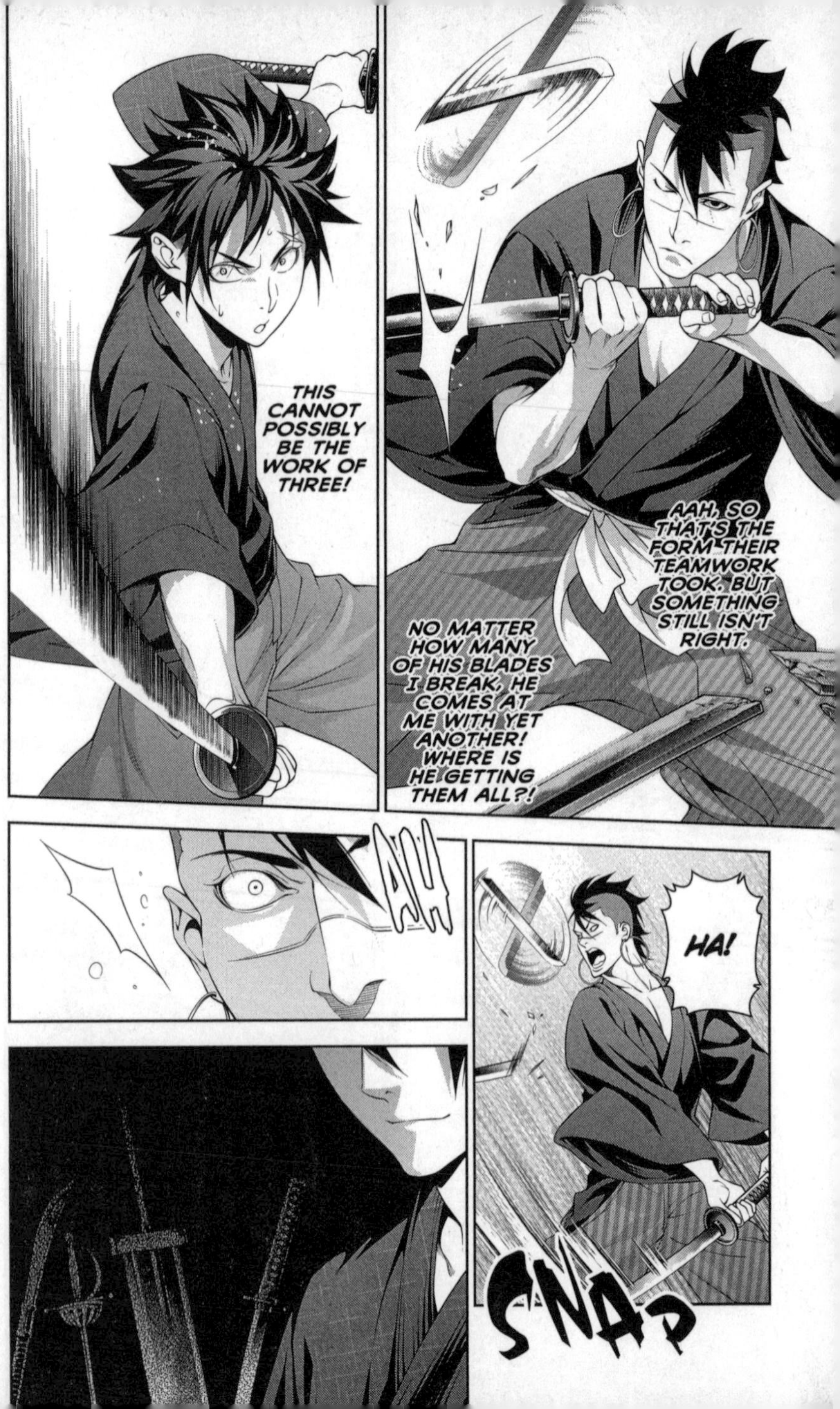
AAH, SO THAT'S THE FORM THEIR TEAMWORK TOOK. BUT SOMETHING STILL ISN'T RIGHT.
NO MATTER HOW MANY OF HIS BLADES I BREAK, HE COMES AT ME WITH YET ANOTHER! WHERE IS HE GETTING THEM ALL?!
THIS CANNOT POSSIBLY BE THE WORK OF THREE!
HA!
SNAP
AAH

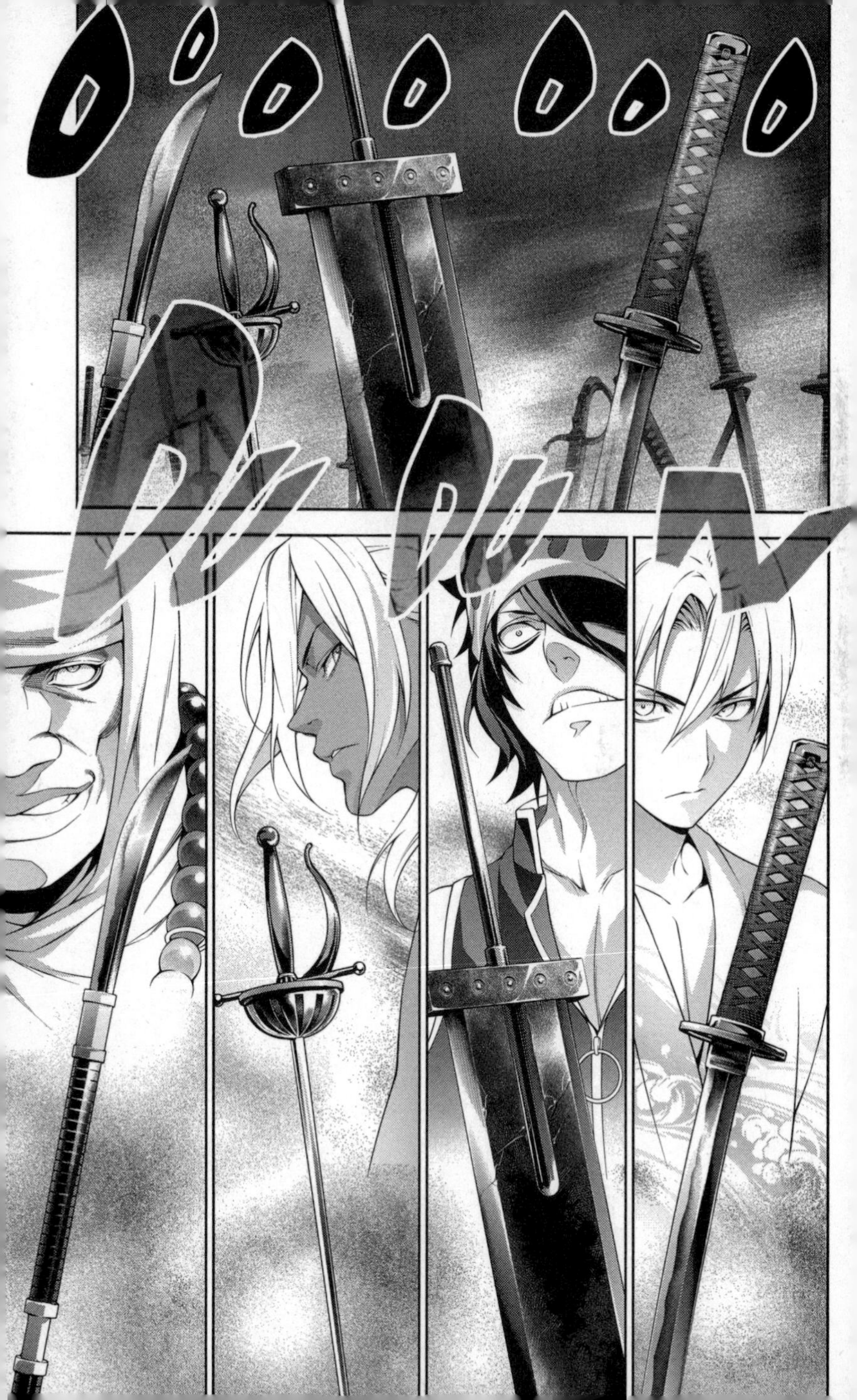

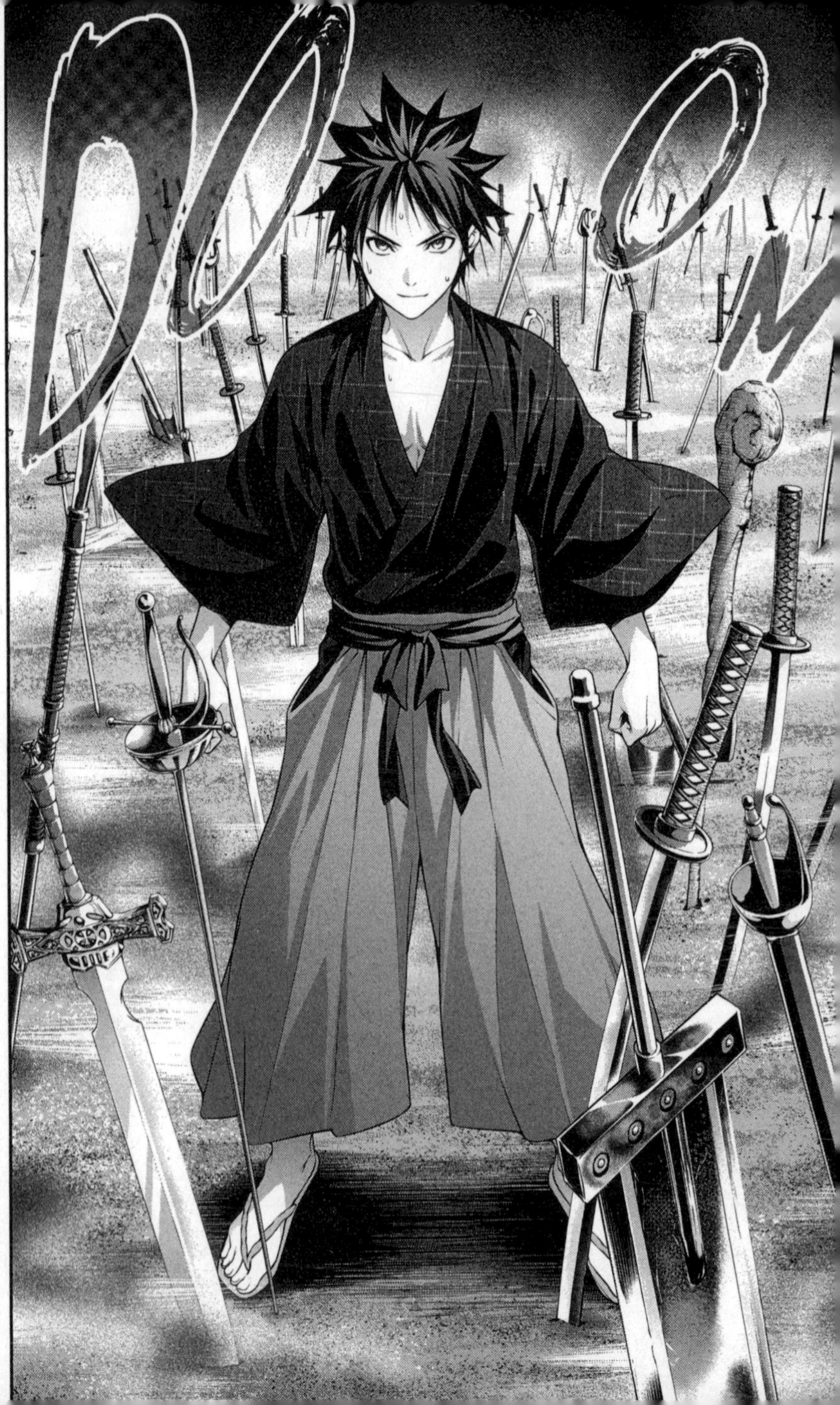
DOOM

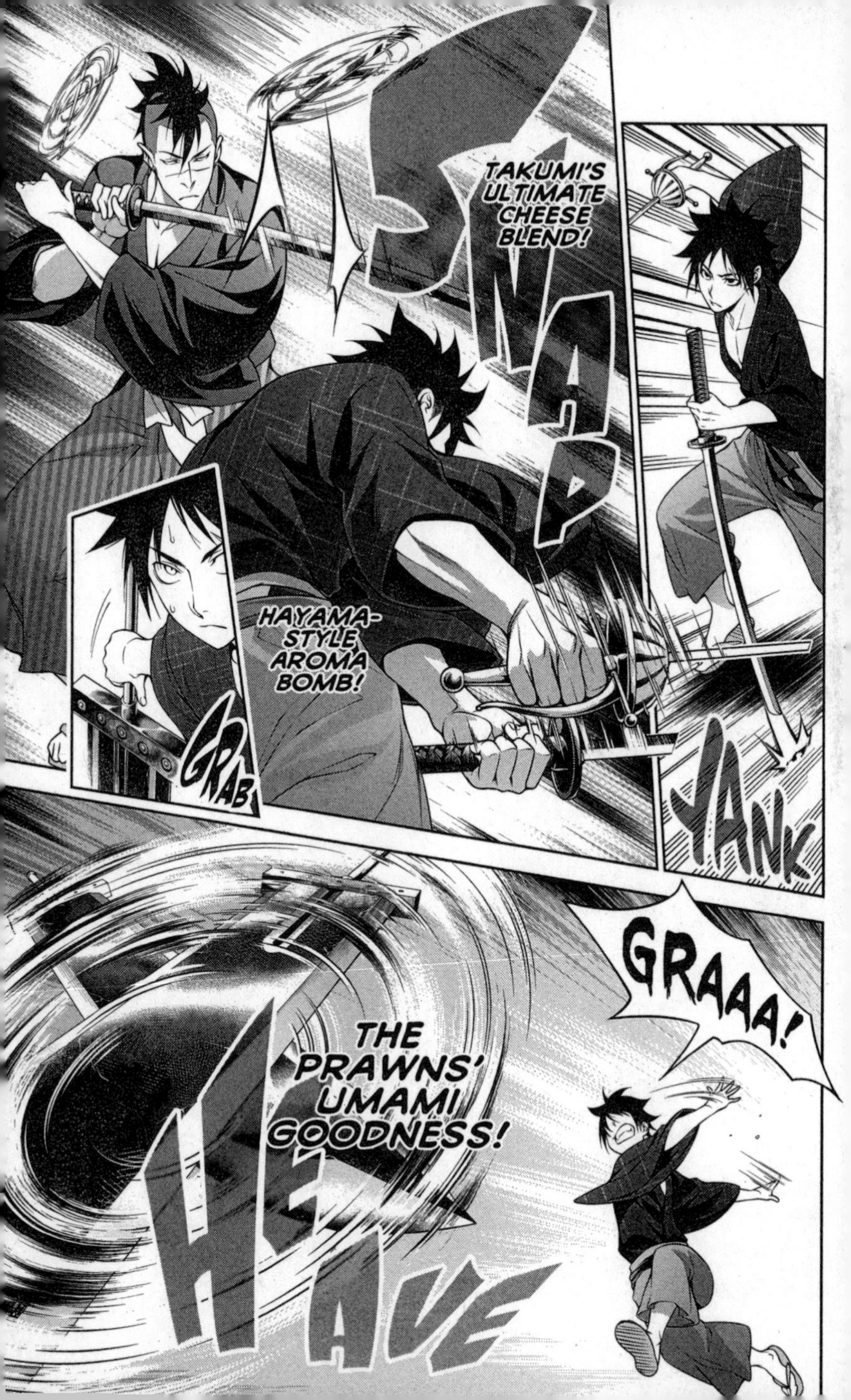
YANK
TAKUMI'S ULTIMATE CHEESE BLEND!
HAYAMA-STYLE AROMA BOMB!
GRAB
GRAAA!
THE PRAWNS' UMAMI GOODNESS!
HEAVE

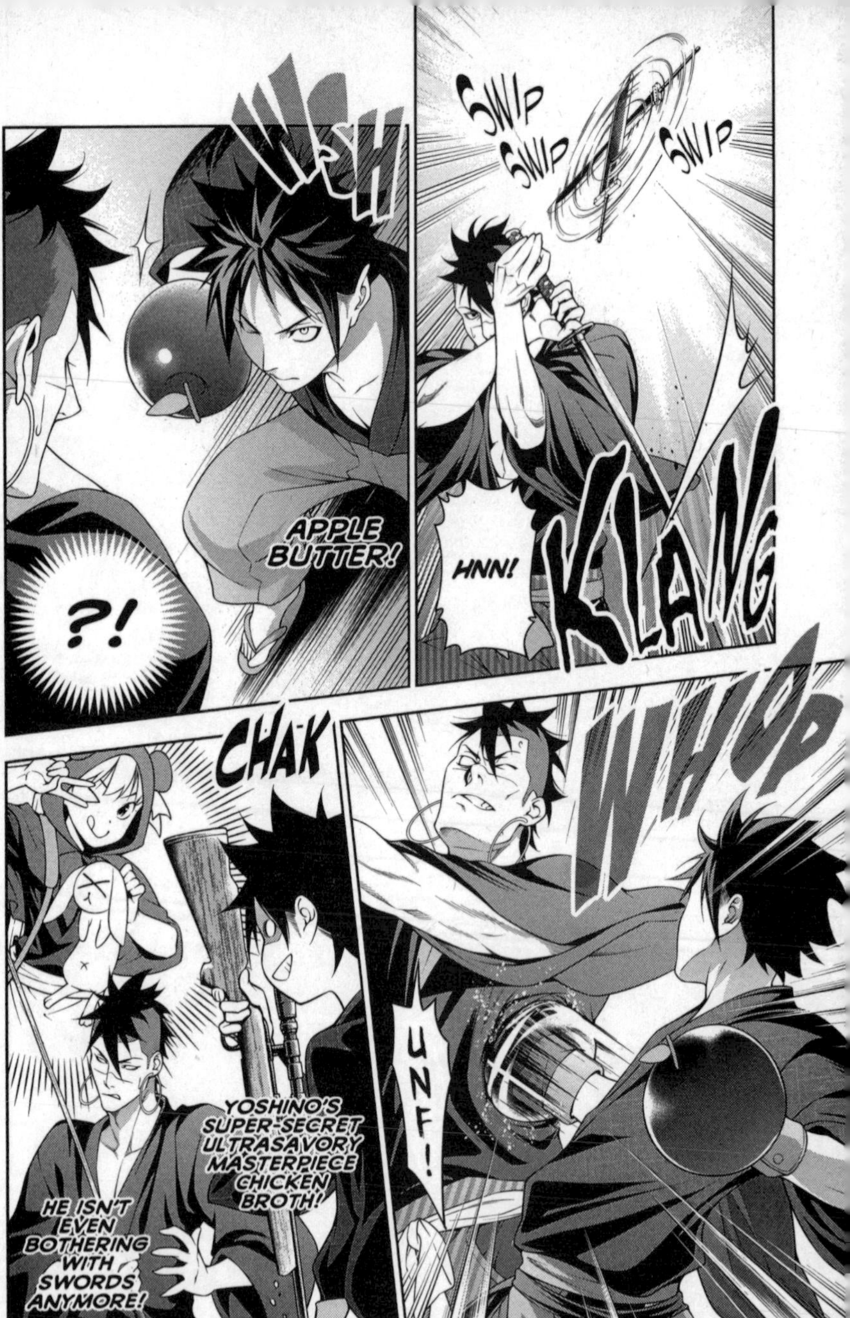
SWIP
SWIP
SWIP
HNN!
KLANG
WHSH
APPLE BUTTER!
?!
WHUP
UNF!
CHAK
YOSHINO'S SUPER-SECRET ULTRASAVORY MASTERPIECE CHICKEN BROTH!
HE ISN'T EVEN BOTHERING WITH SWORDS ANYMORE!

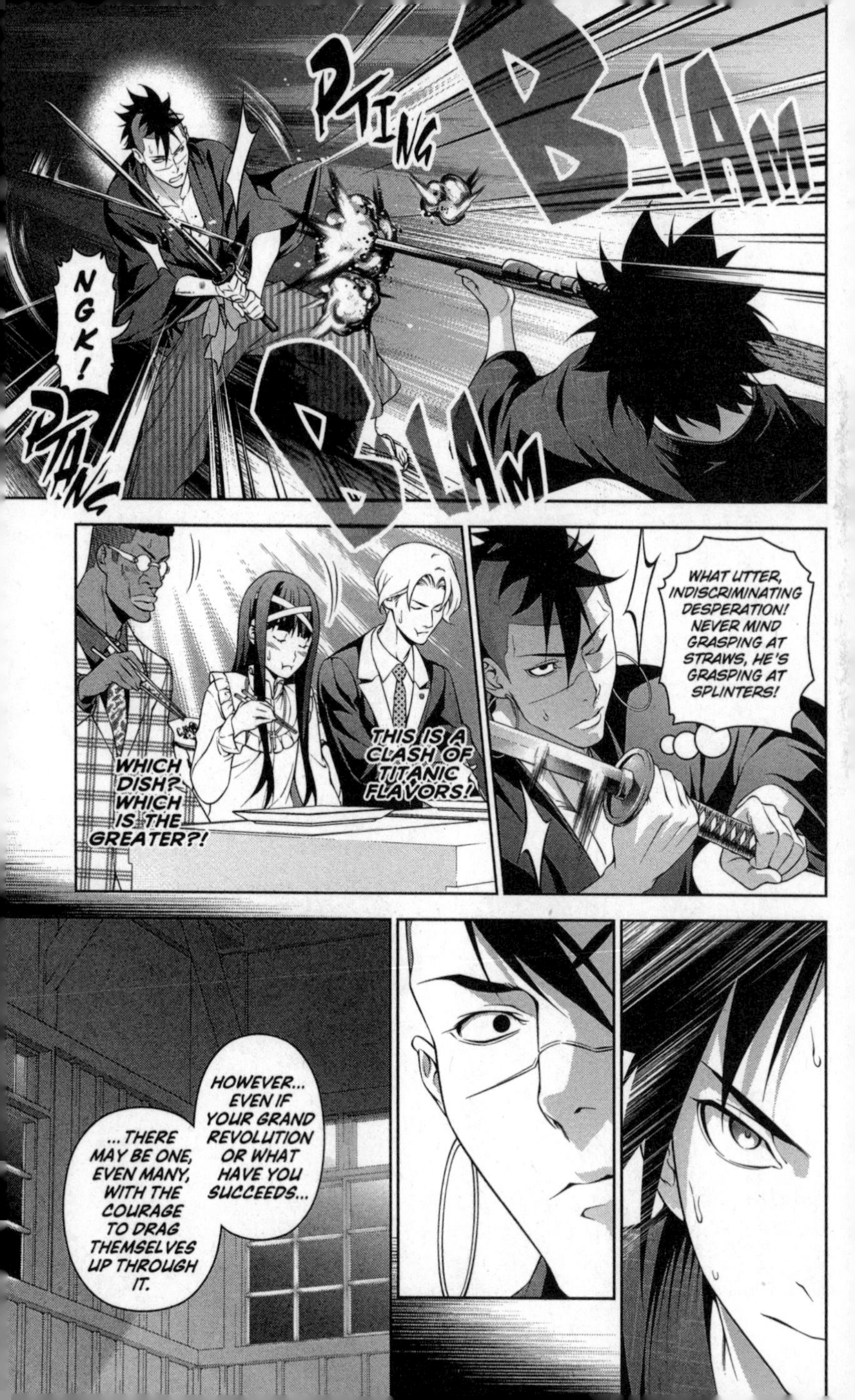
BLAM
PTING
BLAM
NGK!
PTANG
WHAT UTTER, INDISCRIMINATING DESPERATION! NEVER MIND GRASPING AT STRAWS, HE'S GRASPING AT SPLINTERS!
THIS IS A CLASH OF TITANIC FLAVORS!
WHICH DISH? WHICH IS THE GREATER?!
HOWEVER... EVEN IF YOUR GRAND REVOLUTION OR WHAT HAVE YOU SUCCEEDS...
...THERE MAY BE ONE, EVEN MANY, WITH THE COURAGE TO DRAG THEMSELVES UP THROUGH IT.

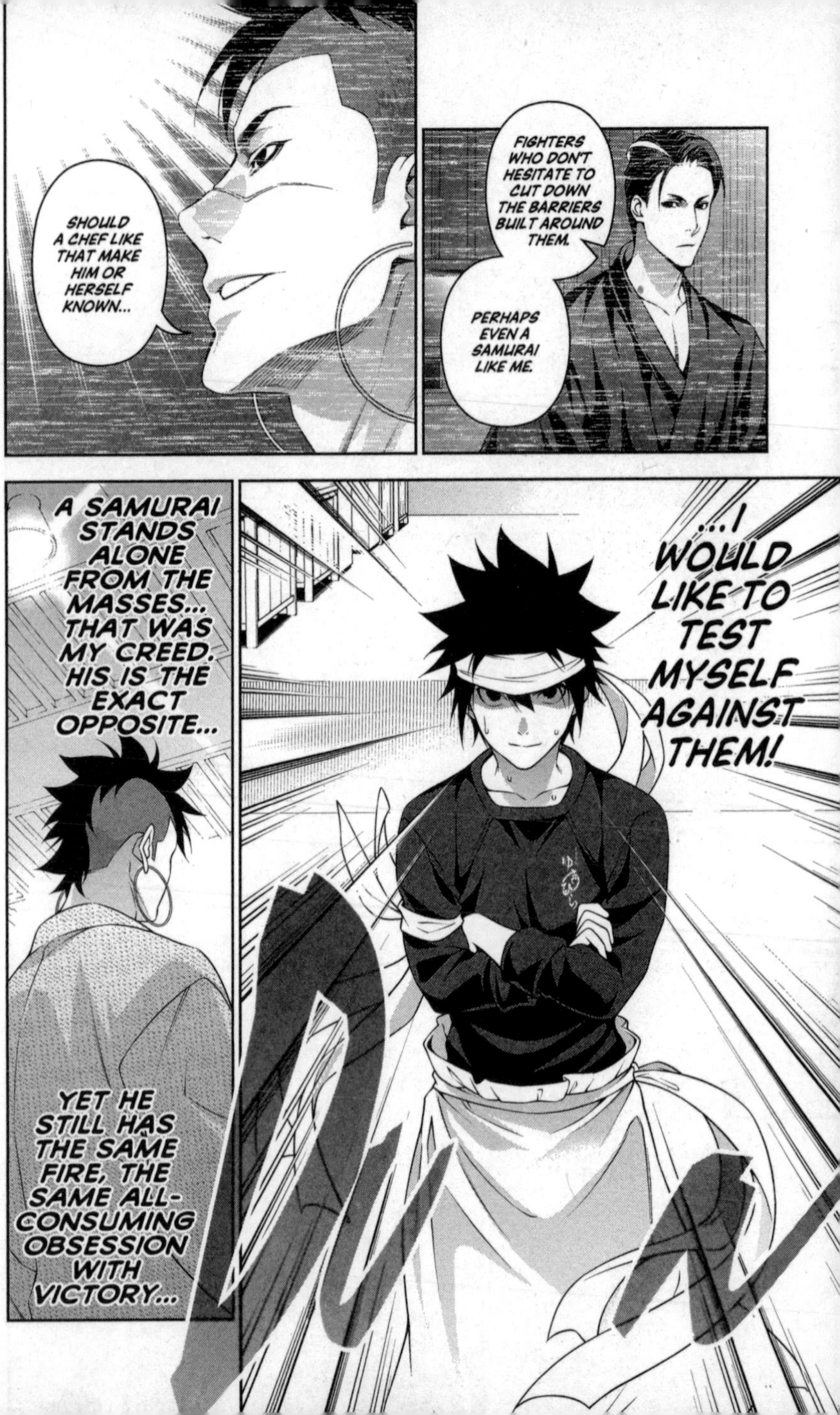
FIGHTERS WHO DON'T HESITATE TO CUT DOWN THE BARRIERS BUILT AROUND THEM.
PERHAPS EVEN A SAMURAI LIKE ME.
SHOULD A CHEF LIKE THAT MAKE HIM OR HERSELF KNOWN...
...I WOULD LIKE TO TEST MYSELF AGAINST THEM!
A SAMURAI STANDS ALONE FROM THE MASSES... THAT WAS MY CREED. HIS IS THE EXACT OPPOSITE...
YET HE STILL HAS THE SAME FIRE, THE SAME ALL-CONSUMING OBSESSION WITH VICTORY...

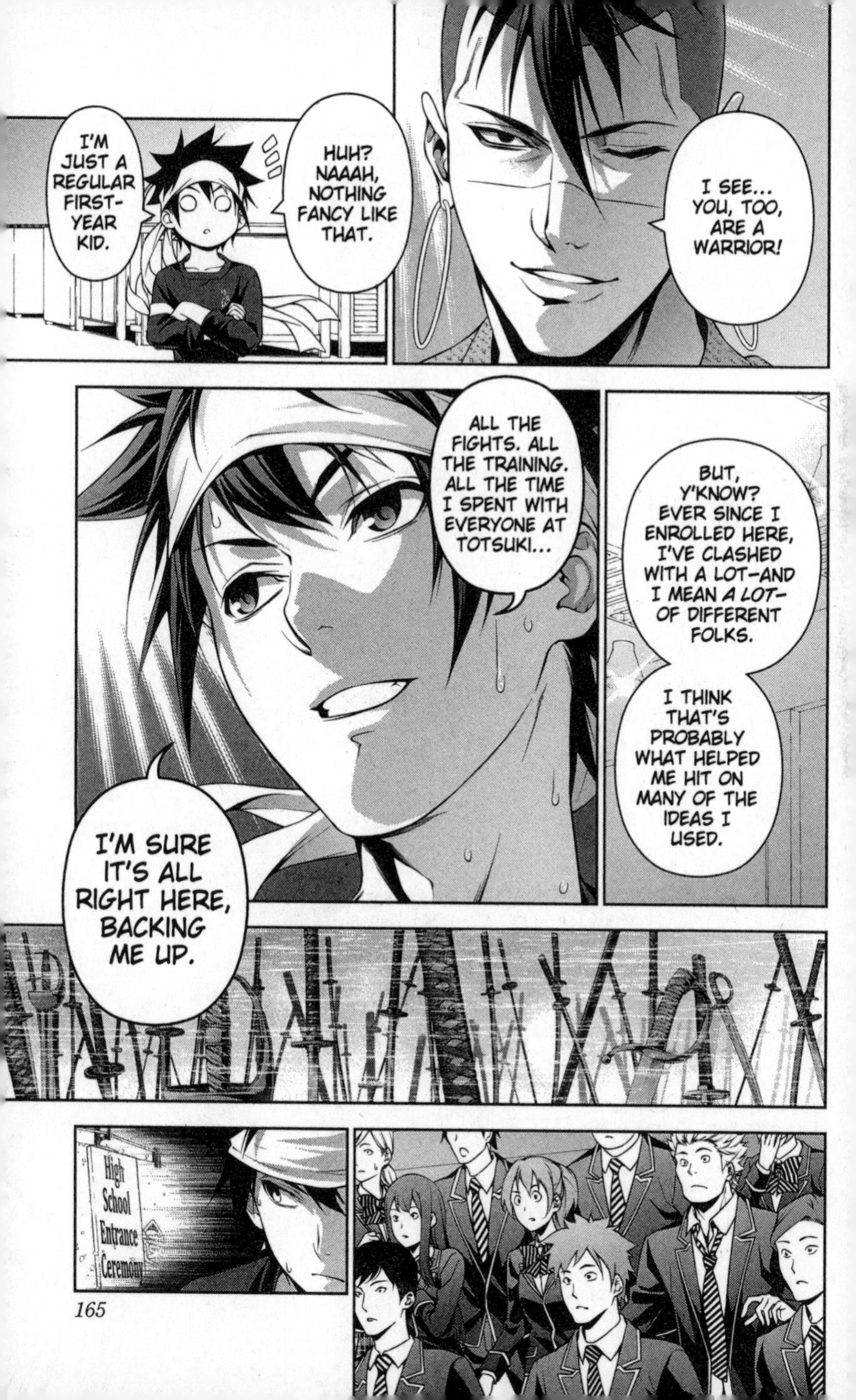
I SEE... YOU, TOO, ARE A WARRIOR!
HUH? NAAAH, NOTHING FANCY LIKE THAT.
I'M JUST A REGULAR FIRST-YEAR KID.
BUT, Y'KNOW? EVER SINCE I ENROLLED HERE, I'VE CLASHED WITH A LOT—AND I MEAN *A LOT*—OF DIFFERENT FOLKS.
I THINK THAT'S PROBABLY WHAT HELPED ME HIT ON MANY OF THE IDEAS I USED.
ALL THE FIGHTS. ALL THE TRAINING. ALL THE TIME I SPENT WITH EVERYONE AT TOTSUKI...
I'M SURE IT'S ALL RIGHT HERE, BACKING ME UP.
High School Entrance Ceremony

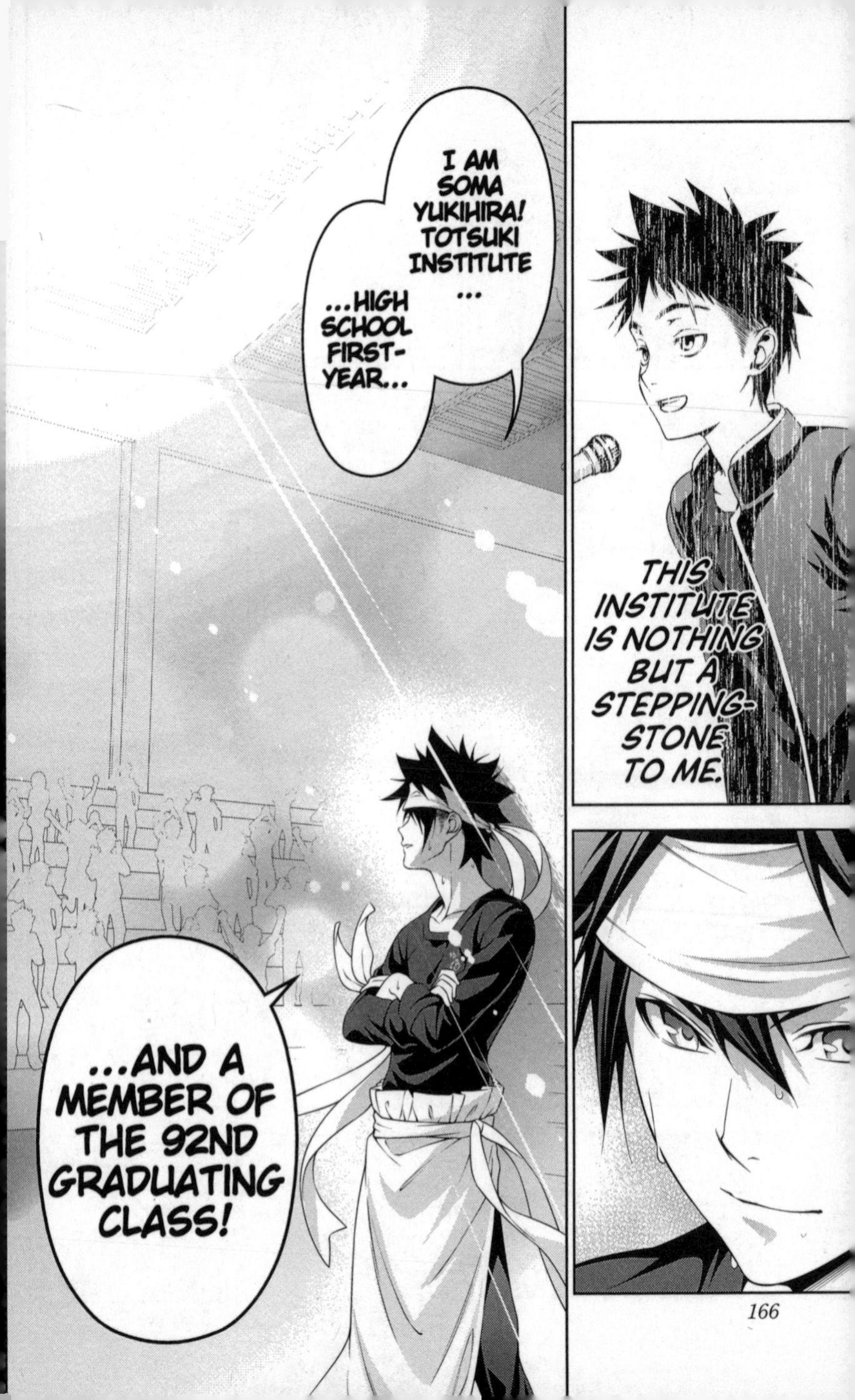
THIS INSTITUTE IS NOTHING BUT A STEPPING-STONE TO ME.
I AM SOMA YUKIHIRA! TOTSUKI INSTITUTE...
...HIGH SCHOOL FIRST-YEAR...
...AND A MEMBER OF THE 92ND GRADUATING CLASS!

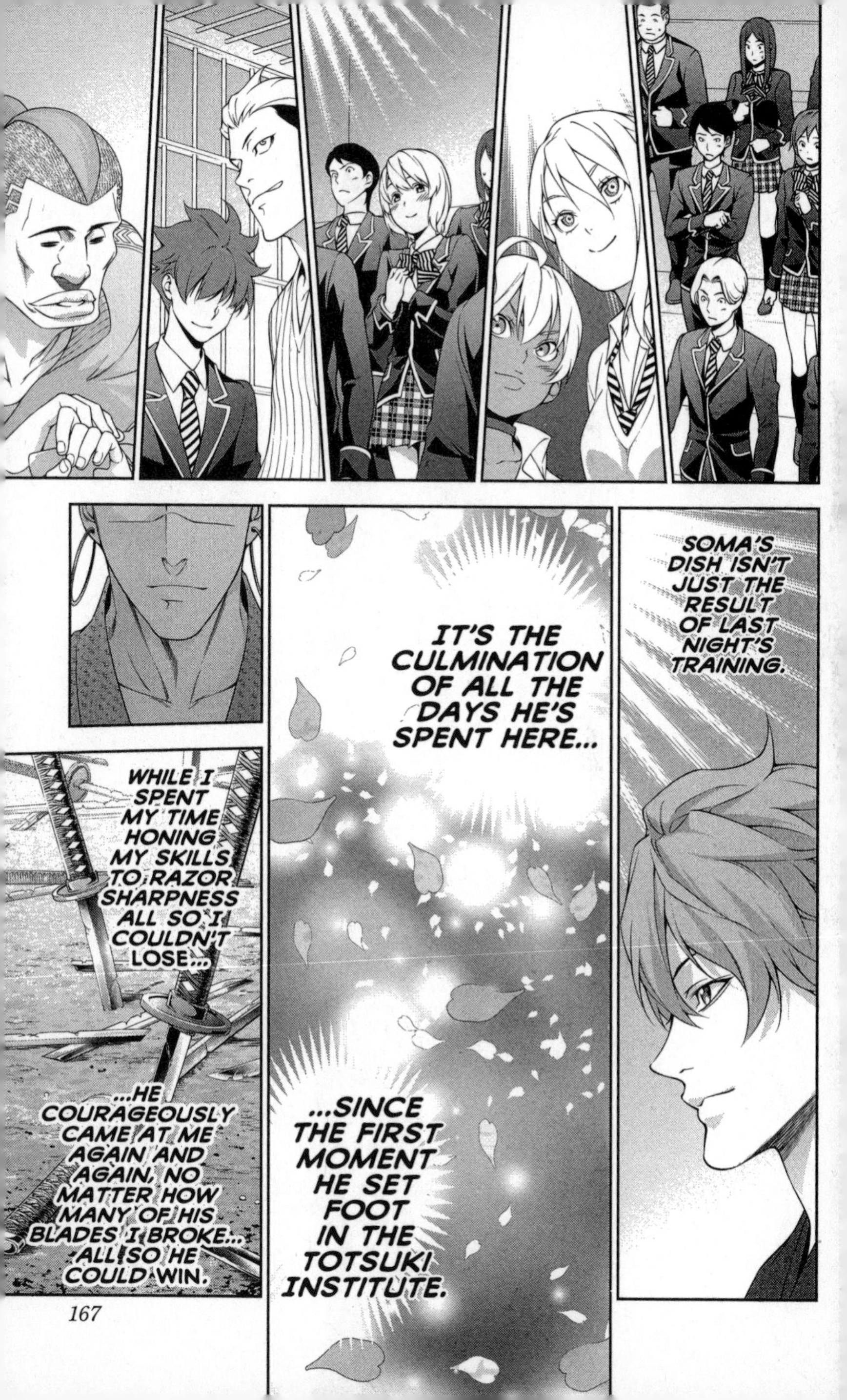
SOMA'S DISH ISN'T JUST THE RESULT OF LAST NIGHT'S TRAINING.
IT'S THE CULMINATION OF ALL THE DAYS HE'S SPENT HERE...
...SINCE THE FIRST MOMENT HE SET FOOT IN THE TOTSUKI INSTITUTE.
WHILE I SPENT MY TIME HONING MY SKILLS TO RAZOR SHARPNESS ALL SO I COULDN'T LOSE...
...HE COURAGEOUSLY CAME AT ME AGAIN AND AGAIN, NO MATTER HOW MANY OF HIS BLADES I BROKE... ALL SO HE COULD WIN.

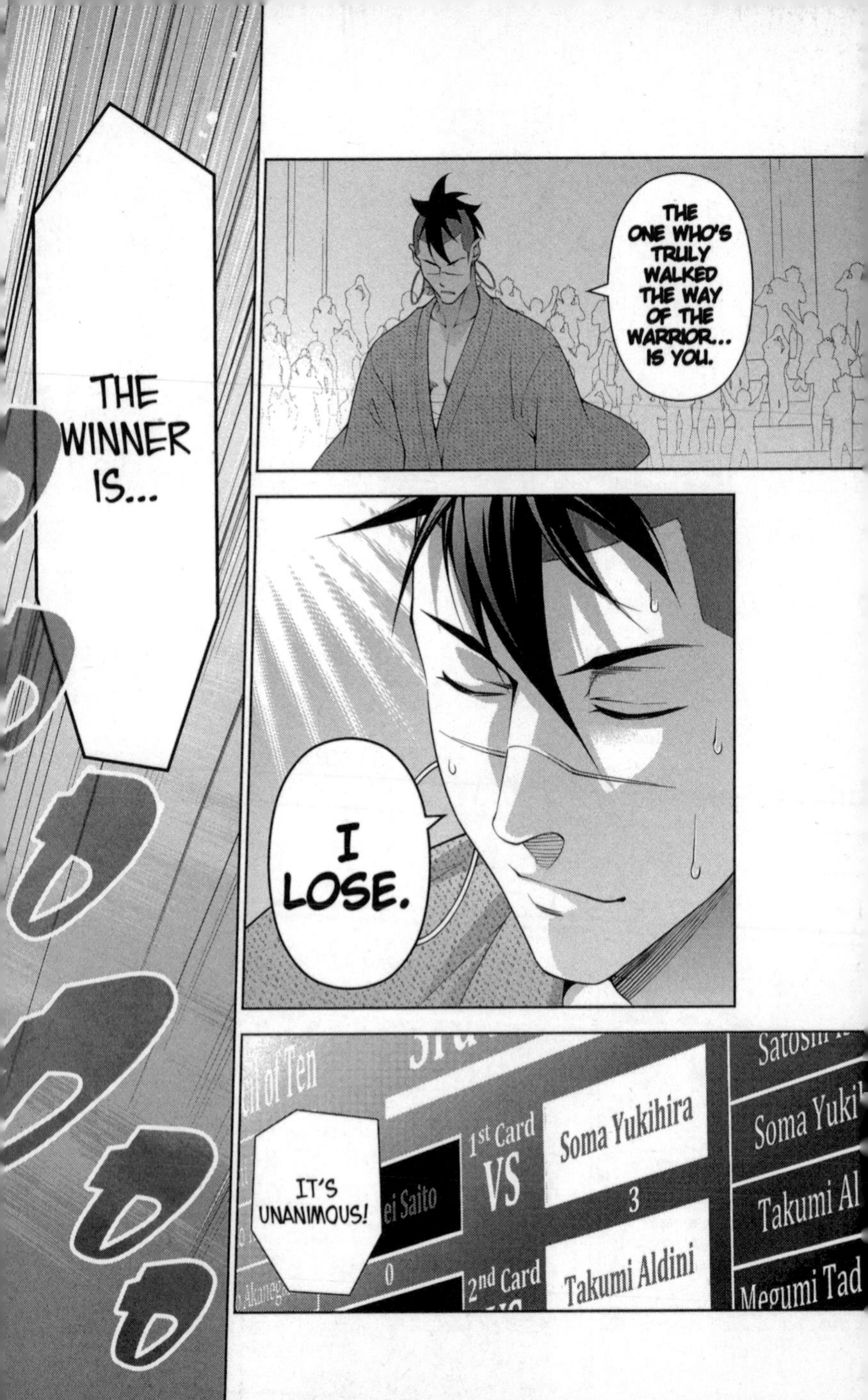
THE ONE WHO'S TRULY WALKED THE WAY OF THE WARRIOR... IS YOU.
I LOSE.
IT'S UNANIMOUS!
1st Card
VS
Soma Yukihira
3
0
2nd Card
Takumi Aldini
THE WINNER IS...

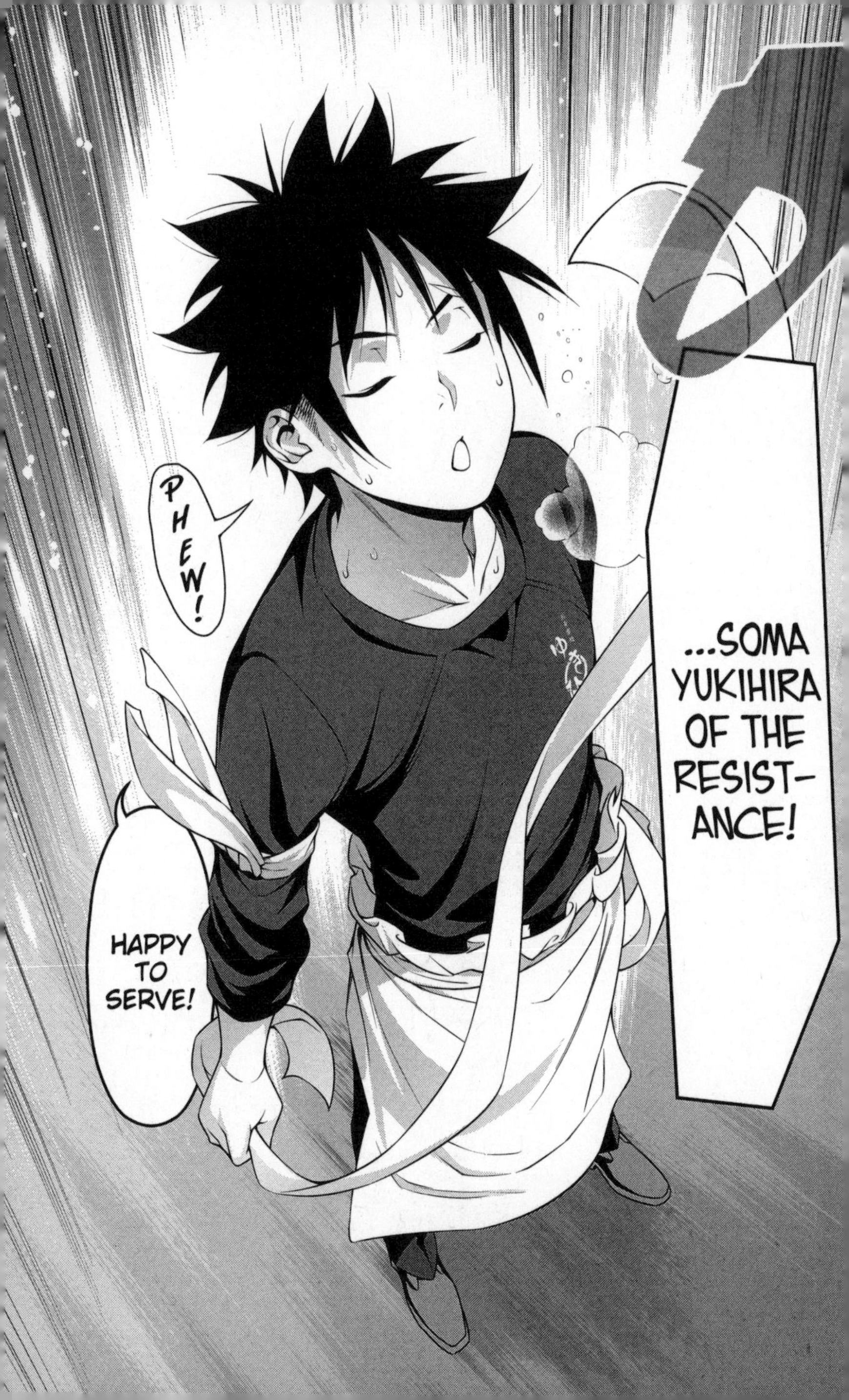
...SOMA YUKIHIRA OF THE RESIST-ANCE!
PHEW!
HAPPY TO SERVE!

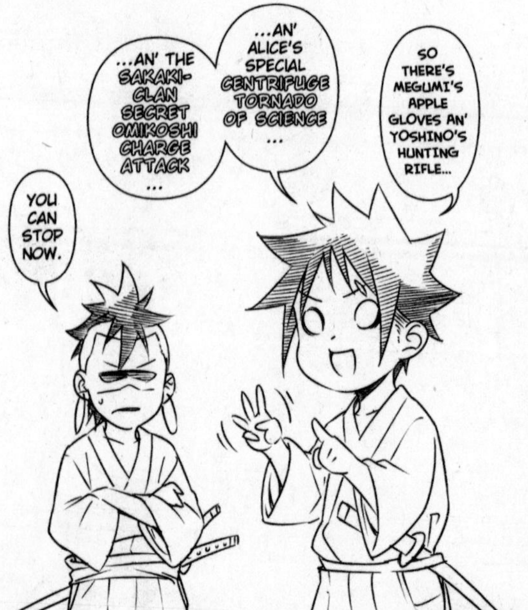
SO THERE'S MEGUMI'S APPLE GLOVES AN' YOSHINO'S HUNTING RIFLE...
...AN' ALICE'S SPECIAL CENTRIFUGE TORNADO OF SCIENCE...
...AN' THE SAKAKI-CLAN SECRET OMIKOSHI CHARGE ATTACK...
YOU CAN STOP NOW.

244 THE FOURTH BOUT

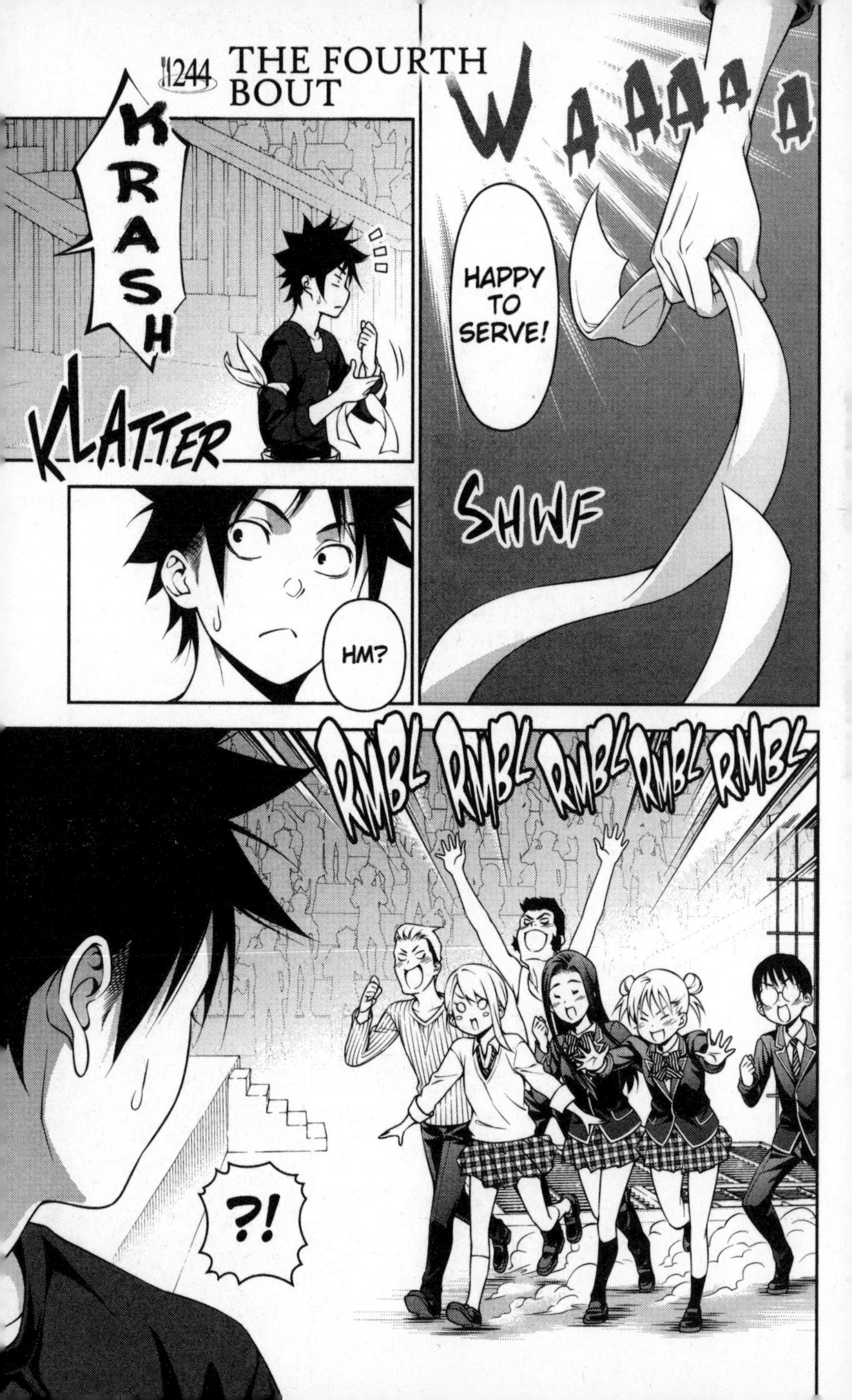
WAAAAA
HAPPY TO SERVE!
SHWF
KRASH
KLATTER
HM?
RMBL RMBL RMBL RMBL RMBL
?!

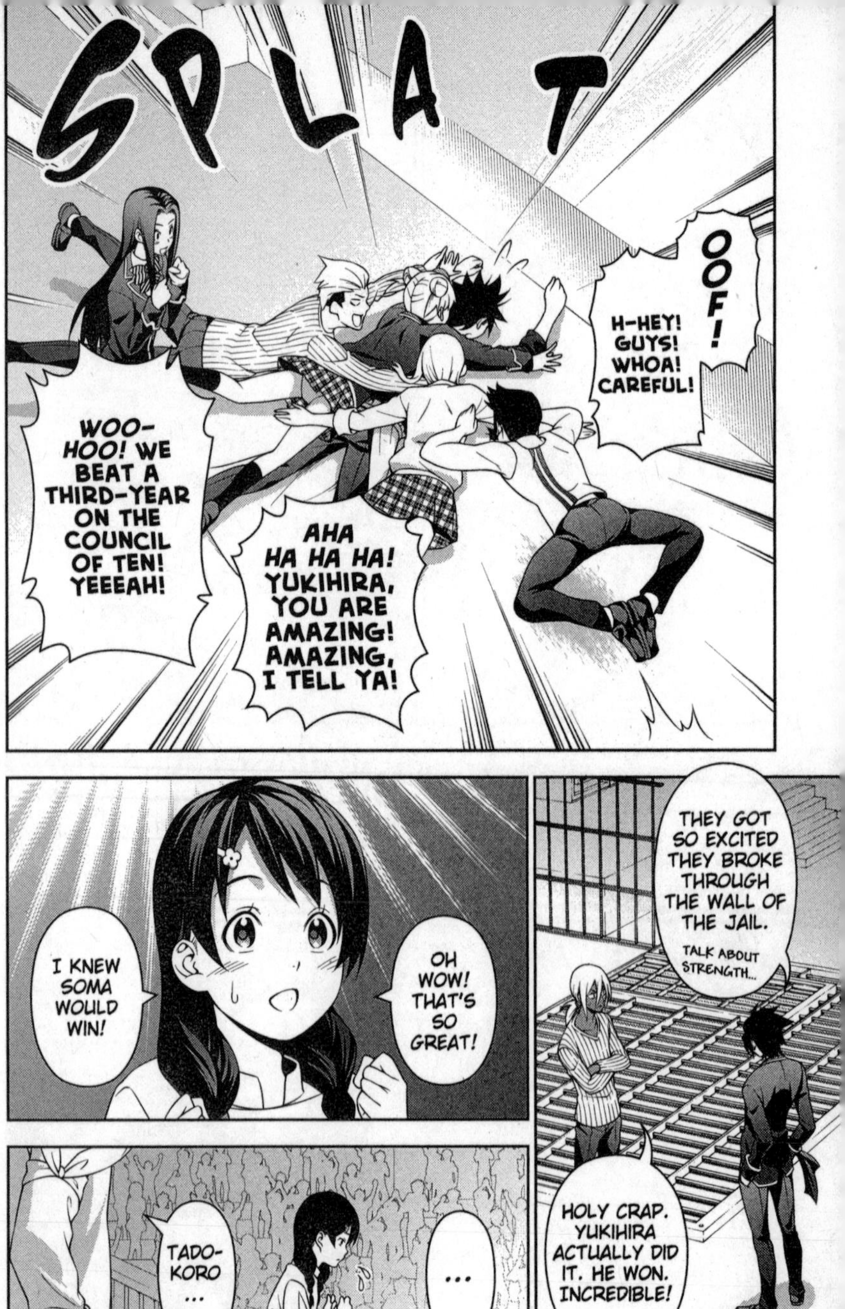
SPLAT
OOF!
H-HEY! GUYS! WHOA! CAREFUL!
AHA HA HA HA! YUKIHIRA, YOU ARE AMAZING! AMAZING, I TELL YA!
WOO-HOO! WE BEAT A THIRD-YEAR ON THE COUNCIL OF TEN! YEEEAH!
THEY GOT SO EXCITED THEY BROKE THROUGH THE WALL OF THE JAIL.
TALK ABOUT STRENGTH...
HOLY CRAP. YUKIHIRA ACTUALLY DID IT. HE WON. INCREDIBLE!
OH WOW! THAT'S SO GREAT!
I KNEW SOMA WOULD WIN!
...
TADO-KORO ...

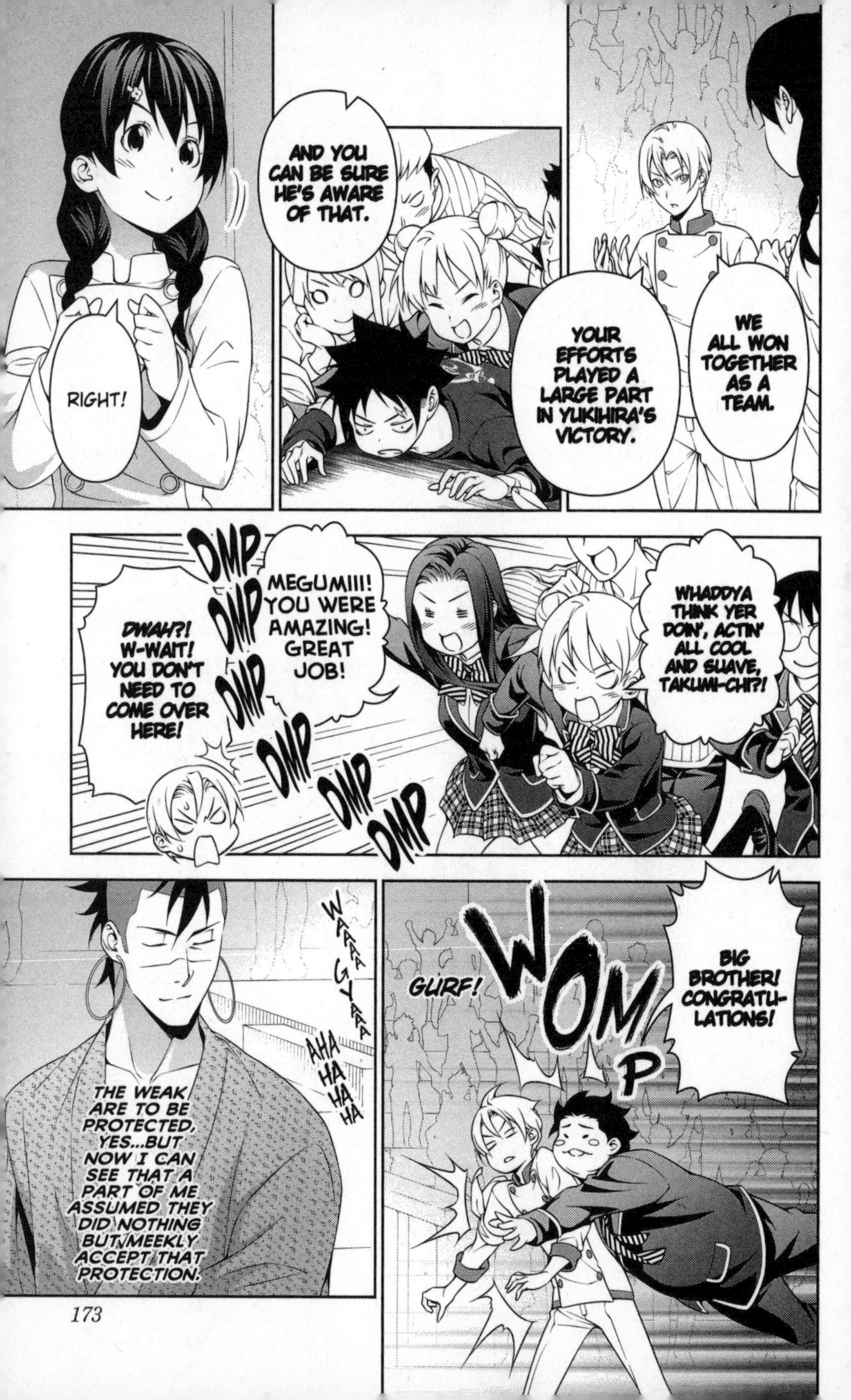
WE ALL WON TOGETHER AS A TEAM.
YOUR EFFORTS PLAYED A LARGE PART IN YUKIHIRA'S VICTORY.
AND YOU CAN BE SURE HE'S AWARE OF THAT.
RIGHT!
WHADDYA THINK YER DOIN', ACTIN' ALL COOL AND SUAVE, TAKUMI-CHI?!
MEGUMIII! YOU WERE AMAZING! GREAT JOB!
DMP DMP DMP DMP DMP DMP
DWAH?! W-WAIT! YOU DON'T NEED TO COME OVER HERE!
BIG BROTHER! CONGRATU-LATIONS!
WOMP
GURF!
WAAAA GYAAAA
AHAHAHAHA
THE WEAK ARE TO BE PROTECTED, YES...BUT NOW I CAN SEE THAT A PART OF ME ASSUMED THEY DID NOTHING BUT MEEKLY ACCEPT THAT PROTECTION.

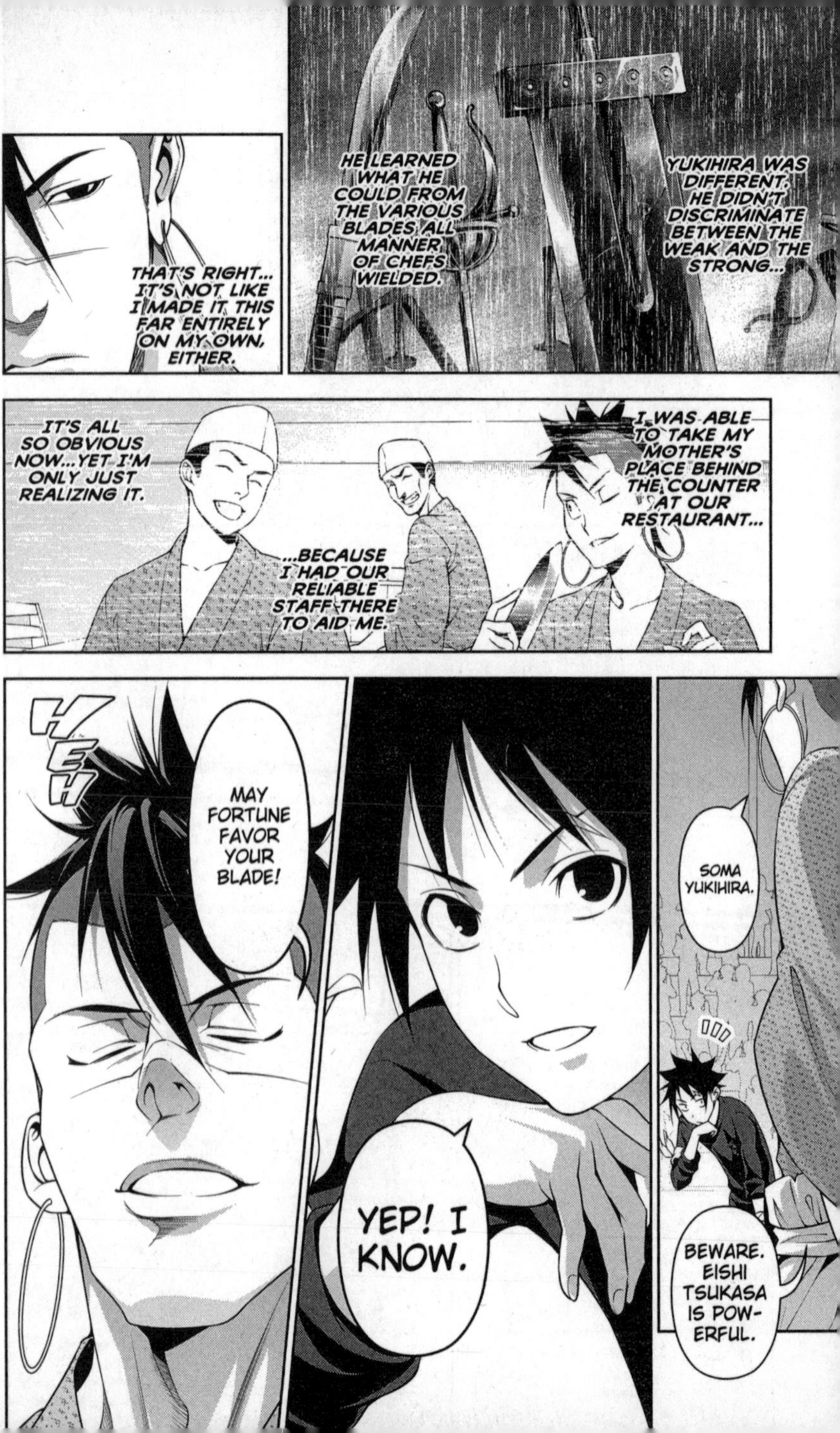

YUKIHIRA WAS DIFFERENT. HE DIDN'T DISCRIMINATE BETWEEN THE WEAK AND THE STRONG...
HE LEARNED WHAT HE COULD FROM THE VARIOUS BLADES ALL MANNER OF CHEFS WIELDED.
THAT'S RIGHT... IT'S NOT LIKE I MADE IT THIS FAR ENTIRELY ON MY OWN, EITHER.
I WAS ABLE TO TAKE MY MOTHER'S PLACE BEHIND THE COUNTER AT OUR RESTAURANT...
...BECAUSE I HAD OUR RELIABLE STAFF THERE TO AID ME.
IT'S ALL SO OBVIOUS NOW...YET I'M ONLY JUST REALIZING IT.
SOMA YUKIHIRA.
BEWARE. EISHI TSUKASA IS POWERFUL.
YEP! I KNOW.
HEH
MAY FORTUNE FAVOR YOUR BLADE!

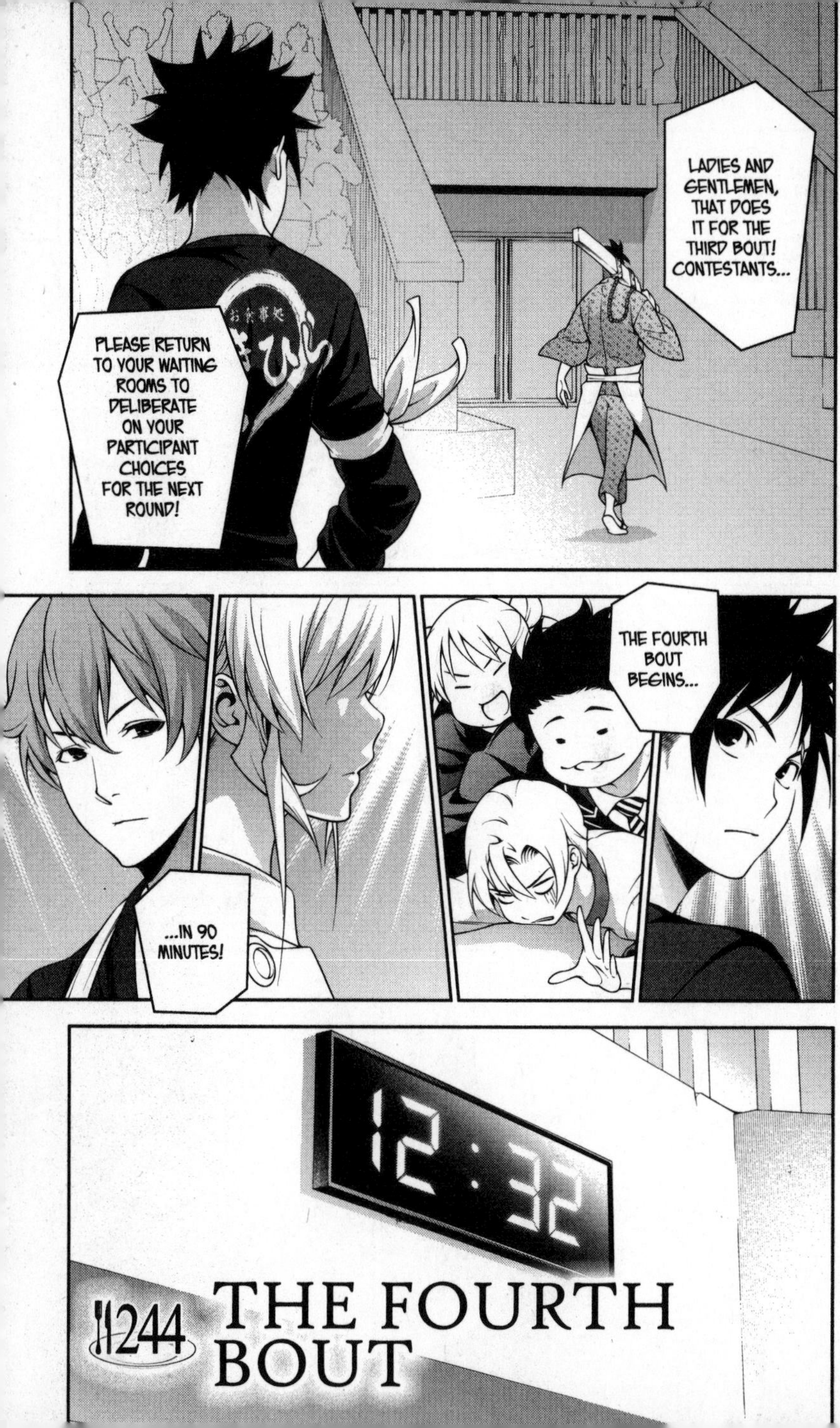
LADIES AND GENTLEMEN, THAT DOES IT FOR THE THIRD BOUT! CONTESTANTS...
PLEASE RETURN TO YOUR WAITING ROOMS TO DELIBERATE ON YOUR PARTICIPANT CHOICES FOR THE NEXT ROUND!
THE FOURTH BOUT BEGINS...
...IN 90 MINUTES!
12:32
244 THE FOURTH BOUT

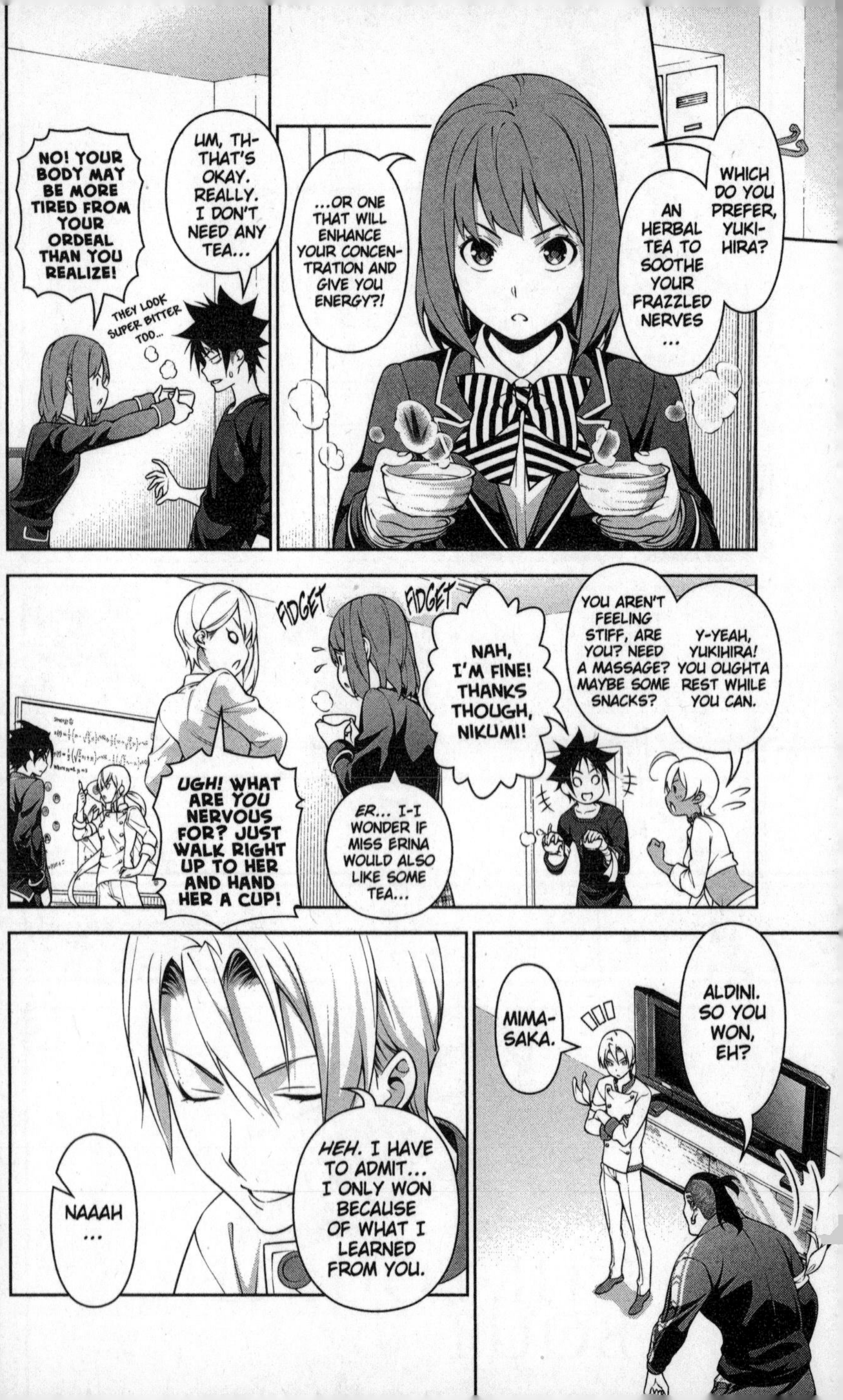
WHICH DO YOU PREFER, YUKI-HIRA?
AN HERBAL TEA TO SOOTHE YOUR FRAZZLED NERVES...
...OR ONE THAT WILL ENHANCE YOUR CONCEN-TRATION AND GIVE YOU ENERGY?!
UM, TH-THAT'S OKAY. REALLY. I DON'T NEED ANY TEA...
NO! YOUR BODY MAY BE MORE TIRED FROM YOUR ORDEAL THAN YOU REALIZE!
THEY LOOK SUPER BITTER TOO...
Y-YEAH, YUKIHIRA! YOU OUGHTA REST WHILE YOU CAN.
YOU AREN'T FEELING STIFF, ARE YOU? NEED A MASSAGE? MAYBE SOME SNACKS?
NAH, I'M FINE! THANKS THOUGH, NIKUMI!
FIDGET
FIDGET
ER... I-I WONDER IF MISS ERINA WOULD ALSO LIKE SOME TEA...
UGH! WHAT ARE YOU NERVOUS FOR? JUST WALK RIGHT UP TO HER AND HAND HER A CUP!
ALDINI. SO YOU WON, EH?
MIMA-SAKA.
HEH. I HAVE TO ADMIT... I ONLY WON BECAUSE OF WHAT I LEARNED FROM YOU.
NAAAH...

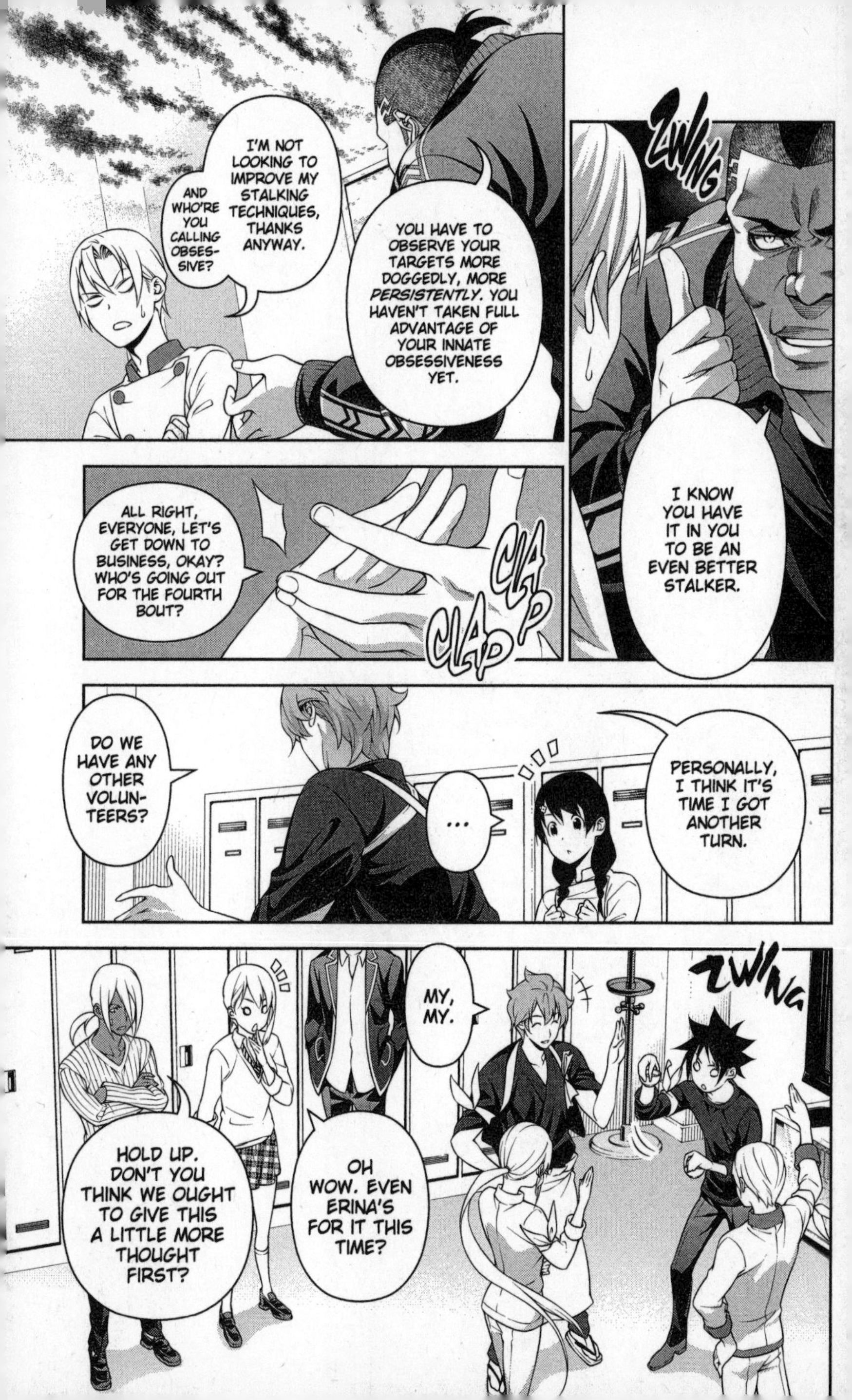
ZWING
I KNOW YOU HAVE IT IN YOU TO BE AN EVEN BETTER STALKER.
YOU HAVE TO OBSERVE YOUR TARGETS MORE DOGGEDLY, MORE *PERSISTENTLY*. YOU HAVEN'T TAKEN FULL ADVANTAGE OF YOUR INNATE OBSESSIVENESS YET.
I'M NOT LOOKING TO IMPROVE MY STALKING TECHNIQUES, THANKS ANYWAY.
AND WHO'RE YOU CALLING OBSES-SIVE?
CLAP
CLAP
ALL RIGHT, EVERYONE, LET'S GET DOWN TO BUSINESS, OKAY? WHO'S GOING OUT FOR THE FOURTH BOUT?
PERSONALLY, I THINK IT'S TIME I GOT ANOTHER TURN.
...
DO WE HAVE ANY OTHER VOLUN-TEERS?
ZWING
MY, MY.
OH WOW. EVEN ERINA'S FOR IT THIS TIME?
HOLD UP. DON'T YOU THINK WE OUGHT TO GIVE THIS A LITTLE MORE THOUGHT FIRST?

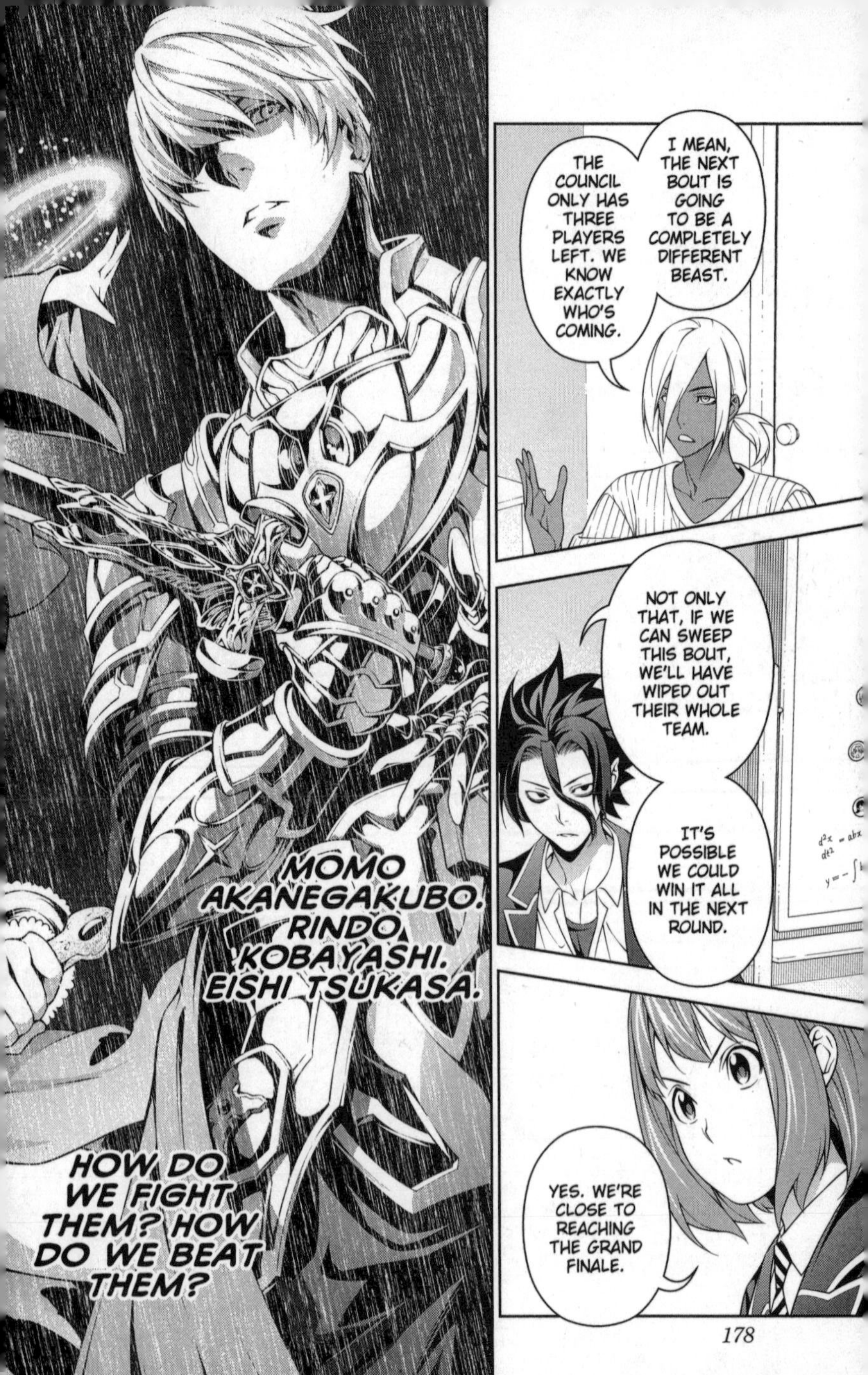
I MEAN, THE NEXT BOUT IS GOING TO BE A COMPLETELY DIFFERENT BEAST.
THE COUNCIL ONLY HAS THREE PLAYERS LEFT. WE KNOW EXACTLY WHO'S COMING.
NOT ONLY THAT, IF WE CAN SWEEP THIS BOUT, WE'LL HAVE WIPED OUT THEIR WHOLE TEAM.
IT'S POSSIBLE WE COULD WIN IT ALL IN THE NEXT ROUND.
YES. WE'RE CLOSE TO REACHING THE GRAND FINALE.
MOMO AKANEGAKUBO. RINDO KOBAYASHI. EISHI TSUKASA.
HOW DO WE FIGHT THEM? HOW DO WE BEAT THEM?

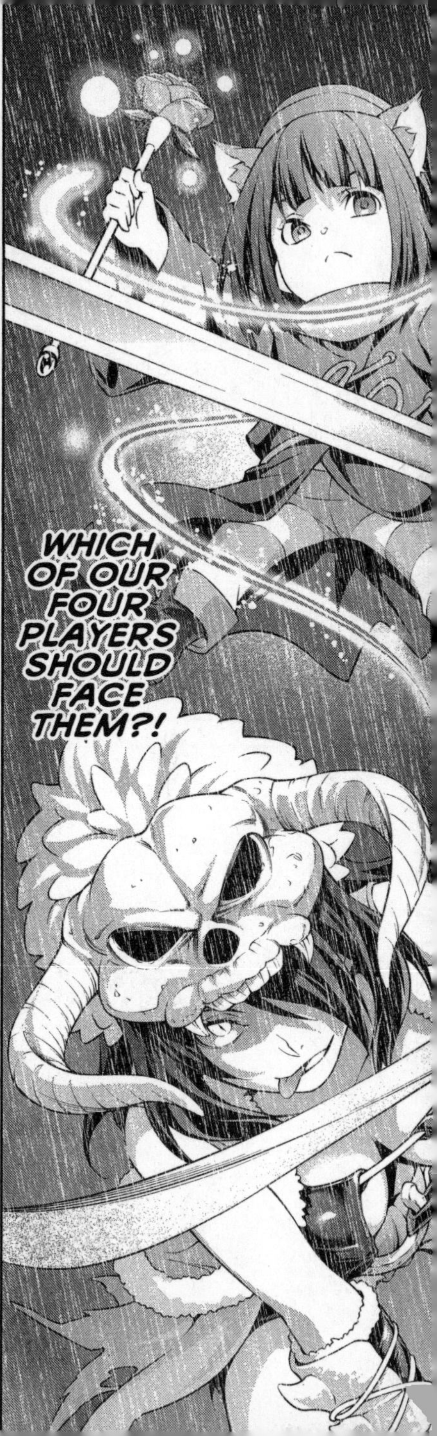
WHICH OF OUR FOUR PLAYERS SHOULD FACE THEM?!

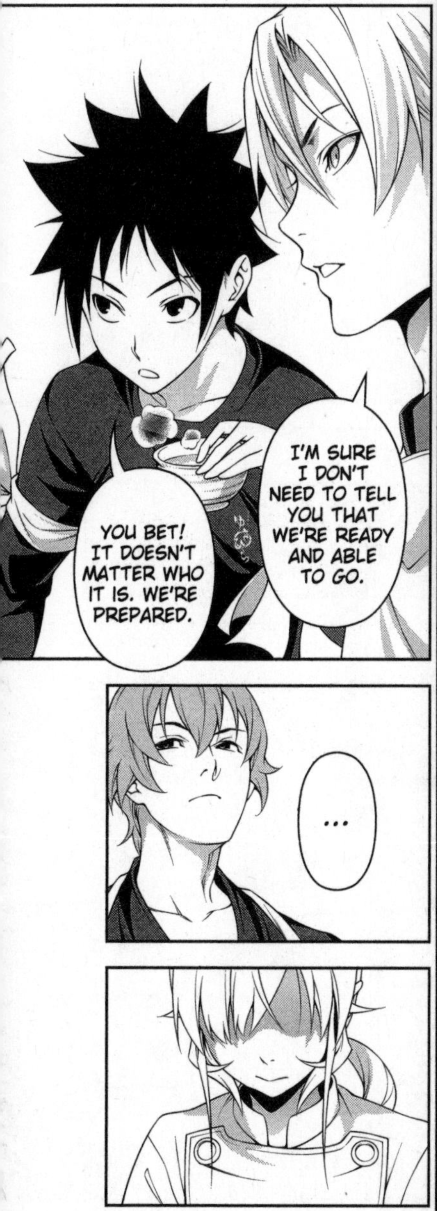
I'M SURE I DON'T NEED TO TELL YOU THAT WE'RE READY AND ABLE TO GO.
YOU BET! IT DOESN'T MATTER WHO IT IS. WE'RE PREPARED.
...

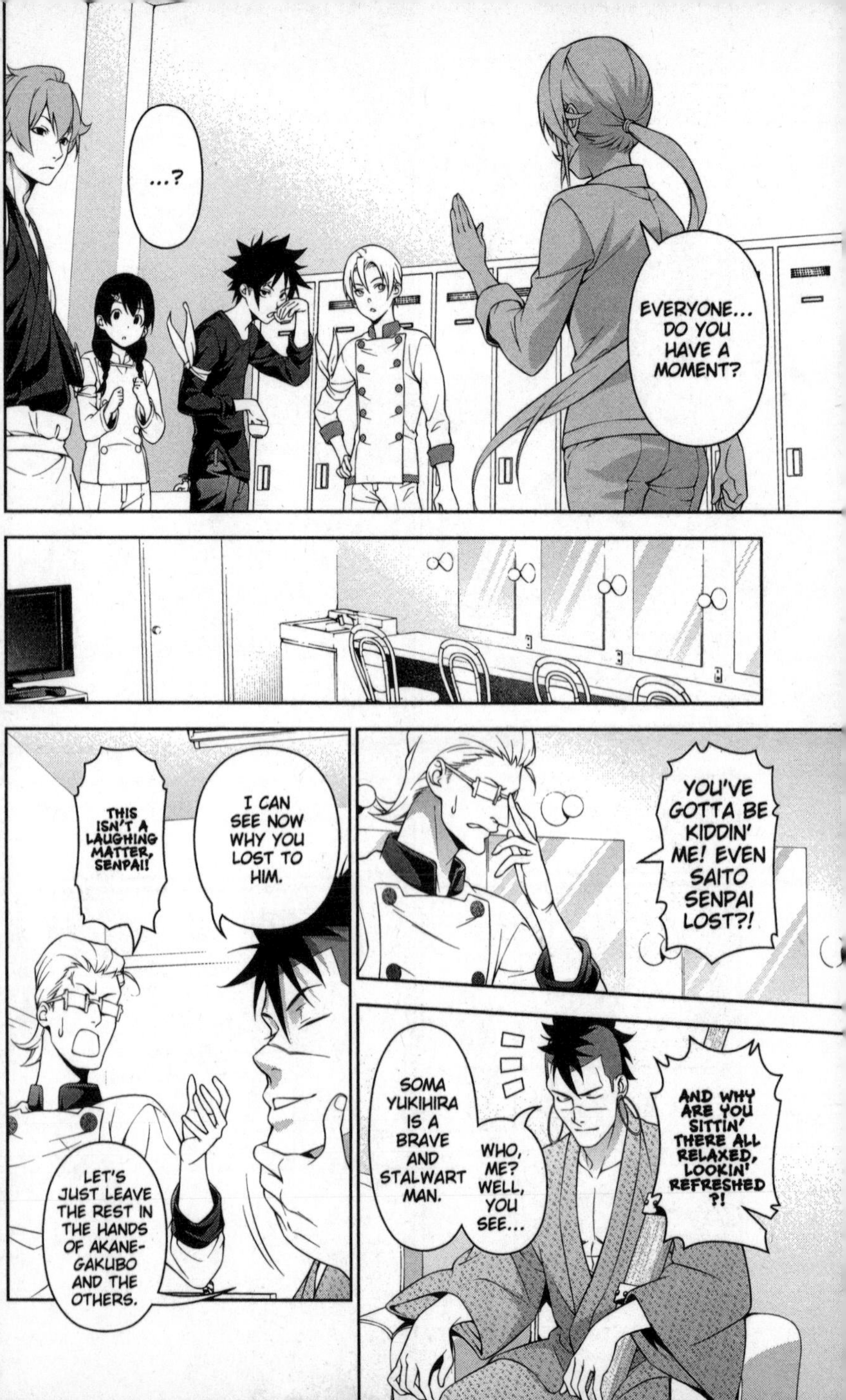
EVERYONE... DO YOU HAVE A MOMENT?
...?
YOU'VE GOTTA BE KIDDIN' ME! EVEN SAITO SENPAI LOST?!
AND WHY ARE YOU SITTIN' THERE ALL RELAXED, LOOKIN' REFRESHED ?!
WHO, ME? WELL, YOU SEE...
SOMA YUKIHIRA IS A BRAVE AND STALWART MAN.
I CAN SEE NOW WHY YOU LOST TO HIM.
THIS ISN'T A LAUGHING MATTER, SENPAI!
LET'S JUST LEAVE THE REST IN THE HANDS OF AKANE-GAKUBO AND THE OTHERS.

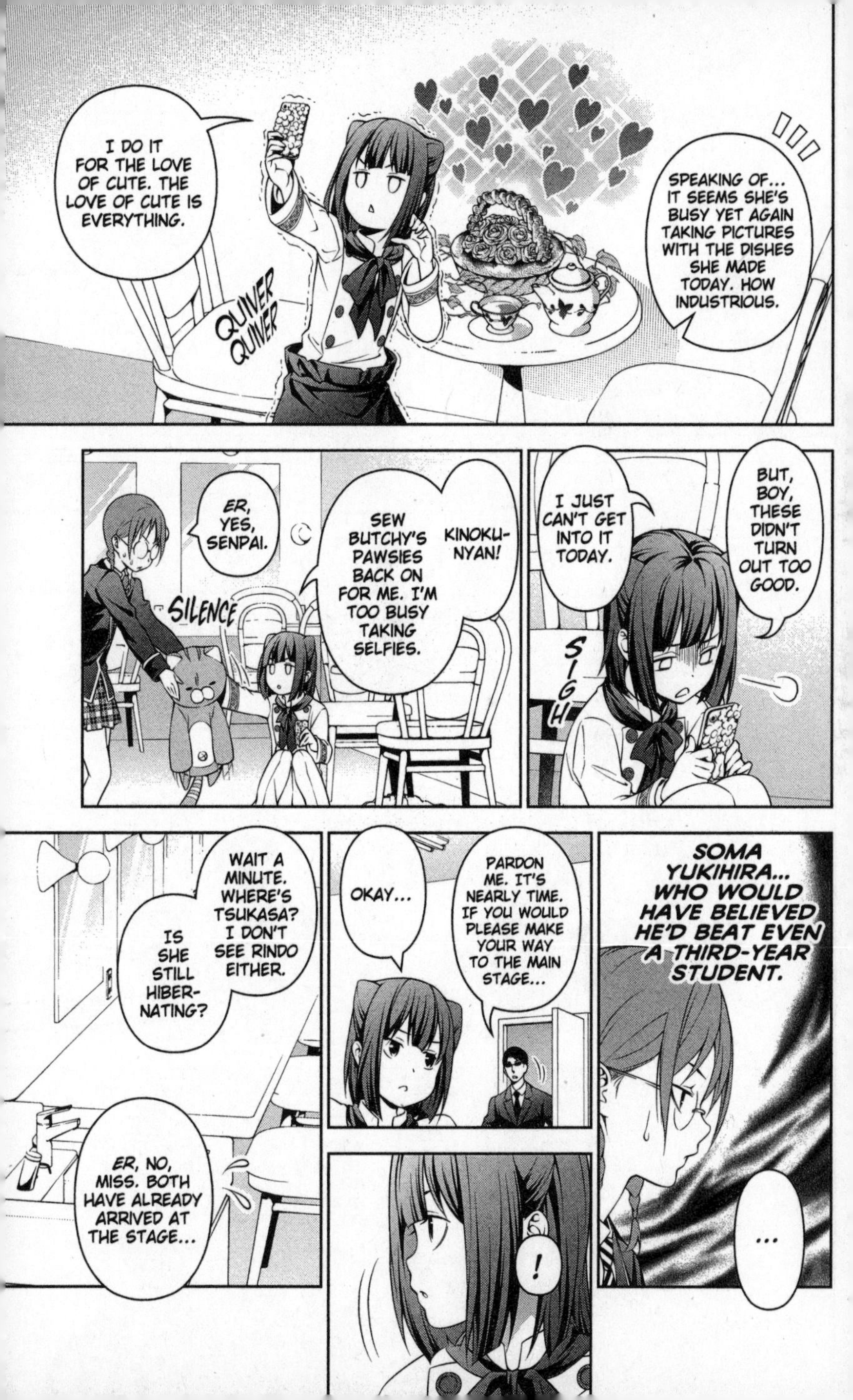
SPEAKING OF... IT SEEMS SHE'S BUSY YET AGAIN TAKING PICTURES WITH THE DISHES SHE MADE TODAY. HOW INDUSTRIOUS.
I DO IT FOR THE LOVE OF CUTE. THE LOVE OF CUTE IS EVERYTHING.
QUIVER QUIVER
BUT, BOY, THESE DIDN'T TURN OUT TOO GOOD.
I JUST CAN'T GET INTO IT TODAY.
SIGH
KINOKU-NYAN!
SEW BUTCHY'S PAWSIES BACK ON FOR ME. I'M TOO BUSY TAKING SELFIES.
ER, YES, SENPAI.
SILENCE
SOMA YUKIHIRA... WHO WOULD HAVE BELIEVED HE'D BEAT EVEN A THIRD-YEAR STUDENT.
...
PARDON ME. IT'S NEARLY TIME. IF YOU WOULD PLEASE MAKE YOUR WAY TO THE MAIN STAGE...
OKAY...
WAIT A MINUTE. WHERE'S TSUKASA? I DON'T SEE RINDO EITHER.
IS SHE STILL HIBERNATING?
ER, NO, MISS. BOTH HAVE ALREADY ARRIVED AT THE STAGE...
!

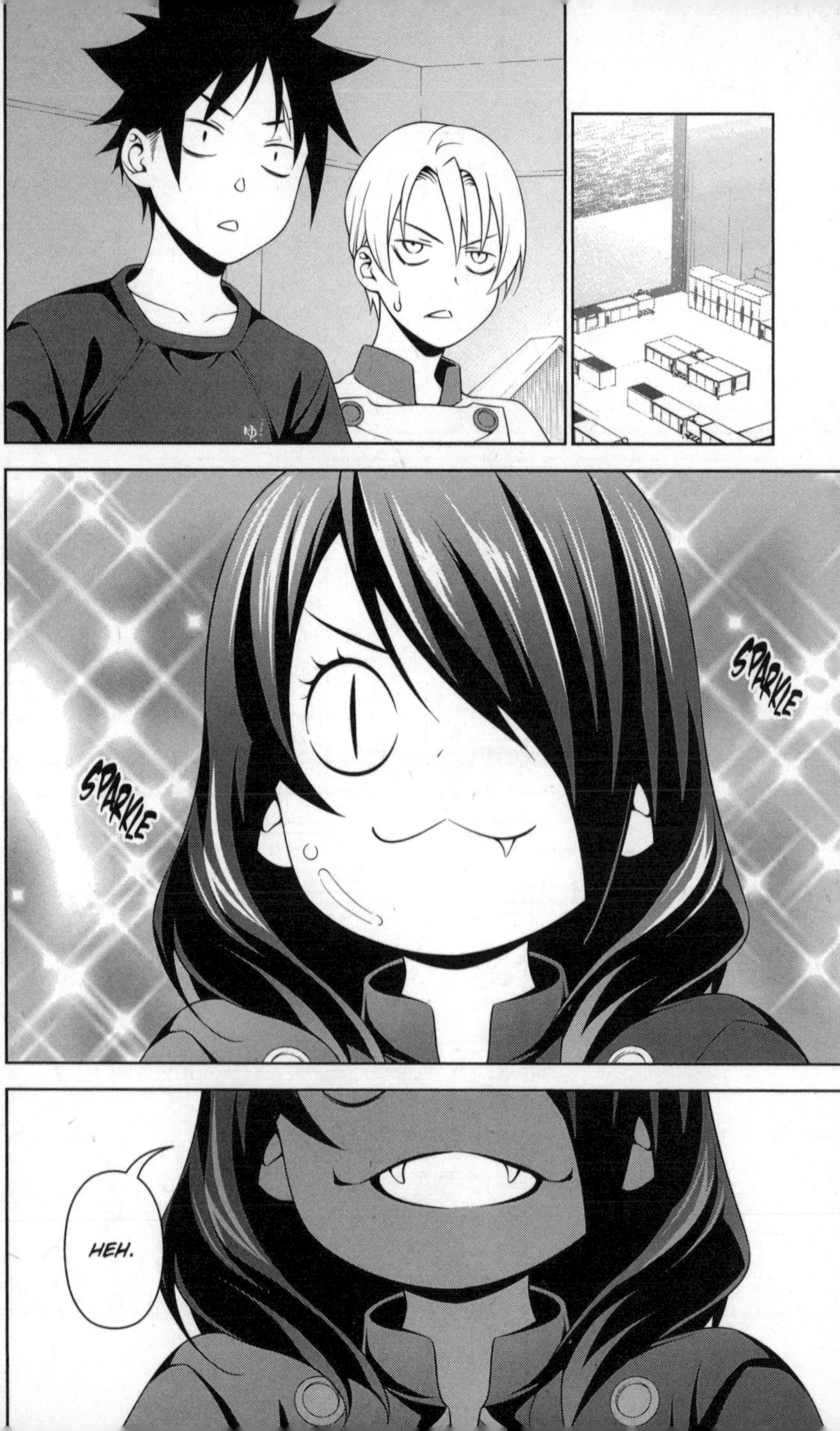
SPARKLE
SPARKLE
HEH.

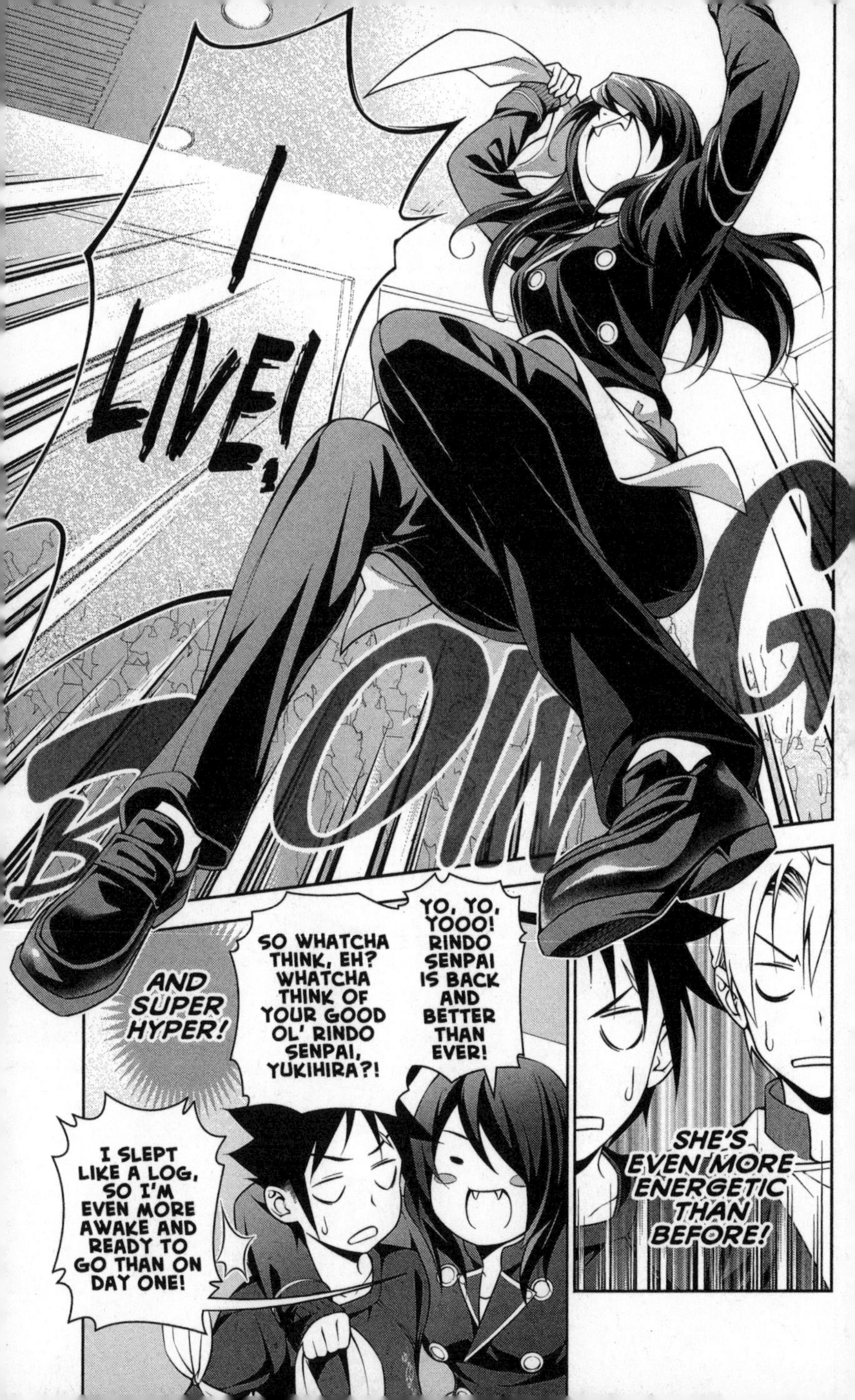
I LIVE!
BOING
SHE'S EVEN MORE ENERGETIC THAN BEFORE!
YO, YO, YOOO! RINDO SENPAI IS BACK AND BETTER THAN EVER!
SO WHATCHA THINK, EH? WHATCHA THINK OF YOUR GOOD OL' RINDO SENPAI, YUKIHIRA?!
AND SUPER HYPER!
I SLEPT LIKE A LOG, SO I'M EVEN MORE AWAKE AND READY TO GO THAN ON DAY ONE!

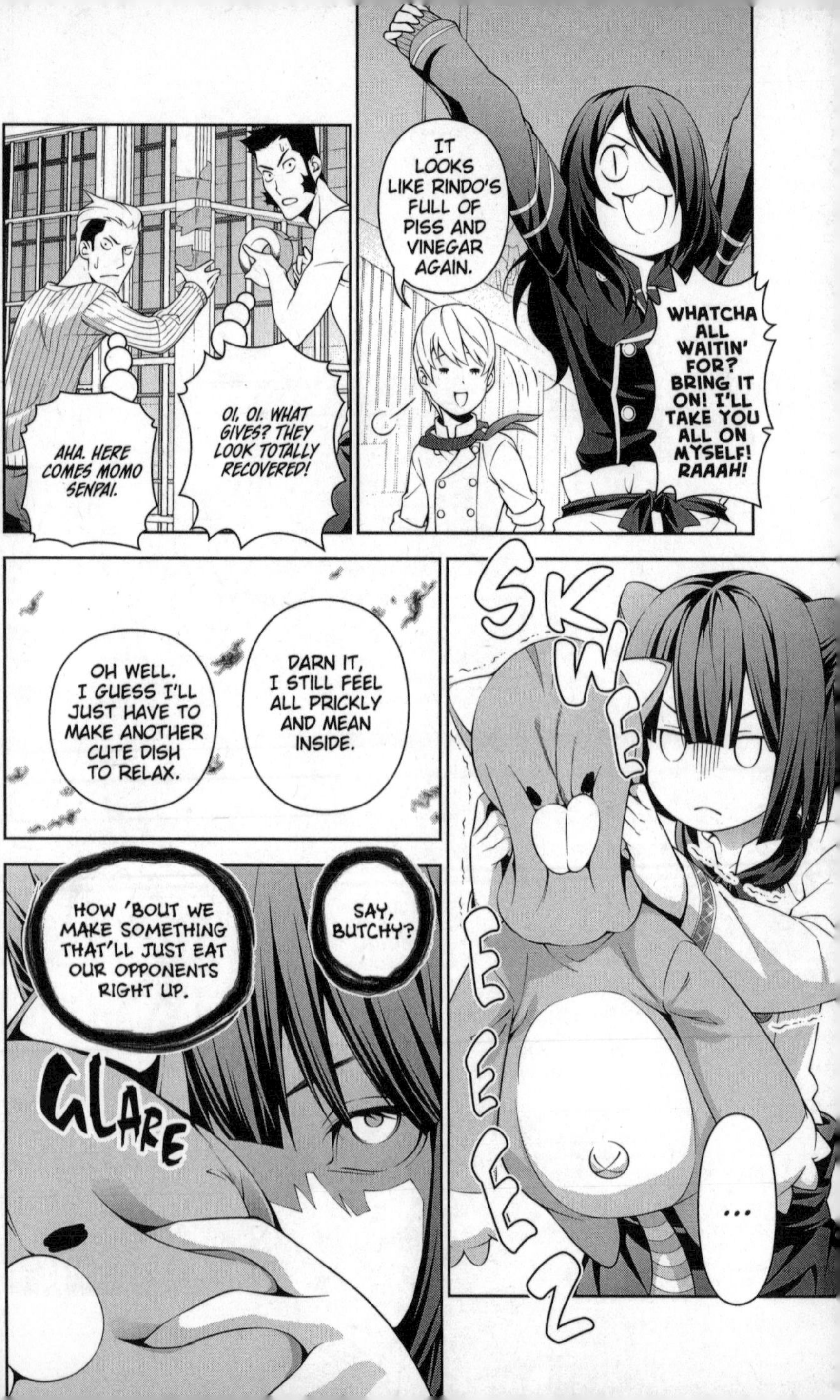
WHATCHA ALL WAITIN' FOR? BRING IT ON! I'LL TAKE YOU ALL ON MYSELF! RAAAH!
IT LOOKS LIKE RINDO'S FULL OF PISS AND VINEGAR AGAIN.
OI, OI. WHAT GIVES? THEY LOOK TOTALLY RECOVERED!
AHA. HERE COMES MOMO SENPAI.
SKWEEEEZE
...
DARN IT, I STILL FEEL ALL PRICKLY AND MEAN INSIDE.
OH WELL. I GUESS I'LL JUST HAVE TO MAKE ANOTHER CUTE DISH TO RELAX.
SAY, BUTCHY?
HOW 'BOUT WE MAKE SOMETHING THAT'LL JUST EAT OUR OPPONENTS RIGHT UP.
GLARE

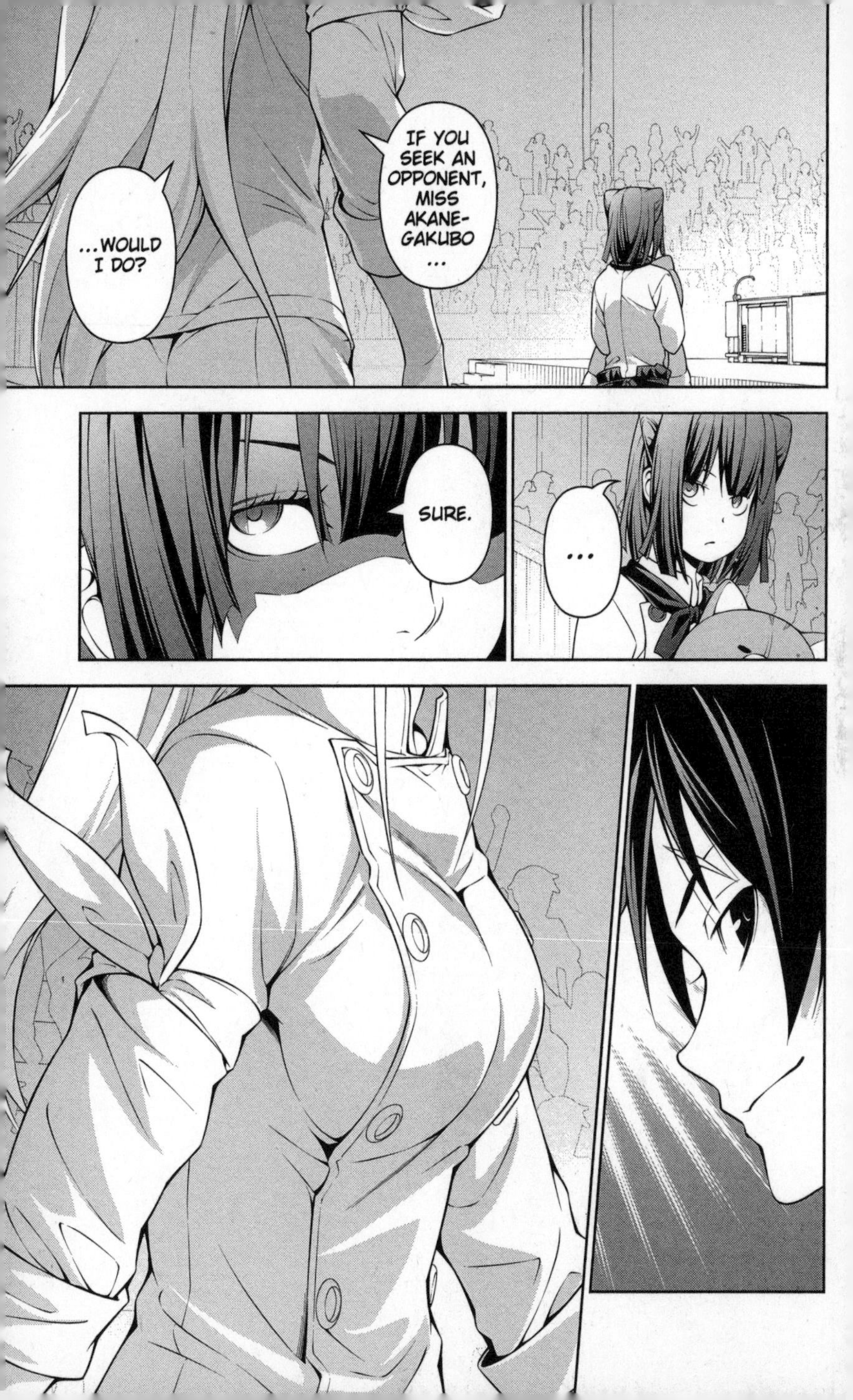
IF YOU SEEK AN OPPONENT, MISS AKANE-GAKUBO ...
...WOULD I DO?
...
SURE.

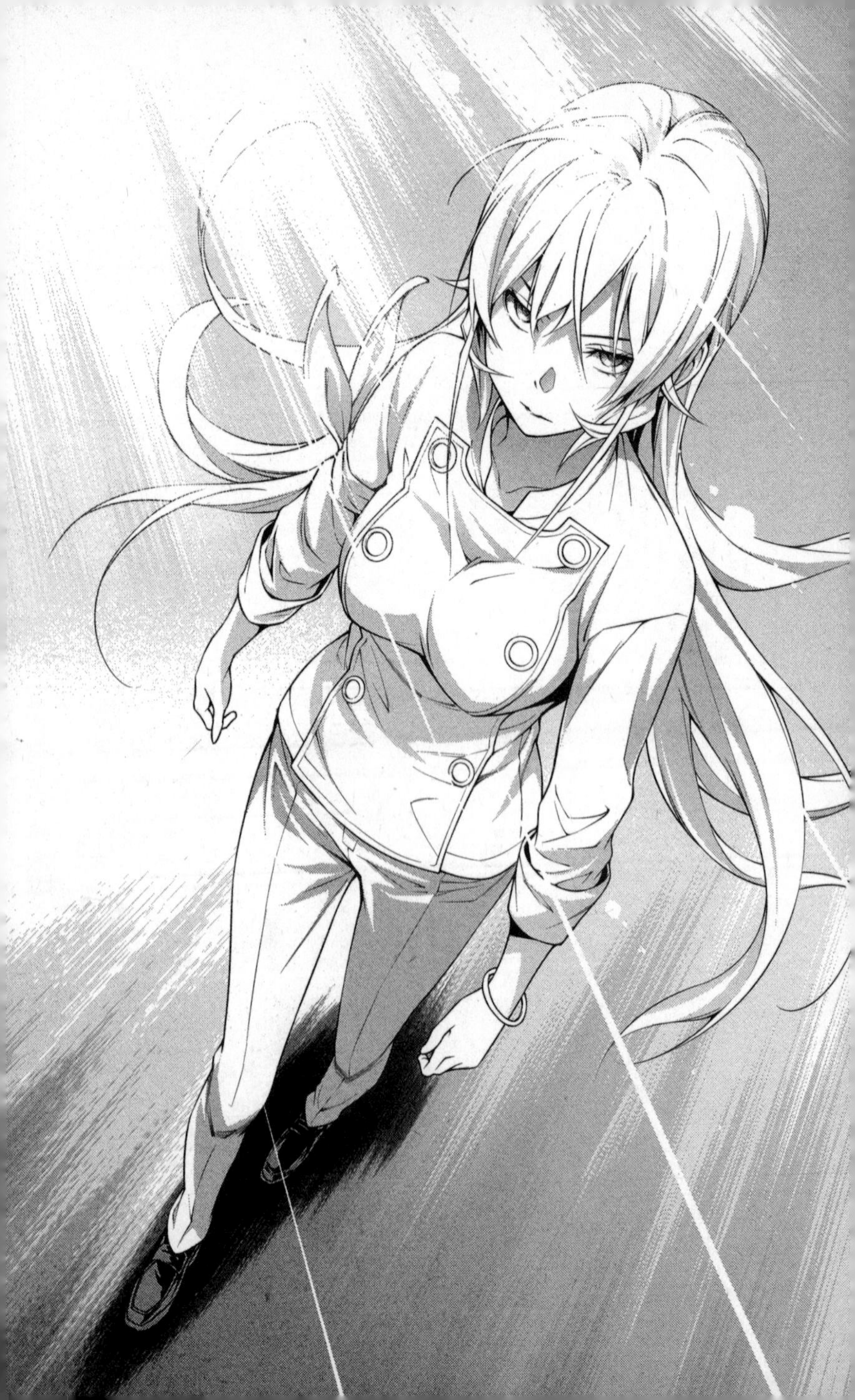

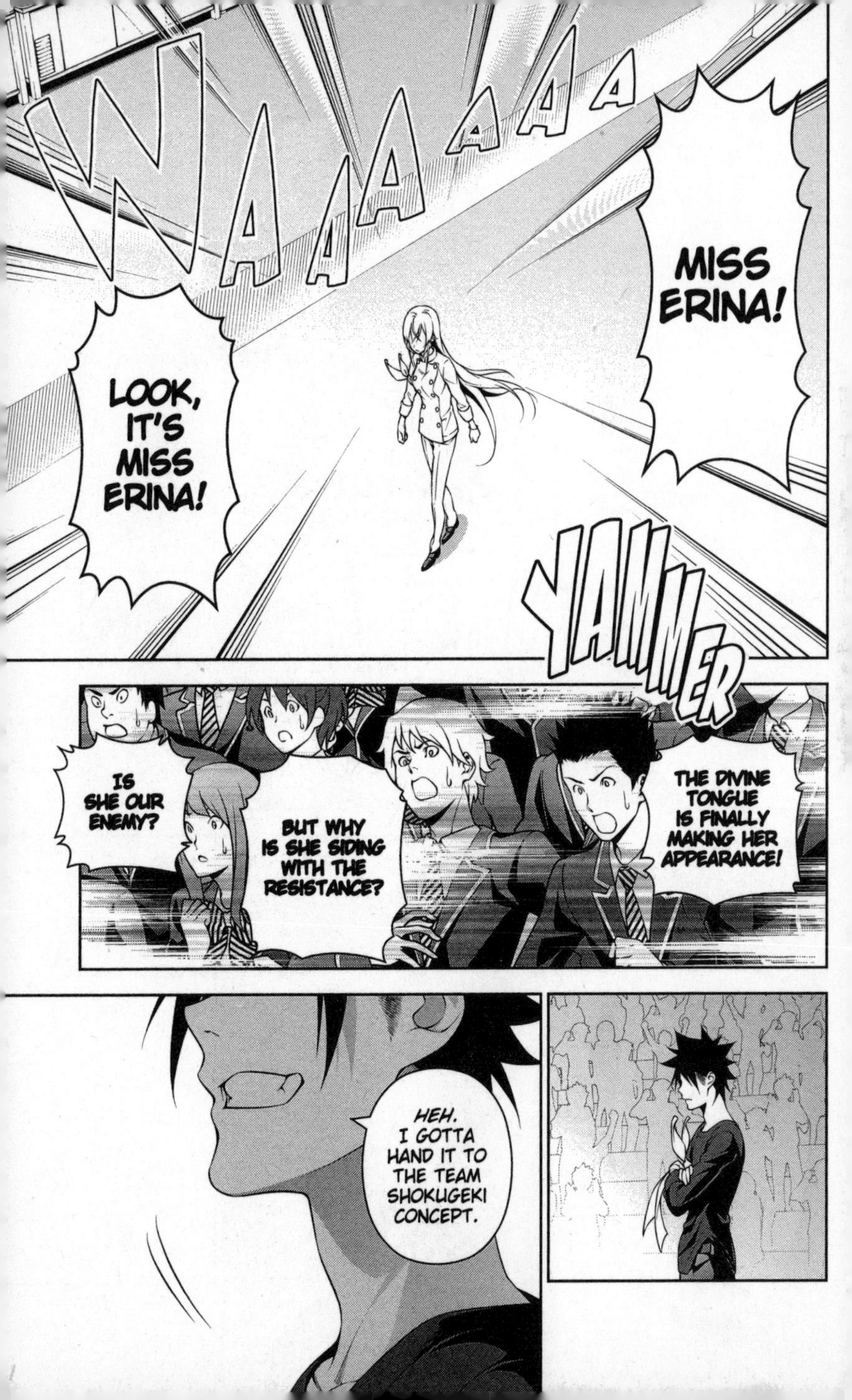
MISS ERINA!
WAAAAAAA
LOOK, IT'S MISS ERINA!
YAMMER
THE DIVINE TONGUE IS FINALLY MAKING HER APPEARANCE!
BUT WHY IS SHE SIDING WITH THE RESISTANCE?
IS SHE OUR ENEMY?
HEH. I GOTTA HAND IT TO THE TEAM SHOKUGEKI CONCEPT.

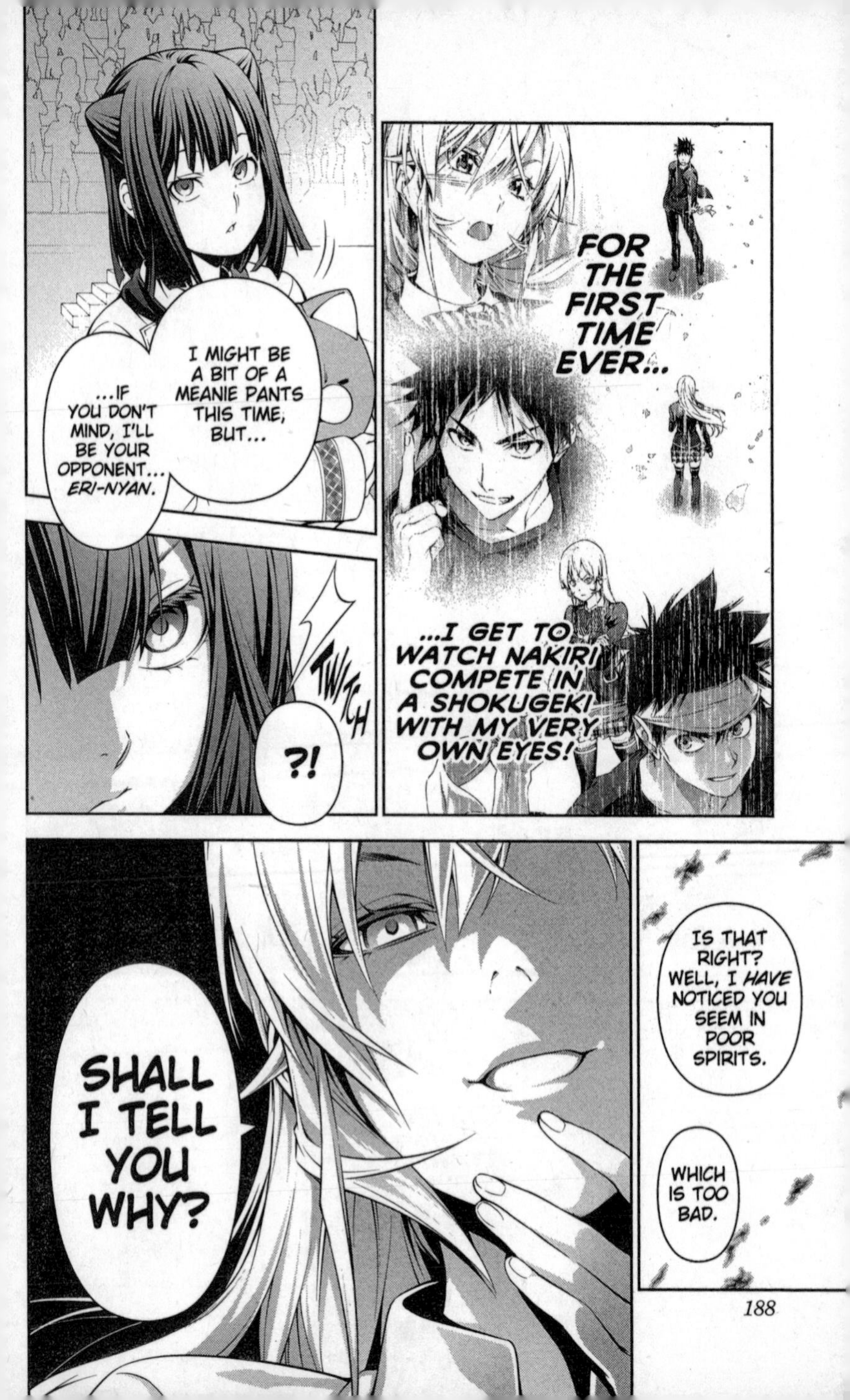
FOR THE FIRST TIME EVER...
...I GET TO WATCH NAKIRI COMPETE IN A SHOKUGEKI WITH MY VERY OWN EYES!
I MIGHT BE A BIT OF A MEANIE PANTS THIS TIME, BUT...
...IF YOU DON'T MIND, I'LL BE YOUR OPPONENT... ERI-NYAN.
TWITCH
?!
IS THAT RIGHT? WELL, I HAVE NOTICED YOU SEEM IN POOR SPIRITS.
WHICH IS TOO BAD.
SHALL I TELL YOU WHY?

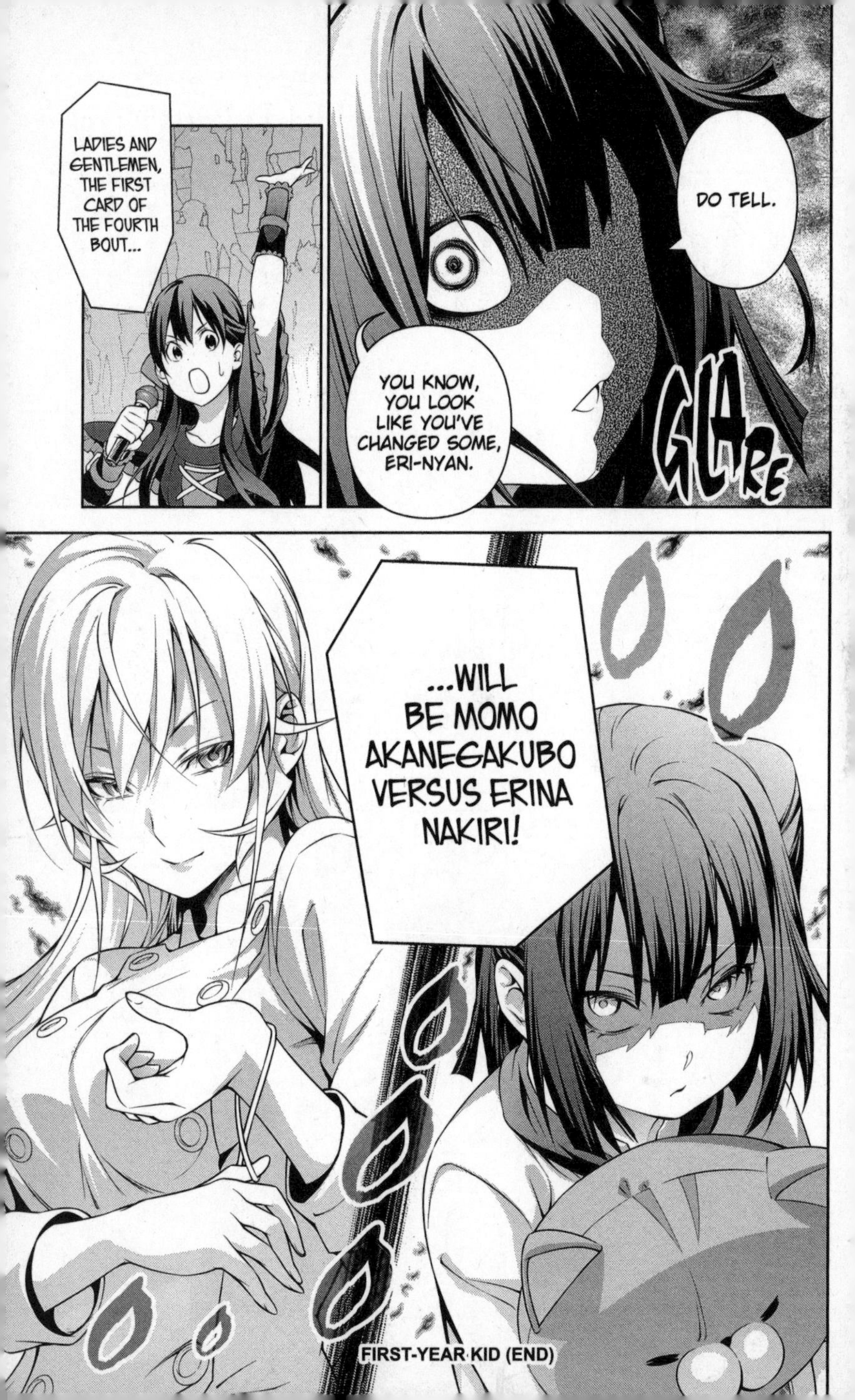
DO TELL.
YOU KNOW, YOU LOOK LIKE YOU'VE CHANGED SOME, ERI-NYAN.
GLARE
LADIES AND GENTLEMEN, THE FIRST CARD OF THE FOURTH BOUT...
...WILL BE MOMO AKANEGAKUBO VERSUS ERINA NAKIRI!

FIRST-YEAR KID (END)

FOOD WARS! 4-YEAR ANNIVERSARY CELEBRATION

WEB POPULARITY POLL RESULTS!

BELOW ARE THE RESULTS FROM THE THIRD OFFICIAL *FOOD WARS!* CHARACTER POPULARITY POLL, AS HELD BY *SHONEN JUMP*+! WHERE DOES YOUR FAVORITE CHARACTER RANK?

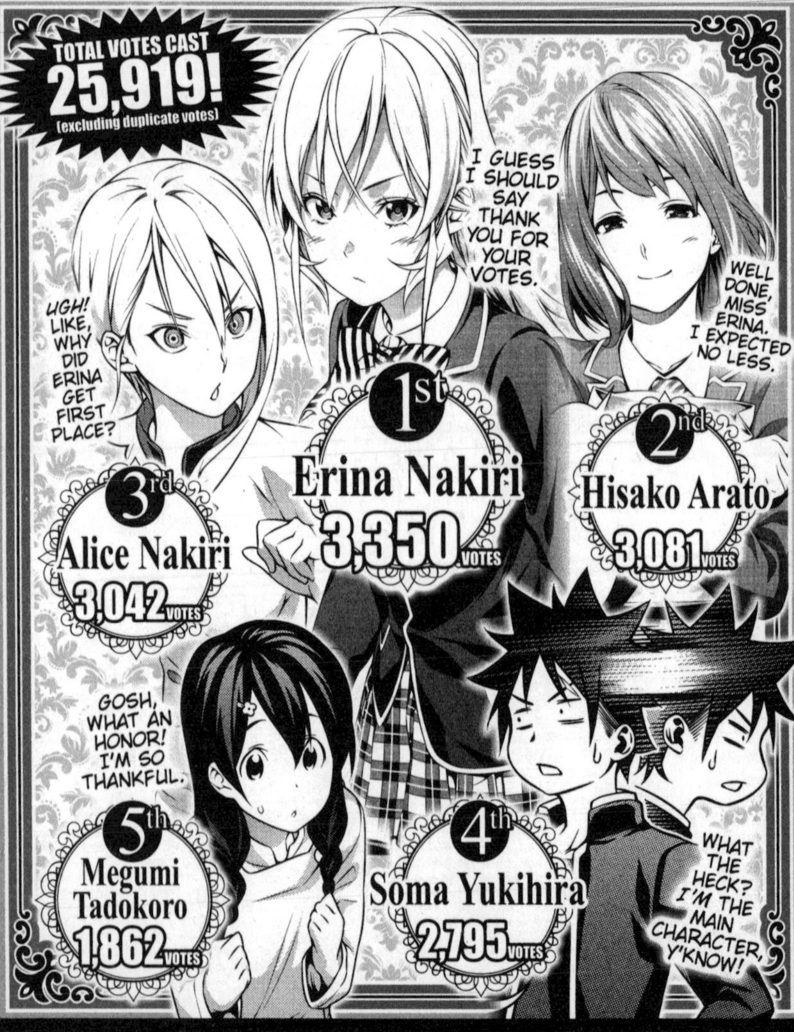
TOTAL VOTES CAST
25,919!
(excluding duplicate votes)
WELL DONE, MISS ERINA. I EXPECTED NO LESS.
I GUESS I SHOULD SAY THANK YOU FOR YOUR VOTES.
UGH! LIKE, WHY DID ERINA GET FIRST PLACE?
2nd Hisako Arato 3,081 VOTES
1st Erina Nakiri 3,350 VOTES
3rd Alice Nakiri 3,042 VOTES
WHAT THE HECK? I'M THE MAIN CHARACTER, Y'KNOW!
GOSH, WHAT AN HONOR! I'M SO THANKFUL.
4th Soma Yukihira 2,795 VOTES
5th Megumi Tadokoro 1,862 VOTES

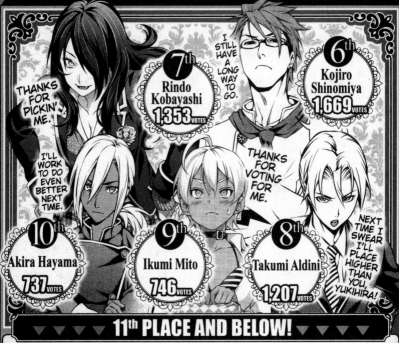

6th
Kojiro Shinomiya
1,669 VOTES
I STILL HAVE A LONG WAY TO GO.
7th
Rindo Kobayashi
1,353 VOTES
THANKS FOR PICKIN' ME.
NEXT TIME I SWEAR I'LL PLACE HIGHER THAN YOU, YUKIHIRA!
8th
Takumi Aldini
1,207 VOTES
THANKS FOR VOTING FOR ME.
9th
Ikumi Mito
746 VOTES
10th
Akira Hayama
737 VOTES
I'LL WORK TO DO EVEN BETTER NEXT TIME.

11th PLACE AND BELOW!

11th Joichiro Yukihira............686 votes
12th Ryo Kurokiba............638 votes
13th Eishi Tsukasa............506 votes
14th Satoshi Isshiki............501 votes
15th Hinako Inui............360 votes
16th Ryoko Sakaki............348 votes
17th Terunori Kuga............290 votes
18th Momo Akanegakubo............279 votes
19th Yuki Yoshino............244 votes
20th Shun Ibusaki............215 votes
21st Gin Dojima............180 votes
22nd Isami Aldini............154 votes
23rd Mayumi Kurase............134 votes
24th Fuyumi Mizuhara............132 votes
25th Jun Shiomi............116 votes
26th Senzaemon Nakiri............102 votes
27th Berta............99 votes
28th Subaru Mimasaka............91 votes
29th Roland Chapelle............74 votes
30th Leonora Nakiri............72 votes
31st Sonoka Kikuchi............64 votes
32nd Cilla............58 votes
33rd Miyoko Hojo............55 votes
34th Soue Nakiri............42 votes
35th Nao Sadatsuka............38 votes
36th Yaeko Minegasaki............37 votes
37th Abel Blondin............34 votes
Kiyoshi Godabayashi
Urara Kawashima
40th Etsuya Eizan............31 votes
Nene Kinokuni
42nd Zenji Marui............27 votes
Kanichi Konishi
44th Azami Nakiri............25 votes
45th Somei Saito............24 votes
46th Taki Tsunozaki............22 votes
46th Fumio Daimido............22 votes
48th Orie Sendawara............20 votes
49th Donato Gotoda............14 votes
Ryushi Yugo
51st Tosuke Megishima............13 votes
52nd Y from Chiba Pref............12 votes
Mitsuru Sotsuda
54th Gao Wei............11 votes
55th Squid & peanut butter............9 votes
56th Tetsuji Kabutoyama............8 votes
Rentaro Kusunoki
58th Shun Saeki............7 votes
Natsume Sendawara
60th Kuga's underlings............5 votes
Yua Sasaki
62nd Shigemichi Kumai............4 votes
Shoji Sato
Mea Yanai
62nd Butchy (Momo's stuffed animal)............4 votes
66th Marui's glasses............20 votes
Mamoru Mitamura
Yuki Morisaki
Soma's cooking knife
Yuya Tomita
Tokuzo eggs
72nd Takumi's mezzaluna............11 votes
Bo Bobo
Isobe Isobei
Taito Kubo
Akari Miyano
The bear-tracker guy
Daigo Aoki
Dogen
Kinu Nakamozu
Yuto Tsukuda
Ryotsu

THESE PEOPLE GOT VOTES TOO!

The girl with the black hair who ate Joichiro's dish in volume 15's "Second Stomach" bonus / honey mustard / Ginzabeth / Chaliapin steak bowl / Jaru Jaru / Sylvette / Bianca / Miss Fumio's first crush / Vegita / McFly McLachlan / sulky Megumi / Yukihira's mom / Rosche / Isshiki senpai's loincloth / Katsumoto Okamoto / Hitoshi Sekimori / The sketch of Kiyoko Shimizu you drew for the *Haikyu!!* project / Chisaki Miyazaki / The girl with the round glasses in the Miyazato Seminar / Jotaro Kujo / The monk who broke fast to eat Joichiro's food / Soma's mash-ups / Soma's dried-squid snacks / advancement exam proctor Hiroi / the little girl who was the first to eat Soma's soufflé during Hell Camp / the little girl who visited Soma's table during the Hell Camp buffet / the Hell Camp flier mascot (evil version) / Gintoki Sakata / plates / Shiro Yamaoka / Rui Kofuru / Kosaki Onodera / Yoshitsugu Matsuoka / The mansion used as the venue for advancement exam stage two / the student expelled from Hell Camp for his hair-care product / Senzaemon's loincloth / Haruki Otori / The meat ruined in chapter 1 / Tadokoro's flower hairpin / Megumi Tadokoro's mom / Kakuei Tanaka / Yoshiaki Nikaido / The undodgeable salmon / The girl whose chef knife Soma got back after his shokugeki with Mimasaka / The gum Mimasaka spit on Takumi's mezzaluna / The girl whose heirloom knife Mimasaka stole / dog-version Soma licking a diamond / Kyoichi Makime / Sonoka Kikuchi's breasts / Izuku Midoriya / Osho

THANK YOU FOR ALL YOUR VOTES!

*AS ORIGINALLY PUBLISHED IN THE DECEMBER 2017 ISSUE OF *WEEKLY SHONEN JUMP*

You're Reading in the Wrong Direction!!

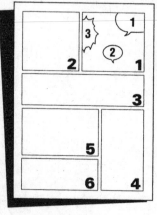

Whoops! Guess what? You're starting at the wrong end of the comic!

...It's true! In keeping with the original Japanese format, **Food Wars!** is meant to be read from right to left, starting in the upper-right corner.

Unlike English, which is read from left to right, Japanese is read from right to left, meaning that action, sound effects and word-balloon order are completely reversed... something which can make readers unfamiliar with Japanese feel pretty backwards themselves. For this reason, manga or Japanese comics published in the U.S. in English have sometimes been published "flopped"—that is, printed in exact reverse order, as though seen from the other side of a mirror.

By flopping pages, U.S. publishers can avoid confusing readers, but the compromise is not without its downside. For one thing, a character in a flopped manga series who once wore in the original Japanese version a T-shirt emblazoned with "M A Y" (as in "the merry month of") now wears one which reads "Y A M"! Additionally, many manga creators in Japan are themselves unhappy with the process, as some feel the mirror-imaging of their art skews their original intentions.

We are proud to bring you Yuto Tsukuda and Shun Saeki's **Food Wars!** in the original unflopped format.

For now, though, turn to the other side of the book and let the adventure begin...!

—Editor

SOMA TAKES CARE OF TAKUMI'S MEZZALUNA ALONG WITH HIS OWN KITCHEN KNIVES.

WIPE
WIPE